PRENTICE HALL
WRITER'S COMPANION
HIGH SCHOOL

Prentice Hall
A Paramount Communications Company
Englewood Cliffs, New Jersey 07632

Prentice Hall
A Paramount Communications Company
Englewood Cliffs, New Jersey 07632

ACKNOWLEDGMENTS

Art credits begin on page 457.

Editorial, design, and production coordination by McClanahan & Company, Inc.

Grateful acknowledgment is made to the following for permission to reprint copyrighted material:

Rudolfo A. Anaya
Excerpts from "A Celebration of Grandfathers" and "In Commemoration: One Million Volumes." Copyright © Rudolfo Anaya. Reprinted by permission of the author.

Bantam Doubleday Dell Publishing Group, Inc.
Excerpts from *The Complete Humorous Sketches and Tales of Mark Twain* by Mark Twain. Copyright © 1961, 1985 by Charles Neider. Excerpts from "A Visit to Grandmother" by William Melvin Kelley. Copyright © 1964 by William Melvin Kelley from *Dancers on the Shore*. Excerpt from *The Actor's Scenebook* edited by Michael Schulman and Eva Mekler. Copyright © 1984 by Michael Schulman and Eva Mekler. Excerpt from "Imagined Scenes" from *Distortions* by Ann Beattie. Originally appeared in *The Texas Quarterly*. Copyright © 1974, 1975, 1976 by Ann Beattie. Reprinted by permission of Bantam Doubleday Dell Publishing Group, Inc.

Susan Bergholz Literary Services
Excerpt from "Straw Into Gold." Copyright © 1987 by Sandra Cisneros. First published under the title "A Writer's Voyage" in *The Texas Observer*, September 1987. Reprinted by permission of Susan Bergholz Literary Services, New York.

David Campbell Publishers, Ltd.
Excerpt from "Letters from an American Farmer" by Michel-Guillaume Jean de Creveoueur. Copyright © Everyman's Library, David Campbell Publishers, Ltd.

Jonathan Clowes Literary Agency
Excerpt from "Through the Tunnel" from *The Habit of Loving* by Doris Lessing. Copyright © 1957 by Doris Lessing. Reprinted by permission. (For Canadian distribution rights.)

Don Congdon Associates, Inc.
Excerpt from *The White Lantern* by Evan S. Connell. Copyright © 1980 by Evan S. Connell. Reprinted by permission of Don Congdon Associates, Inc.

Joan Daves Literary Agency, Inc.
Excerpt from "I Have a Dream" speech by Martin Luther King, Jr. Reprinted by arrangement with The Heirs to the Estate of Martin Luther King, Jr., c/o Joan Daves Literary Agency, Inc. as agent for the proprietor. Copyright © 1963 by Martin Luther King, Jr. Copyright renewed 1991 by Coretta Scott King.

Sandra Dijkstra Literary Agency
Excerpts from "Mother Tongue" by Amy Tan. Copyright © 1989 by Amy Tan. First appeared in *Threepenny Review*. Reprinted by permission of Sandra Dijkstra Literary Agency.

Ann Elmo Agency, Inc.
From "Leiningen Versus the Ants" by Carl Stephenson. Copyright © 1958 by Carl Stephenson. Reprinted by arrangement with Ann Elmo Agency, Inc.

Farrar, Straus & Giroux, Inc.
Excerpt from "Georgia O'Keeffe" from *The White Album* by Joan Didion. Copyright © 1976, 1979, 1989 by Joan Didion. Reprinted by permission of Farrar, Straus & Giroux, Inc.

Graywolf Press
Excerpt from *If You Want to Write* by Brenda Ueland. Copyright © 1938 by Brenda Ueland. Reprinted by permission of Graywolf Press.

Harcourt Brace & Company, Inc.
Excerpt from "A Lincoln Preface" from *Abraham Lincoln: The Prairie Years* by Carl Sandburg. Copyright © 1953 by Carl Sandburg; renewed 1981 by Margaret Sandburg, Janet Sandburg, and Helga Sandburg Crile. Excerpt from "The Jilting of Granny Weatherall." Copyright © 1930 and renewed 1958 by Katherine Anne Porter. Reprinted from her volume *Flowering Judas and Other Stories*. Excerpt from "A Worn Path." Copyright © 1941 and renewed 1969 by Eudora Welty. Reprinted from her volume *A Curtain of Green and Other Stories*. Reprinted by permission of Harcourt Brace & Company, Inc.

HarperCollins Publishers, Inc.
Excerpt from *Pilgrim at Tinker Creek* by Annie Dillard. Copyright © 1974 by Annie Dillard. Excerpt from *An American Childhood* by Annie Dillard. Copyright © 1987 by Annie Dillard. Excerpt from "Through the Tunnel" from *The Habit of Loving* by Doris Lessing. Copyright © 1957 by Doris Lessing. Excerpt from *Of Kinkajous, Capybaras, Horned Beetles, Seladangs* by Jeanne K. Hanson and Deane Morrison. Copyright © 1991 by Jeanne K. Hanson and Deane Morrison. Excerpt from *Games at Twilight* by Anita Desai. Copyright © 1983 by Anita Desai. Excerpt from *Our Town*. Copyright © 1938, 1957 by Thornton Wilder. Excerpt from *Their Eyes Were Watching God*. Copyright © 1937 by Zora Neale Hurston. Reprinted by permission of HarperCollins Publishers, Inc.

William Heineman
Excerpt from *Games at Twilight* by Anita Desai. Copyright © 1983 by Anita Desai. (For Canadian distribution rights.)

David Higham Associates, Ltd.
From *A Child's Christmas in Wales* by Dylan Thomas. Copyright The Trustees of the late Dylan Thomas. Published by J. M. Dent. Reprinted by permission of David Higham Associates, Ltd. (For Canadian distribution rights.)

Henry Holt & Co., Inc.
"Fire and Ice" from *The Poetry of Robert Frost*, edited by Edward Connery Lathem. Copyright © 1969 by Holt, Rinehart and Winston, Inc.; copyright © 1962 by Robert Frost; copyright © 1975 by Lesley Frost Ballantine. Reprinted by permission of Henry Holt & Co., Inc.

Evelyn Tooley Hunt
Excerpt from "Mama Is a Sunrise" from *The Lyric*. Reprinted by permission of Evelyn Tooley Hunt.

Harriet Hurst
Excerpt from "The Scarlett Ibis" by James Hurst. First appeared in *The Atlantic Monthly*, July 1960. Reprinted by permission of Harriet Hurst.

Immigration and Refuge Service of America (IRSA)
Excerpt from "Chee's Daughter" by Juanita Platero and Siyowin Miller. Originally published in *Common Ground*, 1948. Reprinted by permission of Immigration and Refuge Service of America, formerly American Council for Nationalities Service.

Janklow & Nesbitt Associates
Excerpt from "Georgia O'Keeffe" from *The White Album* by Joan Didion. Copyright © 1976, 1979, 1989. Reprinted by permission of Janklow & Nesbitt Associates. (For electronic rights option.)

Kensington Publishing Corp.
Excerpt from *The Dinosaur Heresies*. Copyright © 1986 by Robert T. Bakker. Reprinted by permission of Kensington Publishing Corp.

Little, Brown and Company
Excerpt from *Blue Highways* by William Least Heat Moon. Copyright © 1982 by William Least Heat Moon. By permission of Little, Brown and Company.

(Continued on page 457)

Contents

Writing to Describe

Writing to Narrate

Creative Writing

Writing to Inform

Multimedia Projects

SECTION FOUR Grammar, Usage, and Mechanics
Applying the Rules in Your Writing

Problem Solver

Alphabetized Terms and Lessons

SECTION FIVE Guide to Learning
Taking Charge of How You Learn

Research

Study Skills

College Preparation

Humanities

THE
WRITING
PROCESS

■ ■ ■

Developing Your Technique

Julian Bell Writing, 1928, Duncan Grant
Copyright 1978 Estate of Duncan Grant
Photo, The Charleston Trust

THE WRITING PROCESS

 What is the writing process?

Good baseball players and figure skaters are often so skilled and graceful that their performances look almost effortless. However, anyone who's ever attempted these sports knows the hours of practice behind every good performance. Learning a sport is a process in which athletes gradually overcome their weaknesses and strengthen their abilities. A polished piece of writing can also seem to have been effortlessly created, but most good writing is the result of a process. The writer's ideas and their expression go through a series of changes, or stages. These are prewriting, drafting, revising, proofreading, and publishing.

In **prewriting,** you prepare yourself for writing by exploring ideas using **prewriting techniques,** such as questioning and freewriting. In **drafting,** you write sentences and paragraphs based on your ideas. After finishing your draft, you consider suggestions for improving your writing and then decide which **revisions** you want to make. Finally, when you are satisfied with your writing, you **proofread** it carefully and check for errors in grammar, usage, spelling, and mechanics. Then you make a final copy and **publish** your work.

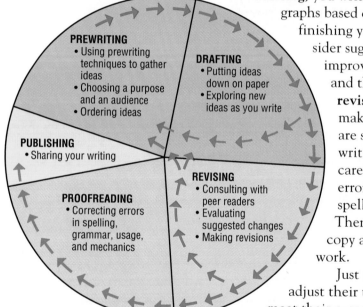

Just as individual athletes adjust their training routine to meet their current athletic goals, you can also adjust your writing process to the needs of your present writing task. You do not have to progress through all five stages in a fixed order. You can backtrack to an earlier stage, temporarily skip a step, or go through the stages in a sequence that suits your particular assignment or frame of mind. To get an idea of what the writing process is like, study the diagram above. The additional arrows in the drafting and revising sections indicate that you can always return to a previous stage.

PREWRITING TECHNIQUES

 How do I find and develop a writing idea?

Argument, persuasion, narration, description, evaluation, or analysis—whatever your writing purpose may be, prewriting techniques can help you find and develop an idea. Experiment with the following strategies. Feel free to combine and adapt them to suit your needs. Each of them can be used for more than one kind of writing assignment.

FINDING IDEAS

Often you'll be writing to fulfill an assignment from your teacher, but assignments usually leave room for your individual ideas. To find specific topic ideas, try any of these techniques.

START A CLIPPING FILE. Collect clippings that amuse you, puzzle you, or make you think. Include articles, photos, other illustrations, and cartoons from newspapers and magazines. Write down appealing lines from songs, films, and books; add bits of conversation and sketches of sights that catch your attention. Make several files with different themes or topics, such as "friendship" or "the environment." Any of these may become sources of writing topics.

VIEW FILMS AND FINE ART. Movies, paintings, and sculptures can be used for personal narrative, analysis, exploration, or comparison-and-contrast writing. Ask yourself questions like the following:

- Does the subject matter remind me of experiences of my own? What are these experiences?
- What message about life or people do I get from the art or film? How do I feel about this message?
- How is the art or film like and unlike other works I've seen?

SKETCH A LIFE MAP. Your own experiences are sources of topics for many kinds of writing assignments. Try creating a life map to help you recall experiences and to explore their meanings for you.

- On the far left side of your paper, write *birth*. Sketch a picture or symbol to stand for your birth.
- Draw a path from your birth to where you are now. Add words, pictures, and symbols to show important events in your life.
- To show where others have crossed your path and changed your life, draw intersecting lines. Where you took one direction instead of another, show a fork in your life path.

- Think of a visual way to present your life as it is now. For example, you may feel as if you are presently in a sheltered valley, setting out toward a far peak, or sailing an uncharted sea.

- On the far right side of your paper, write *future*. Show where you hope to be in ten more years.

FROM A WRITER

66 *You get the facts from outside. The truth you get from inside.* 99

—Ursula K. LeGuin

For more on journal writing, see p. 103.

KEEP A JOURNAL. The thoughts, feelings, experiences, and observations that you record regularly in your journal can give rise to writing ideas. The following tips will help you use your journal to find topics for writing assignments.

- Write about experiences that linger in your memory. Explore what they mean to you. For example, you might describe a friend's voice, the scent of a familiar room, or the view from a window in your home.

- Write about qualities such as integrity, strength, or compassion. When and where have you seen these qualities demonstrated? What do they mean to you?

- Write about an ordinary object or activity, something you see or do every day. What memories, ideas, or feelings does it evoke? How might your life be different without it?

TRY THIS

If you are assigned a general subject, try to narrow it down to a topic you can cover adequately.

For more on narrowing your topic, see p. 11.

DEVELOPING IDEAS

You will have to spend some time developing your ideas on the topic before you are ready to begin drafting. For informative and persuasive writing assignments, developing your topic may require research to gather evidence to support your main idea or point of view. For narrative and descriptive assignments, it may require personal reflection and the recollection of your own experience.

No matter what kind of topic you are developing, you can find ways to explore it on your own, with classmates, with graphic organizers, and with writing aids. The following techniques may be helpful.

BY YOURSELF

ASK QUESTIONS. Ask *who, what, where, when, why,* and *how* about your topic. Then figure out where to look for the answers. If you need advice, ask a teacher or librarian for help. If you are preparing to write an informative report on rockets, for example, you might list the following questions and then visit the library to look for answers.

Who invented rockets?
What purpose did they originally serve?
When did the American space program begin?
Where were the first rockets tested?
Why were German rocket scientists hired by the American space program?
How do rockets work?

READ ACTIVELY. As you read about the topic, keep a pen and paper handy to record ideas that flash through your mind. These may be used for personal, informative, persuasive, and research writing, as well as for responses to literature.

For help with research techniques, see p. 219.

- Stop reading occasionally and daydream. Record where your thoughts have wandered. Try to determine what started your train of thought.

- Jot down questions, thoughts, memories, and opinions triggered by your reading.

- Imagine yourself talking with the author or one of the characters. Write your dialogue and see where it leads.

EXPLORE YOUR INTERESTS. Your own activities and interests can suggest a topic for writing. Explore your connections to the topic by using questions like those that follow.

- What experiences, if any, have I had concerning the topic?

- What have I learned about the topic at school? Outside of school?

- Do I know someone, or could I get in touch with someone, who has information about this topic?

- Has this topic been featured in the news recently?

ASK IMAGINATIVE QUESTIONS. As you explore your topic, you may reach a point where you become stuck, confused about what approach you should take to your subject, or just plain bored with your topic. That's when asking some imaginative questions can help jump-start your thinking, rekindle your enthusiasm, or inspire a more creative approach to your subject. The following examples show "what if" questions that could be used to shake up your thinking on a variety of topics.

- What if a character from my favorite—or least favorite—book became my next-door neighbor?
- What if daylight savings time were in effect year-round?
- What would two historical figures from different eras have thought of each other if they had actually met?
- What if _____ were a _____? For example, what if ambition were a plant? How would it look? How would it grow?

You can also explore and develop your topic on your own by reviewing your clipping file for materials on your topic or by reviewing your journal.

WITH OTHERS

BRAINSTORM. Brainstorming is a useful way for a group of people to generate as many ideas as possible for developing a given topic. When you brainstorm, you'll find that other people's ideas will trigger ideas of your own that you didn't even know you had. After the brainstorming session, each writer can choose details from the list to pursue independently. Follow these steps to conduct a successful brainstorming session.

1. Choose someone to record the group's ideas on the topic.

2. Set a time limit—perhaps five or ten minutes.

3. Have everyone suggest specific ideas related to the topic. Let one idea trigger another.

4. Don't evaluate ideas—just keep them coming. Record them all.

Imagine that a class has been given the assignment of writing a descriptive essay about what the world will be like in A.D. 2100. A group of classmates might generate the following ideas for developing this topic.

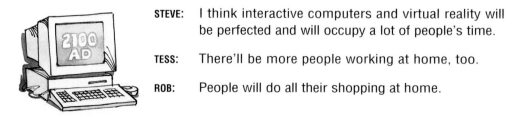

STEVE: I think interactive computers and virtual reality will be perfected and will occupy a lot of people's time.

TESS: There'll be more people working at home, too.

ROB: People will do all their shopping at home.

ANGIE: So why leave home at all? Maybe all the downtowns will be empty or turned into theme parks.

STEVE: What about the outdoors? Will kids still go outside to play?

TESS: I think we'll be eating more genetically altered food.

ROB: Lots of animals are being genetically altered too. Maybe there'll be tiny elephants and giant mice.

Notice that no one stopped to evaluate another person's ideas. They just kept letting one idea lead to another.

DISCUSS ISSUES. Discussions are a great way to develop ideas for a persuasive essay. Discussing your opinions in a group can help you clarify your point of view, find out what opposing arguments you need to address, and discover weaknesses in your argument for which you need to sharpen your reasoning or find better supporting evidence. Discussion is useful for persuasion, argumentation, and debate, essays of opinion, and essays about controversial issues. For example, suppose a class were assigned to write persuasive essays on gun control. A group of students might have the following discussion before they begin drafting their essays.

JULIO: I think there should be laws making it harder to buy guns.

TONY: But then only criminals will have guns. They'll always find a way to get them.

TANYA: But I think I read that most shootings happen between people who know each other. An argument gets out of hand and people end up shooting. If they couldn't get guns so easily, that wouldn't happen.

JULIO: What about that Brady law that was passed? I wonder if it's doing any good? I'm going to check and find out.

TRY ROLE-PLAYING. You and classmates can use role-playing to develop ideas for persuasive papers, problem-solution essays, literary analysis, and fiction and drama, as well as to generate dialogue for short stories or dramas.

- Choose a situation, issue, or conflict, and assign roles. You might choose either a real-life situation or a situation from literature.

- Improvise dialogue and actions based on how each of you would feel in the situation.

- Try trading roles. Notice how your ideas, interpretations, and responses change when your role changes.

For more on dialogue, see p. 97.

INTERVIEW A FELLOW STUDENT. Questioning a fellow student can help both of you develop a topic for character sketches, biographies, news and feature stories, literary reviews, and essays of opinion. Here are some specific interviewing ideas:

For more on interviewing, see p. 244.

- Question a classmate about his or her responses to a literary work that both of you have read or a film that both of you have seen.

- Interview a student with a special skill or area of expertise. Find out how the student developed his or her interest or ability.

- Find an interview partner and take turns questioning each other on a topic you have agreed on.

WITH GRAPHIC ORGANIZERS

SELF PORTRAIT, 1889
Vincent van Gogh
Musee d' Orsay

SELF PORTRAIT, 1887
Vincent van Gogh
KunsthistorischesMuseum
Neue Galerie

SELF PORTRAIT, 1853-90
Vincent van Gogh
Rijks Museum
Kroller-Muller, Otterloo

DRAW OR PAINT THE SUBJECT. Before you begin writing about a person, place, or thing, try drawing or painting it. The images you create may show you new facets of your subject.

- Focus on just one part of your subject. Enlarge that part and include as many details as you can.

- Try placing your subject against different backgrounds. Notice ideas that each background suggests about your subject.

- Create a self-portrait. Which of your qualities will you emphasize? How will you show them?

FILL IN AN OBSERVATION CHART. Things you notice in the world around you can help you generate details that can be used in descriptions and narratives. Try filling in an observation chart like the one that follows. Then reflect on your chart. The scene in the following chart is a kitchen at breakfast time. Choose your own subject, then see what ideas or questions your sense impressions suggest.

SEE	HEAR	TOUCH	SMELL	TASTE
Bright over-head light	Laughter of me and my sisters	Warmth	Oranges	Sweet cereal
My parents and sisters all scrubbed and dressed	Liquid sounds of pouring milk, juice	Bumpy skin of oranges	Grainy smell of cereal	Faint taste of toothpaste
Shiny chrome of toaster	Clatter of silverware, rattle of plastic wrap	Floor slightly sticky under my shoes	Cardboard-and-ink smell of cereal box	Rich, slightly salty, buttered toast

WITH WRITING AIDS

JOT DOWN A LIST. You can develop your topic by listing everything that you can recall or have experienced concerning the topic. Your list may range from the most complex concept to the most commonplace object. Here is an example of a list about a pair of running shoes.

MODEL

bought with my paper-
route money
just white
do they really reduce
stress injuries?
won the 50-meter dash

Coach teases me
purpose of grid pattern
on soles?
lightweight good cushioning
beat-up but comfy

The writer developed the underlined entries on the list into an essay on how shoes are designed to enhance safety and performance.

DO FOCUSED FREEWRITING. When freewriting is used to develop a topic, it is called *focused freewriting*. When you freewrite, you let your mind wander at will and you write down your thoughts as they come to you. Follow these four steps to use focused freewriting to develop a topic.

1. Set a time limit. (At first, five minutes is enough.)

2. Repeat to yourself the key words of your topic and then write whatever comes to mind about them. Don't stop; don't read or correct.

3. If you get stuck, keep writing the last word you wrote, over and over, until a new idea comes.

4. When the time is up, read what you wrote, underlining parts you like best. These may suggest new approaches to your topic or new ideas to research or reflect on.

In the following example, a writer knew that he wanted to write something about the Inuit people of Greenland, but he wasn't sure what approach to take. He decided to do a focused freewriting on his topic, letting himself wonder why the topic interested him.

> ### MODEL
>
> Inuit people, what do I know about them? My Aunt Anna was a teacher in northern Greenland for five years. I've seen her photos: no trees, people wearing anoraks even in summer. Wonder if she knows any Inuit myths. Bet they're pretty different from the myths of sunny Rome. Maybe they feature igloos, walruses, kayaks—hey, do those words come from Inuit languages? Aunt Anna says Inuit languages have about fifty different words for varieties of snow and ice, as English has so many names for kinds of cars. Did she learn the language? Was it hard? I wonder if she writes to anyone she met there. Would she go back?

After reflecting on his freewriting, the writer decided to interview his aunt for a narrative about her experiences living among the Inuit people.

WRITE AN IMAGINARY DIALOGUE. Try making up a dialogue in which two characters—perhaps you and someone else—discuss or debate an issue. When your writing topic involves argument or persuasion, a prewriting dialogue can help you to examine an issue, to consider opposing viewpoints, and to develop your position carefully. When your topic involves narration, description, or literary analysis, a prewriting dialogue can give you insights into characters and their motivations. You can also write or speak a prewriting dialogue with a classmate.

FINDING A FOCUS

How do I find a focus for my paper?

Picture this situation: you're writing a five-page paper about the arts of Japan. After three pages, you start dropping details and even whole subtopics just to have room to mention dance, literature, and other arts.

WARNING! If you find yourself in a similar situation, you can be pretty sure your topic is too broad and lacks a unifying focus.

> To **find a focus** for a paper, frame a precise question or choose a specific angle on a topic.

SUBDIVIDING A TOPIC

To avoid this common pitfall, you must find a specific question or angle on your topic before you begin to write. Having a focused topic will make all the steps of writing a paper easier. Sometimes you can

begin by dividing your topic into parts. Choose one part and then, if necessary, subdivide it further, as in the series of maps shown here. The "topic" of Europe has been subdivided twice, first into Germany and then into Berlin, the capital of Germany. These maps show visually the process of selecting smaller and smaller portions of a topic until you find a subject that is manageable.

Narrowing your topic in this fashion, however, is not enough. You must also come up with a question or issue within this narrower framework. One way to accomplish this task is to combine questioning with a graphic aid such as an inverted pyramid. Write your subject across the top of the pyramid and then continue to ask and answer the questions journalists ask—*who, what, where, when, why,* and *how* questions—until you discover an issue or angle that you can handle in the confines of your paper. The graphic on page 12 illustrates this process.

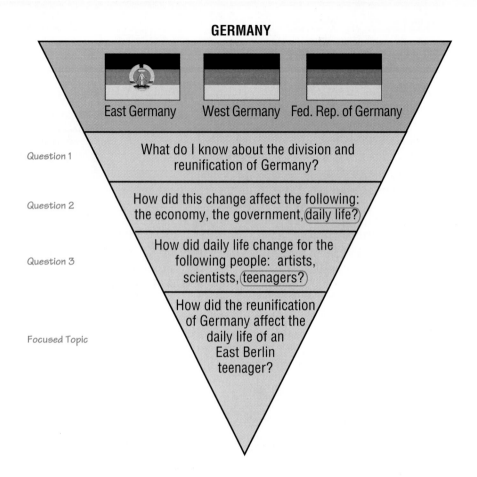

GERMANY

East Germany West Germany Fed. Rep. of Germany

Question 1
What do I know about the division and reunification of Germany?

Question 2
How did this change affect the following: the economy, the government, daily life?

Question 3
How did daily life change for the following people: artists, scientists, teenagers?

Focused Topic
How did the reunification of Germany affect the daily life of an East Berlin teenager?

QUESTIONING FROM DIFFERENT ANGLES

Another strategy you can use is to ask questions that reveal different angles of a topic. If your topic were wolves, for instance, what might be a sheep farmer's perception of wolves? A writer's? A scientist's? A conservationist's? Create a web of your answers as below.

Then select an angle—wolves as literary symbols, for instance—and continue to narrow it by asking questions such as the following:

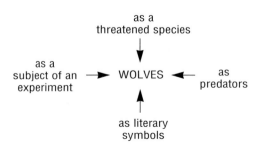

Who used wolves as literary symbols? (*Jack London*) *What* did wolves symbolize in Jack London's short story collection *The Son of the Wolf: Tales of the Far North?*

Once you have found a specific question or angle on a topic, you will be ready to begin gathering material for your paper.

PURPOSE AND AUDIENCE

Why am I writing and who will read my writing?

Imagine that you are going to write two pieces on the same topic: the growing popularity of the sport of soccer among young people. One piece is a research paper for your language arts teacher featuring statistics about the explosion in town leagues and school teams across the country. The other piece is a short story, written for publication in your school magazine, about a teenage girl's attempt to make a highly competitive league team. How would the two pieces differ? The research paper would probably have a direct, informative tone and be filled with facts. The short story might be amusing and use dialogue and suspense to highlight the young girl's struggle.

> Your **purpose** is your reason for writing. Your **audience** is the person or people who read your writing.

Sometimes your purpose for writing will be decided by your teacher. If you must identify your own purpose, however, think of the main goals that you want to accomplish. Remember that most writing has one or more of the following goals: to describe, to explain, to tell a story, to persuade, to inform, or to amuse. For example, if you are writing a letter that accompanies a job application, you will want to inform your prospective employer about your qualifications and persuade him or her to offer you the job.

In addition, different forms of writing tend to be associated with different purposes. For example, forms that usually have the purpose of explaining are the "how-to" essay and the cause-and-effect essay. The form you are using can therefore be a clue to your purpose.

HOW DO I IDENTIFY MY AUDIENCE?

No matter what you write, you're writing with somebody in mind, even if you are writing just for yourself. When you sit down to write, ask yourself who your audience is. Are your readers young, old, naive, sophisticated, liberal, or conservative? Are they inclined to agree with your views? Once you've determined who your audience is, tailor your writing to them.

You might find it useful to make a chart to pinpoint your audience and purpose. Here is a sample chart.

PURPOSE AND AUDIENCE CHART

Form of writing:	school newspaper article
Purpose:	to inform students of new cafeteria menus
Audience:	10th–12th grade students
What does my audience already know?	They know the cafeteria food. They know basic rules of nutrition.
What information does my audience need?	how the menu will change; its effect on student nutrition; effect on the cost of food
What level of language will be suitable?	mixture of formal and informal, following school newspaper rules

Your writing can be adapted to different audiences and purposes.

The writer's purpose is to make a request.

The writer's audience is an adult from whom he wants a favor. His tone is respectful, and his language is informal but polite.

Dear Ms. Tsu,

After spending this week at Santa Cruz, I've decided I definitely want to apply to the University of California here. I need to talk to you about their requirements and admissions procedure. Can we meet next week? I'll be back on the sixth, and I'll call you then to set up an appointment. Thank you so much.

Best wishes,
Duncan McPhail

STAMP

Ms. Roberta Tsu
Wilson High School
101 Monrovia Road
Punta, NM 87196

The writer's purpose is to inform and entertain.

The writer's audience is a relative. His tone is light and humorous, and his language is informal.

Dear Uncle Bryce,

You were right—this place is great! I've decided to apply to your alma mater, UCSC. Can you believe it—I might be a Banana Slug (why did they give their basketball team that name?). I'll call you when we get back.

Dunc

STAMP

Mr. Bryce McPhail
1306 S. 26 Street
St. Louis, MO 63119

How do I focus my ideas?

You probably have a Closet of Doom somewhere in your home. It's the closet where, if you open the door, a lifetime's worth of junk falls out—usually on your head. You can't find anything inside it; it's completely disorganized. Sometimes your writing might remind you of a Closet of Doom. You can't locate your topic, your details are all piled together, your ideas are lost in the clutter. Just as you would use hangers, drawers, shelves, or boxes to organize your closet, you can organize your writing ideas with the help of graphic organizers.

A **graphic organizer** is a visual aid that helps you arrange ideas logically. The graphic organizer you use will depend on your goal and on the type of writing you are doing. This chart will help you choose a graphic organizer that fits your writing situation.

HOW TO USE GRAPHIC ORGANIZERS

GOALS	▶ GRAPHIC ORGANIZER	▶ HELPS FOCUS IDEAS FOR
To analyze aspects of a subject or a piece of writing	Analysis Frame (page 17)	■ Process Analysis ■ Response to Literature ■ Critical Review ■ Comparative Analysis ■ Poetry/Fiction Interpretation
To explore positive and negative aspects of an idea	Pro-Con Chart (page 17)	■ Problem-and-Solution Essay ■ Editorial ■ Persuasive Essay ■ Business Letter ■ Memorandum
To compare and contrast two subjects	Comparison-and-Contrast Chart (page 18)	■ Comparison-and-Contrast Essay ■ Letter to the Editor ■ Comparative Analysis ■ Proposal
To distinguish like and unlike features	Venn Diagram (page 19)	■ Comparison-and-Contrast Essay ■ Comparative Analysis ■ Response to Literature
To outline the steps in a process	Flowchart/ Process Diagram (page 20)	■ Process Analysis ■ Cause-and-Effect Essay ■ Persuasive Essay ■ Research Report ■ Proposal ■ Status Report ■ Technical Description
To explore problems and their possible solutions	Problem-and-Solution Chart (page 21)	■ Problem-and-Solution Essay ■ Editorial ■ Persuasive Essay ■ Business Letter ■ Proposal ■ Memorandum
To make a detailed plan before writing	Outline (page 22)	■ Personal Narrative ■ Story ■ Play ■ Definition ■ News Story ■ Persuasive Essay ■ Response to Literature ■ Research Report ■ Comparative Analysis ■ Status Report

ANALYSIS FRAME

An analysis frame can help you investigate the parts that make up a subject or topic. One way you can use an analysis frame is to analyze a piece of writing. The following example analyzes the elements of the epic poem *Beowulf*.

Beowulf

Main Characters	Settings	Plot
Beowulf (hero, later king of the Geats)	southern Sweden	Beowulf journeys to Denmark to help Hrothgar defeat Grendel and Grendel's mother. He then returns to Geatland (Sweden), where he rules until he dies killing a dragon that threatens his kingdom.
Hrothgar (king of the Danes)	Denmark	
Grendel (monster descended from Cain)		
Grendel's mother		
Wiglaf (Beowulf's friend)		

PRO-CON CHART

A pro-con chart can help you investigate both sides of an issue, a solution, or an idea. The following chart shows the pros and cons of a proposal for national health care.

National Health Care

Pros	Cons
■ All Americans would have health coverage.	■ Government, small businesses, and many individuals would pay more.
■ A centralized system would cut administrative costs and burdensome paperwork.	■ A person's choice of doctors and hospitals would be limited.
■ National caps on spending would cut health care costs.	■ The government would oversee physicians' decisions.

COMPARISON-AND-CONTRAST CHART

When you want to write about similarities and differences between two topics, you can organize your ideas in a comparison-and-contrast chart. The following chart organizes the similarities and differences between solar energy and nuclear energy.

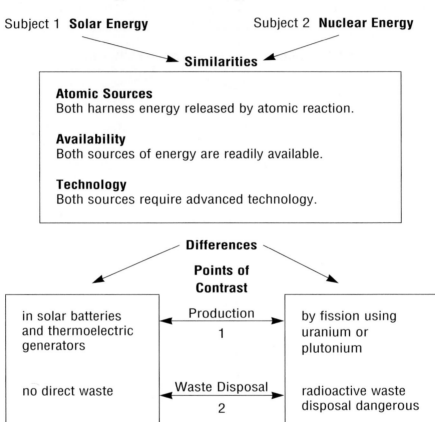

Subject 1 **Solar Energy**   Subject 2 **Nuclear Energy**

Similarities

Atomic Sources
Both harness energy released by atomic reaction.

Availability
Both sources of energy are readily available.

Technology
Both sources require advanced technology.

Differences
Points of Contrast

Solar Energy		Nuclear Energy
in solar batteries and thermoelectric generators	Production 1	by fission using uranium or plutonium
no direct waste	Waste Disposal 2	radioactive waste disposal dangerous
very high	Cost 3	low, once reactors are built
no direct dangers	Dangers 4	high, from accidents and improper waste disposal

VENN DIAGRAM

Another way to compare and contrast two subjects is by using a Venn diagram, named after the English logician John Venn. A Venn diagram has two overlapping circles. In the section that overlaps, you would write the characteristics that the two subjects share. You would write differences in the other sections of the circles. This example compares the French Revolution and the American Revolution.

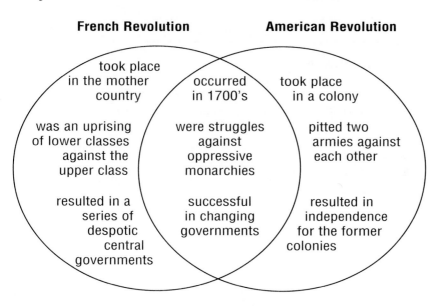

French Revolution

American Revolution

took place in the mother country

occurred in 1700's

took place in a colony

was an uprising of lower classes against the upper class

were struggles against oppressive monarchies

pitted two armies against each other

resulted in a series of despotic central governments

successful in changing governments

resulted in independence for the former colonies

You might occasionally want to consider the characteristics of three subjects. Then you would work with three overlapping circles, like this:

 WRITING FOR MATH

In order to solve a math problem, you might be asked to compare and contrast two geometric figures such as a parallelogram and a rectangle. You might use a Venn diagram as a starting point for your writing. You would then write shared characteristics, such as parallel lines, in the overlapping section of the circles and specific differences, such as the degree of the angles, in the other sections of the circles.

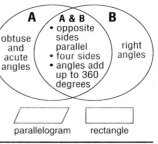

A **A & B** **B**
- opposite sides parallel
- four sides
- angles add up to 360 degrees

obtuse and acute angles

right angles

parallelogram   rectangle

FLOWCHART/PROCESS DIAGRAM

When you want to clarify the steps or stages in a process, you can draw a flowchart or a process diagram to show the steps and outcome graphically. Here is an example of a simple flowchart showing how information is processed through a computer.

Basic Computer Workings

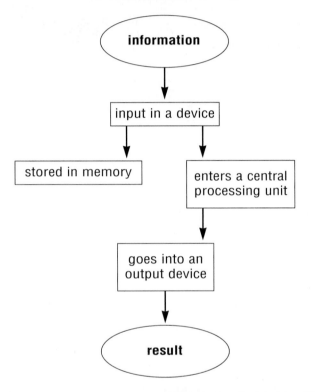

PROBLEM-AND-SOLUTION CHART

When you are writing about a problem and proposing possible solutions, you may find that a problem-and-solution chart helps you evaluate your ideas. The following chart explores the problem of the costs of a college education.

Problem	Goal(s)
The cost of a college education has become too high for most students and conventional loans take too long to pay back.	To find a solution that will enable students to attend college without unduly burdening the government or the taxpayers.

Alternatives	Pros (+) & Cons (–)
The government should offer qualified students free college tuition.	+ Qualified students would receive a college education without mortgaging their future earnings to the government. – Taxpayers would have to subsidize this tuition.
Fewer students should attend college.	+ Government would not be financing student loans. – Talented students would be deprived of educational opportunities.
The government should offer student loans that can be paid back by doing nonsalaried community service work after graduation.	+ Communities would benefit from this nonsalaried service and be able to reduce expenses for salaries. – Performing nonsalaried community service work would restrict graduates' freedom of choice in selecting employers.
The government should try to convince corporations to donate scholarships for deserving and talented students.	+ Neither the government nor the taxpayers would have to pay for the education of certain students. – Allowing corporations to pay for certain students' education may cause business leaders to conclude that they have the right to influence what can be taught in college courses.

Decision(s)	Reason(s)
The government should offer student loans that can be paid back by doing nonsalaried community service work after graduation.	This alternative seems the fairest to deserving students, taxpayers, and local communities.

OUTLINE

A standard outline lists main ideas and supporting ideas for a topic. Here is an outline written in words and phrases.

The Threat of Acid Rain

Thesis statement: Although acid rain threatens plants and animals worldwide, the problem can be solved if people and government work together.

I. Composition of acid rain
  A. Natural acidity
    1. Volcanic activity
    2. Sea spray and decaying vegetation
  B. Introduced acidity
    1. Power plants
    2. Industry
    3. Homes and vehicles

II. Effects of acid rain
  A. Lakes
  B. Forests
  C. Crops
  D. Human health

III. Remedies for acid rain
  A. Liming
  B. Pollution reduction
    1. Coal washing
    2. Desulphurization
    3. Limestone injection
    4. Integrated gasification
  C. Regulation
    1. Federal regulation
    2. Worldwide regulation

DRAFTING

 How do I begin to write?

You have selected a topic and thought about key ideas you want to get across. You have made an outline, used a graphic organizer, or assembled a stack of notecards on which you have jotted down ideas or information. Now it is time to start writing. If you find a clean sheet of paper or a blank computer screen intimidating, remember that at this stage you are writing a draft, or a preliminary sketch. If you don't like what you produce at first, you can change it.

QUICK, LOOSE DRAFT One way to start is to write down your ideas as quickly as possible. Let one thought flow into another, and keep writing without stopping to evaluate. Incorporate new ideas as they emerge.

This technique—writing a quick, loose draft—is helpful if you are the type of person who bogs down in detail. It is also helpful if you want to generate extra copy. Using this technique, you will probably have more material than you need for your final paper. You can revise your draft by selecting the ideas that work best and elaborating on them.

SLOW, STRUCTURED DRAFT If you do not like plunging into projects, or if you have a firm idea of what you want to say and how you want to say it, you might choose to formulate a detailed outline and follow it as you write. Using this drafting technique, you work on one paragraph at a time, making sure the main idea is effectively supported by details. After you complete each section, refer to your outline to make sure your organization is clear and your information complete. When you have finished your draft, you will probably have the right amount of material. However, you will still want to review what you have written and make improvements.

YOUR DRAFTING OPTIONS Another drafting technique is to alternate between a quick, loose draft and a slow, structured draft. For example, you might write a slow, structured draft of the body of an essay, following a detailed outline, but do a quick, loose draft of several possible conclusions.

While drafting, you occasionally may find yourself stuck. One strategy is to retry the prewriting technique that works best for you. You may discover an insight that enables you to continue your draft. Remember that writing is not a one-way process and you can move back and forth between stages.

COMPUTER TIP

If you compose your first draft on a computer, be sure to save an unedited version that you can refer to as you revise your work.

7 ORGANIZATIONAL PLANS

? *What are some organizational plans I can use?*

An **organizational plan** is a method of arranging information for a given topic and purpose.

Sometimes a piece of writing seems to fall "naturally" into a certain structure. A process explanation, for example, typically moves step-by-step in chronological order. Details in the description of a painting, on the other hand, may be presented in spatial order or in the order they are seen by the viewer. Sometimes more than one organizational plan is suitable for a particular writing project, as indicated in the following chart.

TYPE OF ORGANIZATIONAL PLAN	PURPOSE	TYPES OF WRITING
Chronological Order Details and events are presented in the order in which they occur.	To show an unfolding process or series of events	■ biographies ■ process analyses ■ stories ■ narrative poems
Spatial Order Details are presented as seen—for example, top to bottom or left to right.	To help readers visualize what is being described	■ descriptive essays ■ descriptive passages in any type of writing
Order of Importance Details are presented from the least important to the most important, or vice versa.	To help readers understand the importance of different ideas	■ persuasive essays ■ informative essays ■ reports
Main Idea and Details An important idea is followed by facts, reasons, and anecdotes.	To prove or support an idea or opinion	■ persuasive essays ■ informative essays ■ reports
Order of Impression Details are presented in the order in which they catch the writer's attention.	To help readers understand the writer's point of view	■ descriptive essays ■ descriptive passages ■ personal narratives
Question and Answer A question is followed by an answer, which may raise another question, and so on.	To anticipate readers' questions	■ persuasive essays ■ informative essays
Logical Order Ideas are arranged so that their relationship is clear.	To generalize, illustrate an idea, or define a term	■ persuasive essays ■ informative essays

HOW DO THE DIFFERENT PLANS WORK?

Following are descriptions of different types of organizational plans. Remember that you can often combine two or more of these.

CHRONOLOGICAL ORDER When you use chronological order, make sure the sequence of events is clear. If you break the chronological flow to return to an earlier time, shift verb tenses and add transitional words to help readers keep track of time. In the following model, the writer uses a flashback to an earlier time—a technique of fiction writing—to provide background information about the main characters.

MODEL FROM LITERATURE

"My name is Helen Stoner, and I am living with my stepfather, who is the last survivor of one of the oldest Saxon families in England, the Roylotts of Stoke Moran, on the western border of Surrey."

Holmes nodded his head. "The name is familiar to me," said he.

"The family was at one time among the richest in England, and the estates extended over the borders into Berkshire in the north and Hampshire in the west. In the last century, however, four successive heirs were of a

dissolute and wasteful disposition, and the family ruin was eventually completed by a gambler in the days of the Regency."

—Sir Arthur Conan Doyle, "The Adventure of the Speckled Band"

Helen Stoner begins by telling where she is currently living.

As Ms. Stoner continues her story, she tells about a much earlier time. The writer uses phrases such as at one time and in the last century to establish the break in chronological order.

SPATIAL ORDER You can describe a scene using any one of a number of spatial orders: from the right to the left, from the foreground to the background, or even from the perspective of someone moving through a scene. The model on the following page shows movement through time and space from the perspective of a pilot in flight. Notice how this description not only follows a spatial order but also reflects the order in which objects impress themselves on the viewer.

The writer uses words like already and a moment ago to show time passing.

The writer's focus shifts downward to the land below.

In the last sentence, the writer contrasts the swift passage of time with the apparently slow movement of the plane in space.

Night already shadows the eastern sky. To my left, low on the horizon, a thin line of cloud is drawing on its evening sheath of black. A moment ago, it was burning red and gold. I look down over the side of my cockpit at the farm lands of central Illinois. Wheat shocks are gone from the fields. Close, parallel lines of the seeder, across a harrowed strip, show where winter planting has begun. A threshing crew on the farm below is quitting work for the day. Several men look up and wave as my mail plane roars overhead. Trees and buildings and stacks of grain stand shadowless in the diffused light of evening. In a few minutes it will be dark, and I'm still south of Peoria.

—Charles Lindbergh, *The Spirit of St. Louis*

ORDER OF IMPORTANCE With this organizational plan, you can direct attention to the ideas you think are most important. Persuasive writing, for example, often moves from the weakest to the most powerful argument. In other situations, spark interest in your topic by beginning with the most important detail.

MAIN IDEA AND SUPPORTING DETAILS Among organizational plans, main idea and supporting details could be called the "workhorse" plan, steady and proven. Use it to answer almost any question on an essay exam.

ORDER OF IMPRESSION Order of impression reveals *where* and *when* an observer becomes aware of the details of a scene. The emphasis is on the impact of the details, not on factual reporting of what happened. Notice how, in the following passage, Annie Dillard's impressions of a flood affect her various senses in turn.

MODEL FROM LITERATURE

I see rushing, a wild sweep and hurry in one direction, as swift and compelling as a waterfall. The Atkins kids are out in their tiny rain gear, staring at the monster creek. It's risen up to their gates; the neighbors are gathering; I go out.

I hear a roar, a high windy sound more like air than like water, like the run-together whaps of a helicopter's propeller after the engine is off, a high million rushings. The air smells damp and acrid, like fuel oil, or insecticide.

—Annie Dillard, *Pilgrim at Tinker Creek*

> The first impressions are visual.

> The writer becomes aware of the sound of the flood.

> The writer becomes aware of the smell of the damp air.

QUESTION-AND-ANSWER ORGANIZATION Starting with an intriguing question can attract readers' attention and create interest in your answer.

STUDENT MODEL

So what's the problem with plastic? It looks friendly enough, all shiny and helpful, but <u>plastic is no friend of the Earth.</u> Almost none of it is recyclable. Despite many ad claims to the contrary, most plastics will never biodegrade—they are here with us for a very long time. If that's not bad enough, plastic-based foams (like Styrofoam) contain <u>chlorofluorocarbons</u>, or CFCs, that eat away at the ozone layer, letting in more harmful radiation from the sun. Tons of Styrofoam end up in the ocean, where sea animals eat it instead of

> The writer poses a question and provides an answer, which contains the main idea.

> The writer provides a reason that supports the main idea.

> The writer moves to a more important objection against the use of plastic.

The writer restates the main point in more exact words.

food and starve or choke. In short, plastic is helpful to use but harmful to the environment. . . .

You might say, "That's terrible, but what can I do

A question follows logically and leads into the next point in the essay.

about it?" There are several uncomplicated things

you can do. . . .

—Andrew Franklin, Ardmore, Oklahoma

LOGICAL ORDER Any arrangement that shows clear relationships among ideas is logical order. For example, you might begin with simple ideas, explaining basic concepts, and build to more complex ones. You might give examples, incidents, or anecdotes and then make a generalization that crystallizes the connections among the details. In every case, one idea builds on previous ideas or details.

OTHER METHODS OF DEVELOPMENT In particular cases, your purpose for writing may literally shape your organizational plan. **Comparison-and-contrast writing** follows one of two patterns. You might examine all the features of item A and then compare similar features of B. Alternatively, you might compare A and B one feature at a time.

For more on comparison-and-contrast and cause-and-effect writing, see p. 157 and p. 163.

In **cause-and-effect writing,** organizational patterns are also limited. You can begin with a cause and trace its effects, or you can begin with an effect and examine what caused it.

In most other types of writing, however, you are free to select the plan—or combination of plans—that suits your purpose best.

INTRODUCTIONS

 How can I open my paper?

Like the first impression you make when meeting someone, the beginning of a piece of writing is important. That's why introductions to all written work deserve careful planning. If you can win over your readers at the beginning, they'll probably stick with you.

PLANNING YOUR INTRODUCTION

Consider the following points as you think about creating an attention-getting introduction:

THINK ABOUT THE KIND OF WRITING YOU ARE DOING. For example, are you writing a persuasive essay or a short story? Each offers a different set of possibilities. You might focus on a character in a short story introduction. In a persuasive essay, you might begin with an intriguing question.

CONSIDER YOUR PURPOSE. For example, do you wish to amuse your readers—or do you want them to think seriously about a subject? This chart suggests different types of introductions that may be useful for various purposes and types of writing assignments.

PURPOSE	TYPE OF INTRODUCTION	COULD BE USED FOR . . .
To begin clearly and directly	A statement of the main idea (p. 30)	■ Research Report ■ Process Analysis ■ Business Letter ■ News Story
To build interest or suspense	An anecdote (p. 30)	■ Personal Narrative ■ Oral History ■ Biographical Profile ■ Informative Essay
To state your position	A statement of opinion (p. 31)	■ Letter to the Editor ■ Persuasive Essay ■ Editorial
To grab readers' attention	A startling fact (p. 32)	■ Research Report ■ Editorial ■ Cause-Effect Essay ■ News Story

PURPOSE	TYPE OF INTRODUCTION	COULD BE USED FOR . . .
To give your writing authority	A quotation from an expert (p. 32)	■ Research Report ■ Persuasive Essay ■ News Story
To arouse readers' curiosity or persuade readers	An analogy (p. 32)	■ Comparison-Contrast Essay ■ Comparative Analysis ■ Description ■ Persuasive Essay ■ Editorial
To draw readers into a piece	A character description (p. 33)	■ Story ■ Personal Narrative ■ Eyewitness Account
To engage readers	A nonchronological beginning (p. 33)	■ Story ■ Narrative Poem ■ Play

Here are some strategies you might use in your introductions:

STATE YOUR MAIN IDEA. Begin with a direct statement of your main point. It can be as brief as a sentence or as long as a paragraph.

MODEL FROM LITERATURE

The writers state the main idea in the first sentence.

Bedouin nomads have good reason for calling the camel the ship of the desert. This living cargo vessel can move up to 600 pounds of freight during a long workday, and up to 1,000 pounds for short distances. During the cool winter it can subsist for three months without drinking, getting all the moisture it needs from the succulent plants in its diet. In the summer it can go at least ten days without water. . . .

—Jeanne K. Hanson and Deane Morrison, *Of Kinkajous, Capybaras, Horned Beetles, Seladangs, and the Oddest and Most Wonderful Mammals, Insects, Birds, and Plants of Our World*

USE AN ANECDOTE. Telling a brief story that sets a specific tone or mood is an excellent way to hook your readers.

I remember the first time the thought struck me! "There's something very wrong with our dinosaurs." I was standing in the Great Hall of Yale's Peabody Museum, at the foot of the Brontosaurus skeleton. It was 3:00 A.M., the hall was dark, no one else was in the building. "There's something very wrong with our dinosaurs." The entire Great Hall seemed to say that. . . .

—Robert T. Bakker, *The Dinosaur Heresies*

The writer uses an anecdote to introduce his new scientific ideas about dinosaurs and to create an air of mystery.

Dinosaur skeleton at the American Museum of Natural History

TAKE A STAND. Stating a strong opinion at the outset of your paper moves your readers to agree or disagree vigorously.

I have never taken a writing course. I don't believe that anyone can teach another how to write. I believe that writing must be self-taught. . . .

—Vera A. Cleaver, *Speaking for Ourselves*

This controversial opinion prompts readers to agree or disagree.

STARTLE YOUR READERS. Beginning with a startling fact or opinion may raise your readers' eyebrows and compel them to read on.

> **MODEL**
>
> The Steller's sea cow, a 24-foot-long mammal of the Arctic, was discovered by explorers in 1741. Just 27 years later, humans had wiped this animal off the face of the earth.

This shocking fact makes readers want to learn how an animal could be made extinct in such a short time.

QUOTE SOMEONE. Someone else's funny, wise, or striking comment can sometimes make your point and spark your readers' interest.

> **MODEL FROM LITERATURE**
>
> "Where I was born and where and how I have lived is unimportant," Georgia O'Keeffe told us in the book of paintings and words published in her ninetieth year on earth. . . . "It is what I have done with where I have been that should be of interest."
>
> —Joan Didion, "Georgia O'Keeffe"

A quote from a famous artist gives readers the artist's own surprising view of her life.

BEGIN WITH AN ANALOGY. An **analogy** is an extended comparison in which one thing, usually more familiar, is compared to something less familiar. A striking analogy can make a commonplace subject come alive with new meaning.

> **MODEL FROM LITERATURE**
>
> Ships at a distance have every man's wish on board. For some they come in with the tide. For others they sail forever on the horizon, never out of sight, never landing until the Watcher turns his eyes away in resignation, his dreams mocked to death by Time.
>
> —Zora Neale Hurston, *Their Eyes Were Watching God*

This analogy compares men's wishes to ships and suggests that some wishes are granted and others remain forever out of reach.

USE A VIVID, DETAILED DESCRIPTION. A description containing colorful words and strong images can effectively begin many types of writing. Note how the following example from a nonfiction piece sets the scene.

MODEL FROM LITERATURE

Our father's parents lived in Pittsburgh; Amy and I dined with them, rather formally, every Friday night until dancing school swept us away. Our grandfather's name was, like our father's, Frank Doak. He was a banker, a potbellied, bald man with thin legs: a generous-hearted, joking, calm Pittsburgher of undistinguished Scotch-Irish descent, who held his peace.

— Annie Dillard, *An American Childhood*

The writer vividly describes her grandfather's physical characteristics and personality.

START IN THE MIDDLE OR WITH THE END. To get your readers involved in a fiction or nonfiction story, you can plunge them into the thick of the action in the first paragraph or even share the ending with them and then backtrack to provide the rest of the story. This technique works well for stories, personal narratives, biographies, oral histories, and personality profiles. The author of a famous biography of Abraham Lincoln, for example, begins the story of Lincoln's life with the president's dramatic death.

MODEL FROM LITERATURE

In the time of the April lilacs in the year 1865, a man in the city of Washington, D.C., trusted a guard to watch at a door, and the guard was careless, left the door, and the man was shot, lingered a night, passed away, was laid in a box, and carried north and west a thousand miles; bells sobbed; cities wore crepe; people stood with hats off as the railroad burial car came past at midnight, dawn, or noon.

— Carl Sandburg, "Preface," *Abraham Lincoln: The Prairie Years*

To create a dramatic effect, the writer opens the preface of his biography at the end of Lincoln's life rather than at the beginning.

9

ELABORATION

❓ *How can I find details to include in my writing?*

Elaboration is the development of ideas and details to make a written work precise and complete.

Painters develop their works in different ways. Some begin with a basic sketch or outline and add details to complete their vision.

Others begin with some details as a starting point and add other details gradually to enrich their piece.

Portrait of Van Gogh Painting Sunflowers, 1888
Gauguin, Israel Museum, Jerusalem

Portrait of Van Gogh Painting Sunflowers, 1888, Gauguin
Van Gogh Museum, Amsterdam

Writers develop their work in the same ways. You may start out with a strong idea for a piece of writing, or you may build on a detail from your memory or imagination. In either case, you'll have to include more details to help readers understand your subject.

HOW DO I KNOW WHAT TYPES OF DETAILS TO USE?

The following chart suggests types of details that might work for different purposes. You can find examples of these details in the lesson—see the page references in the chart. Then, at the end of the lesson, you will see how to use four types of details in an essay.

PURPOSE	▶ TYPE OF DETAILS	▶ KINDS OF WRITING
To give information	facts and statistics (see p. 36)	■ definition ■ process analysis ■ cause-and-effect essay ■ news story ■ business letter
To make writing vivid	sensory details (see p. 36)	■ journal writing ■ reflective essay ■ personal narrative ■ observation and description ■ lyric poem
To entertain	anecdotes (see p. 36)	■ personal narrative ■ oral history ■ biographical profile ■ story
To prove a point	examples (see p. 37)	■ definition ■ comparison-and-contrast essay ■ problem-and-solution essay ■ letter to the editor ■ response to literature ■ research report ■ comparative analysis
To lend authority or to support an argument	quotations (see p. 37)	■ cause-and-effect essay ■ problem-and-solution essay ■ news story ■ critical review ■ research report
To add emotional depth	personal feelings (see p. 38)	■ journal writing ■ reflective essay ■ personal narrative ■ lyric poem
To make writing personal	memories	■ journal writing ■ reflective essay ■ oral history ■ biographical profile
To enhance understanding	explanation and definition	■ definition ■ process analysis ■ cause-and-effect essay ■ technical writing

TYPES OF ELABORATION

FACTS AND STATISTICS

Facts are statements that can be proven true. Statistics are facts expressed as numbers. Note how this writer uses facts and statistics.

STUDENT MODEL

The writer includes facts that give a more concrete idea of what "health-related problems" means.

The writer elaborates with precise and compelling statistics.

Children with smoking parents develop many more health-related problems than kids with non-smoking parents. ∧ Children of smokers get bronchitis, pneumonia, and other respiratory problems more often than those living in a clean, smoke-free environment. Not only is smoking unhealthy, it is costing the economy billions of dollars. ∧ Every year $13.8 billion is spent on smokers' health care.

—Carrie Hernandez, Beaverton, Oregon

SENSORY DETAILS

Sensory details tell what can be seen, heard, felt, touched, or smelled. The following excerpt from a story appeals to the senses.

STUDENT MODEL

The writer includes details that appeal to the senses of sight and touch.

We sit down on some old worn rocks and wait for the marshmallows to get just right ∧ a little golden-brown on the outside and soft on the inside.

—Klinton Crispen, Bowling Green, Ohio

ANECDOTES

An anecdote is a short account of a funny or interesting incident.

 MODEL FROM LITERATURE

This anecdote uses an incident from the writer's life to illustrate his grandfather's character.

I remember once, while hoeing the fields, I came upon an anthill, and before I knew it I was badly bitten. After he had covered my welts with the cool mud from the irrigation ditch, my grandfather calmly said, "Know where you stand."

—Rudolfo A. Anaya, "A Celebration of Grandfathers"

EXAMPLES

General statements give readers only a broad idea of what you mean. An example makes your meaning clear by offering a specific instance. Notice how this writer uses examples.

MODEL FROM LITERATURE

I've done all kinds of things I didn't think I could do since then. I've gone to a prestigious university, studied with famous writers, and taken away an MFA degree. I've taught poetry in schools in Illinois and Texas. I've gotten an NEA grant and run away with it as far as my courage would take me. I've seen the bleached and bitter mountains of the Peloponnesus. I've lived on a Greek island. I've been to Venice twice.

—Sandra Cisneros, "Straw Into Gold"

With examples, Cisneros shows the variety of things she has done.

QUOTATIONS

Direct quotations are the exact words spoken by someone other than the writer. Quotations from experts can create a sense of authority and authenticity. Notice how Evan S. Connell uses a quotation to confirm his point.

MODEL FROM LITERATURE

Amundsen and Scott . . . got to the Pole within five weeks of each other, which suggests nothing more than good luck and bad luck; but there was such a difference in what happened subsequently that luck cannot explain it. The explanation must be found in the characters of the two men.

Roald Amundsen's opinion of luck is terse and revealing: "Victory awaits those who have everything in order. People call this luck. Defeat awaits those who fail to take the necessary precautions. This is known as bad luck."

—Evan S. Connell, *The White Lantern*

Connell uses Amundsen's own words both to reveal the explorer's character and to show why he thinks Amundsen succeeded.

PERSONAL FEELINGS

Stating your own feelings and reactions can impart a sense of immediacy and humanity to a piece of writing. Such elaboration generally works best when it is used sparingly and is accompanied by facts, examples, and objective details.

MODEL FROM LITERATURE

In revealing his sorrow at the plight of Native Americans, Black Elk makes his message more moving.

I kept on curing the sick for three years more, and many came to me and were made over; but when I thought of my great vision, which was to save the nation's hoop and make the holy tree to bloom in the center of it, I felt like crying, for the sacred hoop was broken and scattered.

—John G. Neihardt, *Black Elk Speaks*

USING TYPES OF ELABORATION

The following chart shows some prewriting notes listing four different kinds of elaboration to use in a feature news story. Similarly, you can use different kinds of elaboration in your writing.

MAIN IDEA Researchers have determined that men and women like to eat different kinds of food.

My Purpose	Types of Details	How to Find
Introduce the idea that males and females have different food preferences	anecdote	memory
Illustrate differences in food preferences	statistic	research
Show that men and women enjoy different sorts of food	example	research
Establish that marketing experts take gender into account when advertising foods	quotation	interview

This excerpt shows how these four types of elaboration were incorporated into the feature story:

I've always found it peculiar that while I, and most of my female friends, would do just about anything to get a taste of something sweet, my brother and his friends snack on potato chips or forgo snacks completely in favor of a big, meat-filled meal. Last Thanksgiving this difference was particularly clear: My mother, aunts, and I ate small amounts to save room for pecan pie, but the men dug into the meat and potatoes as if sugar didn't even exist.

The writer uses a personal anecdote to catch readers' interest.

Now a study shows that this difference really exists. A group of marketing researchers and dietitians have found that when people crave specific foods, women want sweets 48 percent of the time, while men want main dishes 46 percent of the time. Women are also more likely to eat fruit and drink bottled water. Males, on the other hand, prefer meat and soup.

This statistic supports the information the writer is presenting.

These examples support the writer's main idea.

Because of these established differences, market researchers take gender into account when selling food products. A vice-president at NPD Group, a consumer marketing research company, said, "It's odd to think that taste buds would be different among people in the same culture. . . . And yet, there are things that come into play that suggest there are differences between sexes." Small chocolate candy is marketed to women, while hamburger ads are more often aimed toward men.

This quotation brings in an expert's opinion on the subject.

10

CONCLUSIONS

How can I end my paper?

Concluding a piece of writing involves more than just inserting a final paragraph. For one thing, a conclusion generally should give readers a sense that you have pulled everything together. For another, a conclusion should prompt readers to continue thinking about your writing after they have finished reading it.

Concluding an essay is generally different from concluding a narrative. You might end a narrative with the last event or provide a surprise ending. (On rare occasions you might create a dramatic effect by leaving readers hanging.) When you write an essay, however, you want to ensure that readers understand the information you present.

The following model paragraph concludes a persuasive essay about the lack of activities for young people:

> ### M O D E L
>
> In short, this city offers very few activities for young people to engage in in the evening. There should be more for them to do. That way, they would be less likely to get in trouble.

This conclusion is weak because it neither explains the cause-and-effect relationship between the lack of activities and kids getting into trouble nor proposes a solution. The following models show how to rewrite this conclusion with substance and flair.

SUMMARIZE AND RESTATE. Summarize the points you have made in the body of your paper and restate your main idea.

The writer stresses the cause-and-effect relationship and restates a possible solution.

The last sentence reinforces the benefits of this solution.

> ### M O D E L
>
> In short, a lack of evening activities for young people spells trouble. A youth center would offer youngsters a safe place to gather, participate in group activities, and meet people. Keeping kids off the street would help them and the community.

You might use this type of conclusion in a persuasive essay, a comparison-and-contrast essay, an observational report, an informative essay, a research report, or any other type of writing in which you present an explicit main idea.

STATE AN OPINION. Offer an overview of the topic, and share your personal feelings or values.

MODEL

I believe that boredom breeds trouble. The same young people who appear to be just "no-good kids" on a street corner could turn out to be assets to the community if they were given a chance to do something constructive with their free time.

The writer asserts a personal opinion.

The last sentence offers readers a possibility to consider.

This technique is suitable for a personal letter, a reflective essay, a response to literature, a critical review, a persuasive essay, or any other type of writing in which an opinion is appropriate.

CALL FOR ACTION. You've presented your readers with a problem. Now make a suggestion, plea, demand, prediction—or any combination of proposals—to move readers to do something.

MODEL

Without activities, without opportunities to discover their abilities, young people in our city will continue to waste their time and taxpayer dollars. Now is the time to invest in a community youth center that will benefit our whole community.

The writer links a lack of activities with a disturbing prediction.

The writer calls for action—invest in a youth center.

This technique is appropriate when your purpose is to sway your audience. You might use this strategy in editorials, letters to the editor, examinations of controversial issues, or problem-and-solution essays.

ASK A QUESTION. End your writing with a question or a series of questions that will leave your readers thinking about your topic.

The questions get readers to see the issue from a new perspective.

A rhetorical (self-answering) question leads readers to the desired conclusion.

M O D E L

Where would you go if you were sixteen, and you and your friends didn't have much money? Would you hang around on a street corner—or would you watch videos, play basketball, or dance up a storm at a local youth center?

TELL AN ANECDOTE. Use a brief story to bring your point to life.

The anecdote illustrates the writer's main point—a youth center will engage young people in positive activity.

M O D E L

My friends and I worked hard that day, cleaning out the old warehouse that the PTA was fixing up as a youth center. We were covered with dust and sweat—but we were looking forward to the fun we would have when the center opened.

Far from being a tag-on to a piece of writing, this conclusion shows how the final words of an essay or speech can resound through history.

MODEL FROM LITERATURE

When we let freedom ring, when we let it ring from every village and every hamlet, from every state and every city, we will be able to speed up that day when all of God's children, black men and white men, Jews and Gentiles, Protestants and Catholics, will be able to join hands and sing in the words of that old Negro spiritual, "Free at last! Free at last! Thank God Almighty, we are free at last!"

—Martin Luther King, Jr., "I Have a Dream"

11

PEER RESPONSE

How can my classmates help me to improve my writing?

Have you ever been too close to a situation to see it clearly? Perhaps you talked about it with a trusted friend or relative who helped you view the situation objectively. Because it is natural to get attached to your work, you need to see it from another perspective. A fellow student can help you see ways to sharpen your ideas and express them clearly.

You can ask your peers to make their responses in many ways. One way is for one student to read a first draft and discuss it with you. Another is for a group of students to read a more polished piece of writing and then respond orally or in writing. Whether you are submitting your own work or reading someone else's, keep the following guidelines in mind to get the most out of the experience:

FROM A WRITER

❝ *I was afraid to share my work at first, but then I made friends in my response group and I forgot to be frightened.* **❞**

—Sean Gordon, student, Millbrook, New York

GUIDELINES FOR PEER RESPONSE

When you're the writer:

1. **Introduce your work to your readers.**
   - Identify your purpose and intended audience.
   - State whether you are submitting a first draft or a final draft.
   - Identify what specific responses you are looking for. Do you need help with organization or word choices? Do you want readers to point out specific passages that are effective? Point out confusing passages? Discuss their emotional responses to your work?

2. **Let your writing speak for itself.**
   - Don't give away your plot, theme, or main idea.
   - Avoid apologizing for possible problems or weaknesses.

3. **Listen carefully to the comments of your peers.**
   - Don't interrupt. You'll learn more if you let your readers speak freely.
   - Try not to get angry or defensive. Keep an open mind.

4. **When your readers have finished their comments, ask specific follow up questions.**

- Follow up on remarks you didn't understand. If, for example, readers say your writing is unclear, ask them to point out a specific passage.

- Ask for feedback on revisions you are considering, but make your own decisions about how your final draft will read.

TRY THIS

Some writers prefer written responses to their work. Ask your readers for written answers to questions like these:
- **Where does the writing seem the most vivid?**
- **What themes or main ideas come through?**
- **Which sections seem incomplete?**
- **How does the voice strike you?**
- **In what way did the writing affect your opinions or emotions?**

When you're the reader:

1. **Focus on the specific kind of feedback the writer wants, and respond to this request in your review.** If the writer asks for help with organization, for instance, don't focus on grammatical errors.

2. **Take time before responding.** If the writer is reading, listen to the entire work before offering comments. If you have been given a copy of a work, read it at least twice before responding.

3. **Be positive.** Begin your response by pointing out the passages you like best and explaining why they appeal to you.

4. **Be specific.** Point out particularly effective or ineffective words, sentences, and paragraphs. Rather than saying "The writing seems dull," for instance, point out a place where the writer could use a stronger verb: "I'm not sure *walked* is the verb you mean here."

5. **Be honest but tactful.** Don't fake praise just to please the writer. On the other hand, don't be harsh. Offer constructive suggestions for how to improve the work.

HOW DO I USE PEER RESPONSES IN REVISION?

When you've heard or read all your peer responses, follow these steps to revise your writing:

1. If the comments were oral, jot them down while they're still fresh in your mind. Then set them aside for a while.

2. Evaluate all the comments you received by considering the following criteria: Will the suggested change make my writing clearer or more vivid for my audience? Does the suggestion fit my writing voice and style? Can I make this change in the time and space I have for this assignment? Then decide which comments you want to act on, and make changes in your draft. Remember that you're the writer, and you have the final word.

For more on voice and style, see p. 95.

Read the following draft of an essay about a Mexican holiday, noting the handwritten peer responses in the margin. Notice how the writer made changes in response to the comments.

MODEL

On the first of November, just after our Halloween, the Mexican
~~All over Mexico~~ people celebrate a holiday called
the Day of the Dead. People ~~go~~ to cemeteries to
troop
repaint their ancestors' tombs, light candles, and
sprinkle ~~flower~~ petals on the ground. The atmos-
marigold
phere isn't ~~strange~~ at all. Many people have
gloomy ;
picnics and sing songs. Altars are set up to offer
In many houses,
sweet breads and fruits to the souls of the dead.
Children exchange skulls with their names written
tiny sugar
on them and write poems to one another.

Begun in Aztec times, the holiday has changed
very little through the centuries. When I was
we were walking
in Oaxaca last year, ~~we would walk~~ down the street
~~and~~ total strangers ~~would~~ invite us to their homes
d
for a special holiday meal of tamales and black beans. If you
want to get a taste of Mexican tradition and hospitality, plan a visit on
the Day of the Dead.

PEER COMMENTS:
I like your topic.
It's intriguing.
When is this celebrated?

What kind of flower?

Strange sounds judgmental.

Do they use real skulls?

This sentence seems out of place.

I'd like to know more about the meal.

12

REVISING

How do I know what to change?

Here are two strategies you can use to start the revision process:

- **Read your work aloud.** This is an excellent way to catch ideas and details that have been left out and to notice errors in logic.

For more on peer response, see p. 43.

- **Ask someone to read your work.** Choose someone who can point out its strengths as well as suggest how to improve it.

Revising is part of the creative process of writing. It is not about making your writing "correct"; it's about re-seeing it in its entirety (re-vision) and making it more effective. Word processors can correct your spelling—some even detect punctuation errors and identify grammatical tangles. The process of revising, however, requires a human mind. It involves experimenting, exploring, and choosing among possibilities. Your decisions will depend on the subject and purpose of your work, your audience, and the type of writing. Although there is no one "revision formula," there are strategies that you can tailor to your own needs and way of working.

TRY THIS

Try to take at least a one-day break from your writing before you revise it. This will help you see problems and solutions that you overlooked.

For more on revising forms of writing, see Checkpoints for Revising in the lesson on the form of writing you are using.

REVISING FORM AND CONTENT

As you review your writing, think about the purpose of the piece you are working on and the form you have chosen. Fiction and nonfiction are different in content and structure. Forms of nonfiction can also vary greatly. A cause-and-effect essay, for example, has a focus and organization that are different from those of a news article. Nevertheless, certain basic problems tend to plague first drafts no matter what the form, especially problems stemming from lack of unity or lack of coherence. The following chart suggests ways to find solutions to these problems, but you are free to work out your own variations of these strategies.

WRITING PROBLEMS	STRATEGIES FOR SOLVING PROBLEMS
The piece is not unified. The focus shifts from one paragraph to the next.	Write a summary of your thesis (main idea) in one or two sentences. Check to see that every paragraph supports or elaborates on your thesis. Delete or revise passages that do not relate to the thesis.
The first draft does not read well. The arrangement of the parts is not clear or logical.	Create an organizational plan or revise your existing one. Arrange parts in a clear order, such as main idea followed by supporting details or order of importance.
The piece does not get the response from readers that is intended.	Ask yourself what specific effect you want to have on your reader. Do you want to make more of an emotional or intellectual impact? When you're sure of your purpose, add supporting details and language that will create the response you want.

REVISING BY ELABORATING

Elaboration is the process of adding details to support an idea, theme, or opinion. Insufficient elaboration leaves the reader "out of the loop," bewildered and eventually bored. A point that seems obvious to you may not be so obvious to readers whose experience differs from yours. When you revise your work to add relevant details and examples, you bring your topic to life and engage your readers.

For more on elaboration, see p. 34.

FROM A WRITER

66 *Tell me more. Tell me all you can. I want to understand more about everything you feel and know and all the changes inside and out of you. Let more come out.* **99**

—Brenda Ueland

CAUSES OF INSUFFICIENT ELABORATION	STRATEGIES FOR REVISION
You assume your readers know what you know.	Visualize a reader who knows nothing about your topic. Then add what your reader needs to know in order to understand your writing.
You think you have said more than you actually have.	Ask someone to read your draft and point out where you need to fill in information. Add material to close the gaps.
You haven't considered sensory details.	Imagine what you would smell, hear, touch, see, and taste. Add these explicit details to your draft.
You have included all you know about a subject, and it doesn't tell readers enough about your topic.	Do more research. Find out what you need to know in order to inform your readers, and add that information to your work.

When you don't provide enough details, you leave readers with unanswered questions. Note how a writer added information to improve the following paragraph:

MODEL

The writer adds information defining interactive television.

—TV you can order from, play games with, and program—
Interactive television is seen by some as the
∧
wave of the future and by others as a huge waste

The writer details some of the problems facing interactive TV.

Problems include lack of technological know-how and high costs.
of time, money, and effort. Some researchers
∧
believe that those who want interaction will find it

easier and cheaper to use computer hookups rather

than invest in a whole new television/computer.

However, cable companies think that the lure of

being able to interact with a television set will lead

The writer adds details describing what it would be like to use interactive TV.

many viewers to invest in the new technology. After
all, who wouldn't want to be able to sit back in a comfortable easy
chair, choose a program, and have the program respond to their
commands?

REVISING BY CUTTING

Many writers have trouble when they try to add necessary information to their writing. Most writers, however, experience difficulty when they try to cut words. Look for ways to tighten your sentences by removing verbal freeloaders that don't contribute to the main idea or evoke the desired feeling.

PROBLEMS WITH WORDINESS	POSSIBLE REVISIONS
Redundancy (unnecessary repetition) ■ Earthquakes hit without *advance* warning. ■ The monthly newsletter comes out *on a regular basis*.	■ Earthquakes hit without warning. ■ The newsletter comes out monthly.
Empty words and phrases ■ Hamlet seemed to be disturbed *in his mind*. ■ Consumer confidence improves *in connection* with increasing *opportunities for* employment.	■ Hamlet seemed disturbed. ■ Consumer confidence improves with increasing employment.
Several words when one strong word would do ■ *Being in charge of everything* was Macbeth's *constant wish*. ■ Othello opened the envelope *in a state of impatience*.	■ Power became Macbeth's obsession. ■ Othello tore open the envelope.
Overuse of passive voice ■ The play was praised *by the* critics. ■ Special demands *were* imposed on the playwright *by the* Elizabethan stage.	■ The critics praised the play. ■ The Elizabethan stage imposed special demands on the playwright.
Sentences beginning with "There" and "It" ■ *There were* cars inching along the freeway. ■ *It is* the actor's wizardry that often can move the audience to tears.	■ Cars inched along the freeway. ■ The actor's wizardry often can move the audience to tears.

As you review a draft, correct problems with wordiness, using the strategies illustrated in the chart above.

For more on voice, see
p. 95.
For more on adjectives,
see p. 277.
For more on figurative
language, see p. 100.

REVISING BY REWORDING

Word choice, or **diction,** is the writer's most powerful
tool. How you choose and use words gives your writing its
voice—the quality that makes your writing really yours.

PROBLEMS WITH WORD CHOICE	STRATEGIES FOR REVISION
Some words are used too often.	■ Use a thesaurus, or dictionary of synonyms, to find substitute words. ■ Use pronouns to replace nouns.
The vocabulary is limited or lifeless.	■ Replace empty adjectives like *nice* or *great* with precise adjectives: a *quick, spontaneous* smile, for example, rather than a *nice* smile. ■ Use vivid, precise verbs instead of vague, abstract ones, for example, *raced* instead of *went*. ■ Use precise nouns such as *fans* instead of *people, novel* instead of *book*.
The language does not appeal to the imagination or to the senses.	■ Add original similes, metaphors, and other kinds of figurative language. ■ Use words that appeal directly to the senses.

The following essay has been revised. The writer also proofread
the essay to correct errors in spelling, punctuation, and grammar.

MODEL

*Educational
lessons is redun-
dant. Elaboration
makes the thesis
clear: education is
more than acade-
mics.*

"High school's one big party!" That's what

friends told me. As I sit here on my last day of

high school, I am struck by all the ~~educational~~

by joining the "party"—that is, the nonacademic activities.

lessons I have learned in the past four years.

In my junior year, I served on student council

as student body secretary. All school year we met

regularly, yet we never seemed to acomplish

much. I realized that I wanted to be sitting at the

head of the table, not along the sides waiting for somebody else to get things done. I thought I could be a leader if given a chance. ∧ I was soon to get my chance.

This year, I organized the All Sports Awards Banquet, and I was elected captain of my soccer team. I learned how to get the most out of people, without nagging or ~~copping an attitude.~~ playing the tyrant. Those people skills will help me achieve my dream to become a successful exe̲cutive, not an assistant ∧ , but the one who makes the decisions.

Soccer has been
~~Perhaps~~ the most influential activity I've been involved in ~~has been soccer~~ over these past four years. I know that being part of a team means caring about teamates. ∧ Sincerity, Encouragement ∧ and praise are an important part of team success. Insincere words will mean nothing to others. Through sports I've learned that ~~cooperating with teammates and coaches~~ teamwork means success. I've learned to see setbacks as opportunities to ~~find~~ be creative ~~solutions~~. Above all, I learned that consistent, hard work pays off. Our team took first place in the all-league playoffs.

My diploma will not be just a pe̲ace of paper. It will be a symbol of the invaluable lessons I've learned in the past four years. High school gave me an opportunity to discover my talents, fall on my face, and get a taste of success. For me, high school was ~~not one big party; it was a time when I learned a lot.~~ an educational "party."

The added sentence serves as a transition between paragraphs.

The writer replaces slang with precise words.

Elaboration restates the writer's point about leadership.

Moving the key word *soccer* to the beginning of the sentence adds emphasis.

Sincerity is integral to the writer's point about encouragement.

One strong word, *teamwork*, is more effective than five weaker ones.

Deletions strengthen the sentence.

Ending with a striking metaphor makes an impact.

13 PROOFREADING

? *How can I correct my errors?*

Proofreading is the process of reading for errors in grammar, usage, spelling, and mechanics.

Even the most careful writers make mistakes in grammar, spelling, and punctuation. Proofreading helps you perfect your writing so that you produce high-quality work of which you can be proud.

WHAT IS THE BEST WAY TO PROOFREAD?

Try different strategies or combinations of strategies to discover the proofreading methods that work best for you. The following chart lists some strategies you can use to proofread:

GENERAL PROOFREADING STRATEGIES

- Swap papers with a friend and read carefully for grammar, spelling, and punctuation mistakes.
- Read your work aloud to yourself.
- Read your work aloud while a friend reads the piece silently along with you.
- Proofread more than once, looking for specific kinds of errors each time.
- Read your work backwards word for word.

Whatever proofreading method you use, you will need a dictionary and a writer's handbook or other reference to help you correct your mistakes. Be aware of the type of mistake you make most often—for instance, misspelling certain words. You might read your work first for errors you make often, a second time for grammatical errors, and a last time for problems with capitalization and punctuation.

Use the chart on page 53 to help you proofread your writing.

Check Your Grammar and Usage

■ Do your singular subjects have singular verbs and your plural subjects have plural verbs?

Remember that third-person, singular verbs in the present tense usually end in -s, such as *thinks* and *does*.

■ Do all your sentences express complete thoughts?

Make sure every sentence, except imperative sentences, has a main verb and a subject.

■ Have you strung sentences together without punctuation?

Be sure two or more main clauses are linked by a semicolon or by conjunctions like *and*, *but*, and *or*.

■ Have you used the correct past forms of irregular verbs?

Check that helping verbs like *has*, *have*, *had*, *is*, *was*, and *been* are followed by past participle forms, such as *seen, taken, swum*.

Check Your Punctuation and Capitalization

■ Have you used apostrophes where they are needed to show possession or missing letters?

Be sure *it's* is used to express *it is* or *it has*. The possessive pronoun *its* has no apostrophe.

■ Have you used quotation marks to indicate the beginning and end of another's exact words?

Look for places where you are recording speech between characters or repeating words or ideas from another source.

■ Have you begun each sentence or direct quotation with a capital letter?

Watch for quotations that are interrupted by expressions like *he said.* The quoted word following the interruption is *not* capitalized.

Check Your Spelling

■ Have you double-checked the spelling of the names of people and places?

Check your notes and reference sources.

■ Have you used the correct form of words that sound alike but have different spellings and meanings?

Do not just proofread by ear. Look at each word one by one. Be sure you have written the correct form of words like *there, their,* and *they're*.

HOW CAN I USE PROOFREADING MARKS?

Proofreading is not complicated. Just cross out incorrect words or letters and write your corrections in the space above. You can also use a few, simple proofreading marks like the ones in the following chart. These marks make it easy to read your corrected copy.

∧	insert letters or words here
#	insert a space here
∽	switch the order of two letters or words
¶	begin a new paragraph
₿	make this letter lowercase
b̲	capitalize this letter
⌒	link inserted material

Notice how proofreading marks are used to make corrections in the following model:

MODEL

The numbᵉr of people living on the streets without Homes to call their own is a problem in many cities across America. In New York Ctiy in 1990, there were approximately 55,000 homeless peple. Philadelphias homeless numbered about 35,000. Cleveland had about 10,000 people without homes. In San Dieego, there were about 7,000 homeless people and in San francisco, more than 3,000 people *were* are homeless. These *were* are not just single people sleeping on park benches entire families may be homeless, including grandparents, parents, school-age children, and even iffants.

How can I share what I've written?

Some of your writing—for example, journal entries—might be for your eyes alone. However, most writing you do will be for a wider audience, and you can share it by publishing it in some form or another. The following chart lists some of the many ways you can publish your writing:

In Class
- Have a writer's conference with your teacher.
- Trade papers with a partner or read your paper aloud to a small group of fellow students.

At School
- Submit your writing to a school newspaper, literary magazine, or student anthology.
- Read your work aloud at a school assembly, literary club meeting, or debating society forum.
- Arrange to have your work performed at an assembly or a meeting of the drama club.

For Your Community
- Submit your writing to a local newspaper or a regional magazine, especially if your work focuses on topics of local interest.
- Read your work aloud at a meeting of a literary group, a poetry reading, or a public forum.
- Arrange to have your work performed at a community auditorium.

For a Wider Audience
- Submit your writing for publication in a national magazine. Use *Market Guide for Young Writers* by Kathy Henderson for help with selecting an appropriate magazine.
- Enter your writing in a contest. Writing contests for young people are also listed in *Market Guide for Young Writers*.

With Classmates or Friends
- Put together a class collection of writing. You can use a desktop publishing program or a copy shop to print and assemble a booklet of work.
- Start your own student literary magazine.

COMPUTER TIP

With the proper software, use your computer to design and produce professional-looking copies of your written work. You can select different typefaces, change the size of the type, and arrange it in various ways on the page. Some programs even allow you to scan in or create illustrations to accompany your work. Using a desktop publishing program and a good printer, you can create a complete book with an attractive cover, a title page, and a table of contents.

15

REFLECTING ON YOUR WRITING

What can my writing teach me?

Writing can teach you about yourself, about topics you are interested in, and about the processes of writing and learning. After you complete a writing project, take time to think about what you have learned. Ask yourself questions like those in the form below, and record your answers in a journal. By reflecting on your writing, you can gauge your progress as a writer.

Another good way to gauge your progress as a writer is to keep a portfolio of your work. A portfolio is a file folder or computer file for collecting and storing pieces of writing. These may be first drafts you will develop later or finished pieces that are especially important to you. Also, your teacher may tell you which pieces of writing to keep in your portfolio so that the two of you can evaluate your progress as a writer. Consider filling out a portfolio form and attaching it to your written work. The following sample shows what information you may want to record on such a form:

Date:

Title or topic of writing assignment:

What did I learn from writing about this topic?

What do I especially like about this piece of writing?

How does this piece show improvement over previous ones?

What prewriting, drafting, or revising strategies did I use?

How could I improve this piece of writing?

What problems did I solve as I worked on this piece?

How can I apply what I've learned to my next assignment?

THE ELEMENTS OF WRITING

■ ■ ■

Making Paragraphs, Sentences, and Words Work for You

Emblems, c. 1913, Roger de la Fresnaye
The Phillips Collection, Washington, D.C.

16

PARAGRAPHS

How do I create a good structure for a paragraph?

> A **paragraph** is a unit of writing containing a main idea and sentences that develop it.

Can you remember playing with building blocks as a child? Every block you placed became part of your own creation. A writer's building block is the paragraph. Like a building block, a paragraph can function both as a part of a larger structure and as a complete unit.

CREATING THE PARTS

The parts of a paragraph work together to develop one main idea clearly:

- a **topic sentence** states the main idea of the paragraph;

- **supporting details** develop the main idea with reasons, examples, facts, statistics, or incidents.

THE TOPIC SENTENCE

Because this sentence must present the main idea that holds a paragraph together, it must be clear. Here are some typical problems that occur in drafting topic sentences.

PROBLEM:	My topic sentence sounds dull and formulaic.
STRATEGY:	Draw your readers into your paragraph by giving a command or raising a question.
DULL TOPIC SENTENCE:	There are three ways to increase the membership of the Chess Club.
REVISED TOPIC SENTENCE:	If you are wondering how we can increase the membership of the Chess Club, I have three answers.

PROBLEM:	My topic sentence introduces a topic but doesn't say anything about it.
STRATEGY:	Ask yourself about your topic or use a cluster diagram to discover your perspective.
STATING A TOPIC:	Prescription drugs are expensive.
EXPRESSING A PERSPECTIVE:	Prescription drugs should be discounted for patients with below-average incomes.

Implied Topic Sentence

Some paragraphs, especially those in narratives and descriptions, have no topic sentence. Even a paragraph without a topic sentence, however, often suggests a single impression. For example, all the details in this model show that the store and its owner are timeworn:

MODEL FROM LITERATURE

The old store, lighted only by three fifty-watt bulbs, smelled of coal oil and baking bread. In the middle of the rectangular room, where the oak floor sagged a little, stood an iron stove. To the right was a wooden table with an unfinished game of checkers and a stool made from an apple-tree stump. On shelves around the walls sat earthen jugs with corncob stoppers, a few canned goods, and some of the two thousand old clocks and clockworks Thurmond Watts owned. Only one was ticking; the others he just looked at. I asked how long he'd been in the store.

—William Least Heat Moon, *Blue Highways*

SUPPORTING DETAILS

Sentences that add information or details about the main idea expressed in the topic sentence are called **supporting sentences.** Supporting sentences are the pillars or beams of a paragraph because they "hold up" or reinforce the main idea. The paragraph that follows shows a topic sentence and the details that reinforce the topic sentence:

MODEL FROM LITERATURE

Certainly the train was old. The seats sagged like the jowls of a bulldog, windows were out and strips of adhesive held together those that were left; in the corridor a prowling cat appeared to be hunting mice, and it was not unreasonable to assume his search would be rewarded.

—Truman Capote, "A Ride Through Spain"

The details of description, as well as the comparison "sagged like the jowls of a bulldog," reinforce the main idea that the train was old.

Among the types of supporting details you can use are facts, statistics, examples, reasons, and incidents. Which details you choose will depend on your purpose and audience. For example, if you were writing an informative paragraph for an audience unfamiliar with mathematical concepts, you might use facts and examples rather than statistics.

POSITIONING THE PARTS OF A PARAGRAPH

When putting the parts of a paragraph together, you have choices. For instance, you can express the main idea in the first or last sentence or in the body of the paragraph. In the following model, a student writer begins a paragraph with a topic sentence for dramatic effect:

STUDENT MODEL

The writer begins with a short, punchy topic sentence about stress.

The topic sentence is supported by a series of examples.

The conclusion restates and expands on the main idea.

<u>You know what stress is.</u> You're about to give an oral book review or ask the person of your dreams for a date. Your body starts doing weird things. You get sweaty hands, cold feet, and "cotton mouth." Your knees go wobbly and sound like castanets. You get a huge lump in your throat, and you think your friends can hear your heart pounding. And then you get even more stressed at being stressed!

—Chris Green, Danville, Indiana

In the following model, the writer concludes the paragraph with a topic sentence that puts the preceding specific examples in a wider context:

MODEL

In the first three sentences, the writer presents ways of researching family background, or genealogy.

By studying census reports for the years 1790–1920, you can gather critical information about your ancestors' names, ages, occupations, and residences. Land records and tax rolls offer glimpses into a family's economic history, and town histories can help you put specific information into a local context. Learning how to interview your living relatives will allow you to collect firsthand recollections of people, places, and events. In order to trace your family's genealogy accurately, you will need to become familiar with an array of research methods and materials.

The last sentnce is the topic sentence.

The topic sentence below comes in the body of the paragraph:

MODEL

Businesspeople are dressed smartly—the women in skirts and blouses and the men in crisp shorts, knee socks, and jacket and tie. The staff in restaurants and shops politely attend to tourists and native islanders alike. Almost all aspects of Bermuda's public life, in fact, are characterized by a civil, slightly formal manner, traceable to the island's long association with Great Britain. As in England, police officers in Bermuda carry no guns and wear the traditional tall hats of "bobbies." At four o'clock in the afternoon throughout Bermuda, tea is served.

The first and last sentences give examples that support the writer's main idea about Bermuda.

WRITING FOR MATH

Suppose you were asked to explain why the sum of the two nonright angles in a right triangle equals 90°. You could respond with a well-formed paragraph that followed this outline:

Topic Sentence: The sum of the two nonright angles in a right triangle equals 90° because the angles in all triangles must add up to 180°.

Support: Triangle: 3 angles equaling 180°. A right angle equals 90°; 180° minus 90° for the right angle equals 90°.

You might end with a sentence restating what you proved.

UNITY, COHERENCE, AND TRANSITIONS

 How can I make my writing clear and well organized?

Unity refers to a singleness of effect. A paragraph has unity when each sentence relates to the topic. An essay has unity when each paragraph relates to the main idea. **Coherence** refers to the orderly arrangement of ideas within a piece of writing.

Good writers communicate well by focusing on one topic at a time and presenting their thoughts on that topic in a logical way, using a number of transitional devices. The first step in this process is to achieve a consistent, unified effect.

Just as a group of people is unified when each member of the group works toward a common goal, so a piece of writing is unified when all the elements work together to express one main idea. Notice how the writer of the following paragraph gives his writing clarity and grace by making all of his sentences relate to one main idea.

MODEL FROM LITERATURE

The second sentence is a topic sentence that helps organize the paragraph.

Descriptions of land and people illustrate and support the writer's idea about time.

In the concluding sentence, Anaya echoes the topic sentence, maintaining unity.

Newcomers to New Mexico often say that time seems to move slowly here. I think they mean they have come in contact with the inner strength of the people, a strength so solid it causes time itself to pause. Think of it. Think of the high, northern New Mexico villages, or the lonely ranches on the open *llano* [plain]. Think of the Indian *pueblo* [town] which lies as solid as rock in the face of time. Remember the old people whose eyes seem like windows that peer into a distant past that makes absurdity of our contemporary world. That is what one feels when one encounters the old ones and their land, a pausing of time.

—Rudolfo A. Anaya, "A Celebration of Grandfathers"

UNITY IN ESSAYS

To unify a paragraph, formulate a topic sentence and have each sentence in the paragraph illustrate or support it, even if you do not include the topic sentence in the paragraph itself. To unify an essay, introduce the main idea in the first paragraph. The paragraphs that follow should each develop a new idea that supports the essay's thesis.

REVISING FOR UNITY

You need to be concerned about unity at every writing stage. Note how the writer of the following draft of an essay sharpens the focus by eliminating unnecessary details and making sure each paragraph supports the main idea:

MODEL

By the late 1950's, the motion picture industry had been honoring movie actors, actresses, producers, and screenwriters with Oscars for thirty years. Likewise, the television industry had been honoring the best people in the business with Emmy Awards for nearly two decades. It wasn't until 1959, however, that recording artists ~~like Bobby Darin~~ began receiving similar honors. In that year the National Academy of Recording Arts and Sciences (NARAS) handed out its first Grammy. Like the Oscars and the Emmys, Grammys are peer awards. Nominees and winners are picked by NARAS members.

The writer eliminates an unnecessary detail.

The first Grammy Awards ceremony was small and unpretentious. Five hundred members of the recording community showed up for the awards dinner at the Beverly Hilton in Los Angeles. ~~It was raining hard that night.~~ Twenty-eight awards were passed out. Golden gramophones were handed out to Frank Sinatra (for best album) and Ella Fitzgerald (for best jazz vocals). ~~I don't like these artists as much as today's hard rockers and rappers, but maybe these people were actually the best musicians at the time.~~

The writer deletes sentences that contain irrelevant or distracting details.

Today, the Grammy Awards ceremony is an entertainment bonanza. People in more than one hundred countries watch international recording

...AND THE WINNER IS...

GRAMMY AWARDS

artists perform their most popular hits. In the United States alone, millions of people tune in to watch the ceremony. Thousands of people attend the gala black-tie event. More than eighty awards are handed out to artists who work in styles as diverse as classical, country, jazz, pop, and rock. ~~Sting is my personal favorite.~~ Today's Grammys honor a spectrum of musical talent far broader than that of 1959, the year the ceremony began.

The last sentence returns to the origin of the Grammys, tying the first and last paragraphs together.

HOW CAN I MAKE MY WRITING EASY TO FOLLOW?

When writing is coherent, all the elements fit together in a logical way. A coherent paragraph has a topic sentence, and the supporting details are arranged in a clear and rational order. In a coherent essay, paragraphs are arranged according to an obvious plan with clear connections between ideas. In the following paragraph, Jill Ker Conway describes the activities of Australia's ranching families during their occasional visits to the city. Note her clear organization and use of repetition to link ideas.

 MODEL FROM LITERATURE

The paragraph begins with a topic sentence. All other sentences support it.

The repetition of parallel ideas expressed in parallel grammatical structures (see bold type) unifies the paragraph.

Note the repetition of the word unaccustomed in the first and last sentences.

The city was a place of unaccustomed leisure for people who labored hard seven days a week. . . . **For the women there were** the shops, the doctors and dentists for the children, and the luxury of restaurants, fresh fruit and vegetables, seafood, flower stands. **For the children there were** the marvels of electric lights, neon signs, moving pictures, and unlimited candy stores. These were balanced but not outweighed by the ministrations of the dental and medical professions and the ominous crowds. **For everyone there were** sore feet and aching legs which came from wearing one's best shoes on hard pavements, and the unaccustomed feel of city clothes.

—Jill Ker Conway, *The Road from Coorain*

COHERENCE IN NARRATIVES AND ESSAYS

Depending on your audience and purpose, you can choose among a variety of organizational plans. The following chart lists and describes some of these options:

ORGANIZATIONAL PLANS	STRUCTURE OF SUPPORTING INFORMATION
Parts and Whole	Describes the parts that form the whole
Chronological Order	Tells events in their order of occurrence
Spatial Order	Relates details in a clear spatial sequence, for example from top to bottom, clockwise, or from east to west
Order of Impression	Shows details in the order in which they are perceived
Order of Importance	Gives details in order of increasing or decreasing importance
Comparison and Contrast	Describes similarities and differences between two or more items, either feature by feature or subject by subject
Cause and Effect	Presents causes and their effects
Question and Answer	States questions and gives the answers
Pro and Con	Lists positive and negative aspects of a particular process, product, or action
Order of Familiarity	Gives details according to increasing or decreasing familiarity
General Rule and Particulars	Presents a general rule and the particulars that follow the rule, or lists the particulars and then states the general rule

HOW DO TRANSITIONS MAKE WRITING COHERENT?

In order to write a coherent narrative or essay, you must show how your ideas relate to one another. Transitional words can help you do this. The following chart lists transitional words that indicate a variety of relationships:

For more on organizational plans, see p. 24.

TYPE OF RELATIONSHIP	TRANSITIONAL WORDS
Order in Time	before, after, soon, since, once, then, when, first, next, while, finally, slowly, suddenly, now, later, until, at the same time, as soon as, whenever, as
Order in Space	above, below, beside, here, there, across, opposite, next to, near, where
Order of Importance	first, second, last, more important, least, better, best, finally, most of all
Similarities and Differences	like, unlike, likewise, in contrast, similarly, on the one hand, nevertheless, same as, different from, in the same way
Cause and Effect	because, therefore, so, as a result, thus, since, consequently, for that reason
Addition	and, also, again, furthermore, in addition, also, moreover, equally
Example	for example, such as, that is, along with, for instance, like, as, in other words

Note how Amy Tan uses transitions that indicate order in time.

MODEL FROM LITERATURE

I attended more tournaments, each one farther away from home. I won all games, in all divisions. The Chinese bakery downstairs from our flat displayed my growing collection of trophies in its window, amidst the dust-covered cakes that were never picked up. **The day after** I won an important regional tournament, the window encased a fresh sheet cake with whipped-cream frosting and red script saying, "Congratulations, Waverly Jong, Chinatown Chess Champion." **Soon after** that, a flower shop, headstone engraver, and funeral parlor offered to sponsor me in national tournaments. That's **when** my mother decided I no longer had to do the dishes. Winston and Vincent had to do my chores.

—Amy Tan, *The Joy Luck Club*

HOW CAN REPETITION MAKE WRITING COHERENT?

You can repeat words and grammatical structures to make your writing coherent. Repetition of key words and phrases emphasizes important points in a piece of writing and helps readers connect similar concepts expressed in separate sentences. When you repeat grammatical structures, you are using **parallel structure,** which calls attention to and links ideas of equal importance. Note the use of repeated words and parallel structure in the following excerpt:

MODEL FROM LITERATURE

> The people were in despair. They seemed heavy to me, heavy and dark; so heavy that it seemed they could not be lifted; so dark that they could not be made to see any more.
>
> —John Neihardt, *Black Elk Speaks*

The repetition of heavy *and* dark *and the parallel structure ("so* heavy/*so* dark*") emphasize the mood of despair.*

OTHER STRATEGIES FOR COHERENCE

Other strategies that help to improve coherence in your writing include using pronouns to refer to earlier nouns and using **synonyms,** words with similar meanings. For example, in an essay on the military, you can refer to *the commander-in-chief* by using the pronoun *he* in the course of a paragraph. In a piece about a road race, you can substitute synonyms like *dash* or *run* for the word *race.*

Note how pronouns and synonyms build coherence in the excerpt from an essay that follows:

MODEL

It has been nine years since my Uncle Luke sold his <u>farm</u>, but I can still remember just what <u>it</u> looked like. We moved to Chicago the year after the <u>land</u> was sold, and I haven't been back to <u>Wisconsin</u> since, but if I close my eyes I can picture the rolling <u>acres</u>. Memory is useful that way. It gives you the illusion that you can go back to a place, even if you know you can't.

The opening paragraph establishes the essay's thesis.

The writer builds coherence by using a pronoun and synonyms to refer to Uncle Luke's farm.

18

SENTENCES

 How do I recognize a sentence?

> A **sentence** is a group of words that expresses a complete thought.

Because sentences help communicate ideas clearly, you are expected to use them in school reports, essays, and most other writing that you do. Of the following groups of words, only the first expresses a complete thought and, therefore, qualifies as a sentence:

Dave Barry is a popular humorist.

His weekly columns in many newspapers.

Has also published several funny books.

To express a complete thought, a sentence must contain a subject and a predicate. The subject tells who or what the sentence is about. The predicate tells what the subject is or does.

SUBJECT	PREDICATE
Dave Barry	makes his home in Miami.
He	often writes about his two dogs.
His "main dog"	is named Ernest.
His "backup dog"	is named Zippy.

WHAT MAKES A SENTENCE EFFECTIVE?

Good communication requires not only that you write complete sentences, but also that your sentences say exactly what you mean. Here are some guidelines for writing effective sentences:

1. An effective sentence provides clear and complete information.

LESS EFFECTIVE: The popularity of Barry's columns resulted in *Dave Barry's Greatest Hits.*

MORE EFFECTIVE: The popularity of Barry's columns resulted in his best-selling book *Dave Barry's Greatest Hits.*

2. An effective sentence is concise, making its point in as few words as possible.

LESS EFFECTIVE: Because his mocking and humorous column is carried by more than 150 newspapers, it is well known that he is considered somewhat of an authority on the perils and troubles of modern life in America.

MORE EFFECTIVE: Because more than 150 newspapers carry Barry's irreverent column, he is considered an expert on the pitfalls of modern American life.

3. An effective sentence emphasizes its main point or most important detail. In a short sentence such as "He is very funny," all the details inevitably receive emphasis. In a longer sentence, however, the most important point or detail should be placed in a prominent position. You can usually emphasize a detail by placing it last.

LESS EFFECTIVE: Barry also belongs to a not quite serious writers' band that performs now and then.

MORE EFFECTIVE: Barry also performs now and then in a not quite serious writers' band.

You can also emphasize a detail by putting it first.

LESS EFFECTIVE: The band, which also features Amy Tan and Stephen King, plays rather loud rock-and-roll music.

MORE EFFECTIVE: Amy Tan and Stephen King also perform in the band, which plays rather loud rock-and-roll music.

The most important detail in the first pair of sentences is the not quite serious writers' band. The most important detail in the second pair is the participation of Amy Tan and Stephen King.

Stephen King

♦ **WHEN YOU WRITE** ♦

Use your first draft to get your thoughts on paper and to organize them. Once you have decided what you want to say, turn your attention to saying it in complete and effective sentences. Make sure your sentences provide clear, concise information. Also decide which detail you want each sentence to stress, and place that detail in a prominent position.

19

SENTENCE PROBLEMS

 How do I recognize when a sentence isn't working?

When your sentences are not finely tuned, there is a loss in the quality and clarity of your communication. The following lesson examines eight common sentence problems that prevent writers from communicating effectively and presents strategies for correcting those problems.

PROBLEM 1: SENTENCE FRAGMENTS

A **sentence fragment** is a group of words that is punctuated as a sentence but lacks a subject, a verb, or both and fails to express a complete thought. In the following passage, everything but the final sentence is a fragment:

For more on sentence fragments, see Problem Solver, p. 261.

Problem Passage: Sentence Fragments

Intrepid mountain climbers scaling a tall peak. Climb higher and higher. Up the frozen slopes. When they reach the top. They can look forward to an even more treacherous descent.

To correct a fragment, add the necessary subject or verb or both to complete the thought. Often you can do this by combining the fragment with a nearby sentence or another fragment.

Revision: Sentence Fragments

Intrepid mountain climbers **are** scaling a tall peak. **They** climb higher and higher **up** the frozen slopes. When they reach the top**,** **they** can look forward to an even more treacherous descent.

PROBLEM 2: RUN-ON SENTENCES

For more on run-on sentences, see Problem Solver, p. 260. For more on clauses, see p. 297.

A **run-on sentence** has two or more main clauses incorrectly punctuated as a single sentence. In the following passage, each sentence is a run-on:

Problem Passage: Run-on Sentences

Mountain climbers need years of training, good judgment is essential. The hazardous terrain includes sheer rock walls taller peaks also have snow and ice. Warm clothing is essential, the weather conditions are usually bad. The climbers reach high altitudes, they greatly appreciate thermal underwear.

There is more than one way to correct a run-on. You can divide the main clauses into separate sentences, using periods and capital letters; add a semicolon between the main clauses; or use a comma and a coordinating conjunction between them. Sometimes you can also introduce a subordinating conjunction to make one clause subordinate to the other, creating a complex sentence.

For more on semicolons, see p. 379. For more on conjunctions, see p. 322.

Revision: Run-on Sentences

Mountain climbers need years of training. **G**ood judgment is essential. The hazardous terrain includes sheer rock walls; taller peaks also have snow and ice. Warm clothing is essential**, for** the weather conditions are usually bad. **After** the climbers reach high altitudes, they greatly appreciate thermal underwear.

PROBLEM 3: STRINGY SENTENCES

A **stringy sentence** contains too many ideas connected by words like *and, so, then, and so, or,* and *then*. Stringy sentences are repetitious and hard to follow because the relationships between ideas are unclear.

Problem Passage: Stringy Sentences

Mount Everest is in Asia's Himalaya mountain range, and it is the world's tallest mountain, and so climbing it was a great challenge, and Edmund Hillary and Tenzing Norgay first climbed it in 1953, and then all the world celebrated their triumph.

To correct a stringy sentence, decide which ideas are closely related and which are not. When the ideas are not closely related, place them in separate sentences. When they are closely related, combine them in one sentence by adding a subordinating conjunction that clarifies their relationship.

Revision: Stringy Sentences

Mount Everest is in Asia's Himalaya mountain range. **Because** it is the world's tallest mountain, Mount Everest was a great challenge to climbers. **When** Edmund Hillary and Tenzing Norgay first climbed it in 1953, all the world celebrated their triumph.

PROBLEM 4: CHOPPY SENTENCES

Choppy sentences are a series of short sentences that create an abrupt, jerking rhythm. They are often boring, repetitive, and hard to follow because every idea is given equal emphasis and the relationships between ideas are unclear.

Problem Passage: Choppy Sentences

Icy slopes have few natural footholds. They are hard to climb. The climbers must use an ice ax. They chop out footholds. Then the climb can progress. Rocky slopes often have natural footholds. Climbers still must insert iron spikes into the rock surface. These spikes are called pitons. Rings are attached to these spikes. The rings hold the climbers' ropes.

To correct choppy sentences, combine sentences that express closely related ideas. You can link related sentences with a conjunction that makes their relationship clear or turn one sentence into a phrase and combine it with a related sentence. Vary sentence lengths and structures to make your writing more interesting.

For more on phrases, see p. 350.

Revision: Choppy Sentences

Because icy slopes have few natural footholds, **they** are hard to climb. The climbers must use an ice ax **to chop** out footholds **before** the climb can progress. Rocky slopes often have natural footholds, **but** climbers still must insert iron spikes **called pitons** into the rock surface. The rings **attached to these spikes** hold the climbers' ropes.

PROBLEM 5: WORDY SENTENCES

A **wordy sentence** includes words that do not add meaning. These extra words slow the reader down and obscure the message. To correct the problem, drop the wordy expressions or replace them with something shorter or more to the point. The chart on page 73 illustrates and corrects many common examples of wordiness:

WORDY SENTENCE	REVISION
People climb mountains **in spite of the fact that** many have died in the attempt.	People climb mountains **even though** [or **although** or **though**] many have died in the attempt.
Frostbite is always a danger **because of the fact that** temperatures are so cold.	Frostbite is always a danger **because** [or **since**] temperatures are so cold.
Icy slopes are treacherous on **account of the fact that** you can easily slip and fall.	Icy slopes are treacherous **because** [or **since**] you can easily slip and fall.
The reason why the Himalayas are a challenge **is that** they are the world's tallest range.	The Himalayas are a challenge **because** [or **since**] they are the world's tallest range.
Tenzing Norgay, **who was** a Sherpa guide, helped Edmund Hillary scale Everest in 1953.	Tenzing Norgay, a Sherpa guide, helped Edmund Hillary scale Everest in 1953.
The Himalayas go through Nepal, **which is** the homeland of the Sherpa people.	The Himalayas go through Nepal, the homeland of the Sherpa people.
What I want to say is that my sister enjoys rock climbing.	My sister enjoys rock climbing.
She **is a woman who** [or She **is someone who**] has gone rock climbing often.	She has gone rock climbing often.
She climbs rocky ridges **in a** bold **manner.**	She climbs rocky ridges bold**ly**.
What she seeks **is** adventure, but **what** she may have **is** rocks in her head.	She seeks adventure, but she may have rocks in her head.

PROBLEM 6: EMPTY SENTENCES

An **empty sentence** provides little information either because it repeats an idea or because it makes a statement without adding supporting facts, reasons, or other details. Correct empty sentences by eliminating the repetition or by adding supporting details.

EXAMPLE:	Daring French mountaineers scaled Annapurna in 1950. They were very adventurous.
ANALYSIS:	The second sentence is empty because it repeats information; **adventurous** means **daring.**
REVISION:	Daring French mountaineers scaled Annapurna in 1950.
TECHNIQUE:	Eliminate the repetition.

EXAMPLE:	*Annapurna,* a book about the expedition, is a classic since it is a noted book on mountain climbing.
ANALYSIS:	The sentence is empty because it is repetitive and does not provide details to explain *why* the book is a classic.
REVISION:	*Annapurna,* a book about the expedition, is a classic since it **gives one of the most accurate and dramatic accounts of real-life mountain climbing.**
TECHNIQUE:	Support opinions or generalizations with details.

PROBLEM 7: LACK OF PARALLEL STRUCTURE

Good writers use **parallel structure,** or similar grammatical form, to express similar ideas. The similarity in form helps readers recognize the similarity in content and also makes the content easier to read and remember. The use of parallel structure is often called **parallelism.**

FAULTY PARALLELISM:	The Himalayas are located in India, Tibet, Bhutan, and they also go through Nepal.
REVISION:	The Himalayas are located in India, Tibet, Bhutan, **and Nepal.**

FAULTY PARALLELISM:	At night the Himalayas can be freezing cold, but they are often extremely hot in the day.
REVISION:	At night the Himalayas can be freezing cold, **but in the day they are often extremely hot.**

FAULTY PARALLELISM:	Avalanches pose a threat, and another peril is seasonal monsoons.
REVISION:	Avalanches pose a threat, **and seasonal monsoons are another peril.**

FAULTY PARALLELISM:	Other ranges popular with climbers include the Andes, Caucasus, and the Alps.
REVISION:	Other ranges popular with climbers include the Andes, **the** Caucasus, and the Alps.

PROBLEM 8: UNNECESSARY SHIFTS

An unnecessary change in verb tense or in the person, number, or gender of pronouns often confuses and distracts readers. In the following passage, the verbs and pronouns are in bold print:

Problem Passage: Confusing Verb Tense and Pronoun Shifts

According to local legends, a mysterious creature **dwells** in the Himalayas. **Its** local name **is** Yeti; some **call it** the Abominable Snowman. Judging from **his** footprints, **he was** a creature of monstrous size.

The first two sentences in the problem passage use the present-tense verbs *dwells*, *is*, and *call*, but then in the third sentence there is a shift for no reason to the past tense with the verb *was*. Similarly, the passage first uses the third-person neuter pronouns *its* and *it* to refer to the creature but then shifts for no reason to the male pronouns *his* and *he*. Both of these unnecessary shifts have been corrected in the following revision.

Revision: Verb Tense and Pronoun Shifts

According to local legends, a mysterious creature **dwells** in the Himalayas. **Its** local name **is** Yeti; some **call it** the Abominable Snowman. Judging from **its** footprints, **it is** a creature of monstrous size.

For more on verb tense and pronoun shifts, see p. 265 and p. 266.

SENTENCE COMBINING

How do I avoid dull or choppy sentences?

Imagine that you came across this description in a novel: "The fire raced down the mountain. It raced with tremendous speed. It consumed homes. It consumed cars. It consumed trees. It left nothing behind but hot, white ash. Also, it left a row of blackened chimneys." Would you be likely to get caught up in the action, or would you wish the author would get to the point a bit quicker?

Now imagine that the sentences were combined to read like this: "The fire raced down the mountain with tremendous speed, consuming homes, cars, and trees and leaving only hot, white ash and a row of blackened chimneys."

Both descriptions say exactly the same thing, but the second will more likely get you to turn the page. Like the fire, the sentence rushes headlong, propelling the reader into the action.

Short sentences can be powerful and dramatic, but they can lose effectiveness when strung together unimaginatively, repeating the same subject-verb structure in sentence after sentence. Instead, you can add rhythm and variety to your writing by combining short sentences in many different ways.

SENTENCES WITH COORDINATING CONJUNCTIONS

For more on conjunctions, see p. 322.

If the ideas expressed in two short sentences are of equal importance, you can join the sentences with a **coordinating conjunction** such as *and*, *but*, or *or*. A coordinating conjunction links words or groups of words of equal rank, as shown in the following examples:

1. If the ideas in the two sentences are similar, use a comma and the conjunction *and* to join them:

> My friend Kim is a great ski jumper. He wants to try out for the Olympic team.
> **COMBINED:**   My friend Kim is a great ski jumper, **and** he wants to try out for the Olympic team.

2. If the sentences express differing ideas, use a comma and the conjunction *but*:

> He's only seventeen. He's strong and powerful, though.
> **COMBINED:**   He's only seventeen, **but** he's strong and powerful.

3. If the sentences express a choice, use a comma and the conjunction *or*:

Kim might compete in next year's Winter Olympic games.
Kim might wait for the games four years later.
COMBINED: Kim might compete in next year's Winter Olympic games, **or** he might wait for the games four years later.

SENTENCES WITH SUBORDINATING CONJUNCTIONS

Sometimes the ideas expressed in two sentences are of unequal importance; one sentence states an idea, and the other clarifies, expands, or limits the idea. You can join pairs of sentences (or main clauses) like these by adding a subordinating conjunction before the sentence containing the less important, or subordinate, idea. Choose the subordinating conjunction that reflects the relationship between the two sentences.

For more on clauses, see p. 297.

Subordinating Conjunctions

TO EXPRESS TIME:	before, after, when, while
TO EXPRESS LOCATION:	where, wherever
TO EXPRESS A CAUSE-EFFECT RELATIONSHIP:	because, since, as, so
TO EXPRESS CONDITION:	although, unless, if

I heard about Kim's victory. I was thrilled.
COMBINED: **When I heard about Kim's victory,** I was thrilled.
(time relationship)

He'll make the Olympic team. He may or may not be lucky.
COMBINED: He'll make the Olympic team **if he is lucky**.
(conditional relationship)

◆ WHEN YOU WRITE ◆

To add variety to your sentences, you can also reverse the order of the clauses, sometimes beginning with the subordinate clause and at other times with the main clause. An introductory subordinate clause should always be followed by a comma, as in the first example in the sentences that follow:

If he is lucky, he'll make the Olympic team.
I was thrilled *when I heard about Kim's victory.*

JOINING SENTENCES BY ADDING WORDS

In addition to joining whole sentences, you can join sentence parts, eliminating wordiness and making your writing more concise.

1. In sentences with identical subjects, eliminate the subject or subjects in the second sentence and join the two verbs with a coordinating conjunction such as *and, but,* or *or:*

> On Saturdays Tanjou and I go to the rink. Tanjou and I practice there for at least four hours.
> **COMBINED:**   On Saturdays Tanjou and I **go** to the rink **and practice** there for at least four hours.

2. In sentences with identical verbs, eliminate the verb in the second sentence and combine the two subjects with a coordinating conjunction:

> Tanjou is a speed skater. I'm a speed skater, too.
> **COMBINED:**   **Tanjou and I** are speed skaters.

3. Sometimes you can combine three or more sentences with identical subjects or verbs. In these cases, be sure to separate the verbs or subjects in your new sentence with commas, adding a coordinating conjunction before the last verb or subject.

For more about using commas in a series, see p. 305.

> Jean practices her starts. Luis practices his starts. Nadra practices her starts.
> **COMBINED:**   **Jean, Luis, and Nadra** all practice their starts.

4. You can also join sentences in which the subjects and the verbs are identical but the modifiers (such as adjectives or adverbs) are different.

> **ADJECTIVES:**   Tanjou is daring. She is also powerful.
> **COMBINED:**   Tanjou is **daring and powerful.**
>
> **ADVERBS:**   I would like to skate as fast as she can. I would like to skate as gracefully as she can.
> **COMBINED:**   I would like to skate as **fast and** as **gracefully** as she can.

5. In some cases, you can combine sentences by adding modifiers that you have created from other parts of speech. For instance, you can create **present participles** (ending in *-ing*) or **past participles** (ending in *-ed*) from verbs.

For more on participles, see p. 348.

Tanjou heads into the stretch. She pants.
COMBINED: **Panting,** Tanjou heads into the stretch.

On the third lap she passed a skater. The skater was winded.
COMBINED: On the third lap she passed a **winded** skater.

You can also change an adjective to an adverb.

I watched as Tanjou raced for the finish line. I was nervous.
COMBINED: I watched **nervously** as Tanjou raced for the finish line.

Here is a revision in which the writer combines short, choppy sentences to make longer, more rhythmic ones:

M O D E L

Two athletes in our school are trying out for the Winter Olympics. Like all top athletes, they are strong. ~~They are also~~ dedicated and determined to win. Tanjou Smith ~~is a~~ speed skater. ~~So is Earl Williams.~~ During training, they practice six hours a day. ~~Somehow they~~ still manage to keep up with their studies. ~~They are~~ disciplined and uncomplaining. ~~They~~ push their bodies to the limit.

(editorial insertions: "and Earl Williams are", "and")

The writer combines sentences by creating a series.

The writer combines two subjects.

The writer combines two verbs.

The writer adds participles to the main sentence.

JOINING SENTENCES BY ADDING PHRASES

Another way to combine sentences and improve the flow of your writing is to take a group of words from one sentence and add it to another.

1. You can combine sentences by using one to create an **appositive phrase**—a noun or pronoun and its modifiers that rename a preceding noun or pronoun.

For more on appositives, see p. 290.

I always watch the downhill skiing during the Winter Olympics.
Downhill skiing is my favorite event.
COMBINED: I always watch the downhill skiing, **my favorite event,** during the Winter Olympics.

For more on preposi-
tional phrases,
see p. 354.

2. Sometimes you can combine two sentences by taking a prepositional phrase from one sentence and inserting it into the other.

Downhill courses are exciting and dangerous. The courses are filled with steep drops and tight turns.

COMBINED: **With their steep drops and tight turns,** down-hill courses are exciting and dangerous.

For more on participial
phrases, see p. 348.

3. Sometimes two sentences can be combined by changing a verb and its modifiers in one sentence to a participial phrase and adding it to the other sentence. A **participial phrase** is made up of a participle and all its modifiers. **Present participles** end in *-ing* and most **past participles** end in *-ed*. Be sure that you place the participial phrase as close as possible to the word it modifies in the combined sentence.

The skiers are leaning precariously into their turns. They are barely in control.

COMBINED: **Leaning precariously into their turns,** the skiers are barely in control.

Here is a model showing how to combine sentences by adding various types of phrases:

The writer adds an appositive phrase.

The writer combines sentences by adding a prepositional phrase.

The writer combines two sentences with a past participle.

The writer combines two sentences with a present participle.

> ## MODEL
>
> ⌒, a ski jumper,
> Doug Park is also trying out for the Winter
>   ∧
> Olympic team. ~~He is a ski jumper.~~ He learned to
> ski jump as a child. ~~He practiced ski jumping~~ in
> his backyard. His father built him a long ramp.—
>   practicing
> ~~It was~~ made of scrap lumber. Often ~~he practices~~
>   ⌒,
> more than forty jumps a day∧ ~~H~~e wins first place
> in the state championship every year.

JOINING SENTENCES BY ADDING CLAUSES

Another way to make your writing more concise and varied is to convert one main clause to an adjective clause. An **adjective** or **relative clause** is a group of words that contains a subject and a verb and begins with a relative pronoun such as *who, that,* or *which.*

JOINING SENTENCES WITH <u>WHO</u> If the subject of the main clause is a person or persons, begin the subordinate clause with the relative pronoun *who*.

When the details in the adjective clause are **essential** to the meaning of the main clause, you do not need to set off the subordinate clause with commas. When the details in the clause are **not essential,** however, you must separate the subordinate clause from the main sentence with commas.

ESSENTIAL:	Only athletes **who are in top physical and mental condition** can qualify for the Winter Olympics.
NONESSENTIAL:	The Scandinavians**, who are champion skiers,** will probably win many medals this year.

JOINING SENTENCES WITH <u>THAT</u> OR <u>WHICH</u> If the subject of the main clause is an object or idea, begin the subordinate clause with the word *that* or *which*.

Use *that* when the information in the subordinate clause is **essential** to the meaning of the sentence. Use *which* when the information in the subordinate clause is **nonessential** to the meaning of the sentence; separate the clause with commas.

ESSENTIAL:	Everyone cheered for the Jamaican luge team **that qualified last year.**
NONESSENTIAL:	Jamaica**, which never gets an inch of snow,** seems an unlikely place for a sledding team.

Here is a model that shows how to incorporate adjective clauses:

MODEL

Seventeen-year-old Chris Woods has been figure ⁀, who grew up in a small town in Idaho, ∧ skating since he was five. ~~He grew up in a small town in Idaho.~~ Coaches say he is one of the most who know a lot about technique ∧ ever promising skaters they have seen. ~~The coaches know a lot about technique.~~ Woods routinely performs the triple axel. ⁀, which is one of the most difficult jumps in figure skating. ~~It is one of the most difficult jumps in figure skating.~~ Next year he hopes to that perform the quadruple axel. ~~It~~ will be the key to his qualifying for the Winter Olympics team.

The writer adds a nonessential clause beginning with *who,* an essential adjective clause beginning with *who,* a nonessential adjective clause beginning with *which,* and an essential clause beginning with *that.*

21   SENTENCE VARIETY

How do I vary my sentences?

You are riding in a car through the desert. It's flat and hot. There are no trees, no mountains, nothing but sand and sky and a row of telephone poles marking the horizon. You probably find the view monotonous. Writing, too, can be dull if all the sentences are as alike as a row of telephone poles. Good writing depends on variety—in sentence structure and sentence length and especially in the way sentences begin.

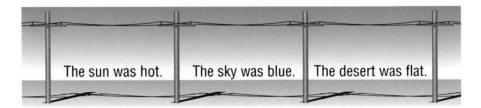

The sun was hot. | The sky was blue. | The desert was flat.

TYPES OF SENTENCE STRUCTURES

To vary your sentences, first learn the four basic sentence structures:

1. A **simple sentence** has one main clause. A **main clause** contains a subject (S) and a predicate (P) and can stand alone as a sentence.

     S   P
Jordan **led his horse into the ring.**

2. A **compound sentence** has two or more main clauses linked by the coordinating conjunctions *and, but,* and *or* or by a semicolon. The conjunctions are usually preceded by a comma.

> For more about clauses, see page 297.

   S   P   S   P
He **squeezed with his knees,** and the horse **broke into a trot.**

3. A **complex sentence** has one main clause and one or more subordinate clauses. A **subordinate clause,** underlined here, has a subject and a predicate but cannot stand alone as a sentence.

     S   P   S   P
<u>After he **checked the length of the stirrups**</u>, he **swung into the**

saddle.

4. A **compound-complex sentence** has two or more main clauses and one or more subordinate clauses.

      S   P   S
<u>When the horse **had trotted once around the ring**</u>, Jordan

  P   S   P
clicked his tongue and the horse **broke into a gallop.**

VARYING SENTENCES

You can vary the sentences in your writing in two ways:

SENTENCE STRUCTURE AND TYPE Try to write a mix of simple, compound, complex, and compound-complex sentences. Also, use exclamatory and interrogative sentences as well as declarative sentences. For more about sentences, see p. 380.

SENTENCE LENGTH Providing a variety of long and short sentences keeps readers interested. If most of your sentences are short and choppy, you can lengthen them by

- combining two or more sentences.
- elaborating—that is, adding descriptive details, quotations, facts, and examples. For more about elaboration, see p. 34.

If most of your sentences are long, you can consider dividing some of the compound and complex sentences into simple sentences. Remember that one way to emphasize an important point is to express it in a sentence that is much shorter than the surrounding sentences.

Note how this paragraph was revised for sentence variety:

MODEL

The spectators cheered, as Jordan led his horse into the ring. He checked the length of his stirrups, and Then he swung himself into the saddle. To warm up, Jordan trotted his the horse once around the ring. He clicked his tongue, and Then he urged broke the horse into a gallop, as They approached the jump. The horse lengthened its stride and stretched its neck eagerly. "Hooray!" Jordan shouted as The horse soared over the jump.

The writer makes a complex sentence.

The writer makes a compound sentence.

The writer makes a compound-complex sentence.

The writer adds a direct quotation.

VARYING SENTENCE BEGINNINGS

Here are some ways to add variety to sentence beginnings:

1. Begin with an adverb.

Gracefully, the horse soared over the jump.

2. Begin with a prepositional phrase.

With great ease, the horse soared over the jump.

For more about prepositional and participial phrases, see p. 354 and p. 348.

3. Begin with a participial phrase.

Gathering its strength, the horse soared over the jump.

4. Begin with a subordinate clause.

As Jordan held his breath, the horse soared over the jump.

5. Begin with a question.

"Will I make it?" Jordan asked himself as the horse soared over the jump.

Here is the second paragraph of the model on the previous page. Notice the variety of sentence beginnings.

M O D E L

The writer begins with a subordinate clause.

The writer begins with an adverb.

The writer adds prepositional and participial phrases.

When
All the riders had finished, ~~Then~~ the rails on
Nervously,
the jumps were raised. Jordan awaited his turn.
One of the contestants missed a jump, and a rail
With a lump in his throat,
clattered to the ground. Jordan urged his horse
forward. He cleared the jumps with inches to
Nodding to the judges,
spare. He left the ring.

◆ WHEN YOU WRITE ◆

After you have revised your sentence beginnings, reread your draft to make sure you have not created any misplaced modifiers. Every introductory participial phrase must modify the noun or pronoun that follows it.

INCORRECT: **Grinning proudly,** the blue ribbon was awarded to Jordan by the judges. [Was the blue ribbon grinning proudly?]

CORRECT: **Grinning proudly,** Jordan accepted the blue ribbon from the judges.

How do I know which word to use?

Which of these sentences better describes the painting below? The pond has flowers floating in it. The surface of the pond is dotted with many delicate water lilies.

Both sentences tell something about the painting. The second sentence, however, describes the painting with greater detail. When you write, choose words that do the following:

1. Say exactly what you mean.

2. Fit your purpose—whether it is to amuse your readers, impress them with your knowledge, or create a mood.

3. Suit your audience. There is no use in saying exactly what you mean if you use words your audience will not understand.

Waterlilies at Giverny, 1908
Claude Monet, private collection

GENERAL VERSUS SPECIFIC WORDS

General words describe large concepts (like *freedom*) or large categories (like *flower*). Sometimes it is useful and appropriate to use such words. Often, however, it is desirable to replace a general word like *plant* with a more specific word like *hyacinth*. Note the pairs of general and specific nouns, adjectives, and verbs below:

---

music or **reggae?** **Reggae** is a particular kind of **music** that has unique rhythms and a specific origin.

Jimmy Cliff was the first popular artist to sing ~~music~~ *reggae* in America.

---

sad or **mournful?** **Mournful** gives a precise description of **sadness** involving loss.

The barn owl's ~~sad~~ *mournful* hoot echoed over the fir trees.

---

ran or **sprinted?** **Sprinting** is a specific kind of **running** that calls for a burst of effort over a short distance.

We ~~ran~~ *sprinted* down the hall to get to class.

You'll also want to replace vague, unclear words with specific, precise words that come as close as possible to your meaning. Avoid overused, vague words such as *really, nice, fine, good, bad, kind of, sort of,* or *great.* In addition, replace vague phrases with specific single words.

◆ WHEN YOU WRITE ◆

The writer George Orwell once said, "Prose consists less and less of *words* chosen for the sake of meaning, and more and more of *phrases* tacked together like the sections of a prefabricated henhouse." When you write, select specific words rather than standard phrases.

            about
■ I am writing ~~in regard to~~ my job application.

      believe
■ ~~I am of the opinion~~ that I am the best candidate for the job.

This model replaces general words with specific words.

MODEL

The writer replaces general words such as writer, place, people, mail, stop, person, tell, and thoughts with specific words that reveal more about Grandma and her relationships with others.

                                   poet.
    Maxine Renier is a well-known ~~writer.~~ She is
                                    home
also my grandmother. I grew up in the same ~~place~~
with her, and I never knew she was famous.
Fans
~~People~~ wrote to her all the time—I never wondered
               hundreds letters.
why she got ~~lots~~ of ~~mail.~~ People would recognize
                      pester
her on the street and ~~stop~~ her. I had no idea why.
                                warm, wonderful woman
To me, she was Grandma—a ~~nice person~~ to whom I
   confide   *secrets.*
could ~~tell~~ all my ~~thoughts.~~

CONCRETE VERSUS ABSTRACT WORDS

One way to be specific is to use concrete words instead of abstract words whenever possible. A **concrete** word refers to something you can perceive with your senses—the color red for example. An **abstract** word refers to qualities that cannot be perceived by the senses—for instance, the quality of fairness. To talk about sophisticated ideas, you need to use abstract words. Be sure, however, that your meaning is clear.

DENOTATION AND CONNOTATION

A word's **denotation** is its dictionary definition or literal meaning. Many words also have an underlying emotional association, or **connotation**. The word *graveyard*, for example, is defined as "a place where bodies are buried." That is its denotation. For many people, the word also carries a connotation, or emotional charge, of fear or sorrow. These synonyms have similar meanings but very different connotations:

Positive	Negative
slender	skinny
fragrance	odor
popular	vulgar
firm	tough

TRY THIS

Try substituting *synonyms*, words with similar denotations, in your sentence to figure out which word has the right shade of meaning for the context.

When you choose words, consider their connotations. Shades of meaning can change the emotional effect of a passage, as in the following model:

MODEL

> The fish swam ~~actively~~ (fierce) in circles. Behind it, the ~~shadow outline~~ (loomed) of the shark ~~moved~~ (suspected). The fish ~~knew~~ it was in ~~trouble,~~ (danger,) but it wasn't until the ~~big mouth~~ (huge jaws) ~~opened around~~ (encircled) it that ~~eater~~ (predator) changed to ~~eaten~~ (prey).

The writer's use of words that have negative, suspenseful connotations creates a frightening effect on the reader.

ONOMATOPOEIA

The sound of the words you choose can also influence readers' reactions to your writing. Poets pay special attention to sound effects, but you can use **onomatopoeia**, or words that imitate or suggest the sounds they describe, to make your prose come alive. Notice how this writer uses onomatopoeic words to suggest the sounds of nature.

For more on onomatopoeia, see p. 145.

MODEL FROM LITERATURE

> When she came the beauty of the llano unfolded before my eyes, and the **gurgling** waters of the river sang to the **hum** of the turning earth.
>
> —Rudolfo A. Anaya, "A Celebration of Grandfathers"

The onomatopoeic words *gurgling* and *hum* suggest the sounds they describe.

VARIETIES OF ENGLISH

? *How are different varieties of English used?*

Diplomats around the world speak it. So do sugarcane workers in Jamaica, journalists in India, and schoolchildren in Louisiana, Scotland, and Australia. English is one of the most widely spoken languages in the world; yet if you put a Yorkshire coal miner in the same

room with a pizza chef from Chicago, there would be no guarantee they would understand each other.

English is as varied as the people who speak it. As any teenager who's tried to communicate with his or her forty-something parents knows, even people who live in the same house don't always use the same words. What's "dis" to one person may be "insulting" to another.

STANDARD AND NONSTANDARD ENGLISH

Even **standard English**, which follows the most widely accepted rules of grammar, usage, and mechanics, comes in more than one variety. There is **formal English**: the language used in public speeches, textbooks, and school papers. There is also **informal English**: the language used in letters to friends and in family conversations.

Notice the long, complex sentences, absence of contractions, and sophisticated vocabulary in the following example of formal English:

MODEL FROM LITERATURE

Here individuals of all nations are melted into a new race of men, whose labors and posterity will one day cause great changes in the world. . . . The American is a new man, who acts upon new principles: he must therefore entertain new ideas, and form new opinions. From involuntary idleness, servile dependence, penury, and useless labor, he has passed to toils of a very different nature, rewarded by ample subsistence—this is an American.

—Jean de Crèvecoeur, *Letters to an American Farmer*

By contrast, notice the short sentences (including some fragments), simpler vocabulary, and contracted verbs in this example of informal English:

The young fathers are waiting outside the school. What curly heads! Such graceful brown mustaches. They're sitting on their haunches eating pizza and exchanging information. They're waiting for the 3 P.M. bell. It's springtime, the season of first looking out the window. I have a windowbox of greenhouse marigolds. The young fathers can be seen through the ferny leaves.

—Grace Paley, "Anxiety"

Another variety is **nonstandard English**, which consists of all the **dialects,** or versions of English, spoken across the world that do not conform to standard grammatical rules. Appalachian farmers speak a distinct dialect of English; so do taxi drivers from the East End of London and Cajun fishers in Louisiana.

WHICH VARIETY OF ENGLISH SHOULD I USE?

Many people are comfortable in using at least two—and sometimes three—varieties of English. A teenager from Baton Rouge, for instance, may speak a Cajun dialect at home, use informal standard English with his friends, and write his school papers in formal standard English.

From time to time, you may get into situations in which you are uncertain about the variety of English to use. For example, should you say "I am honored to make your acquaintance" when you are introduced to a friend's parents or "It's very nice to meet you"? Should you write "previous employment history" on your résumé or simply "job experience"?

When you are writing, choosing the appropriate variety of English depends largely on your audience and your purpose. If you're sending a résumé to a prospective employer or writing a research paper or theater review, use formal English. Remember, though, that no one will be impressed if your language sounds stiff and pretentious. Try to strike a balance between naturalness and the proper degree of formality. (See the revised model at the end of this lesson for an example of the standard English that is appropriate for most school papers.)

TYPES OF INFORMAL STANDARD ENGLISH

In informal speech and writing, people often enliven their language by adding colorful words and phrases. The following are some of the most commonly used examples of informal expressions:

COLLOQUIALISMS Does your little brother always *tag along* with you? Do you eat *skimpy* meals? Does classical music *get on your nerves*? The italicized expressions are examples of **colloquialisms**, informal words and phrases characteristic of everyday speech. Playwrights and novelists incorporate colloquialisms into their dialogue to make it sound natural and authentic. Some journalists and essay writers also use colloquialisms to give their pieces a personal or common touch.

For more on clichés, see p. 100.

IDIOMS AND CLICHÉS Did the new student in class *catch your eye*? Did your friend's comment *rub you the wrong way*? Does that TV commercial *drive you up the wall*? Have you been feeling *under the weather*? The italicized words are **idioms**, expressions whose meanings cannot be taken literally. Idioms are a particularly lively form of colloquial speech. Used wisely, they can add spice to your writing, but beware of **clichés**—trite, overused expressions. If you say it's been *raining cats and dogs* or that a character *slept like a log*, your readers will quickly get bored.

"I've heard that the proof is in the pudding, but I sure couldn't find it."

SLANG If you're describing something you like, do you say it is *cool, slick, def, trick, far-out, neat, phat, groovy,* or *peachy-keen*? Which word might your parents or grandparents use? Slang is a highly informal variety of language created by a particular age or social group. It is the most changeable form of informal speech in which new words and meanings are continuously created and dropped. A few slang words and expressions, like *snapshot*, eventually become part of the standard vocabulary; most fall out of use or change meanings as time passes. For example, how many of the italicized words in the first sentence above do you use? When you are thinking of including slang in your writing, bear in mind that it can date your work and limit your audience. In writing, slang can indicate a particular time as quickly as clothing or hairstyles can in a movie. Used selectively, however, slang can add authenticity and immediacy to your writing.

TYPES OF NONSTANDARD ENGLISH

Like novelist Amy Tan, many Americans grow up with and use more than one variety of English. The most common form of nonstandard English is a **dialect**, a version of English spoken by a group of people who share a heritage. These dialects are not "incorrect"; they simply differ from standard English in their vocabulary and pronunciation and sometimes in grammar and usage. They develop slowly, over decades or even centuries, among people who live in the same region or who have similar social, economic, or ethnic backgrounds. The dialect spoken in parts of Appalachia, for instance, contains Elizabethan words and expressions used by the English immigrants who settled there in the seventeenth century. Black English, a dialect spoken by some African Americans, contains words and syntax derived from the West African languages spoken by captives shipped across the Atlantic and sold as slaves. Cajun English is peppered with French expressions spoken by immigrants who moved from French-speaking regions of northeast Canada to Louisiana two hundred years ago. Jamaican English, otherwise known as Patois, contains influences from West African languages and the Portuguese spoken by some slave traders.

Notice the nonstandard use of the verb *to be* and the variations in subject-verb agreement and in past-tense verbs—all typical of Black English—in this excerpt from a story about an old woman from Mississippi coming across a scarecrow in a field:

FROM A WRITER

66 *Language is the tool of my trade. And I use them all—all the Englishes I grew up with.* 99

—Amy Tan, "Mother Tongue"

MODEL FROM LITERATURE

"Ghost," she said sharply, "who be you the ghost of? For I have heard of nary death close by."

But there was no answer—only the ragged dancing in the wind.

She shut her eyes, reached out her hand, and touched a sleeve. She found a coat and inside that an emptiness, cold as ice.

"You scarecrow," she said. Her face lighted. "I ought to shut up for good," she said with laughter. "My senses is gone. I too old. I the oldest people I ever know. Dance, old scarecrow," she said, "while I dancing with you."

—Eudora Welty, "A Worn Path"

WRITING FORMAL ENGLISH FOR SCHOOL

The writing you do for school usually requires formal standard English. Avoid both informal language and language that is too stiff.

MODEL

About 46 million Americans—roughly one in four—smoke cigarettes. ~~A lot~~ Many of those smokers ~~be kids~~ are teenagers. If tobacco companies had their way, more and more ~~kids~~ teenagers would light up every day. With the number of ~~grown-up~~ adult smokers shrinking, the ~~big guns in~~ executives of the tobacco industry are ~~jumping over backwards~~ rushing to expand the teenage market.

Ads are the key. Billboards display cartoon ~~personages~~ characters designed to appeal to children. Now one company has come up with a new female character to make smoking attractive to ~~young females~~ girls. Dr. Joycelyn Elders, ~~our~~ the surgeon general, thinks the advertising campaign is ~~truly gross~~ appalling. ~~There's lots of~~ Several studies ~~that~~ show that advertising lures young smokers. The Journal of the American Medical Association just published a study that ~~shows that~~ showing teenage girls are influenced to smoke by ads targeted directly to young women. A ~~bunch~~ number of companies are marketing special cigarettes that make smoking ~~look~~ appear feminine and ~~cool~~ sophisticated.

What can be done to keep teens from ~~jumping on the~~ smoking ~~bandwagon? Maybe nothing.~~ ? But one solution might be to ban cigarettes ~~for good. Folks~~ entirely. Researchers at the Food and Drug Administration are thinking about classifying cigarettes as addictive drugs. If they did, then nobody, from ~~your~~ a twelve-year-old ~~kid~~ girl ~~sister~~ to ~~your~~ an eighty-year-old grandfather, could ~~get off on~~ legally indulge in this dangerous substance.

How do I create tone and mood in my writing?

What emotional reactions do you have when you look at Walker's painting? Do you find the scene happy or sad, amusing or serious? Would you enjoy being part of this scene? Your reactions are the result of specific choices that the artist made while painting. When you write, you too can make choices that influence the effect your work will have on your readers.

> **Tone** is the writer's attitude toward his or her subject and toward readers. **Mood** is the emotional quality, or atmosphere, of a piece of writing.

Selling Fruit, Highway 1, Barbados, Jill Walker, Sardcon Gallery, New York

WHAT IS THE TONE OF A LITERARY WORK?

A writer's tone, for instance, may be formal or informal, serious or lighthearted, engaged or detached, happy or angry or sad. The tone you adopt in a particular piece of writing usually depends on three factors: the subject you are writing about, your purpose in writing, and the audience you are writing for. For example, if your subject were recent bicycle thefts at your school, your tone might be angry—especially if you were one of the thief's victims. However, if you were a reporter for the school newspaper and you had to give an objective account of events, you would adopt a more detached, unemotional tone.

You create a tone largely through **diction**, or word choice. For example, you can choose among the following types of diction:

Words with Negative Connotations	Words with Positive Connotations
cowardly	prudent
sly	clever

Formal Words	Informal Words
craven	chicken
clandestine	sneaky

or more on word
noice, see p. 85.

Sentence structure also influences your tone. Short, simple sentences can convey a childlike tone, whereas longer sentences convey a more serious tone.

WHAT IS THE MOOD OF A LITERARY WORK?

The mood of a work may be uplifting, joyous, gloomy, suspenseful, or whimsical, among other things. The words, images, and other details you choose all contribute to the mood. You create the mood based on the specific effect you wish to have on readers. Works of nonfiction, as well as fiction, can create very specific moods or feelings. For example, for a personal essay about your first date, you might use informal language and comical, exaggerated images to establish a whimsical or lighthearted mood. For a detective story, you might choose dynamic action verbs and ominous imagery to establish a suspenseful mood.

For more on imagery,
see p. 100.

As you read the following model, consider how the writer's words, images, and other details help to create a particular mood.

MODEL FROM LITERATURE

Words with positive connotations, like *springtime* and *gentled*, work with images like "peach trees...shedding fragrance and pink blossoms" and "tender young grass" to create a warm mood.

Springtime transformed the mesas. The peach trees in the canyon were shedding fragrance and pink blossoms on the gentled wind. The sheep no longer foraged for the yellow seeds of chamiso [a dense desert shrub] but ranged near the hogan [Navajo house] with the long-legged new lambs, eating tender young grass.

—Juanita Platero and Siyowin Miller, "Chee's Daughter"

❖ *How do I achieve my own voice and style?*

Imagine this scene: You and your arch-rival, the person with whom you have the least in common, are both running for class president. On the day before the election, you both give final campaign speeches to the student body. How do your speech and delivery differ from your rival's?

The differences in the way you and the other candidate speak reflect differences in who you are. Just as people's speaking voices vary, so do their writing voices. The **voice,** or identity, that you reveal in your writing is a result of your writing **style.** Your writing style, in a turn, is affected by your use of diction, tone, sentence structure, and grammar and mechanics.

DICTION Contrast the following examples of **diction,** or word choice. Which tells you more about the writer's personality?

For more on diction, or
word choice, see p. 85.

VAGUE DICTION:	I ate lunch.
SPECIFIC DICTION:	I devoured four huge slices of pizza.

Vague, unimaginative words like *ate* and *lunch* have no personality because they are too general and are used too often to have much of an effect on the reader. Specific, concrete words make a stronger impression on the reader and reveal more of the writer's personality.

TONE The **tone** of your writing reflects your attitude toward your subject and audience. For example, your tone may be critical or admiring, formal or informal. An effective style demands that you use a tone suited to the audience and the occasion. Which of the following examples has a tone better suited to an objective restaurant review? Which has a tone better suited to a newspaper ad aimed at budget-minded young diners?

Chez Shay's offers large portions at reasonable prices.

Go to Chez Shay's for humongous portions at
incredibly low prices!

For more on tone, see
p. 93.

SENTENCE STRUCTURE The lengths and types of sentences you use also affect the personality you convey in your writing. Too many short simple sentences can make your writing seem childish or abrupt; too many long compound-complex sentences can make your writing seem dull or preachy. To achieve a natural voice and style, use a variety of sentence structures.

GRAMMAR AND MECHANICS Errors in grammar, spelling, or punctuation may create negative impressions that will draw the reader's attention away from your true voice and style. To ensure that your personality shines through, correct such errors when you proofread your writing.

As you read the following passage from a reflective essay, consider how elements of style help the writer convey his voice, or writing personality:

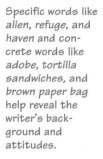

MODEL FROM LITERATURE

Specific words like *alien, refuge,* and *haven* and concrete words like *adobe, tortilla sandwiches,* and *brown paper bag* help reveal the writer's background and attitudes.

The writer uses a reflective yet fairly informal tone suitable for this type of essay.

A variety of sentence lengths and types helps the writer to reveal his natural voice.

Those were exciting times. Around me swirled the busy world of the university, in many respects an alien world. Like many fellow undergraduates, I sought refuge in the library. My haven during those student university years was the reading room of the west wing of the old library. There I found peace. The carved vigas [roof beams] decorating the ceiling, the solid wooden tables and chairs, and the warm adobe color of the stucco were things with which I was familiar. There I felt comfortable. With books scattered around me, I could read and doze and dream. I took my breaks in the warm sun of the portal, where I ate my tortilla sandwiches, which I carried in my brown paper bag. There, with friends, I sipped coffee as we talked of changing the world and exchanged idealistic dreams.

—Rudolfo A. Anaya, "In Commemoration: One Million Volumes"

What is dialogue?

"The Great and Powerful Oz has spoken."
"Make my day!"
"Love means never having to say you're sorry."
"After all, tomorrow is another day."
"Beam me up, Scotty."

A scene from *Star Trek*

These lines of dialogue bring scenes from movies, television shows, and books vividly to life. Whenever you write a story, essay, or personal narrative, use dialogue to create a feeling of realism and to heighten your reader's sense of involvement. Try to write dialogue that sounds natural—the way real people talk, as in the following example.

MODEL FROM LITERATURE

A tall, thin man said, "Closed up. For good," and started to shut the door.

"Don't want to buy anything. Just a question for Mr. Thurmond Watts."

—William Least Heat Moon, "Nameless, Tennessee"

In addition to sounding realistic, good dialogue can also

- reveal the speakers' personalities and backgrounds.
- keep the plot or action moving.
- show relationships among people.

HOW CAN DIALOGUE REVEAL CHARACTER?

For more on varieties of English, see p. 88.

When you want dialogue to reveal the speakers' personalities or backgrounds, try these techniques.

1. Use distinctive varieties of English, such as slang, dialect, or formal English. These speech patterns will tell readers something about your speakers' backgrounds.

2. Indicate, when appropriate, *how* the people in your work speak. For instance, do they murmur, shout, advise, console, whine? Their manner of speech reveals as much about their personalities and emotions as the words themselves.

MODEL FROM LITERATURE

The character's broken English indicates that she is new to the United States.

The words *quietly* and *concluded at last* suggest that she is intelligent and discerning.

My mother patted the flour off her hands. "Let me see book," she said quietly. . .

"This American rules," she concluded at last. "Every time people come out from foreign country, must know rules. You not know, judge say, Too bad, go back. They not telling you why so you can use their way go forward. . . ."

—Amy Tan, *The Joy Luck Club*

HOW CAN I USE DIALOGUE TO KEEP THE ACTION MOVING?

Instead of just telling the reader what will happen next, use dialogue to advance the action. Let the speakers' words *show* what is happening.

MODEL FROM LITERATURE

This conversation reveals that one character is dying. It sets up the conflict in the story.

"How long will it be?" he heard his grandmother say.

"Before the end of summer."

"Are you sure?"

"Yes. You should have sent for me long ago."

"I've passed my threescore and ten years. I'm eighty-four."

—Grant Moss, Jr., "Before the End of Summer"

HOW CAN DIALOGUE SHOW RELATIONSHIPS?

You can show how characters feel about each other by letting their words speak for them. If one character speaks gently to another, that probably indicates fondness or love. Characters who interrupt each other and speak harshly demonstrate a different relationship.

MODEL FROM LITERATURE

He stopped her. "It's too late."

"But you don't understand."

"What don't I understand? I understood then; I understand now."

Tears now traveled down the lines in her face, but when she spoke, her voice was clear. "I thought you knew. I had ten children. I had to give all of them what they needed most." She nodded. "I paid more mind to GL [your brother]. I had to. GL could-a ended up swinging if I hadn't. But you was smarter. . . ."

—William Melvin Kelley, "A Visit to Grandmother"

This brief exchange reveals a strained relationship between mother and son.

The writer characterizes the mother's tone of voice as "clear." This word suggests that the mother feels she did the best she could for each of her ten children.

HOW DO I PUNCTUATE DIALOGUE?

When you write dialogue, you are recording the exact words of your characters. Therefore, the rules governing the punctuation of direct quotations apply to dialogue.

1. Place quotation marks around each person's exact words.

2. If the tag line (the words that identify the speaker and his or her tone of voice) follows the dialogue, place punctuation inside the final quotation mark. If the tag line appears before the dialogue, place a comma before the opening quotation mark.

For more on punctuating quotations, see Quotation Marks, p. 372.

3. Begin a new paragraph when the speaker changes.

MODEL FROM LITERATURE

"What did you say? I didn't hear you."

"I said that I had been thinking about something."

"About what?"

"About the priest sprinkling holy water for Grandpa. . . ."

—Leslie Marmon Silko, "The Man to Send Rain Clouds"

27

FIGURATIVE LANGUAGE

What is figurative language, and how can I use it?

Figurative language is lively language that goes beyond the literal, dictionary meanings of words.

You probably use figurative language all the time without realizing it. For example, if you say that someone is a string bean, you are using a comparison to make his or her tall, thin appearance easier to picture. However, this comparison is a **cliché**, an expression used so often that it has lost its impact. Good writers use figurative language that is fresh and imaginative.

TYPES OF FIGURATIVE LANGUAGE

Examples of figurative language are called **figures of speech**. Two of the most common kinds of figures of speech are similes and metaphors. A **simile** compares two apparently different things by using the words *like, as,* or *more . . . than.* A **metaphor** makes a comparison by talking about one thing as if it *were* another.

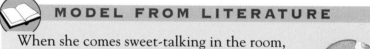 **MODEL FROM LITERATURE**

The poet uses a simile to compare the mother's approach to eating grits.

The poet also uses a metaphor: *Mama is a sunrise.*

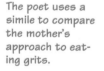

When she comes sweet-talking in the room,
   she warms us
   like grits and gravy,
   and we rise up shining.
Even at night-time Mama is a sunrise
   that promises tomorrow and tomorrow.
     —Evelyn Tooley Hunt, "Mama Is a Sunrise"

Hyperbole is figurative language that uses exaggeration not meant to be taken literally. **Personification** is a type of figurative language that talks about something nonhuman as if it were human.

The poet uses personification when he describes *hunger* as if it were a person.

MODEL FROM LITERATURE

. . . hunger searches you out.
It always asks you,
How are you, son? Where are you?
Have you eaten well?
     —Simon J. Ortiz, "Hunger in New York City"

A **symbol** is a person, place, event, or object that represents something beyond its literal meaning. Usually it stands for an abstract idea or a range of related ideas. The writer rarely states directly what the symbol means.

MODEL FROM LITERATURE

After they had dived and come up, they swam around, hauled themselves up, and waited their turn to dive again. They were big boys—men, to Jerry. He dived, and they watched him; and when he swam around to take his place, they made way for him. He felt he was accepted and he dived again, carefully, proud of himself.

—Doris Lessing, "Through the Tunnel"

The details in the second and third sentences and Jerry's pride, described in the last sentence, all suggest that the diving symbolizes maturity .

USING FIGURATIVE LANGUAGE

Figurative language can explain something unfamiliar in more familiar terms or provide a concrete image for something abstract. A good figure of speech can be effective in essays as well as in poetry and fiction.

MODEL FROM LITERATURE

At other times, in other places, when I have been privileged to be with the old ones, to learn, I have felt this inner reserve of strength upon which they draw . . . . I have felt the same power when I hunted with Cruz, high on the Taos mountain, where it was more than the incredible beauty of the mountain bathed in morning light, more than the shining of the quivering aspen, but a connection with life, as if a shining strand of light connected the particular and the cosmic.

—Rudolfo A. Anaya, "A Celebration of Grandfathers"

By comparing the spiritual connections Anaya felt with a shining strand of light, the simile helps readers understand an abstract idea.

TYPES
OF WRITING

■ ■ ■

How to Do Your Writing Assignments

Girl Writing, 1941, Milton Avery
The Phillips Collection, Washington, D.C.

EXPRESSIVE WRITING: JOURNAL WRITING

28

How do I keep a journal?

Whether your journal is a clothbound book, a sketch pad, a spiral notebook, or a computer file, it is a private place to write informally and freely.

> A **journal** is a record of your thoughts, feelings, experiences, and observations.

> March 21, 8:30 P.M. —Just got home from Greg's house. It's a family of seven—Greg's the second of five kids. Everyone in his family is very frank and open and talks a lot. Greg's sister Yolanda seems to be living out the most interesting drama of all. While helping her best friend recover from an accident, she's campaigning hard for Class President—and may win!
>
> VOTE

WHAT GOES INTO A JOURNAL?

What goes into your journal is entirely up to you. Here are types of entries suitable for a journal:

- reactions to local, national, and international events
- responses to books, poems, plays, and stories you read
- details or impressions of day-to-day events
- memories of past events
- plans or wishes for the future
- thoughts about friends and family members
- reflections on school subjects and what you're learning
- ideas for your own stories, poems, and essays

Some people like to include newspaper clippings, letters, photos, ticket stubs, and other such items in their journals. Others make sketches, drawings, or collages on journal pages. Some people keep

FROM A WRITER

66 Good journal writing is fishing the river of your mind. 99

—Dan Kirby and Tom Liner, *Inside and Out*

two separate journals—one for personal ideas and memories and another to record responses to literature, progress in a sport, or reflections on school subjects. Others combine different types of entries in one journal. Since there are so many possibilities, feel free to use any technique that works for you. Remember too, that you have the right to keep journal entries private.

The following journal entry was written by a student traveling with her family on a road trip. Note how the student recorded feelings, thoughts, and observations about the trip and her family.

STUDENT MODEL

May 11, 12:30 p.m.—We just went to a drive-thru. I swear my hamburger was gray inside. Dad wouldn't even let us stop and stretch. Dad's like a maniac. He's determined to make this trip in as short a time as possible. Mom's not saying much. She just sits there next to Dad, in front of me, reading a romance novel. All I can see of her is her curly blond hair peeking over the headrest.

—Alice Reagan, Swampscott, Massachusetts

HOW DO I USE A JOURNAL?

People use their journals in a variety of ways. As you get used to keeping a journal, you'll probably find yourself referring to it more and more. The following chart describes how your journal can help you with your writing:

PURPOSE	STRATEGY
writing to express your thoughts, feelings, and observations about people and events	Write in your journal as regularly as possible so that you'll have a detailed record of how you grow and change.
creating a story, poem, essay, or play	Skim your journal for anecdotes, descriptions, and topics.
trying out a kind of writing you've never attempted before	Freewrite in your journal, experimenting with words and ideas.

KEEPING A DOUBLE-ENTRY JOURNAL

A double-entry journal helps you engage in a give-and-take with the literature you read. On the left-hand pages of this journal, write as you read, jotting down words, phrases, and images from the text that catch your attention or spark your curiosity. Use the right-hand pages of your journal to respond freely to whatever you've written on the left-hand side. This kind of journal can help you think and feel more deeply about what you are reading.

Here's an example of a double-entry journal:

TRY THIS

Occasionally review journal entries. Make notes next to old entries. Perhaps an event recorded long ago has new meaning for you now.

"The Jilting of Granny Weatherall" by Katharine Anne Porter	
"The children huddled up to her and breathed like little calves..." (p. 84, para. 1)	I remember the soft-eyed calves at the farm I visited.
"The pillow rose about her shoulders and pressed against her heart and the memory was being squeezed out of it: oh, push down on the pillow, somebody: it would smother her if she tried to hold it." (p. 84, parag. 3)	Granny must be trying not to remember something. I think this must be the key to the story.
"...her features were swollen and full of little puddles." (p. 85, para. 1)	What does this mean? Was she crying?

Whatever form your journal takes, you'll find that you revisit it often to find ideas and to reflect on your reading and writing.

WRITING FOR SCIENCE

In science class, you may be asked to set up a journal to record your observations of nature or of a specific phenomenon. For example, you might be required to note how the moon changes from night to night. With a scientific journal, it is important to make observations regularly and to write the date and time of each observation. You might also make labeled sketches or diagrams of what you observe. If your journal includes a variety of observations, consider the following:

• Use all your senses to observe. Record what you hear, feel, and smell as well as what you see.
• Make observations at different levels. Look high, look low, and look under objects on the ground.
• Bring field guides with you for reference.
• Use a hand lens to observe small items.
• Use binoculars or a telescope to observe distant objects.
• If you usually make observations alone, try observing with a friend; if you usually make observations with others, try observing alone.

29

EXPRESSIVE WRITING: REFLECTIVE ESSAY

What is a reflective essay?

Thoughtful and conversational, reflective essays can help you clarify your thoughts about yourself and the world. As you explore the deeper meanings of your experience in your essay, you invite your readers to share the reflective process that led to your insights.

Like all personal writing, the reflective essay is a means of self-expression, yet it does have important features you should keep in mind as you plan your writing.

> In a **reflective essay,** a writer explores the meaning of an observation or personal experience to gain fresh insights into life.

GUIDELINES

A reflective essay

► vividly describes an observation or a personal experience.

► explores the meaning of this observation or experience to gain insights into life.

► is conversational in style and thoughtful in tone.

► is written from the first-person point of view.

HOW CAN I FIND A SUBJECT TO WRITE ABOUT?

Novelist Virginia Woolf reflected on a moth on her windowsill. Dylan Thomas wrote about throwing snowballs at cats. Amy Tan explored her mixed feelings about her ancestral language, Chinese. Any topic, large or small, is worthy of consideration in a reflective essay.

If you're trying to come up with a subject and are drawing a blank, consider these strategies:

CREATE A PERSONAL TIMELINE. Include mileposts showing important stages in your life. Which of these experiences will have the greatest appeal for your readers?

1980 I'm born in Cincinnati, Ohio.
1985 My grandparents sell their farm.
1987 We move to Chicago.
1989 I win first place in track.
1990 My brother is hurt in motorcycle accident.
1991 I place second in state math contest.
1994 My mom gets new job at the bank.

SIFT THROUGH YOUR OLD KEEPSAKES. These might include ribbons, trophies, photographs, souvenirs, and so on. Look for a memento of a personal experience that affected you deeply. Freewrite in your journal about the experience. How did it change you as a person?

CHAT WITH A RELATIVE OR FRIEND. Recall an experience you shared. It might be a camping trip, a scary encounter, or a conflict you helped resolve. What was special about this experience for you and for your companion? How did it influence you?

BROWSE THROUGH A BOOK OF QUOTATIONS. Look up authors or subjects that interest you. Do any of the quotations remind you of a significant experience of your own?

HOW DO I INTERPRET MY EXPERIENCE?

Reflective essays don't just narrate an event. They explore its significance. Like a painter studying a landscape day after day, the writer of a reflective essay sees more meaning in the experience or observation each time he or she reflects on it.

To help you see the true significance of your subject, try creating a chart. First, briefly describe the experience or observation you have chosen to explore. Then try to recall the thoughts and feelings prompted by the experience, and write them down. Next, spend some time reflecting on the meaning of this experience. Has your interpretation of what happened changed over time? If so, how? Write down two or three insights or questions triggered by your experience. Finally, try summing up what you have learned. You may discover that your final insight is quite different from your initial reaction to the event.

The following chart is an example of prewriting notes exploring the meaning of an event:

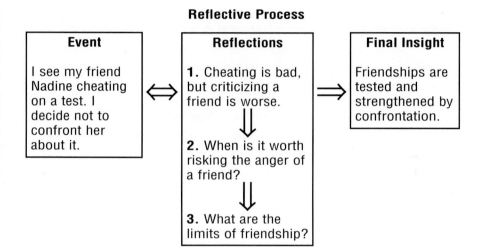

Reflective Process

Event	Reflections	Final Insight
I see my friend Nadine cheating on a test. I decide not to confront her about it.	**1.** Cheating is bad, but criticizing a friend is worse. ⇩ **2.** When is it worth risking the anger of a friend? ⇩ **3.** What are the limits of friendship?	Friendships are tested and strengthened by confrontation.

HOW DO I DRAFT MY ESSAY?

Once you have chosen your experience or observation and have begun to explore its meaning, you're ready to begin drafting your essay. Remember that it is important to present *both* your experience or observation and your reflections on it. There are different strategies for doing this. Brief descriptions of some of these strategies follow. However, keep in mind that what you write about will help determine your strategy.

One useful strategy for a reflective essay is to narrate a single experience, pausing several times during the narration to reflect on the meaning of what you have just related. This is a good approach if you are writing about a complex experience or sequence of events and want to reflect on different aspects of it. This strategy is used in the model at the end of this lesson.

A second useful strategy is to narrate the complete experience or observation in detail, suggesting how it affected you, and then draw conclusions by reflecting on the experience as a whole. This is a good approach to use if the experience leads you to a single, important insight or realization that has application beyond your personal experience. One student used this strategy to reflect on the meaning of having her father called up to fight in the Gulf War.

A third useful strategy is to describe several related experiences that, when reflected on together, suggest a common meaning. This strategy is useful for reflective essays that relate more than one experience or observation. One student used this strategy to explore the emotional impact a series of moves from home to home and school to school had upon him.

WRITING FOR SOCIAL STUDIES

Sometimes in a social studies class you may be asked to write an analysis of a historical event. Try applying a reflective writing strategy to your social studies essay. A good historical analysis both describes an event and reflects on its broader meaning and effects: how it affected the social, political, and economic conditions immediately after the event and in the decades, even centuries, that followed. In fact, one of the reasons people study history is to reflect on how events in the past have influenced life today.

HOW DO I END MY ESSAY?

Generally, your reflective essay should conclude by returning to the observation or concrete incident described in your introduction. This is your opportunity to interpret its deeper significance in light of the insights you have gained. Consider ending your essay with a dramatic quotation, a thought-provoking question, or a strong statement about the lessons your experience has taught you.

Amy Tan begins a reflective essay on language by telling how she was made "keenly aware" of "the different Englishes" she uses. Then, at the conclusion of her essay, she returns to this idea and remembers how she became a better fiction writer by learning how to use these "Englishes":

MODEL FROM LITERATURE

I began to write stories using all the Englishes I grew up with: the English I spoke to my mother, which for lack of a better term might be described as "simple"; the English she used with me, which for lack of a better term might be described as "broken"; my translation of her Chinese, which could certainly be described as "watered down"; and what I imagined to be her translation of her Chinese if she could speak in perfect English, her internal language. . . . I wanted to capture what language ability tests can never reveal: her intent, her passion, her imagery, the rhythms of her speech and the nature of her thoughts.

Apart from what any critic had to say about my writing, I knew I had succeeded where it counted when my mother finished reading my book and gave me her verdict: "So easy to read."

—Amy Tan, "Mother Tongue"

HOW DO I REVISE MY ESSAY?

As you revise, ask yourself the following questions:

CHECKPOINTS FOR REVISING

▶ Have I based my essay on an experience or observation that will interest my readers?

▶ Have I vividly described this experience or observation?

▶ Have I thoughtfully explored this experience to gain new insights?

▶ Does my exploration lead logically to the insights I express?

▶ Is my essay written in a clear, conversational style?

This last paragraph of a reflective essay shows the revisions the writer made to make the conclusion tighter and flow more logically:

MODEL

I've come to understand that ~difficult~
~Talking about~ things doesn't necessarily hurt
friendships, it can make them ~stronger.~ It's easy
think
to ~get the idea into your head~ that friendship is
fun together
just about good times, about having ~a blast and~
stuff ~and pretty much~ nothing else. I realize now
decided not to
that when I ~didn't~ talk to Nadine I missed out on
important. having a problem
something Maybe she was ~unhappy;~ maybe she
needed my help.

Friendships are only worth having if you're willing to risk losing them.

The writer moves a sentence and adds a closing thought to make the final insight clear.

The model that follows is the final draft of a reflective essay:

I never suspected that it would happen. My friend Nadine was a model student; she studied hard and got good grades. So when I saw her cheating on a French exam—she had photocopied parts of the textbook and hidden them under her test paper—I didn't know what to do. I thought about telling her what I'd seen, but I didn't want to jeopardize our friendship. Did I do the right thing? Now I'm not so sure.

I didn't mean to catch Nadine cheating. I saw her by accident when I passed by her desk on my way out of the room. She looked up at me, her eyes narrowing as if to say, "Don't give me away." If I had thought about it as carefully then as I have since, I would have talked to her right away.

Later that day, I saw Nadine eating lunch alone. She's usually surrounded by friends at lunchtime. Was something wrong? I wondered. Did she feel guilty? Maybe she'd had a problem at home and didn't have time to study. I should have talked to her, but I was afraid she'd get angry.

It's easy to think that friendship is just about good times, about having fun together and nothing else. I realize now that when I decided not to talk to Nadine, I missed out on something important. Maybe she was having a problem; maybe she needed my help. I've come to understand that talking about difficult things doesn't necessarily hurt friendships; it can strengthen them. Friendships are only worth having if you're willing to risk losing them.

The writer begins with a statement that immediately engages readers' interest.

The writer clearly describes the incident that inspired the reflection.

The writer begins the reflective process by questioning an initial response to the incident.

The writer returns to the incident and reflects further on it.

The writer discovers a new level of meaning in the experience.

The writer has gained an insight into the larger significance of the experience.

30

WRITING TO DESCRIBE: DESCRIPTIVE AND OBSERVATIONAL WRITING

How is descriptive writing related to observational writing?

Descriptive and observational writing are closely linked but not identical. Observational writing identifies the subject the writer observed, conveys the vantage point from which the observation was made, tells when and where it occurred, and uses sensory details to describe it. All observational writing is descriptive, but not all descriptive writing is based on actual observation. Good writers can describe things that they have visualized only in their imaginations, as in the following passage:

> **Descriptive writing** uses vivid details to re-create a person, place, scene, object, or emotion in words. **Observational writing** describes a writer's firsthand perceptions of a subject.

The Shipwreck, c. 1805, J.M.W.Turner

MODEL FROM LITERATURE

... the terrific funnel, whose interior, as far as the eye could fathom it, was a smooth, shining, and jet-black wall of water ... speeding dizzily round and round with a swaying and sweltering motion, and sending forth to the winds an appalling voice, half shriek, half roar. ...

—Edgar Allan Poe, "A Descent into the Maelstrom"

HOW CAN I USE DESCRIPTIVE WRITING?

You can write a descriptive essay to bring to life for readers specific people, places, things, and events. In addition, you can use descriptive details in all kinds of writing. For example, when you write a story, you vividly describe characters, settings, and events so that readers can experience them, in their imaginations. In a news article, you can use descriptive details to help readers feel like eyewitnesses to the important events that you are reporting. When you report the results of a science project, you present details from an experiment that you observed and recorded.

Using descriptive details doesn't mean scattering a handful of adjectives and adverbs throughout your writing. It means helping readers experience a scene. You can breathe life into a description by choosing the right details and making the most appropriate comparisons.

GUIDELINES

A good description

▶ relies on all five senses, not only on sight.

▶ uses vivid, specific details and comparisons to bring a subject to life.

▶ is carefully and clearly organized.

▶ can create a strong mood or atmosphere.

▶ improves all kinds of writing, both fiction and nonfiction.

A good piece of observational writing

▶ identifies the subject.

▶ conveys the vantage point, or angle, from which the subject is observed.

▶ identifies the specific time and place in which the observation occurs.

▶ uses sensory details to re-create the writer's observations.

HOW DO I CHOOSE A SUBJECT?

If you want to write an essay that is entirely descriptive, here are some ways to choose a topic:

LOOK AROUND YOU. The easiest things to describe are those you experience firsthand. For example, look closely at something you see every day. Use your other senses as well to examine your subject.

EXPAND YOUR HORIZONS. Look at photographs. Leaf through books and magazines. Listen to music. What scenes do these sights and sounds evoke?

SEARCH YOUR MEMORY. Think of places and people from the past. Draw a sketch or make an audiotape to recall your impressions in sharper detail.

Navajo girl, Monument Valley, Arizona

USE YOUR IMAGINATION. Take a fantasy trip to another place or time—even to another planet. Freewrite about whatever comes into your mind. Later you may want to build on some of your thoughts and images to make what you imagined come alive for a reader.

WHAT KINDS OF DETAILS DO I INCLUDE?

The kinds of descriptive details you choose and the way you present them depend on your audience and your purpose for writing. In most kinds of nonfiction writing, factual details must be presented in a clear, objective fashion. This kind of writing is called **literal description**.

In fiction writing and in personal essays and personal narratives, however, the details you emphasize will depend on your thoughts and feelings about your subject. This kind of writing, called **subjective description**, requires further thinking about your purpose and your audience. What mood or atmosphere do you want to create in your description? Do you want to evoke a gloomy, tense, wild, peaceful, or mysterious feeling? Do you want to make your audience laugh, cry, or feel angry? Which details about the person or scene will evoke those responses in your audience?

Notice how Mark Helprin uses descriptive details to create an exhilarating, hopeful mood in the opening paragraph of his story "Katherine Comes to Yellow Sky."

MODEL FROM LITERATURE

Like a French balloonist who rides above in the clear silence slowly turning in his wicker basket, Katherine rode rapidly forward on a steady-moving train. It glided down depressions and crested hills, white smoke issuing lariat-like from the funnel, but mostly it was committed to the straightness of the path, the single track, the good open way. And as an engine well loved, the locomotive ran down the rails like a horse with a rider.

—Mark Helprin, "Katherine Comes to Yellow Sky"

Figurative language uses imaginative comparisons to evoke feelings in readers. For an example of a subjective description using figurative language, see the student model on page 118.

For more on figurative language, see p. 100.

WRITING FOR SCIENCE

Objective observations and descriptions of laboratory work in science classes must be focused on measurable changes (or the lack of changes) in experimental materials. Furthermore, results must be presented in a standardized, objective format, using statistical data and measurements from which scientific conclusions can be drawn. Laboratory reports do not allow for subjective descriptions.

If you are assigned to write field notes based on your observations of the natural world, however, you may be given permission to combine accurate, detailed scientific observations with your subjective views. You can also use your field notes as source material for the creative writing you are doing.

HOW CAN I "SHOW" RATHER THAN "TELL"?

Your subjective description should show what you are describing. The more details you include, the more complete a picture your readers will draw in their minds. What is the difference between the sentence below and the model that follows it?

The thin old man had white hair and dark eyes.

STUDENT MODEL

The man looked like a scarecrow, all bones and skin—wrinkled brown skin, at that. His nose was bent crookedly to one side, and tobacco stains had yellowed his teeth, but he had some redeeming features. They were, namely, short-cropped, snow-white hair with a hint of a wave, and wise, kind, dark eyes.

—Cynthia Lewis, Sweetwater, Texas

The first sentence is a flat statement. It tells a few facts about a person but provides nothing that would help readers distinguish him from any other man of his age and general appearance. The student model, on the other hand, uses concrete details and comparisons to create a unique, vivid, and memorable picture of a particular individual. It shows rather than tells. In providing a vivid portrait of the man's physical appearance, the student focuses on particular features, such as the man's eyes, that also offer insight into his personality.

HOW DO I ORGANIZE MY DESCRIPTION?

The following questions will help you plan and organize an effective description:

- Are your details mainly visual? If so, you may wish to give your description a spatial organization.

- Are you describing an incident? If so, you may wish to organize your description in chronological order.

- Do you want to suggest meaning beyond the literal? If so, you may wish to arrange your details in their order of significance.

STUDENT MODELS

The sand of the shoal is the color of pummeled stone, the overhanging banana trees a weathered green. Above is a haze so fine that it fades into blue imperceptibly. The light is strong salt-gray.

—Michelle Johnson, Sarasota, Florida

Using spatial order, the writer describes the scene from the bottom up.

By the time the old man reached the mailbox, the morning sun hung high in the sky. Metal burned hot against his skin as he opened the box. Reaching his gnarled hand inside, he felt nothing except dry aluminum. He shut it back nonchalantly, though his face was tight with disappointment.

—Cynthia Lewis, Sweetwater, Texas

The writer describes events in chronological order.

Just a couch at the window, its tasseled pillows tossed to one side. A rocker, forlornly rocking in the sympathetic wind. And the glass bottle ships sitting proudly on the mantel—the only objects in the house that were free of dust.

—Summer Woodford, Strafford, Maryland

The writer uses fragments and describes the most important objects last.

HOW DO I REVISE MY DESCRIPTION?

Just as a narrative is shaped by a point of view, observational writing is shaped by the writer's location. In order to rethink your description, imagine viewing the same scene from a different vantage point. This exercise may give you ideas for revising your description.

In addition, try showing your description to a friend. Then reread it along with your friend's comments, keeping these questions in mind:

CHECKPOINTS FOR REVISING

▶ Have I used the five senses in my description?

▶ Have I used imaginative comparisons?

▶ Have I used details that show rather than tell?

▶ Have I presented the details in an orderly way?

STUDENT MODEL

The writer identifies her subject and uses a simile that elicits an overall impression.

Vivid verbs like *swoops, glides,* and *slinks* add movement to the scene.

Words like *fallen, brown, lone, bare, peeling,* and *sagging* reinforce the mood and setting.

The writer appeals to the senses of hearing (*chirping*), touch (*embraces*), and smell (*rotten*) and describes things that catch her eye, creating a patchwork effect resembling a gypsy's shawl.

My spacious back yard lies spread out before me like a gypsy's shawl. I hear the faint chirping of robins, and occasionally one swoops down from a tree and glides to the other side of the yard. From time to time, the wind picks up fallen brown leaves and swirls them away to one of the overgrown flower beds. A lone tomcat slinks craftily along the fence, his gray striped belly brushing bare patches of earth. A peeling picnic table sits crookedly in a large circle of dirt where a swimming pool used to be. Beyond the ancient table lies a sagging clothesline, which a yellow delicious apple tree embraces with its twisted branches. Rotten apples decorate the base of the tree like Christmas gifts. A Styrofoam archery target leans crazily against a shed, waiting for a strong gust to send it careening.

—Ami Palmer, Boise, Idaho

WRITING TO DESCRIBE: BIOGRAPHICAL PROFILE

31

How can I capture a person in writing?

Would you like to meet a famous quarterback? The director of an Oscar-winning film? Chances are you will never meet them, but you can get to know them a little by reading biographical profiles. A good biographical profile makes readers want to know more about the person.

> A **biographical profile** is a brief article that creates a vivid portrait of a real person.

GUIDELINES

A biographical profile

▶ focuses on someone of interest to you or to the public.

▶ usually includes a physical description, impressions of the subject's personality, and biographical information.

▶ reveals the writer's attitude toward the subject.

WHOM CAN I WRITE ABOUT?

Anyone can be a suitable subject for a biographical profile—as long as the person interests you and you can interest your readers. Your choice of subject depends both on your purpose and your audience. If you're writing a profile for the school yearbook, for instance, a classmate is a more appropriate subject than a Hollywood actress.

WRITING FOR SCIENCE

Scientists make excellent subjects for biographical profiles. Is there a chemistry or geology teacher at your school with an interesting background? Have you heard of a scientist in your community who discovered something or developed an innovative solution to an environmental problem? Remember to keep your purpose and audience in mind as you write your profile. Ask your subject to explain his or her research in simple, graphic language. Use reference sources to verify that the scientific background you provide in your profile is accurate.

Stephen Hawking, physicist

HOW DO I GET INFORMATION ABOUT MY SUBJECT?

Your strategies for gathering information will vary depending on your choice of subject. Here are some suggestions:

Someone you know personally	After explaining your writing plan, set up a mutually convenient time to talk to your subject. Jot down quotations, anecdotes, and mannerisms that reveal personality.
A national or international celebrity	Read interviews with and articles about your subject.
A public figure in your community	Read published interviews and other pro-files. If possible, watch the person on television or arrange for an interview.

HOW DO I ORGANIZE A BIOGRAPHICAL PROFILE?

You can organize a profile in several ways. Here are just a few options:

HOW CAN I BRING MY PROFILE TO LIFE?

Once your first draft is finished, look through it to make sure your information is accurate and complete. If necessary, strengthen the tone of your profile by adding appropriate direct quotations, anecdotes, and concrete examples. As you revise your profile, consider the following questions:

CHECKPOINTS FOR REVISING

▶ Do I show why this person is intriguing?

▶ Do I capture my subject's character traits and physical appearance?

▶ Is the biographical information I include accurate?

▶ Do I reveal my attitude toward the subject?

Here is an example of a biographical profile

MODEL

Rosa James has never bought a tube of paint—not one. She has never taken an art class. "Waste of time," she says. Yet she's one of the hottest artists in Los Angeles. Her sculptures, made from discarded objects, are displayed in local galleries.

The writer introduces an interesting subject and establishes a sympathetic tone.

Born in St. Louis, James came west "when Nixon was president" and has spent twenty years living in downtown L.A. She made her first sculpture out of Pepsi cans "stitched" together with coat hangers. "I call it my freedom quilt," she says, "because it's red, white, and blue."

The writer includes biographical information to begin building a portrait.

Tall and gray-haired, with bright eyes and quick hands, James is a familiar figure downtown. Stores and local residents donate castoff materials for her sculptures, and two elementary schools have asked her to teach an art class.

The writer provides a physical description of the subject.

"I'm too busy to teach right now," says James as she hammers a hubcap into a canoelike shape. "Maybe someday, when I slow down." Does she mind being called the junk lady? "I don't mind," she laughs. "Some of the finest-looking things in this world are thrown away. There's art everywhere, if you just look around."

The writer uses quotations and details from the subject's daily life to reveal her personality .

32

WRITING TO NARRATE: PERSONAL NARRATIVE

 How can I show what a personal experience meant to me?

A **personal narrative**—or an **autobiographical incident**—presents an experience from the writer's life and shows its importance.

Imagine your life as an autobiography in progress. How does your life story read so far? Pick one of the episodes from your "story": your first ride on a two-wheel bike or a painful quarrel with your best friend. What did the incident teach you about life? About yourself? Writing a personal narrative can help you understand who you are and maybe even give you an insight into the direction your life is taking.

GUIDELINES

A personal narrative

▶ tells about a meaningful incident.

▶ relates events truthfully and in a clear order.

▶ uses vivid details to re-create people, places, and events.

▶ uses a first-person point of view.

▶ suggests or explains the importance of the writer's experience.

WHICH EXPERIENCES ARE IMPORTANT?

So far you have lived through five or six thousand days. That is an impressive amount of raw material for a personal narrative. How can you select an experience to write about? Thinking about the following kinds of incidents in your life will be helpful:

A CONFLICT THAT WAS ULTIMATELY RESOLVED For example, you and your best friend quarreled about her decision not to attend college. How was your conflict settled? Did it affect your friendship?

A DISCOVERY YOU MADE For example, you remember your first time on stage, at age seven. You discovered that you could make other kids laugh. How did it feel?

A CHANGE YOU EXPERIENCED For example, you find some old photographs of yourself in a family album. In what ways are you now different from the child you see in the album? What caused those changes?

AN EXPERIENCE THAT MOVED YOU For example, you remember a pleasant visit with your best friend. What made that visit memorable?

WHAT SHOULD I INCLUDE IN MY NARRATIVE?

A personal narrative has the same basic elements as a short story—plot, characters, and setting. In the case of a personal narrative, however, you do not have to create these elements out of your imagination. Instead, you re-create them from your memory. Use the following strategies to bring alive the people, places, and events from your past:

PEOPLE If possible, get a photograph or make a sketch of each individual in your narrative. Attach the picture to a sheet of paper, and link physical characteristics and specific character traits.

| Grandad: | twinkling blue eyes; dimples—merry, teasing sense of humor; strong jaw—kind, outgoing, understanding |
| Grandma: | shy smile, wide sweet mouth—reserved but loving; large golden-brown eyes—determined, gentle, challenging |

PLACES Use a wheel chart to generate details about places involved in your narrative. For example, one student created a wheel, placing the words *OUR FAMILY CAR* at the hub. The spokes of the wheel were labeled *Sights, Sounds, Smells, Tastes, Temperatures,* and *Textures.* Each spoke had a box at its far end, identifying details such as these:

Sights: faded green upholstery; empty pretzel bags on the floor; dusty windshield

Sounds: hiccupping motor; tapes of 1960's folk music; honking traffic; road-bump thumps

Smells: car deodorizer; salt-sea air; axle grease

Tastes: saltwater taffy; fried clams; chewing gum

Temperatures: overheated air; cool glass windows

Textures: wrinkled, sweaty clothing; lumpy upholstery

WRITING FOR SOCIAL STUDIES

In social studies you will be reading personal narratives—journals and other first-person accounts. Sometimes you may be asked to write a personal narrative from the point of view of a historical personage—either a specific famous person or a character who typifies a historical period. Read accounts that reveal details about the period in which he or she lived as well as the person's personality, judgment, and relationships with others. Draw a picture of that person, and use a wheel chart to generate details about the historical period.

EVENTS List the events, both major and minor, that occurred during your experience. Write down everything everyone did in the order in which the events happened. You might consider using a timeline or a flowchart to represent these events.

For more on graphic aids, see p. 15.

Briefly describe any conflict or problem along with its resolution. Finally, write a sentence about why the experience was important to you. You may choose not to include that sentence in your final narrative, but referring to your statement will help you stay focused as you write.

Example: Discovering that I could make people laugh made me feel confident for the first time in my life.

HOW DO I DRAFT MY NARRATIVE?

Now that you have chosen an experience to re-create, you can begin to write your narrative, keeping the following in mind:

FIRST-PERSON POINT OF VIEW In a personal narrative you are the narrator as well as the central character. Write your narrative from the first-person point of view, using such pronouns as *I, my, mine, me, we, our,* and *us.* Remember that you, the first-person narrator, cannot tell what other people in your story are thinking unless they tell you.

CHRONOLOGICAL ORDER Narration generally follows chronological order but includes some room for variation, particularly in the opening section. You can begin a chronological narrative with the first event, but you can also begin with any exciting event. You would then describe in chronological order the events that preceded or followed the exciting one. You may also vary chronological narratives with flashforwards to later events. When you include a flashforward, you interrupt the chronological order to describe something that happened later on—perhaps a long-term effect of the incident you are relating. Keep any sequence of events clear by using transitions such as *first, later on, the next morning,* and *at last.*

DIALOGUE When you are writing a personal narrative, try to re-create what people actually said as naturally and as accurately as you can. Be sure to punctuate your dialogue correctly and to begin a new line for each change of speaker. Notice the format of this dialogue from a personal narrative by Dylan Thomas, a Welsh poet:

For more on writing dialogue, see p. 97.

MODEL FROM LITERATURE

"I bet people will think there's been hippos."

"What would you do if you saw a hippo coming down our street?"

"I'd go like this, bang! I'd throw him over the railings and roll him down the hill and then I'd tickle him under the ear and he'd wag his tail."

—Dylan Thomas, *A Child's Christmas in Wales*

HOW DO I REVISE A PERSONAL NARRATIVE?

As you review your personal narrative, make sure that you have made clear to the reader your reason for telling the story. You can state this reason or you can suggest the importance of an incident.

- The nature of an experience may suggest its importance—your first day at school or your last time with a grandparent.
- You might also suggest the importance of an experience by showing its effects, showing rather than telling how it changed your life. For example, a writer who wants to indicate that she suddenly gained confidence from her discovery that she could make people laugh could establish her shyness before the discovery and then show confident behavior afterward.
- You can use powerful language and figures of speech to highlight the importance of the event.

Use the following checkpoints as you revise your narrative:

CHECKPOINTS FOR REVISING

▶ Is the order of events clear?

▶ Are there enough details to make people, places, and events come to life?

▶ Do I use the first-person point of view throughout my narrative?

▶ Have I suggested or explained why the experience is important to me?

Here is a personal narrative in which a student writer explains why acquiring a particular piece of jade mattered greatly to him:

The writer uses the first person.

When I was ten, New York's Chinatown seemed like my home away from home. Every so often, my family would take trips there to do grocery shopping and see pieces of our Chinese heritage come alive. Upon arriving, I always looked for the beautiful and lustrous jade pendants that hung around the necks of everyone, from little children to wizened widows. Each had its own unique feature, whether hung from a red string or a twenty-four karat pure gold chain. Somehow this stone had enchanted me, even more than the little plastic figurines that were the rage for boys my age. In a sense, it represented a connection with my culture that I had not yet understood, growing up in America.

Visual details help readers see the jade pendants and suggest the writer's deep appreciation of them.

The writer explains why the experience of obtaining a jade pendant would be important to him.

Jade in Chinese is pronounced <u>yu</u>, a smooth and warm sound that reflects the nature of the stone. I also learned that it is cherished more than any other stone by Chinese people. Some Confucian* scholars describe <u>yu</u> as having the characteristics of a virtuous man: benevolence, justice, courage, and wisdom. Indeed, after much inquiry I found I was not the first to be mesmerized.

Background information indicates the significance of jade in Chinese culture.

I never really showed my desire to have a <u>yu</u> because it is not good to want something too much, nor is it proper to ask for anything. For an entire

---

* <u>Confucian</u>: pertaining to the Chinese philosopher Confucius (551–479 B.C.)

year, I kept the love to myself—nearly bursting. Nevertheless, the opportunity arrived when my dear grandmother asked me to choose my own present for the holidays we'd missed together. I replied only by staring at the small jade shop across the street, owned by a family friend. For three hours, I sifted through the long display case full of jade pieces of every imaginable shape, size, and color. Then I found it, my <u>bao yu</u>, my treasured jade. A true example of Chinese craftsmanship, it was the <u>yu</u> I had seen in my dreams for one whole year.

Even as I wear it today, I still remember how I kept my feelings inside and how a part of me was reunited with myself. Like a mother who has found her long-lost son, my lovely piece of jade had finally found me.

—Edward Kai Chiu, New City, New York

The writer creates suspense by telling how he kept his wish to himself for a whole year.

The writer clarifies time relationships with transitions such as *For three hours, Then,* and *today.*

The narrative ends with a memorable simile: Jade is compared to a mother.

33 WRITING TO NARRATE: EYEWITNESS ACCOUNT

❓ *What is an eyewitness account?*

An **eyewitness account**, whether oral or written, is a firsthand account that re-creates an event in such compelling detail that audience members feel as if they have experienced it.

Edward R. Murrow, an American radio and television broadcaster, became famous during World War II when he broadcast directly from London as German bombers descended nightly upon the city in a relentless attack known as the Blitz. Murrow developed an on-the-scene reporting style that gave a sense of urgency, immediacy, and authenticity to his radio broadcasts. His firsthand reporting was punctuated by the piercing scream of air-raid sirens, the thunderous explosion of incendiaries, and the crackling roar of raging fires. With his voice booming over the noise, Murrow would give vivid descriptions of events as they occurred, often interviewing participants and giving his listeners the feeling that they were actually right there in London with him.

Edward R. Murrow (left) interviews a soldier.

GUIDELINES

An eyewitness account

▶ makes the audience feel that they are witnessing a newsworthy event.

▶ usually is organized chronologically.

▶ includes objective, accurate information, sensory details, anecdotes, and quotations that convey a sense of immediacy.

▶ usually is told by a first-person narrator.

▶ has a beginning that hooks the reader's attention and an ending that summarizes the significance of the event.

WHAT IS A GOOD SUBJECT FOR AN ACCOUNT?

You don't have to be an international correspondent to find good subjects for an eyewitness account. Commonplace events, from the blooming of spring's first crocus to a graduation party for this year's senior class, can provide you with excellent subject matter. Check school and local newspapers for upcoming events you may observe as an eyewitness. Here are some suggestions:

Sporting events: football, soccer, field hockey, lacrosse, rugby, a swim meet, a diving competition, basketball, boxing, gymnastics, ice hockey, baseball, tennis, golf

Civic or political meetings: a student council meeting, school board meeting, village or city council meeting, speech of a local or national politician, election-day events at polling places or party headquarters

Social events: a school dance, victory party after a sporting event, cast party, firefighters' or police officers' ball, church or temple picnic or social, fund-raising dinner for a local charity

Special performances or seasonal events: a concert, dance performance, play, poetry reading, art fair, parade, carnival, state or county fair, religious observance, neighborhood festival; signs of changing seasons, such as planting or harvesting crops, the first frost, the migration of various animals

Unexpected events: floods, tornadoes, fires, ice storms, power failures, insect plagues, earthquakes, volcanic eruptions

HOW CAN I COLLECT INFORMATION?

The ability to observe is essential to good eyewitness reporting. Pay attention to everything around you—sights, sounds, smells, tastes, and textures. Keep a pencil and pocket-sized notebook handy to jot

down all of your observations. If you can speak quietly and unobtru-
sively, tape-record your observations. A camera can also be
useful. Such equipment is especially helpful if you decide to
interview participants or spectators.

For more on observation-
al writing, see p. 113.

Whether you write or tape-record your observations, use the following chart as a guide for collecting and recording essential data:

Type of Data	Examples
FACTS:	the names or general categories of partici-pants and spectators; the name and purpose of the sponsors (if applicable)
NARRATIVE SEQUENCE:	a detailed, chronological description of what happens during the event; photographs to aid memory
SENSORY DETAILS AND ANECDOTES:	any and all details that describe the setting, portray the mood, give a sense of drama, or let readers feel they are at the scene
QUOTATIONS, QUESTIONS, AND RESPONSES:	quotations taken from informal and formal interviews arranged during or after the event (always get permission to quote)

HOW DO I DRAFT AN EYEWITNESS ACCOUNT?

Your main purpose in writing an eyewitness account is to bring
readers into the scene of a significant event. Although an eyewitness
account is usually written in the first person and colored by the narrator's reactions and responses, its main focus is not on the
reporter's feelings but on the wider, public meaning of the event.

For more on writing a
news story see p. 177.

Organization is an important element of an eyewitness account.
Include chronological cues so your readers can easily follow the chain of
events. You may want to make an outline or a timeline before you begin
drafting to make sure you do not leave out any important events. You
also may consider using spatial order to organize descriptions of objects
or scenes so that readers will have the sense they are looking through a
camera lens.

As you write, refer to your notes for details that will make the
events unfold before your reader's eyes. Use sensory details appropriate
to your subject. Choose forceful, precise verbs, and spice your account
with quotations that accent key points and keep the narrative moving.

Include an engaging beginning and a thought-provoking conclusion. Hook readers' interest by drawing them into the scene, and end by summing up the mood, drama, or significance of the event.

WHAT CHANGES SHOULD I MAKE AS I REVISE?

As you revise your account, ask yourself the following questions:

CHECKPOINTS FOR REVISING

▶ Does my eyewitness account present an event in vivid, compelling, and accurate detail?

▶ Is my account told by a first-person narrator?

▶ Does my introduction immediately draw the reader into my account?

▶ Is my account organized chronologically?

▶ Have I woven together objective information, sensory details, anecdotes, or quotes, giving a sense of immediacy to the writing?

▶ Does my conclusion help convey the significance of the event?

Read the following introduction to an eyewitness account.

STUDENT MODEL

I had a very <u>unusual</u> fifteenth birthday. During my birthday week, the end of April, I was traveling with 5,000 high school students from around the world, visiting concentration camps in Poland. I learned more there than I learned during my entire life in school; once I stepped out of a gas chamber, I became a different person. When I turned fifteen, I discovered that no matter how much you read about the Holocaust, nothing can ever be like seeing it with your own eyes. The day after my fifteenth birthday was the turning point of my life. I was at Majdanek, one of the largest Nazi concentration camps. And I will never forget it.

—Dara Horn, Millburn, New Jersey

The first sentence piques readers' curiosity by using the word *unusual*.

The writer heightens the suspense by telling how her life was changed by the experience she is about to describe.

34

WRITING TO NARRATE: ORAL HISTORY

 What is an oral history?

An **oral history** is a personal recollection of an important event, period, or process, recorded on or transcribed from audiotape.

Oral histories give a personal dimension to history that cannot be obtained through reading and research. Often such histories are part of a larger project to record people's remembrances about a particular place, time, or subject. For example, your class might be studying the effect of early television shows on the 1950's American family. As part of that project, you might obtain oral histories from a number of people to see how such shows affected them.

GUIDELINES

An oral history

▶ consists of a person's memories of a historical period or past event.

▶ provides unique information about a topic that gives a personal dimension to history.

▶ helps answer larger questions about a period or event.

▶ is recorded or transcribed in a way that is easy to read.

HOW DO I CHOOSE SOMEONE TO INTERVIEW?

Imagine that you and your classmates *were* doing the project on early television and the American family. Your next step would be to find people who have strong feelings, either positive or negative, about the impact of television. It wouldn't make sense to choose people who aren't interested in or have no opinion on your topic. Besides choosing people who have specific, detailed information about your topic, you should also consider the following qualifications:

• The person is a willing and interesting speaker. People of few words, poor memories, or little enthusiasm are not good subjects for an oral history.

• The person is available for you to interview.

HOW CAN I PLAN FOR AN ORAL HISTORY INTERVIEW?

Contact the person you want to interview—your subject—by letter or by telephone. If you don't know the subject personally, introduce yourself, briefly describe your project, and ask if he or she would be interested in giving an oral history. Then, set up a convenient time and place for the recording.

Before you do the interview, find a tape recorder and a blank tape, and practice with the equipment to make sure you can get a high-quality recording. You will also need to devise a brief list of thought-provoking questions. Since you want to draw out reminiscences about your topic, plan to ask a few broad, open-ended questions rather than a long series of specific ones. The idea is to encourage your subject to talk at length and not just briefly answer a specific question. However, the questions should be focused enough so that the answers will fit with the general purpose of your project. The following sentences show how to focus questions for an oral history interview on the influence of television on the American family:

TOO BROAD:	What are some of your best childhood memories? What did your family do for recreation when you were a child?
TOO NARROW:	What was your favorite television show? When, during the day, did you watch TV?
FOCUSED:	What do you remember about the time your family got its first television set? How did having a television change life for you and your family?

HOW DO I CONDUCT AN ORAL HISTORY INTERVIEW?

Before you begin your oral history interview, you may wish to chat informally with your subject to put you both at ease. When you both feel comfortable, ask your subject's permission to turn on the tape recorder. Prior to recording, however, test the equipment briefly.

At the beginning of the recording, give the date, topic, and possibly some background information on your subject. Ask your question or questions and encourage your subject to speak freely and respond fully. Jot down notes for follow-up questions that may help your subject to elaborate on important details or flesh out interesting anecdotes. However, don't interrupt your subject. Hold your follow-up For more on interviewing, see p. 244. questions until the subject has finished answering or can't think of anything more to say. Your job in an oral history interview is to encourage the subject to provide his or her perspective on events.

TRY THIS

Use three ellipsis points to indicate where a word or words are missing from a sentence. Use four ellipsis points to show words are missing from the end of a sentence or that whole sentences have been cut.

HOW DO I PREPARE AN ORAL HISTORY?

Your final product will be either an edited audiotape or an edited transcript of the taped interview. If you are going to work with tape, make a copy or two of the original that you can use to edit. Label originals and copies appropriately. Listen to the original and note down sections you want to delete, such as long pauses or gaps, interruptions, unnecessary repetitions, or material that doesn't relate to the topic. Then listen to the tape again, referring to your editing notes. Use the counter to figure out where to start and stop erasing material. You can get rid of the gaps you create by making a third tape, using the counter to determine when to stop and restart. Label the final tape with the topic, subject, and date of the oral history.

If your final product will be a written transcript, the first step is to listen to the original tape and write down or type what you and your subject say, word for word. Also include in parentheses important information on nonverbal communication, such as laughter, tears, meaningful pauses, or other clarifying clues. Then play the tape again, correcting your transcript where necessary. As with a tape, edit your transcript to get rid of irrelevant or repetitive information. Use ellipsis points to show where you have deleted words or sentences.

HOW SHOULD I REVISE MY ORAL HISTORY?

Whether you are making an audiotape or a written transcript, the most important revision step is to check your edited version against the original interview. Make sure that you haven't deleted or changed any important information and that your edited version remains true to the original interview. Also, use the following checkpoints for revising:

CHECKPOINTS FOR REVISING

► Have I correctly labeled and identified the subject, topic, and date of my oral history?

► Does my oral history include my subject's specific, personal memories about a historic topic or past event?

► Is my edited version true to the original interview?

► Does my oral history contribute to my larger purpose or project?

► Have I indicated any additions, sounds, or other nonverbal clues with parentheses and any deletions with ellipsis points?

The following oral history is one of a series collected from Japanese Americans about their experiences during World War II. At that time, many Japanese Americans were ordered to leave their homes and livelihoods and live in distant internment camps.

MODEL FROM LITERATURE

I remember another thing. We had our Fourth of July program. Because we couldn't think of anything to do, we decided to recite the Gettysburg Address as a verse choir. We had an artist draw a big picture of Abraham Lincoln with an American flag behind him. Some people had tears in their eyes; some people shook their heads and said it was so ridiculous to have that kind of thing recited in a camp. It didn't make sense, but it was our hearts' cry. We wanted so much to believe that this was a government by the people and for the people and that there was freedom and justice. So we did things like that to entertain each other, to inspire each other, to hang on to things that made sense and were right.

—Mary Tsukamoto from *And Justice for All*
by John Tateishi

The specific, personal memories of the speaker illuminate the meaning of the larger historic event.

Detention center for Japanese Americans,
Manzanar, California, 1942

35

CREATIVE WRITING: STORY

 What do I need to do to write a story?

A **story** is a brief work of fiction that has a simpler plot and setting than a novel and reveals character through a crucial incident.

When you write a story, you can revisit an incident from your own life, or you can travel into the world of fantasy. Your readers want only to enjoy or to be moved by the experience you share with them.

As a writer, you should be aware of the story elements that combine to produce a unified effect. The following guidelines include the basic elements of a story:

GUIDELINES

A story

- ► requires a **plot**, a series of related events.
- ► focuses on a struggle, called a **conflict.**
- ► includes one or more **characters,** usually people or animals.
- ► occurs in a **setting,** or time and place.
- ► is told by a **narrator,** a storyteller who has a **point of view.**
- ► expresses a **theme,** a central message about life.

HOW CAN I FIND IDEAS FOR A STORY?

Start with a person, place, situation, problem, or feeling that appeals to you. Jot down ideas and then periodically scan them to try to spark your imagination. Here are some techniques:

START WITH A CHARACTER:

Retell or invent an incident involving a family member or a friend; observe strangers and try to imagine what their lives are like; imagine a character from literature or television in a new situation.

START WITH A SETTING:

Imagine what a familiar place would be like at another time, and try to picture the people and problems you would find there. As an alternative, imagine that you've moved to a place that you've always wanted to explore.

START WITH A SEQUENCE OF EVENTS:

Choose an experience and then rearrange the details or events; borrow a situation from a fictional work and create your own outcome; change one aspect of the real world by developing a "What if?" scenario.

HOW DO I DEVELOP MY STORY?

Flesh out your story idea by developing concrete, specific pictures of your characters, setting, and plot.

CHARACTERIZATION In order to create strong characters, answer the following questions:

- Who are my characters and how are they related to one another?
- How does each one look, move, talk, and dress?
- What are the main personality traits of each character?
- What do the characters in the story want and what obstacles do they face?

SETTING Answering the following questions will help you create a vivid setting:

- Where and when does the story take place?
- What features does the setting include?
- What is the weather like?
- What problems does the setting present?
- What atmosphere, or feeling, does the setting create?
- What sensory details make the setting come alive?

PLOT STRUCTURE AND CONFLICT Your plot must be more than a series of events. Something must connect the events and give them momentum. In many stories, the events are propelled by a **conflict,** a struggle between opposing characters or forces. Once you have decided on the conflict, map your plot.

The conflict should become apparent early in the plot because subsequent events will grow out of the conflict. In a story about a family escaping from a flood, you might show the conflict against nature intensifying as the floodwaters rise, the levee collapses, and the family's chances of rescue grow slim. As the conflict builds, the suspense increases until it reaches its high point, or **climax.** For example, the climax could be the family's narrow escape seconds before their house floats away. After the climax, the conflict is usually settled, and the story winds down to a satisfying **resolution,** or working out of all the problems.

WHAT ELSE WILL MY STORY NEED?

When writing your story, you should also consider your narrator's point of view and the theme, or insight into life, you want to convey.

POINT OF VIEW When you choose a **first-person point of view,** your narrator uses the pronoun *I* and reveals his or her thoughts and feelings. A first-person narrator does not know the thoughts of other characters.

When you use a **third-person point of view**, your narrator is not a story character and refers to a character as *he* or *she*. A third-person narrator can be *omniscient*, meaning that the narrator knows the thoughts and feelings of all the characters in the story. In contrast, a *limited third-person* narrator reveals the thoughts and feelings of only one character.

THEME Write a statement expressing your theme to guide you in making decisions about the plot, characters, and setting.

HOW DO I DRAFT MY STORY?

Review your notes about character and setting, your plot diagram, and your decisions about point of view and theme.

BEGINNING THE STORY Here are several ways of starting a story:

Use details to describe a character:

MODEL FROM LITERATURE

The hat told the story, the big, black, drooping Stetson. It was not at the proper angle, the proper rakish angle for so young a Navajo.
—Juanita Platero and Siyowin Miller, "Chee's Daughter"

Provide some details of the setting:

MODEL FROM LITERATURE

It was still too hot to play outdoors. They had had their tea, they had been washed and had their hair brushed, and after the long day of confinement in the house that was not cool but at least a protection from the sun, the children strained to get out.
—Anita Desai, "Games at Twilight"

Begin with dialogue, or conversation between characters:

MODEL FROM LITERATURE

"I've unlaced my boots and I'm standing barefoot on a beach with very brown sand, ocean in front of me and mountains in the distance, and trees making a pretty green haze around them."
"Pretty," David says.
—Ann Beattie, "Imagined Scenes"

Begin in the middle and then use a flashback—a return to events:

MODEL FROM LITERATURE

Chig knew something was wrong the instant his father kissed her . . . . Ten days before in New York, Chig's father had decided suddenly he wanted to attend his college class reunion, twenty years out.

— William Melvin Kelley, "A Visit to Grandmother"

SHOWING, NOT TELLING Follow your plot design, adding complications or events to keep the plot moving toward a climax. Use details, actions, and dialogue to show, rather than tell, what happens and what the characters feel. The sentence that follows tells rather than shows: I was frightened, trapped like a prisoner. However, note how a student writer shows the same idea:

STUDENT MODEL

I peered out from under the car at the two sets of feet that imprisoned me.

— Drake Bennett, Exeter, New Hampshire

DIALOGUE To write natural-sounding dialogue, listen to how people speak, and note what makes each style unique: repeated phrases, short or long sentences, or slang. Make your characters' speech fit their backgrounds and personalities, and also look at ways of setting it off from other text. Here each shift in speaker begins a new paragraph:

STUDENT MODEL

In a few minutes, I heard Dr. Castor's voice outside the door. "Hey there, Tiger, how's it going?" He came over and shook my hand. I felt a little better. Not a lot of people took the trouble to shake the hand of a four-year-old.

"Fine." My smile was weak.

— Drake Bennett, Exeter, New Hampshire

ENDING THE STORY As your story approaches its climax, use details, actions, and dialogue that increase the main character's conflict. The **climax** is the moment at which the crisis reaches its peak. After the climax, show how the conflict is finally settled.

HOW DO I REVISE MY STORY?

Revision is as much a part of the creative process as the initial burst of inspiration. Here are some ways to start the revision process:

- Imagine your story as a short film. Should events be rearranged?
- Ask a friend to read the story and give you an opinion.
- Tape-record your story. Does the dialogue ring true?

Ask yourself the following questions as you revise your story.

CHECKPOINTS FOR REVISING

▶ Does my opening seize the reader's attention? Does it establish the point of view from which the story is being told?

▶ Do the characters behave consistently? Are their motives clear?

▶ Is the setting described in enough detail, and is its role clear?

▶ Are there instances in which a passage that only "tells" can be replaced by details, action, or dialogue that "shows"?

▶ Does the story's resolution follow convincingly from the climax?

▶ Do I resolve the conflict effectively, without leaving "loose ends"?

STUDENT MODEL

Homer?

The story begins with dialogue in the middle of the action.

"Your turn, Michael," said our coach Mr. Hogue. I had hoped and prayed that the inning would end before I got my turn at bat, but no such luck.

The writer uses a first-person point of view.

My name is Mike, and I am a catcher for the Lean Mean Baseball Bashin' and Fly Catchin' Machines of North Riverdale (for short, the L.M.B.B.F.C.M.N.R.). It was a Saturday afternoon several years ago in Shiloh Park. The summer had been very dry and as a result the baseball field

---

was parched. It was the bottom of the ninth inning in a game against the Really Awesome All-Star Totally Cool Never-Lost-A-Game Baseball Players of Middle Riverdale (for short, the R.A.A.S.T.C.N.L.A.-G.B.P.M.R.). The score was tied at six to six. For the first time this season, I would get a turn at bat.

You see, I was Riverdale's best catcher. But wouldn't you know it, I was awful at another essential skill of baseball: hitting. The previous year I had hit the ball only twice out of about a million times at bat.

I chose a wooden bat, and again it felt far heavier than I thought it would. As I stepped up to the plate, beside myself with fear, I tried to distract myself by dusting off home base with my cleats. But the diversion didn't work. So I positioned myself and the bat, tensed all my muscles, and readied myself for the pitch.

The pitcher eyed me suspiciously. But soon his look turned to one almost of amusement. I noticed his lip curl. I was such a terrible hitter, and he could tell by my frantic shaking that I was terrified and couldn't hit anything he pitched. It was now or never! I stepped forth and swung the bat as hard as I could. Then I heard a tremendous crack! I saw the pitcher bury his face in his glove, and I was overwhelmed with joy. For once I had actually hit the ball and on my first swing to boot! I dropped the bat and headed for first base. Then the race began. I was running at full throttle.

A flashback establishes the conflict, which involves the narrator's poor hitting record.

Mike has a conflict within himself. He also has a conflict with the pitcher.

Sensory details add to the excitement of the hit.

"Keep on go . . ." yelled the third base coach,
his words a blur in my race toward home.

The catcher jumped up and opened his glove like
a Venus' flytrap . . . . Suddenly, something
whizzed past my head. The ball! The round, white
projectile surged ahead of me, directly in line with
the catcher's mitt, now opening like a shark's
mouth. I attempted to speed up again but simply
couldn't do it.

I was as good as out unless I could find a way
to get past the ball. Millisecond thoughts shot
through my brain. Finally, it hit me (no, not the
ball). There was only one thing to do: I stopped
running and sent my legs forward. The ball was
nearly to its goal when I began my slide. My feet
kicked up a tidal wave of powdery dirt, sending
huge clouds into the catcher's face. He coughed
several times and was engulfed by the dust.

The clouds were all around me. I couldn't see
what had happened. I couldn't even see home
base! All I know is that during my slide, I heard
the loud clap of the ball entering the catcher's
mitt. Had I been tagged? When the dust cleared,
all my teammates came and dragged me back into
the dugout, smiling and shouting victorious words
at me all the way. Although I didn't know for
sure, I had apparently hit my first home run and
the winning hit for our team that game.

—Mike Arbagi, Dayton, Ohio

CREATIVE WRITING: LYRIC POEM

36

How do I write a lyric poem?

A lyric poem, according to Wallace Stevens, is like a meteor. It flies across the page, leaving a streak of light and a vivid impression. Lyric poems can be sad or joyful, frivolous or profound. They may rhyme or they may not. All lyric poems, though, express the thoughts of a single speaker and are filled with vivid images. Lyrics celebrate the spoken word and use its sounds, rhythms, and layers of meaning to create a strong mood or feeling.

> A **lyric poem** is a short, musical, poem expressing the thoughts and feelings of a single speaker.

Consider the images, sounds, and mood of this lyric poem:

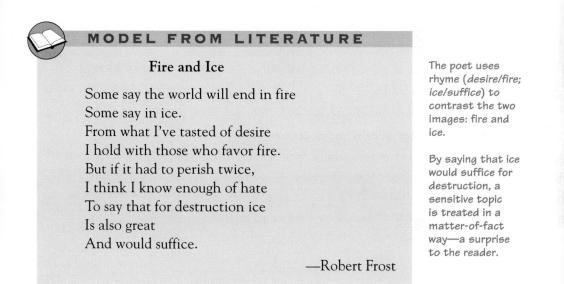

MODEL FROM LITERATURE

Fire and Ice

Some say the world will end in fire
Some say in ice.
From what I've tasted of desire
I hold with those who favor fire.
But if it had to perish twice,
I think I know enough of hate
To say that for destruction ice
Is also great
And would suffice.

—Robert Frost

The poet uses rhyme (*desire/fire; ice/suffice*) to contrast the two images: fire and ice.

By saying that ice would suffice for destruction, a sensitive topic is treated in a matter-of-fact way—a surprise to the reader.

HOW CAN I FIND AN IDEA FOR A LYRIC POEM?

Great themes, such as how the world will end, aren't the only suitable themes for a lyric poem. Try looking for ideas in ordinary, everyday things you see and do. Denise Levertov, for instance, wrote a poem about a highway, Carl Sandburg wrote about a splinter, and James Wright wrote about lying in a hammock. Just remember that a lyric usually has a single subject. In lyric poetry, less is more. It's better to narrow your focus than to try to cover too much.

TRY THIS

From your closet pull out an object at random. Think about what it means to you. Perhaps it will spark a memory or idea.

HOW DO I DRAFT MY POEM?

Once you've come up with a subject for a lyric poem, think about the best way to put it down on paper. First, you may decide how you want the poem to look and sound. Is it to be tight and formal, with regular lines and stanzas and clear patterns of rhyme and rhythm? Or will it be free and loose, with ragged lines and few if any rhymes? A helpful rule in poetry is that the sound often echoes the sense. If you're writing a poem about a funeral, for instance, you probably wouldn't want to give it a rollicking rhyme and rhythm, unless it was a very unusual funeral.

The following pointers will help you when drafting your poem:

TRY SAYING EACH LINE OUT LOUD. Pay attention to the sounds of words and the feelings they evoke.

THINK ABOUT THE MOOD OF YOUR POEM. Do you wish it to be angry, thoughtful, melancholy, or joyful? Try to choose words that enhance the mood you have chosen, and discard those that do not.

CONSIDER THE MESSAGE OR THEME OF YOUR POEM. Not every poem has a theme you can sum up in a sentence. However, every line of a poem should contribute to the effect of the poem as a whole.

HOW DO I POLISH MY POEM?

Like jewelers polishing precious stones, poets strive to give depth and brilliance to every line. After drafting your poem, you can add to its luster in several ways:

USE PRECISE LANGUAGE. A poem is a distillation of your thoughts and feelings. Use words sparingly, cutting out everything that's not essential. Choose specific words rather than vague ones (*finch* rather than *bird*; *scooted* rather than *moved*). Include images that help your readers see, hear, touch, taste, and smell what you are describing.

USE FIGURATIVE LANGUAGE. Poets help us see the world in new and fresh ways by connecting things that appear to be unrelated. When Emily Dickinson says that "hope is the thing with feathers," she helps us to picture an abstract idea. This nonliteral use of words takes several forms:

For more about figurative language, see p. 100.

Metaphor: a figure of speech that describes one thing as if it were another ("Hope is the thing with feathers.")

Simile: a figure of speech that uses *like* or *as* to compare unlike things ("A poem is like a meteor.")

Personification: a figure of speech that gives a nonhuman thing human characteristics ("The engine wheezed.")

EXPLORE THE CONNOTATIONS OF YOUR WORDS.

Connotations are the emotional associations that a word suggests. For instance, "determined" and "stubborn" have very different connotations, though their dictionary meanings are similar. Choosing words with the right connotations gives power and precision to your poems.

LISTEN TO THE SOUNDS OF YOUR WORDS. Poets choose words not just for what they mean but for how they sound. Consider these devices when polishing your poem:

Repetition and Parallelism: **Repetition** (repeating the same word) and **parallelism** (using a similar phrase or line) can give rhythm and unity to a poem. They can also bring emphasis to its underlying meaning or message.

Alliteration, Consonance, and Assonance: **Alliteration** is the repetition of consonant sounds at the beginning of words (*green, grape*); **consonance** is the repetition of consonant sounds at the end or in the middle of words (*black, creak*); and **assonance** is the repetition of vowel sounds (*scream, mean*). All can enhance the mood and meaning of a poem.

Onomatopaeia: Words that are **onomatopaeic** imitate the sounds they describe (*swish, crack*). They add color and liveliness to a poem.

Rhythm and Meter: In spoken English, some syllables are stressed, and others are not. Poets use this natural **rhythm,** arranging words so that stressed and unstressed syllables fall into regular patterns, known as **meter.** In Robert Frost's "Fire and Ice," for instance, each un-stressed syllable (marked ˘) is followed by a stressed syllable (marked ´):

> Some say the world will end in fire
> Some say in ice.
> From what I've tasted of desire
> I hold with those who favor fire.

Used with care, rhythmical patterns can help tie ideas together and call attention to the key ideas of a poem.

Rhyme: **Rhyme** is the repetition of sounds at the ends of words: *fire/desire, twice/ice, hate/great.* Sometimes rhyme is used randomly, but often it follows a pattern, as in Frost's "Fire and Ice." Like rhythm, rhyme can unify a poem and make it memorable.

PAY ATTENTION TO THE MOOD OF YOUR POEM. Mood, or **atmosphere,** is the feeling created in the reader. Word choice, rhythm, and rhyme all influence a poem's mood; so can the poet's tone, or attitude toward his or her subject. A lyric poem expresses a single mood (or, in some cases, the contrast between two moods). If you find that some element of your poem—the rhythm, the sounds of the words, or the choice of images—works against the mood, try to revise the poem so that form and mood work in harmony. Eliminate heavy rhythm, for instance, if the dominant mood of your poem is light and playful.

WHAT FORM SHOULD MY POEM TAKE?

Many traditional poetic forms with fixed rules of meter and rhyme, such as sonnets, elegies, and odes, are still used today. Some contemporary poets, however, prefer the flexibility of **free verse**—poetry that doesn't adhere to fixed patterns of meter and rhyme. Like traditional verse, free verse is written in lines and stanzas. Poets writing free verse, however, can break lines wherever they wish. Likewise, they can utilize rhythms, rhymes, and repetitions whenever they like. The only rule is that the poem's rhythm and form should contribute somewhat to its meaning.

Notice how a student writer experiments with images and sound devices in this draft of a free-verse poem.

STUDENT MODEL

The Last Mustangs

Personifications (time pulls, thirsty cacti) add color to the poem.

Time pulls the pale sun
Over the dun landscape
Barren except for
Lonely tumbleweeds
and thirsty cacti.

Images of heat, drought, and silence enhance the lonely mood.

Hazy heat slides up
off the far mesa.
Its steady rise
occasionally broken
by the lazy turns
of a hungry vulture.

The wind is dry
as it listlessly

harrows the dust.

Suddenly a break in the silence!

The rhythmic beat

of proud hooves

reverberating

through the parched soil

The rumble builds until . . .

There! Can you see the mustangs?

Glorious manes

Flashing eyes

Graceful frames

Beneath the lurid sky

Fly in unison

Across the plains.

—Kelly Dane, Hudson, New Hampshire

With the sound of the horse's hooves, the poet introduces a sharp change in mood.

The poet directly addresses readers, pulling them into the poem.

Parallel phrases (*glorious manes, flashing eyes, graceful frames*) draw attention to the beauty and motion of the animals.

HOW DO I REVISE MY POEM?

As you read this revised version, note how the student has tightened and polished the poem:

The Last Mustangs

The poet sharpens the language through the use of more specific words like *drags* and *slithers*.

Time drags the sun
over the dun landscape—
barren and lonely
except for tumble-
weeds and thirsty cacti.

The poet condenses the language by eliminating unnecessary adjectives and adverbs.

Heat slithers
off the mesa,
its steady rise stopped
by the swoop
of a vulture.
A dry wind harrows
the dust.

The poet rearranges a stanza for drama and clarity. The new stanza introduces a new mood, one of liveliness.

The poet eliminates the word *mustangs*, forcing readers to picture the subject from the descriptions.

By adding the word *solitary*, the poet underscores the contrast in the poem's two moods.

Then a break in the silence!
The beat of hooves
reverberates
through the parched soil.
The rumble builds until . . .
There! Can you see them?
Glorious manes,
flashing eyes,
graceful limbs
fly in solitary unison
across the plains.

—Kelly Dane, Hudson, New Hampshire

37

WRITING TO INFORM: EXTENDED DEFINITION

How do I define a term or concept?

Imagine that you want to explain what the ocean is to someone who has never seen it. You might start by providing a dictionary definition of the word *ocean*: "the entire body of salt water that covers nearly three-fourths of the earth's surface." After hearing this definition, however, the person would still not have a clear picture of an ocean and so you might want to provide an extended definition of the term.

> An **extended definition** is a definition enhanced with details such as sensory descriptions, facts, statistics, comparisons, and examples.

GUIDELINES

An extended definition should

► include a basic definition of the term or concept.

► include sensory descriptions, facts, statistics, comparisons, examples, and other details that flesh out the meaning of the term or concept.

► be organized clearly and logically.

HOW DO I CHOOSE A SUBJECT?

If your purpose is to learn something, choose a subject that you are curious about. If your purpose is to share what you know with others, choose a subject that you already know a great deal about. In either case, you might use the following questions to help you choose terms or concepts for extended definitions:

• Are you interested in the arts or fashion? A term in one of these fields might be the subject of your extended definition.

• Do you have strong feelings about a particular personal value or political, environmental, or societal goal? Such an abstract term can be an interesting subject for an extended definition.

• Are you interested in knowing more about an unusual word or expression? It too could be the subject of your extended definition.

HOW CAN I GATHER INFORMATION?

The following cluster diagram shows the kinds of information you may want to collect for an extended definition:

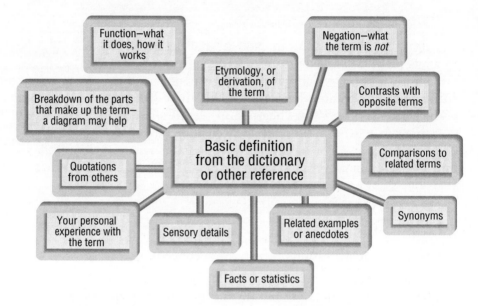

Search for such information in dictionaries, encyclopedias, almanacs, nonfiction books, newspaper or magazine articles, and other printed or electronic sources. You also might interview experts or others who have a special interest in your topic. Consider too your personal experiences and observations, and incorporate them if they seem relevant. Record information in a notebook or on note cards so that you can locate it quickly and easily when you are ready to draft your extended definition.

HOW DO I DRAFT MY EXTENDED DEFINITION?

When deciding which details to include in your definition, select those that will be most helpful and relevant to your particular audience. For instance, if you are defining a slang term for your peers, you might include the latest examples of how the term is used. If your audience is your teacher or other adults, you may choose to emphasize how the word developed its present meaning and then compare it to slang terms that were used when your readers were in their teens.

For more on organizational plans, see p. 24.

Start with a brief definition of the term you are defining, either quoted or paraphrased from a dictionary or another reference source. Then organize the rest of your definition in a logical order that makes your ideas clear.

HOW CAN I REVISE MY EXTENDED DEFINITION?

As you revise your extended definition, ask yourself the following questions:

CHECKPOINTS FOR REVISING

▶ Does my definition fulfill my purpose for writing?
▶ Is my definition suited to my audience?
▶ Have I started with a basic definition and extended it, using a variety of details to give a complete picture of my subject?
▶ Have I organized my details clearly and logically?

WHEN SHOULD I USE AN EXTENDED DEFINITION?

You can use an extended definition whenever you need to define a term that has many facets. These kinds of definitions are especially useful when you write about social studies, science, music, art, literature, and other subjects in which special terms often require elaboration.

WRITING FOR MUSIC

Musical concepts can be hard to put into words and can thus warrant extended definition. In writing such definitions, consider these guidelines:

• Determine how much your audience knows about music, and provide any necessary explanations.
• For a general audience, describe how the music sounds. Consider using figurative language to enhance your description.
• After checking a term's basic definition in a dictionary, consult reference works such as *Grove's Dictionary of Music and Musicians, Baker's Biographical Dictionary of Musicians,* and *The Penguin Encyclopedia of Popular Music.* To find articles and reviews by subject, you can consult the *Readers' Guide to Periodical Literature* or the more specialized *Music Index.*
• Many musical terms have changed their meaning over time or have both specific, technical meanings and broad, less technical meanings. You can therefore often organize an extended definition by tracing a term's meaning chronologically or by moving from broad and nontechnical meanings to specific and technical ones or vice versa. For example, in defining *blues,* you might move chronologically from African American folk music through jazz to current forms of blues, or you could begin with a specific technical definition that focuses on keys and chords and then move to a less technical one that focuses on lyrics and mood.

In writing an extended definition of the term *weed* the author of the following model tells how a nutritious plant, the dandelion, came to be viewed as a notorious pest.

The author begins by quoting a standard gardening definition and refuting it with a brief example. She then gives her own definition.

MODEL FROM LITERATURE

The gardening definition of a weed is "a plant growing in the wrong place." I can't agree with that. A chrysanthemum may grow in the wrong place, but I can dig it up and be done with it. If weeds were so amenable to interference, they would not be weeds. A weed is a plant that is not only in the wrong place, but intends to stay.

The author next cites an agricultural definition, which she also refutes, this time with a lengthy example.

In the economic terms agriculturalists use to define weeds, a weed is any plant that is not useful and which, by competing with useful crops, reduces yield or increases costs for labor and materials. True, weeds cost. But the definition still lacks rigor. As elders lament, values change, and the value of a weed is no exception. . . .

What was a dandelion when it appeared at Jamestown? To colonists in the starving time of year, this early spring riser can only have been a savior. Its leaves contain nine times the scurvy-battling vitamin C in lettuce, three times the anemia-preventing iron in spinach, and forty-two times the vitamin A in ordinary iceberg. . . .

I have thought quite a bit about the present plight of dandelions. Maybe their descent to weeddom can be traced to the American dream, a home of one's own and a perfect lawn. . . .

To support her own idea of what a weed is, the author gives the example of the prickly pear, an attractive wild plant in America that has become an invasive, unwanted plant— or weed—in Australia.

In 1839 a pretty little prickly pear . . . was moved to Australia in a flower pot. Cuttings from this single plant were rooted and transplanted to grow into hedges around homesteads. By 1925 prickly pear had spread by its own means to cover, sometimes impenetrably, sixty million acres of land. Thus can a move make a weed. . . .

—Sara B. Stein, *My Weeds*

WRITING TO INFORM: PROCESS ANALYSIS

38

What is a process analysis?

Imagine that a person from the 1700's has been beamed forward in time. You have to explain something about modern life to him—how to use a computer, for example, or the way a car engine works. How would you explain such processes to someone who knows nothing of your subject? You could write a process analysis and tell him, step by step, how the process works.

> A **process analysis** explains how to do something, how something happens, or how something works.

No matter what type of process analysis you write, your goal is a clear, simple explanation. Here are some guidelines to keep in mind:

GUIDELINES

A process analysis

- ▶ clearly introduces its subject and purpose.
- ▶ explains a process by describing the steps in chronological order.
- ▶ clarifies the steps by breaking them down into simple actions.
- ▶ uses transitions to show the relationships between steps.
- ▶ defines any unfamiliar words or concepts.
- ▶ concludes by explaining the results of the process or the benefits of knowing how to perform it.

HOW DO I GET STARTED?

TRY THIS

If possible, videotape the process and take notes on each step or phase. As an alternative, draw pictures to help you understand the process, or diagram it using a flowchart.

CHOOSE A PROCESS TO EXPLAIN. In some cases, you may be assigned to analyze a specific process. If, however, the subject is up to you, you may choose to analyze a process you already understand or one that you want to learn more about.

DECIDE ON YOUR PURPOSE. Consider which of the following purposes your writing will have:

- to explain how something works or happens

- to instruct readers how to make or do something

CONSIDER YOUR AUDIENCE. Decide what your readers already know about the subject and what they need to know.

ANALYZE THE PROCESS. First, list what you know and what questions you have. Then research and perform the process, taking notes. Break the process into individual steps.

Here are some prewriting notes on how a TV picture is created:

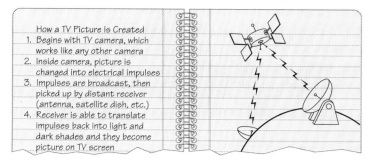

How a TV Picture Is Created
1. Begins with TV camera, which works like any other camera
2. Inside camera, picture is changed into electrical impulses
3. Impulses are broadcast, then picked up by distant receiver (antenna, satellite dish, etc.)
4. Receiver is able to translate impulses back into light and dark shades and they become picture on TV screen

HOW DO I DRAFT A PROCESS ANALYSIS?

Follow these steps as you draft:

1. Introduce the subject in an interesting way.

2. Select the appropriate point of view. You may narrate a how-to essay in the first person—"I begin by …"—or in the second—"You begin by…." Generally, however, explanations work best in the third person, using the pronouns *he, she, it,* and *they.*

3. Present the steps in the order in which they occur or in which they are performed. Explain how each contributes to the whole.

4. Include important details and define any unfamiliar terms.

5. Use transitions—such as *first, second, next, then, after that, as soon as, later,* and *finally*—to clarify the order of the steps.

6. Conclude by explaining the results of the process or the benefits of understanding it.

Notice how the writer revised this draft:

M O D E L

> I've often
> ~~Have you ever~~ wondered how ~~the~~ that picture gets
>
> onto ~~your~~ my TV screen? From research, I learned
>
> how a camera picks up an image and transmits it
>
> to become a picture on my screen.
>
> TV cameras ~~get~~ take in images by reflecting shades of
>
> light and darkness. The light and dark signals are
>
> then ~~translated~~ transformed into electrical impulses.
>
> In the next step,
> The electrical impulses are ~~then~~ transmitted as
>
> radio waves through the air to a receiver. ~~It~~ The receiver might
>
> be the antenna in your TV set or the cable con-
>
> nected to your set.

The writer changes the opening to make it more personal.

The writer changes words to clarify meaning.

A transition is added to clarify the order of the steps.

The term receiver *is defined by examples.*

WRITING FOR MUSIC

You might be asked to write an essay explaining why a particular musical instrument is well suited for playing certain types of music. Your essay could include a process analysis, showing the steps through which the instrument produces sound:

- what the musician does
- how the instrument responds
- how the instrument's response produces a certain kind of sound or series of sounds

You could then explain why the instrument's sound is appropriate for a particular kind of music.

HOW DO I REVISE MY PROCESS ANALYSIS?

Check the order of the steps and the clarity of your explanation by reading the process analysis and performing the steps, if possible, or checking them against your research notes. Better yet, ask someone else to read your process analysis and try to perform the process you have explained. Then have your reader explain the process in his or her own words and tell you whether any part of your analysis is confusing. In addition, look through the Checkpoints for Revising feature on the following page.

CHECKPOINTS FOR REVISING

▶ Does the introduction clarify my subject and purpose?

▶ Are all the necessary steps included and in the correct order?

▶ Are transitions used to clarify the order of the steps?

▶ Are important details included and unfamiliar terms explained?

▶ Does the conclusion sum up the results or the benefits of the process?

Here is the finished process analysis:

MODEL

The introduction announces the subject in an interesting way.

I've often wondered how that picture gets onto my TV screen. From research, I learned how a camera picks up an image and transmits it to become a picture on my screen.

Each succeeding paragraph deals with a separate step in the process.

TV cameras take in images by reflecting shades of light and darkness. The light and dark signals are then transformed into electrical impulses.

Each new step is introduced with a transitional expression.

In the next step, the electrical impulses are transmitted as radio waves through the air to a receiver. The receiver might be the antenna in your TV set or the cable connected to your set.

In the final stage of the process, the electrical impulses are transformed back into light and dark signals. These signals appear on your screen as the same image that the TV camera picked up.

This process is repeated 30 times every second, resulting in a rapid series of images. Each image is replaced so quickly that what we see on the TV screen appears to be moving as we watch.

The conclusion shows what the writer gained from the process analysis.

My research satisfied my curiosity. Now when I watch TV I know how the picture got to my screen!

WRITING TO INFORM: COMPARISON-AND-CONTRAST ESSAY

39

How can I write effectively about similarities and differences?

Seeing two people side by side sometimes reveals something new about each of them. When we compare and contrast people or objects, we can surprise our readers and ourselves by discovering unanticipated likenesses and differences. Writing a comparison-and-contrast essay gives us the chance to see things from a new perspective.

> In a **comparison-and-contrast essay**, a writer explores both the similarities and the differences between two (or more) items.

GUIDELINES

A comparison-and-contrast essay

► explores the similarities and differences between two (or more) related items.

► reveals unexpected relationships between items.

► can be written for one or more of the following purposes: to inform, persuade, evaluate, or entertain.

► uses specific examples to show similarities and differences.

► is organized clearly.

► uses transitions to clarify similarities and differences.

WHAT SHOULD I COMPARE AND CONTRAST?

You've heard the expression, "That's like comparing apples and oranges!" It's a shorthand way of saying, "The two things you are comparing are so different that there's no point in talking about them in the same breath." Actually, there might be a point in comparing apples and oranges: They're both fruits, they're both tasty, they're approximately the same size, and so on. However, it would be hard to see any point in comparing apples and airplanes, or oranges and orangutans. The items you discuss should be similar enough to make a comparison-and-contrast essay worthwhile.

 ## WRITING FOR SOCIAL STUDIES

When you are asked in social studies to compare and contrast two historical figures, events, social trends, or political movements, you have a wide choice of subject matter. One way to find an appropriate topic for your essay—that is, two items with at least a few things in common—is to use this modified pie chart. Spin the outer wheel and match the heads on the wheel with the categories in the center of the chart. Then list specific ideas for the pairs you create. (Some categories may match better than others.) For instance, by pairing "People" with "In Our Culture, In Other Cultures" you might choose to compare and contrast women's rights around the world.

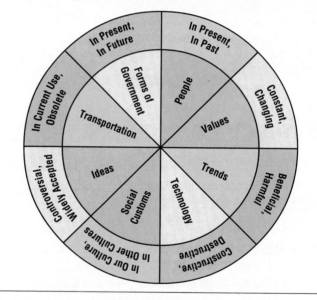

HOW DO I GATHER INFORMATION FOR MY ESSAY?

Once you've chosen the items you will compare and contrast, consider making a Venn diagram to pinpoint similarities and differences between the items. Draw overlapping circles. In the "inner space," where the circles overlap, list the qualities that the two items share. In the "outer space," where the circles do not overlap, list the qualities that are unique to each item. The Venn diagram shown on the next page shows similarities and differences between two kinds of dinosaurs:

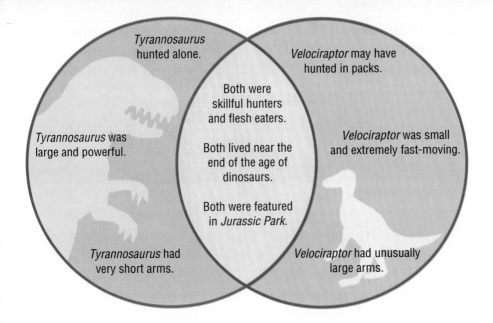

You can spark observations by answering the following questions:

- If I wrote about each item, which qualities would I focus on?
- Which important qualities do the items share?
- Which qualities are unique to each? What differences become apparent?
- Which similarities and differences might surprise my readers?

HOW DO I DRAFT MY ESSAY?

WRITING THE INTRODUCTION In writing a comparison-and-contrast essay, it is easy to get bogged down detailing all the similarities and differences you discover. Answering the following questions will help you get a perspective on the information you have gathered:

- Overall, which seems more important—the similarities or differences between the two items? Why?
- Has my comparison-and-contrast essay suggested a generalization I can make about the two items?
- What is my main purpose in writing? To evaluate the items? To persuade, inform, or entertain?

COMPUTER TIP

Make a chart like the one below and store it in your glossary. Then you can copy it when you need to.
Item #1 _____
Item #2 _____
Similarities
_____
Differences
_____
My Insight
_____

ORGANIZING THE BODY There are two basic ways to organize a comparison-and-contrast essay. You may describe the key qualities of the first item and then describe the qualities of the second. Or you may compare and contrast the items feature by feature, pointing out similarities and differences. An essay comparing and contrasting two dinosaurs, for example, could be set up in the following ways:

FIRST ONE ITEM THEN THE OTHER	FEATURE BY FEATURE
Para. 1: Introduction	Para. 1: Introduction
Para. 2: *Tyrannosaurus*—what it ate, its size and other physical attributes, its ferocity	Para. 2: Feature—Eating habits (similarities between *Tyrannosaurus* and *Velociraptor*)
Para. 3: *Velociraptor*—what it ate, its size and other physical attributes, its ferocity	Para. 3: Feature—Size and Mobility (contrasts between *Tyrannosaurus* and *Velociraptor*)
Para. 4: Conclusion	Para. 4: Conclusion

TRY THIS

Reread the body of your essay and ask yourself "So what?" Use your answer to develop the conclusion.

WRITING THE CONCLUSION Do not simply repeat the similarities and differences you developed in the introduction and body of your paper. Instead, tell your readers what the similarities and differences suggest. Describe any new insights you have gained. For example, an essay comparing and contrasting the *tyrannosaurus* and the *velociraptor* could end by indicating which predator seems more terrifying.

HOW DO I REVISE MY ESSAY?

As you revise your essay, insert transitions to clarify relationships between ideas. The following transitions are useful in writing about similarities and differences:

To Emphasize Similarities:
like; likewise; similarly; in the same way; also; as; just as; both

To Emphasize Differences:
unlike; on the other hand; in contrast with; however; but; instead; rather than; whereas

As you revise your comparison-and contrast-essay, ask yourself the following questions:

CHECKPOINTS FOR REVISING

▶ Have I explored genuine similarities and differences between two (or more) related items?

▶ Have I revealed unexpected relationships between these items?

▶ Have I fulfilled my main purpose—informing, persuading, evaluating, or entertaining?

▶ Have I given specific examples of similarities and differences?

▶ Is my essay consistently organized, either item by item or quality by quality? Would a different organization better suit my purpose?

▶ Have I used transitions to clarify similarities and differences?

MODEL

Finny and Gene: Two Classic Characters

Ever since it was first published in 1959, readers of John Knowles's A Separate Peace have been fascinated by the similarities and differences between the two main characters, Finny and Gene. Though they are best friends, attend the same school, and influence each other's lives, they are opposites in many ways.

A casual observer, watching Gene and Finny walk through the Devon campus carrying their schoolbooks, might hastily conclude that the two teens are very much alike. Both characters are sixteen-year-old white males attending a privileged New England prep school in the war year of 1942. They study the same subjects, belong to a club that they founded together, and play blitzball, a sport of their own invention. In their conversations, Finny and Gene often have differing views, but they share the same general concerns. For example, although Finny pretends not to believe that the war is going on and Gene does believe in it,

The introduction indicates the purpose: to compare and contrast the characters Finny and Gene.

The essay uses a feature-by-feature organization.

This paragraph discusses the similarities between the two characters.

both characters are concerned about how the war might affect them in the future.

This paragraph discusses the differences between the characters.

Most of these similarities, however, are only on the surface. They result from the fact that Gene and Finny come from extremely similar backgrounds. The truth is that, as individuals, they are as different as any two people can be. Gene is good at academics, while Finny is a great athlete. Gene is plagued by self-doubts and insecurities, whereas Finny is amazingly confident. Gene forces himself to do brave things (such as jumping from the tree branch into the river), especially when others are urging him on, but Finny does them easily and fearlessly. Gene is a follower; Finny is his leader. Finny doesn't care much about following rules; in one scene he wears the school tie as a belt. In contrast, Gene admires that kind of non-conforming behavior but would not do it himself.

Transitions such as while, whereas, but, and in contrast highlight differences.

Finny, on the one hand, is a much more magnetic, charming, attractive character than Gene. On the other hand, Gene seems more real. Real people do have self-doubts and mixed feelings. Finny, meanwhile, is presented as an ideal character. His combination of physical ability, moral values, and individualism make him extremely popular. Gene has to settle for being a regular person who struggles through life and has to face his imperfections. Perhaps Finny represents the way every young man would like to be, and Gene, the way most young men really are.

The conclusion offers the author's opinion that Gene is a more realistic character than Finny, who is an ideal character.

WRITING TO INFORM: CAUSE-AND-EFFECT ESSAY

40

How do I write about relationships between causes and effects?

What makes an economic recession occur?

What if the dinosaurs had survived?

What will happen to a car engine if there is an oil leak?

Why was Lincoln elected President in 1860?

How has the free-agent system changed professional sports?

"Why?" "What if?" "How?" These questions shape many of our thoughts and much of our casual conversation. They lead us to think about the reasons for certain events; they make us wonder about the probable results of particular actions, from the personal to the cosmic. These kinds of questions are also the basis of the cause-and-effect essay.

> A **cause** is an event, condition, or situation that makes something else happen. An **effect** is the result or outcome of a particular event, condition, or situation.

CAUSE

EFFECT

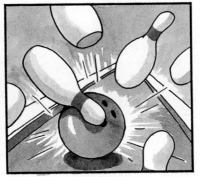

GUIDELINES

A cause-and-effect essay

► explores and explains the causes and effects of certain events, conditions, or situations.

► supports explanations with specific evidence.

► presents the evidence in a well-organized, logical sequence.

► makes cause-and-effect connections clear with transitional words like *as a result, consequently, because, due to,* and *therefore.*

HOW DO I FIND A TOPIC FOR MY ESSAY?

If you aren't given a topic, anything that arouses your curiosity is possible material for a cause-and-effect essay. Try the following strategies to find a topic:

FOLLOW THE DAILY NEWS. Look for intriguing questions in newspaper stories or on television or radio broadcasts.

NOTICE THE HUMAN DRAMAS GOING ON AROUND YOU. Observe people's behavior, both ordinary and unusual, and think about why they act as they do.

REFER TO YOUR JOURNAL OR LEARNING LOG. Which of your observations would you like to explore in greater depth? Journals or learning logs from your science or social studies classes are bound to contain excellent topics.

THINK OF A KEY EVENT IN HISTORY. Imagine what would have occurred if the event had turned out differently.

WRITING FOR SOCIAL STUDIES

If you need a cause-and-effect topic for your history class, list on a timeline the political, economic, and social events that occurred during a particular period. Then color-code events that might be related to one another as causes or as effects. This strategy may give you a good idea for a cause-and-effect essay.

HOW DO I DISTINGUISH AMONG CAUSES?

"Which came first, the chicken or the egg?" You don't have to solve that ancient riddle, but you do have to be able to distinguish among the remote, underlying, and immediate causes of events before you can understand a cause-and-effect relationship. A **remote cause** is a cause far removed from the event. An **underlying cause** is one that is not immediately apparent. An **immediate cause** is an event that comes immediately before the effect and plays a role in bringing it about. For example, you could trace the causes of the Civil War to the establishment of slavery in the English colonies of North America, but reaching that far back to explain a conflict that occurred at a much later time would not explain why slavery became an institution in the South. Similarly, identifying the immediate cause of the Civil War as

the firing on Fort Sumter would not point to other, more fundamental causes of the Civil War. Instead, you would focus and organize your essay by deciding what underlying cause-and-effect relationships were most critical.

STRATEGIES FOR FOCUSING AND ORGANIZING

Depending upon your topic, you may focus and organize your essay in any of several ways. In some cases, you may describe a chain, a series of events in which each cause has an effect that in turn causes another effect and so on. Here is an example of a cause-and-effect chain dealing with the whaling industry:

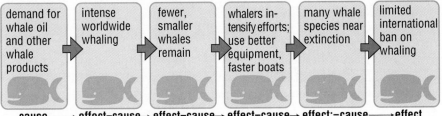

In other cases, you may begin with a single cause—an event, situation, or condition—and then investigate the various effects that it has produced:

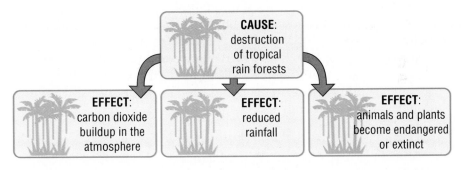

Another way is to look for the causes behind a particular effect:

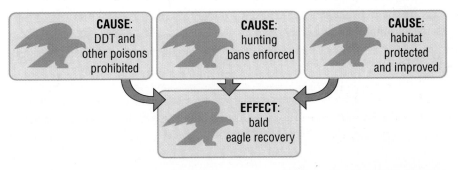

EXPLORATION STRATEGIES

As you focus and organize, you can explore cause-and-effect relationships in the following ways:

- **Do research.** If you want to know why the school board voted against building a new high school gym, begin by reading local newspaper coverage of the issue.
- **Ask questions and make observations.** To follow up your research on the school-board vote, observe the next board meeting and set up interviews with individual board members.
- **Speculate and develop theories of your own.** Ask yourself some questions: Did the school board pay attention to community opinion? Did they seem to give more weight to certain portions of the community than to others? If so, why?

AVOIDING FALLACIES

Fallacies are illogical conclusions based on unproved assumptions. In exploring causes and effects—trying to determine why things occurred—you must watch out for some pitfalls:

- *Post hoc, ergo propter hoc* ("After this, therefore because of this") This error in thinking involves identifying one event as the cause of another just because the first occurs before the second. For example, night is always followed by dawn. However, dawn is not caused by night but by the rotation of the earth on its axis.
- Do not assume that the first cause you find is the only cause or the main cause. Similarly, do not assume that a cause has only one effect.
- Beware of "conventional wisdom," or what "everyone" thinks. Sometimes such widely held opinions are correct, but not always. (Sixty years ago, many people thought mild exposure to radiation was actually healthy!) Keep an open mind and use your critical-thinking skills to evaluate what seems obvious or easy.

HOW DO I DRAFT A CAUSE-AND-EFFECT ESSAY?

For more on thesis statements, see p. 222. Begin the drafting process with these three steps:

WRITE A ONE- OR TWO-SENTENCE THESIS STATEMENT.
Express the main point of your essay and your focus (on causes, effects, or a cause-and-effect chain).

PICTURE YOUR AUDIENCE. What do they need to know about your topic? What tone will make them most comfortable?

DECIDE ON YOUR PURPOSE FOR WRITING. Are you explaining a cause-and-effect relationship or making a larger point or general observation?

SUPPORTING INFORMATION

Use specific supporting information to educate your audience and add credibility to your views. Such support includes statistical data, examples, and expert opinions. For example:

- **Statistical Data:** A National Institutes of Health panel sought data to determine whether any commercial diet program had proved to be effective. None was. Over the course of the study, 100 percent of the plans failed to result in permanent weight loss.

- **Examples:** Dieting is not the only cause of eating binges. For example, people who skip breakfast or lunch often end up overeating later in the day.

- **Expert opinion:** Gayle Najarian, M.D., tells her patients that eating three meals a day is the best way to avoid binges.

ORGANIZATIONAL STRATEGIES

You can organize an essay about causes and effects in one of the following ways:

- **Chronological order**—time order—tells about events in their order of occurrence. You should consider using chronological order if you are explaining a *cause-and-effect chain* or are discussing the various *effects* of a single event, condition, or situation.

- **Reverse chronology** (going backward in time) works well if you are analyzing the *causes* of an event, condition, or situation.

- **Order of importance** places the most crucial information either at the beginning of a discussion or at the end. By using order of importance when discussing several causes or effects, you can stress a particular cause or effect.

USING TRANSITIONAL WORDS

In a cause-and-effect essay, your most important objective is to make sure readers can follow the connections you are trying to make between one situation or event and another. One good way to help readers follow a series of causes and effects is to use transitional words such as *therefore, because, as a result, consequently,* and *so that.* These words alert readers that a cause or an effect is about to follow. If your essay is organized according to order of importance, transitional words such as *most important* and *more significant* can also help your readers follow your thinking. If your essay is organized in chronological order, time words such as *first, then, yesterday, now,* and *later* are helpful.

On page 168 there is an example of a cause-and-effect paragraph organized in chronological order. Transitional words are underlined.

Lyme disease is caused by the bite of a tiny tick that lives in woods and tall grass. The effects of the disease vary according to how long it is left untreated. <u>At first</u>, the infected person may notice only a tiny red pimple that later turns into a burning rash. If the victim begins taking antibiotics at this point, the infection can be stopped in its tracks. If left untreated, however, lyme disease can cause fever, swelling, muscle and joint pain, and fatigue. <u>After several weeks</u>, the disease may even attack the nervous system. <u>As a result</u>, the victim may experience facial paralysis, depression, and even damage to the heart.

HOW DO I REVISE MY CAUSE-AND-EFFECT ESSAY?

Before you revise your essay, ask yourself these questions:

CHECKPOINTS FOR REVISING

▶ Is my purpose clear? Does my audience know whether I am writing about a cause-effect chain or whether I am primarily concerned with showing causes or effects?

▶ Have I given readers unfamiliar with my topic as much information as they need to understand what I am saying?

▶ Have I clarified the relationships between the causes and effects I discuss? Are there any fallacies or gaps in my analysis?

▶ Do I need more transitional words to make my writing flow better and to clarify relationships between causes and effects?

WRITING FOR SCIENCE

When you write up a lab report based on a science experiment, you are both reporting your observations and drawing conclusions about causes and effects, based on your observations. Be sure to include charts or graphs showing your observations and to weave statistics from these graphic aids into your writing to support your conclusions.

In the following excerpt, a science writer explains the effects that changes in the earth's atmosphere have had on life on this planet.

MODEL FROM LITERATURE

Viewed from the distance of the moon, the astonishing thing about the earth, catching the breath, is that it is alive. The photographs show the dry, pounded surface of the moon in the foreground, dead as an old bone. Aloft, floating free beneath the moist, gleaming membrane of bright blue sky, is the rising earth, the only exuberant thing in this part of the cosmos. If you could look long enough, you would see the swirling of the great drifts of white cloud, covering and uncovering the half-hidden masses of land. If you had been looking for a very long, geologic time, you could have seen the continents themselves in motion, drifting apart on their crustal plates, held afloat by the fire beneath. It has the organized, self-contained look of a live creature, full of information, marvelously skilled in handling the sun.

The writer uses a vivid description of the earth and its atmosphere to draw the reader into the essay.

It takes a membrane to make sense out of disorder in biology. You have to be able to catch energy and hold it, storing precisely the needed amount and releasing it in measured shares. . . .

When the earth came alive it began constructing its own membrane, for the general purpose of editing the sun. . . .

The writer introduces his main idea: The atmosphere is like a breathing membrane that manages light and air and makes life possible.

The earth breathes, in a certain sense. Berkner suggests that there may have been cycles of oxygen production and carbon dioxide consumption, depending on relative abundances of plant and animal life. . . . An overwhelming richness of vegetation may have caused the level of oxygen to rise above today's concentration, with a corresponding depletion of carbon dioxide. Such a drop in carbon dioxide may have impaired the "greenhouse" property of the atmosphere, which holds in the solar heat otherwise lost by radiation from the earth's surface. The fall in temperature would in turn have shut off much of living, and, in a long sigh, the level of oxygen may have dropped by 90 per cent. Berkner speculates that this is what happened to the great reptiles; their size may have been all right for a richly oxygenated atmosphere, but they had the bad luck to run out of air.

Now we are protected against lethal ultraviolet rays by a narrow rim of ozone, thirty miles out. We are safe, well ventilated, and incubated, provided we can avoid technologies that might fiddle with that ozone, or shift the levels of carbon dioxide. Oxygen is not a major worry for us, unless we let fly with enough nuclear explosives to kill off the green cells in the sea; if we do that, of course, we are in for strangling.

It is hard to feel affection for something as totally impersonal as the atmosphere, and yet there it is, as much a part and product of life as wine or bread. Taken all in all, the sky is a miraculous achievement. It works, and for what it is designed to accomplish it is as infallible as anything in nature. . . .

It breathes for us, and it does another thing for our pleasure. Each day, millions of meteorites fall against the outer limits of the membrane and are burned to nothing by the friction. Without this shelter, our surface would long since have become the pounded powder of the moon. Even though our receptors are not sensitive enough to hear it, there is comfort in knowing that the sound is there overhead, like the random noise of rain on the roof at night.

—Lewis Thomas, "The World's Biggest Membrane"

The writer cites expert opinion to explain a chain of causes and effects that occurred millions of years ago, resulting in the disappearance of dinosaurs.

The writer uses the word now to signal a transition to a description of the effects the earth's atmosphere has on life today and what might happen if we destroy our atmosphere.

The writer concludes by summarizing his main idea and by leaving the reader with one more dramatic effect of the earth's atmosphere to think about.

41

WRITING TO INFORM: PROBLEM-AND-SOLUTION ESSAY

What is a problem-and-solution essay?

Something's vexing you. You're worried about wasted resources and wonder what your community can do to conserve energy and encourage recycling. Writing an essay may help.

> A **problem-and-solution essay** states a problem and offers a practical solution.

HOW DO I WRITE A PROBLEM-AND-SOLUTION ESSAY?

Writing a problem-and-solution essay will help you focus your thoughts on a problem so that you can analyze it in a clear, logical way and propose a solution. The analysis you present in your essay may suggest one or more solutions. Examining their pros and cons will help you decide which solution is most practical for you, your school, or your community.

GUIDELINES

A problem-and-solution essay

▶ states a problem clearly and analyzes it logically.

▶ proposes a solution based on the analysis of the problem.

▶ shows why the solution will work.

WHAT PROBLEMS SHOULD I WRITE ABOUT?

You can tackle a wide range of issues, from personal peeves to school and community problems and political and environmental concerns. You can even write an essay to help you solve a physics problem or to design a system of traffic lights for your neighborhood. Remember that your essay will have a wide appeal if you focus on a problem that concerns other people and that lends itself to a concrete solution.

HOW DO I FIND IDEAS?

What things would you like to change in your life, in your school, or in your community? If nothing occurs to you right away, follow these suggestions for finding ideas:

FOR PERSONAL PROBLEMS Search the advice column of your local newspaper. Trade ideas with your friends. Jot down personal topics discussed on television talk shows or dealt with in works of literature you have read.

FOR PROBLEMS AT SCHOOL Poll students in your class or school to find out what problems bother them most. Think about specific kinds of problems, such as the expansion of the football field at the expense of the softball diamond or the enforcement of the local noise ordinance in the school parking lot or on school grounds. Look at editorials and opinion pieces in your school newspaper to see which problems are being written about.

FOR SOCIAL AND POLITICAL ISSUES Find out what people are talking about in your community by reading the local newspaper, listening to talk radio, and watching the local news on TV. Sit in on a meeting of the city planning board, arts commission, or parks committee. Contact a local outreach program (say, a center for teen runaways), and find out what problems the staff faces each day.

FOR SCIENTIFIC AND ENVIRONMENTAL PROBLEMS Look through newspapers and magazines. Speak with your science teacher. Contact local environmental organizations or speak with the staff of a science museum. Remember that a relatively small problem— how to measure the noise level in the school parking lot or how to protect the local bluebird population—can be as challenging and difficult to solve as a large one.

WRITING FOR MATH

On math tests you may be asked to write a problem-and-solution essay that describes the procedures you used to solve each problem. Try using a chart or another kind of graphic organizer as part of the "prewriting" or "presolving" stage. This may help you see how all the parts of the problem fit together. You could then refer to it as you write a "rough draft" of a solution that you will revise after you have carefully analyzed the problem and checked all your calculations.

HOW DO I EXAMINE THE PROBLEM?

Once you choose a specific problem for your essay, you'll need to examine it to be sure that you understand it. Only when you have a thorough understanding of the problem will you be able to propose a realistic solution.

One way to examine your problem is to try to see it from several angles or points of view. Every problem has a number of facets, just as a cube has different faces. For instance, one writer was concerned that classmates who had access to expensive computers had an unfair advantage over classmates who didn't. As he examined the problem, he thought of solutions and then weighed each solution from different points of view in order to find the best one.

POSSIBLE SOLUTIONS

- Ban the use of all sophisticated computers.
- Buy more computers for the school computer lab so that every student will have access to the latest technology.
- Expand access to the school's computers.

He sketched the following graphic cubes showing three possible solutions and mapped out the three perspectives involved in each solution: that of students with computers (1), that of students without computers (2), and that of the school administration (3).

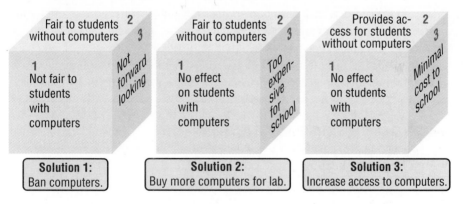

Once you've mapped out the pros and cons of each solution, decide on the solution you will recommend and develop your ideas for implementing your solution.

HOW DO I ORGANIZE MY ESSAY?

Keep these points in mind when you organize your essay:

1. Introduce the problem. Be specific. Try to define the problem in a sentence or two. Catch your readers' attention with a striking

TRY THIS

Not all problem-and-solution essays need to address weighty social concerns. Try writing a humorous essay. For ideas, take a look at the amusing essays of Mark Twain, James Thurber, E.B. White, Erma Bombeck, and Roy Blount.

quotation, anecdote, or description.

2. Elaborate on the problem. Keep your audience in mind as you write. Are they familiar with the issue? If not, provide some background—but don't overload readers with unnecessary detail.

3. Present your solution, which should flow logically from your analysis. State it briefly, and give practical suggestions for carrying it out. Back up your opinion with facts, statistics, examples, or quotations. Then address any objections that readers could raise to your proposal.

4. Wrap up your argument. Conclude your essay with a strong statement that supports your solution. Consider ending with a quotation or a thought-provoking question.

 WRITING FOR SOCIAL STUDIES

Whenever you write about the struggles faced by a person in the past— Harriet Tubman's quest to end slavery, for instance, or Robert Peary's attempts to reach the North Pole— you're in effect writing a problem-and-solution essay. Leaf through some history books, and look for people who tackled problems in a courageous or ingenious way. Try to analyze their problems as they perceived them and explain how they surmounted their difficulties. You can also offer your own solution to one of the problems they faced— as long as it's feasible and realistic. If you prefer, you can write about someone who faced a daunting challenge but failed to meet it. (Amelia Earhart's attempt to fly solo around the world is one example.) What made the challenge so difficult? Why did the person fail?

HOW DO I REVISE MY ESSAY?

Set your draft aside for a few hours, and then look it over again with a fresh eye, keeping these points in mind:

CHECKPOINTS FOR REVISING

- ▶ Have I stated and analyzed the problem clearly?
- ▶ Have I shown how the solution flows logically from the analysis of the problem?
- ▶ Have I shown how the solution can be carried out?
- ▶ Have I answered any objections readers may have to my solution?
- ▶ Is my conclusion brief and strong?

Here is a final draft of a problem-and-solution essay:

MODEL

There's at least one in every class—a guy or girl who regularly uses state-of-the-art computers with the latest word processing and graphics programs, laser printer, CD-ROM research tools, and online databases to research and write papers. Meanwhile, the rest of us struggle along with our typewriters.

The writer defines the problem in a striking way to grab readers' attention.

When I see some of the results that the computer whizzes get, I'm green with envy. Their papers look so impressive, but the method of production seems so unfair to students who can't afford to use it. It seems to me that either every student should have access to the latest technology—or nobody should.

For a while, I thought that banning such equipment for homework assignments was the answer. Then I talked to a couple of computer nerds, one of whom said, "You can't stop progress. It's the wave of the future, and I want to explore it. Besides, it would be unfair to keep me from using equipment that belongs to me." I had to admit that he had some good points.

The writer proposes one solution and then presents an opposing viewpoint.

Then I decided that the answer was for the school to buy more computer equipment so that everyone could have a shot at using the latest technology. Our principal, Mr. DeMarco, however, told me that my dream of an expanded computer lab was not likely to come true. "The legislature hasn't passed a school levy in years," he said,

The writer proposes a second solution and then shows why it will not work.

"and if it does, the money will be allocated to buying textbooks and hiring teachers."

The writer proposes a third solution and presents support from a teacher to back up the proposal.

Then one afternoon, as I was trying to finish an assignment in the computer lab, the final bell rang. After grumbling in frustration, I complained to Mr. Schwartz, the computer teacher. "I've offered to keep the lab open nights," he said, "but so far the administration hasn't taken me up on it. It wouldn't cost the school much because the building is open nights for adult education classes. Maybe if you organized a petition drive, the administration would realize that there is a demand for more computer time."

I knew immediately that he was right. By expanding computer lab hours, the school administration would give everyone at Edgemont High access to the latest equipment, and the cost would be small—especially considering the benefit the extra hours would bring to almost the entire student body.

The writer ends with a recommended solution.

How do I write a news story?

A photograph and a headline like those below can tell a lot about a news event—but they don't tell everything. Who, for example, is a Navajo surgeon and pioneer? How is this person a pioneer? Why is she an important person?

> A **news story** is a brief, factual, and objective report on a current event or issue.

A news story can answer these questions by telling readers that the person is Dr. Lori Cupp, the first Navajo woman to become a surgeon and to combine traditional Navajo methods of healing with modern medicine. This news story might also add other details about Dr. Cupp in order to give readers an interesting and well-rounded portrait of her.

Navajo Surgeon and Pioneer

Stories like this one may be picked up by newspapers that cover national news. Other newspapers mainly focus on local stories. The news in your school newspaper reflects what happens in your school and what is currently of interest to you and your fellow students. This might include local, national, and international news. All news stories, however, follow the same basic rules.

GUIDELINES

A news story

► tells about a recent event or issue of interest to readers.

► provides accurate facts.

► answers six basic questions, known as "the five W's and H":

Who was involved?	**Where** did it happen?
What happened?	**Why** did it happen?
When did it happen?	**How** did it happen?

► reports on other people's opinions without taking sides or making judgments.

► has an interest-catching headline.

FINDING THE NEWS

An event is newsworthy if

- **it's unusual.** If the debate team wins the state championship for the first time ever, it's news.

- **it affects readers.** If the school system introduces a twelve-month school year, students will want to know about it.

- **it's recent.** Last year's dress code is old news. This year's new student lounge is more interesting now.

- **it's local.** The opening of a new landfill will interest readers if it is in their neighborhood.

To search out the news, you'll have to be alert. Look carefully at local newspapers, posters, and bulletin boards. Watch for changes in your community. Ask people you meet about issues that interest them. Finally, cultivate sources by becoming friends with people in key positions and then calling them regularly to see if they have any news.

For more about interviewing, see p. 244.

Here are ways to gather information for a news story.

Observe	Record	Interview	Read
If you know that an event is about to happen, try to witness it firsthand to gather details that will capture readers' interest.	Always keep a notebook handy. Jot down information under the headings *Who, What, When, Where, Why,* and *How.*	If an event has already happened, interview people who were there. Compare accounts to get a complete story.	Background information can help you put a news story in context so that your readers can understand its importance.

SHOULD I WRITE A NEWS ARTICLE OR A FEATURE?

A news story can be written either as a news article or as a feature. A news article stresses the immediate and the factual. It is a straightforward account of what happened. A feature article is usually based on research or interviews. It can provide any or all of the following:

- background information on a newsworthy event.
- historical information.
- biographical details about a newsworthy person.
- firsthand impressions of an event.

Imagine, for example, that you are assigned to write about a visiting dance troupe. You might write a news article telling where the troupe is from, who the dancers are, where they will perform, what pieces they will do, and why they have come to this town. Or you could write a feature article telling the life story of the founder of the troupe or describing your visit to a rehearsal. The news article should be objective, but the feature article can include your own ideas and opinions.

HOW DO I ORGANIZE MY NEWS STORY?

A news story has three main parts: the headline, or "head," the lead, or first paragraph, and the body. The story is structured like an upside-down pyramid, with the most important information first.

The Three Parts of a News Story

HEAD

LEAD

BODY

THE HEADLINE (HEAD) The headline is the first thing a reader sees but often the last part written. It catches the reader's attention and briefly tells the main idea. Make your headlines short and specific. Often, you can leave out a subject or a verb. Many headlines have humorous puns or allusions that grab readers' attention.

THE LEAD The lead is the first paragraph of the news article. It contains much of the story's vital information. Your lead should keep the reader's interest by stressing the timeliness, the unusualness, or the importance of your story. On page 180, you will find five ways to write a lead for your news story.

1. Surprise.

The woman in the green Saab whisked off a black beret, patted her hairnet and plunked on a wig, a Liza Minelli number—all the while cruising down the Saw Mill River Parkway at 55 miles an hour.
—*The New York Times*, February 8, 1994

2. Quote an expert.

Acknowledging that Japan's reform effort is in imminent danger of derailment, the new Prime Minister, Tsutomu Hata, said today that "people are seized with uncertainty and a sense of crisis," and warned that after a year of national upheaval, "the new order is still not in sight."
—*The New York Times*, May 11, 1994

MODELS

3. Summarize.

Naturalist Karim Ali reported the first sighting of a woolly flying squirrel in northern Pakistan since 1924.

4. Amuse.

When 100-year-old Alaskan Matilda Arik was asked what she wanted for her January fourth birthday, she didn't hesitate for a moment. "Summer!" the centenarian replied.

5. Question.

What looks like the Loch Ness monster, acts like the Loch Ness monster, and is found in Loch Ness? Would you believe—a sturgeon?

THE BODY The body of a news story gives details about the five W's and H. Most news stories present events or details in descending order of importance, using the **inverted pyramid** as a model. When you organize a story this way, place the most important facts first and the least important details last. This method gives readers the most vital information right away. As you can see from the graphic on page 179, this organizational method also allows editors to cut the story easily if it runs too long, by deleting less important details at the end.

When you are deciding which facts to present first in your news story, keep these questions in mind:

Is the detail timely? If so, place it near the beginning.

Is it vitally important to the story? Place it near the beginning.

Does it include names or dates? Place it near the beginning.

Does the detail present a conflict? The placement depends on the importance of the conflict to the story.

Does it contain human interest? It can probably go near the end.

Is the detail humorous? It can probably go near the end.

You can also present events in a news story in chronological order. This method is best for stories that occur over a period of time. In a **chronological news story,** you write the events in time order, from first to last.

Still another way to organize information is the **composite news story,** which combines two or more news events that share a similar theme. For example, a reporter could write a composite story about the 1994 Olympic Games by describing similar accidents that occurred in the bobsled and luge events.

 ## WRITING FOR SCIENCE

You may be asked to write a news story on a scientific experiment or discovery for a science class. Science articles answer the basic five W's and H questions. Often more space in a science article must be devoted to answering *how* questions than in other articles because scientific processes are complex and many readers are not experts in the field. As you write, other points to consider are the following:

Specialized terms or jargon Be sure to define any difficult scientific terms you use. Remember that many in your audience may not know a lot about your topic.

Graphs, charts, and tables Use graphic aids to compare numbers, show changes over time, and clarify details for readers. Be sure your graphics illustrate important points and help readers understand the topic.

Significance of the event or discovery Be sure to quote an expert discussing the significance of the scientific finding. Readers will want to know why this event or discovery is important and how it will affect their lives.

Factual accuracy It is always important to get your facts right. Check your sources again if you are unsure about anything.

Human-interest details Since science stories often tend to be abstract, readers will appreciate any human-interest details you can provide. For example, does a scientist you are discussing have any special pursuits that will help bring the story to life? Does he or she have lively opinions that are worth noting?

HOW CAN I REVISE MY NEWS STORY?

Consider these points when you revise:

CHECKPOINTS FOR REVISING

▶ Does my headline state the main idea of the story?

▶ Does my lead keep my readers' interest?

▶ Do I answer the questions *who, what, when, where, why,* and *how?*

▶ Have I organized my material in a way that suits my story—either chronologically or in descending order of importance?

▶ Is my information accurate and objective?

▶ Have I checked names, dates, titles, and quotations carefully?

Here is a news story based on what a writer witnessed.

MODEL

The headline tells the main idea of the story.

Unexpected Fire Alarm Empties Building

In the lead, the writer tells *who, what, when, where,* and *why.*

All students were unexpectedly evacuated from the high school on Tuesday when electricians installing new wiring accidentally set off the fire alarm. The false alarm disrupted classes for twenty minutes while the fire department investigated.

The writer uses a quotation to tell *how.*

"I'm proud of our students," said Principal Isaiah Braithwaite. "Their response was quick and orderly."

The writer presents events in chronological order.

At first, most students did not realize that anything out of the ordinary was happening. Moments later, when firefighters arrived, students saw that the threat of fire was real. Class groups waited outside until the team of firefighters emerged to report all clear.

A quotation from an observer adds personal interest.

"I never took fire drills that seriously," said Pete Yaches, a senior. "This made me realize they're important."

WRITING TO INFORM: WRITTEN EVALUATION

43

How do I write an evaluation?

Though you may not be aware of it, you make evaluations every day of your life. Whenever you buy a particular running shoe, advise against seeing the latest action movie, sign a petition, or select a book for a friend or relative, you make an evaluation.

A written evaluation is more formal. First, you choose a subject—for instance, the Chicago Bulls. Then you analyze it, comparing, say, the Bulls to other professional basketball teams and assessing their strengths and weaknesses using specific standards such as athletic ability, coaching, teamwork, and performance last season. On the basis of your analysis, you form a judgment and back it up with facts and examples.

> A **written evaluation** is an essay that analyzes and judges the value of a product, performance, book, idea, or other subject.

GUIDELINES

A written evaluation

- expresses the writer's judgment about a book, performance, product, idea, or other subject.
- describes the subject in as much detail as needed.
- identifies criteria, or standards, by which the subject can be judged.
- evaluates the subject by applying the criteria consistently.
- supports the evaluation with evidence, including comparison and contrast with other subjects, personal experience, examples, and the opinions of authorities.
- conveys a confident tone.

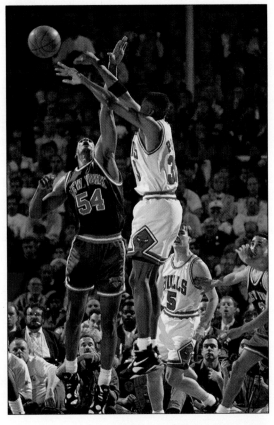

WHAT CRITERIA DO I USE FOR EVALUATING?

Criteria means "the standards for judging." In order to develop your own set of criteria, take a look at the ways professionals assess their subjects.

FOR PRODUCTS Look up an article about your product in *Consumer Reports*, and note the criteria used to judge its value. Efficiency, durability, safety, and price are common criteria for judging products.

FOR PERFORMANCES Read reviews of performances in newspapers or magazines, and note the criteria used to evaluate the work. Common criteria include originality, skill and artistry, and emotional impact on the audience.

FOR BOOKS Look up some reviews of books of the same genre as the one you are trying to evaluate (fiction, nonfiction, poetry, mystery, or fantasy, for example), and note how the reviewer assesses the work. Does he or she evaluate its plot, style, tone, authenticity, or suspense, for instance?

FOR IDEAS Search for newspaper editorials and magazine articles about your subject. If you are evaluating proposed gun control legislation, for instance, note what criteria editorial writers use to judge its merit. It is useful to ask whether a piece of legislation has been designed to achieve the purpose for which it is being proposed.

WHAT SHOULD I INCLUDE IN MY EVALUATION?

A written evaluation has three main components: an introduction to the subject, an evaluation, and a recommendation.

The introduction, usually not longer than a paragraph or two, should include the following:

- an opening hook such as a thought-provoking question or a striking anecdote or quotation that catches readers' attention.

- information that readers will need to understand the subject (for instance, the author, title, and basic plot of a book or play; the name of a software program, its manufacturer, the hardware with which it is compatible, and its price).

- the aspect of the subject that will be discussed (for instance, the Chicago Bulls' upcoming season).

The **evaluation** is the meat of the essay. Here you explain your criteria and assess your subject in one or more ways:

COMPARE AND CONTRAST. For instance, you could compare the new compact disc by your favorite heavy metal group to the last disc the group released or to discs by other heavy metal bands.

ANALYZE. Use your criteria to examine your subject. If you have decided to evaluate the technical aspects of a new movie, for instance, you might analyze its lighting, sound, camera work, special effects, and editing.

For more on comparison and contrast, see p. 157.

EXPLORE PERSONAL EXPERIENCES. If you're evaluating a product, you might test it or interview people who have used it. Try to avoid rash judgments and purely subjective opinions, however. Give specific details about how long the product was used and under what conditions.

CONSULT EXPERTS. Look up reports, studies, or reviews of your subject, and select quotations and results to bolster your judgment.

To make your written evaluation stronger, pay close attention to your tone. Choosing the right tone is a critical part of writing an evaluation. **Tone** is the writer's attitude toward his or her subject. Keep in mind that a confident tone will lend credibility to your judgment. The more carefully you have studied your subject, the better you will be able to project an air of authority. In the chart that follows, notice how differences in tone can alter the effect of a book review.

For more on tone, see p. 93.

Tentative

I found *The Broken Cord* **quite** moving. A true story about a tragic situation **tends** to make me cry. This book would **probably** affect most people the same way.

Confident

A major strength of *The Broken Cord* is its emotional impact. The book, which chronicles one man's struggles to raise a severely disabled child, has tremendous power.

The **recommendation** is usually the third part of a written evaluation. Many writers choose to close with recommendations based on their assessments, but others begin their essays with strong negative or positive statements. A recommendation, like a judgment, can be explicit or implicit. If you have supported your evaluations with evidence, your recommendation need not be stated.

FROM A WRITER

❝ *This is not a novel to be tossed aside lightly. It should be thrown with great force.* **❞**

—Dorothy Parker

WRITING FOR MUSIC

To evaluate a concert, a new compact disc, or a song, you need a keen ear, an open and analytical mind, and enough background to understand your subject. Think about these suggestions as you plan your evaluation:

- **Narrow your subject.** Instead of choosing all the music of Jimi Hendrix, try to compare and contrast two versions of "Purple Haze."
- **Select your criteria.** If you're unsure of how to analyze, say, the improvisational technique of trumpet player Wynton Marsalis, read reviews of his concerts or a book of jazz theory.
- **Refine your judgment.** Remember that your readers will be less interested in superficial impressions ("Bonnie Raitt has a terrific voice.") than they will be in specific judgments supported by facts.

HOW CAN I MAKE MY EVALUATION EFFECTIVE?

The credibility or authority of your evaluation depends on your ability to maintain consistency throughout your evaluation, to offer sufficient evidence, and to know your readers.

Consistency of judgment means "maintaining criteria for evaluation throughout the review." For example, if you praise the environmental organization Greenpeace for adopting radical tactics in its fight to save whales, you will confuse readers if later in your essay you accuse Greenpeace of tactical excesses in another campaign.

Sufficient evidence means "citing relevant facts and examples and giving enough background information about your subject to support your opinion." If you are reviewing a book, performance, or idea, use quotations selectively to help illustrate your points and to make the subject come alive for your readers. If you are evaluating a product or an idea, you can use statistics, diagrams, or charts to give weight to your argument. Be sure, however, that your figures are accurate, relevant, and up to date.

Knowing your readers means "keeping the concerns of your audience in mind as you write." For example, if you are reviewing a play that contains material that might be objectionable to your readers, alert your audience. If your audience has a special interest, point out aspects of your subject that are related to that interest. For instance, if you are writing an evaluation of two candidates for the City Council for your school newspaper, summarize each one's stand on issues that affect young people, such as recreation and schools.

Use these checkpoints to help you revise your evaluation:

> **COMPUTER TIP**
>
> To ensure the consistent application of criteria as you move from one point to the next in your first draft, input your standards and periodically call them up on a split screen as you write.

CHECKPOINTS FOR REVISING

▶ Does my introduction provide essential information about my subject?

▶ Does my evaluation focus on a significant aspect of the subject?

▶ Do I develop suitable criteria and apply them consistently?

▶ Are my judgments clearly stated?

▶ Do I provide sufficient evidence to support my judgment?

▶ Is my evaluation written in a confident, authoritative tone?

Here is an evaluation of a book. Notice how the evaluation contains descriptions that underscore the writer's positive judgment.

MODEL

The writer weaves information—author, title, and subject—into the description.

The writer focuses on Dorris's personal story and his investigation of FAS. The word *compelling* conveys a positive evaluation of the book.

The writer gives readers the necessary background for understanding the review.

An example from the book reveals the emotional power of Dorris's personal experience and the effects of FAS.

In a confident tone, the writer assesses the book in terms of two key criteria: emotional impact and scope.

The closing sentence can be read as a strong recommendation of the book.

When Michael Dorris adopted Adam, he simply wanted to be a father to the child. Before long, however, he was drawn into a tragedy. Adam had FAS (Fetal Alcohol Syndrome), a devastating but preventable condition. The Broken Cord is the compelling story of Adam's life and Dorris's crusade to reveal the facts about FAS.

When Dorris adopted Adam in 1971, the boy was small for a three-year-old. He could barely talk and wasn't toilet trained. Dorris denied that these signs meant something was wrong. Then Adam began to have seizures. Dorris could no longer deny the truth: Adam's problems stemmed from his mother's heavy drinking while pregnant.

Dorris expected to find some precocious talent in Adam that would "make up for" the FAS. He found none. Instead, Adam fell further behind. He could not reason. If a T-shirt and shorts were fine in summer, Adam assumed they were fine in winter too. Dorris felt the loss of what his son could have been.

A major strength of The Broken Cord is its emotional impact. Dorris takes the reader on his personal odyssey, sharing his heartbreak and anger about Adam's irreversible injury. The book's scope goes beyond a personally moving story to educate readers about FAS. Reading the last page of The Broken Cord is like saying goodbye to a good friend. If we're lucky, Dorris will write more memoirs like this one.

WRITING TO PERSUADE: LETTER TO THE EDITOR

44

What is a letter to the editor?

If you look at a newspaper or magazine, you may see stories on homelessness, health care, poverty, violence, education, technology—issues on which you may have strong opinions. If you want to express your opinions about a current issue, you can write a letter to the editor.

> A **letter to the editor** states an opinion on an issue and is written for publication in a magazine or news-paper.

GUIDELINES

A letter to the editor

▶ responds to an article, a story, or an editorial in a magazine or news-paper.

▶ aims to persuade readers of the writer's point of view or to provide information not given in the original published piece.

▶ supports opinions with evidence.

▶ uses language and tone appropriate for the magazine or newspaper you are writing.

▶ uses standard business letter form.

HOW DO I WRITE A LETTER TO THE EDITOR?

A letter to the editor has three main parts: the introduction, the body, and the conclusion.

THE INTRODUCTION Your introduction should identify the article to which you are responding. Mention the title, the writer's name, and the date of publication. Then state your opinion as briefly and as clearly as possible. Use language that suits the backgrounds and concerns of your audience. If you are writing to *Forestry* magazine, for example, you can assume that your readers know the terms *clearout* and *firebreak*.

THE BODY The body of your letter should include facts, statistics, examples, and reasons that reflect your purpose. If your goal is to persuade your readers to believe or act as you do, you will need to offer strong evidence to convince them. Even if your purpose is simply to inform your readers of additional facts, you must provide them with accurate, detailed information from a reliable source. For example, if you were writing a letter about the amount of virgin forest that remains in the Pacific Northwest, you would probably quote statistics from the United States Forest Service rather than a local timber company.

THE CONCLUSION In your conclusion you should summarize your position or make a recommendation. If your purpose is to persuade, you can recommend a point of view or plan of action. If your purpose is to inform, you should restate your main point in your conclusion.

HOW DO I REVISE MY LETTER TO THE EDITOR?

After you've completed your letter to the editor, look it over and make any necessary changes or additions. Ask yourself these questions as you reread it.

CHECKPOINTS FOR REVISING

▶ Have I followed the guidelines for writing to the editor given in the magazine or newspaper to which I am writing?

▶ Have I made my point clear to readers?

▶ Have I made a concise, reasoned argument?

▶ Is my position supported with facts, examples, and other appropriate evidence?

▶ Is my tone reasonable and informative and my language appropriate for readers of the newspaper or magazine?

▶ Have I used the correct business letter form?

Here is an example of a letter to the editor.

412 Hurley Street

Tempe, Arizona 85282

January 16, 199-

The writer uses correct business letter heading and salutation.

NewsFlash Magazine

1102 High Street

Los Angeles, California 90036

Dear Editor:

I am responding to Kit Aldridge's article of November 9, 199-, "Guns for Toys? Get Real!" In her article, Aldridge mocked the idea of trading guns for certificates to toy stores. I do not agree!

The introduction to the letter states the name of the article, date of publication, and author.

The writer states her opinion firmly.

Shooting crimes are frequent, and often innocent bystanders—even children—are wounded or killed. Reports show that in areas where the "Guns for Toys" program has been tried, there is up to 40 percent less violent crime. That means lives have been saved. I think that the saving of even one life makes the whole program worthwhile.

The writer backs up her opinion with statistics.

The writer's tone is firm and reasonable.

If "Guns for Toys" had been tried elsewhere, there might be fewer shooting victims of all ages. Handguns are a menace, and any program that results in fewer guns on the street is a good one. Instead of criticizing "Guns for Toys," Aldridge should encourage it. Everyone should encourage it.

The writer concludes with a call to action.

Sincerely,

Renata Baldwin

Renata Baldwin

45

PERSUASIVE ESSAY

How can I express my opinion in a convincing way?

| A **persuasive essay** is an essay written to convince an audience to think in a certain way or to take a particular action. |

A good persuasive essay is like a charming person: It wins readers over to a particular viewpoint without offending them. To do this, it must present arguments or show evidence that will sway its audience. Appealing to an audience's emotions is also an effective way to persuade, as long as such appeals are responsible and don't stir up feelings that are harmful. Because different audiences respond to different arguments and varying emotional appeals, a persuasive essay must build its case forcefully and intelligently for its particular audience.

"Junior's writing has improved. His letters from college, pleading for more money, are forcefully and flawlessly written."

GUIDELINES

A persuasive essay

► begins with a concise statement of position on an issue that will interest the audience.

► supports this position with valid evidence and logical arguments (facts, statistics, examples, reasons, expert opinions) and responsible appeals to emotion.

► addresses an audience whose views may differ from the writer's.

► anticipates opposing arguments.

► ends in a way that prompts readers to change their thinking or to take a certain course of action.

WHAT ISSUE SHOULD I WRITE ABOUT?

The point of a persuasive essay is to change your readers' minds. If all your readers already agree with you about an issue, then whom are you persuading? If you have not already been assigned a topic and wish to find one that hits a nerve, try any of these strategies:

- Scan the editorial pages of your newspaper for a controversial issue such as a social or political problem that affects you or someone you know.

- Research some of the ethical dilemmas arising from technological or scientific advances such as genetic research.

- Tune in to a radio talk show and list the gripes that callers have. Is there a caller to whom you would like to respond?

- Conduct a class survey to find out what issues are of concern to your peers.

Once you have chosen an issue, you must develop your position, or **thesis statement.** Developing your thesis statement now will help you focus on your issue as you draft your essay. You should include your thesis statement in the introduction of your essay to let your readers know what issue you have chosen and what your position is. Narrow your position to one strong, clear statement. One way to formulate your position and focus on an issue is to ask yourself the question, "What should be done about it?" Keep revising your answer until you can state your conclusion in one sentence.

FROM A WRITER

❝Writing comes more easily if you have something to say.❞

—Sholem Asch

AN UNFOCUSED OPINION		A FOCUSED STATEMENT OF POSITION
Smoking is a terrible habit.	**What Should Be Done About It?**	Smoking should be banned from cafés and restaurants as well as from other public places.
They ought to do something about the panhandlers downtown.		The public should give panhandlers food vouchers instead of cash.

For more on focusing your topic, see p. 11.

Once you have formulated your thesis statement, you are ready to begin developing the body of your paper.

WHAT SHOULD I INCLUDE IN MY ESSAY?

You should begin your essay by defining the issue you will address. Try to use facts, examples, anecdotes, or statistics to show your readers what the issue entails and why it is important. If you have chosen a controversial issue, summarize the controversy. Then state your position, and develop your supporting argument.

HOW DO I DEVELOP MY ARGUMENT?

Once you have stated your position, you must make a case for it. As you build your argument, you should provide logical proofs. You may also want to appeal to your readers' emotions; however, you should not use such appeals in place of good arguments and you should not stir up feelings that are harmful or dangerous. The proportion of logic to emotion that you should use will depend entirely on your audience, your purpose, and your subject.

◆ WHEN YOU WRITE ◆

As you plan your argument, consider the following:

■ **Subject** Can you make your point by using valid arguments that appeal to logic, and at the same time appeal responsibly to emotion? For example, effectively mobilizing people to work toward ending world hunger requires valid arguments that are logically convincing and emotionally motivating.

If you have chosen a controversial issue, you know that the issue is charged with emotion. Rather than focus on the emotional aspects of the issue, you could probably win your readers' confidence by basing your arguments on careful thinking and by using emotional appeals sparingly, only to indicate your concern over the issue.

■ **Audience** Are you addressing scientists who expect to hear hard evidence or an audience that is apathetic about a serious problem? Consider your audience when you are composing your arguments.

■ **Purpose** Do you want readers to see something in a different way, or do you want to motivate readers to take action? How urgent is your issue? The proportion of reason to emotion should be tailored to your particular purpose.

Here are some tips to help you write valid arguments that will appeal to both logic and emotion:

ESTABLISH COMMON GROUND. When you are addressing an audience that disagrees with your thesis, search for a **common ground,** or area of agreement. If you want to ban smoking in restaurants and all other public places in your town, and you are addressing an audience of smokers, you might argue that town government has a responsibility to safeguard public health. Since most readers would agree with this statement, they might be more inclined to consider your argument that smoking, as a public health hazard, should be banned in public places.

DISTINGUISH FACTS FROM OPINIONS. Facts are statements that can be proved or verified. When citing a fact to prove a point, ask yourself: Is this fact accurate? Is it relevant? Opinions are personal judgments. Do not use opinions as the sole basis of your argument.

> *Argument Based on Opinion:* Goat's milk tastes better than cow's milk. [Taste is a matter of opinion or personal preference.]

> *Argument Based on Fact:* Goat's milk is cheaper than cow's milk. [This reason can be verified.]

USE STATISTICS ACCURATELY. Statistics are facts based on numbers. Because statistics can be confusing, double-check such information in more than one source. When writing on a current topic, note the publication dates of your sources to be sure your statistics are up-to-date. Be aware that the statistics you choose *not* to include can alter your case. Advertisers often manipulate statistics to make their point.

BUILD CREDIBILITY. Citing reliable sources gives your writing validity. When quoting an expert, ask yourself, "Does this person's knowledge help me prove my point?" "Is this opinion unbiased?"

SET AN EFFECTIVE TONE. Your **tone,** or attitude toward your subject, can help you to win readers' respect. Tone is revealed through the connotations of the words you choose and through the care with which you develop your arguments. Establish a tone that shows you are confident, reliable, and committed to your position.

For more on connotations, see p. 87.

CHECK YOUR LOGIC. A valid argument must follow logically from one step to another. If your readers cannot follow your argument, they may not be persuaded. Map out the steps of your argument before writing. Check to make sure your essay has included all of them.

For more on logical fallacies, see p. 437.

To use **inductive reasoning,** present specific evidence and then draw a general conclusion based on it. To use **deductive reasoning,** start with a generalization and then develop its specific implications.

EVALUATE YOUR POINTS. Find a way to emphasize the strongest point of your argument. For example, you may want to devote more space to it, to use a memorable image to illustrate it, or to place it last in your essay so that your readers will remember it.

ANTICIPATE OPPOSING ARGUMENTS. You need to anticipate the arguments that will be leveled against yours. You can strengthen your case by acknowledging valid dissent or by refuting invalid arguments. In the following excerpt, a professional writer clears the way for her argument by conceding to the opposition on several points.

MODEL FROM LITERATURE

The writer states her thesis.

She anticipates valid arguments and concedes their truth.

These concessions enable her to return to her thesis and sharpen the focus.

We have become the most overpackaged society in history. . . .

Make no mistake: packaging is important. It protects products from damage, ensures that they remain sanitary, prevents tampering, provides space for production information, and offers convenience (can you imagine carrying home all the soft drinks if they didn't come in six-packs?). But the manufacture, use, and disposal of packaging materials contribute to many environmental problems, from litter to acid rain.

—Julia Hailes, *The Green Consumer*

USE RESPONSIBLE APPEALS TO EMOTION. Another effective way to persuade your audience is to try to stir the heart as well as the mind. Emotion, however, can be as dangerous as a combustible chemical. It is important to use it sparingly, so that it does not ignite feelings that are unreasonable or harmful.

HOW DO I REVISE MY PERSUASIVE ESSAY?

CHECKPOINTS FOR REVISING

▶ Does my essay contain a clear definition of my issue and a statement of my position?

▶ Does every point I make help build my case?

▶ Have I supported my points by using valid arguments and making responsible appeals to emotion?

- Do I acknowledge valid opposing arguments or respond to invalid ones?
- Have I organized my essay clearly and logically?
- Does my conclusion challenge readers to think in a new way or to take action?

Notice how one student caps an argument developed by facts, statistics, and logical reasoning with a responsible appeal to emotion.

STUDENT MODEL

What smokers don't always consider is that they not only endanger themselves by smoking—they endanger others around them also! According to Current Health (November 1988), adult nonsmokers who are married to smokers run a 34% higher risk of developing lung cancer than they would if they were living in a smoke-free environment.

The writer states her thesis.

The writer cites a reliable source. The writer uses statistics she has verified to back up her argument.

Not only is smoking unhealthy, it is costing billions of dollars. Every year, $13.8 billion is spent on health care for smokers; another $25.8 billion is blown away in lost wages and other costs of smoking-related illnesses. The country's six major cigarette companies spend $1.5 billion each year on advertising alone.

The writer expands on her thesis with facts and statistics.

Some smokers argue that they should be free to take risks with their health. However, in many family situations, other people, including young children, would be victims of the polluted air.

The writer anticipates and refutes one key counterargument.

Smoking is a dangerous habit, not only for the smoker but for the people sharing the air with him or her. It must come to an end. We deserve to have smoke-free air and our friends and family alive.

—Carrie Hernandez, Beaverton, Oregon

The writer uses a responsible appeal to emotion by emphasizing love and the fear of loss rather than blaming smokers or urging readers to dislike them.

46

WRITING ABOUT LITERATURE: RESPONDING TO LITERATURE

? *How can I express my responses to a work of literature?*

> A **response to literature** explores your feelings and expresses your thoughts about a literary work.

When a movie director reads a great book, she or he may want to make it into a movie to communicate his or her feelings about it. As a reader, you can communicate your response to a work of literature by writing about it. As you draft your response, you will explore the effect that a work has had on you. This will deepen your understanding of both the work and yourself. Your purpose is not to persuade other readers to react the way you did. Rather, it is to express your feelings and thoughts to a community of readers and writers who appreciate and respect one another's opinions.

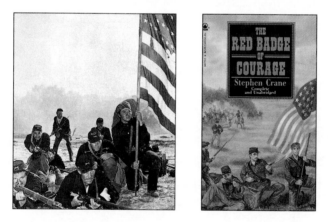

(left) *Scene from* The Red Badge of Courage, 1951, *a film directed by John Huston*

(right) *Book cover for the novel by Stephen Crane*

Here are some guidelines to consider when you write a response to literature:

GUIDELINES

A response to literature

- ▶ identifies the work by title, author, and genre.
- ▶ when necessary, summarizes the work or passage(s) explored.
- ▶ explores your response; that is, your thoughts and feelings about the work.
- ▶ gives examples from the work to illustrate your response.
- ▶ explains the reasons for your response.

HOW CAN I DEVELOP MY RESPONSE?

If you have no response to a given work, you may be better off selecting another one to discuss. If the text is assigned, however, try rereading it with a classmate, asking your partner for help in understanding difficult or ambiguous passages. Look for scenes in which a character says or does something you can relate to. Try to find some common ground between you and the text.

If you have a strong response to a text, you might record it in a double-entry journal. Here is one page of a reader's double-entry journal showing the reactions to the Civil War novel *The Red Badge of Courage*.

Passage/Quote	My Response
scene: The main character, Henry Fleming, runs away from battle	How would I have reacted?
"the line [of men] curled and writhed like a snake stepped upon . . ."	Snakes frighten me. I hate them.
"It seemed that the dead men must have fallen from some great height to get into such positions. They looked to be dumped out upon the ground from the sky."	I've noticed that when I've seen newscasts. I hope there are no wars in my future.

Another way to explore your reactions is to write open-ended questions like the following examples:

- What is surprising or new to me in the work?
- Which part is closest to my own personal experience or observations?
- What memories came to me as I read?
- What other works of literature does the work recall?
- Which images made a strong impression on me?
- Which images or ideas were agreeable or disagreeable to me?
- What passage or line is hard to understand?
- How have my feelings changed since my first reading?

TRY THIS

If you are having trouble with your response, act out a crucial scene or draw it in order to capture the mood of the literary selection.

Answering open-ended questions will often enable you to see parallels between the work and your own experience. Once you have found a link, use follow-up questions to develop your ideas and to focus your written response.

OPEN-ENDED QUESTION	STRONG REACTION	FOLLOW-UP QUESTION	FOCUSED RESPONSE
Which images made a strong impression on me?	Henry Fleming's first battle—sensory details are still with me!	Why can't I forget Fleming's first battle ?	Crane's description is so vivid that it frightens me. I hope I never have to fight a war.

You can focus on any significant aspect, element, or passage from the work. For example, the focused response in the preceding chart tells what image stood out for one reader—the author's frightening description of a battle. Another reader might focus on Fleming's courage. Still another might focus on the historical accuracies of the novel. In a response-to-literature essay, your individual concerns and perceptions are what count most.

WHICH STRATEGIES SHOULD I FOLLOW?

Your focus can help you decide which strategies to use to develop your written response. For example, if you appreciate the vivid description of a place, you might cite examples of sensory words, figurative comparisons, or other descriptive details the author uses to bring the place to life. Here are some other strategies:

SUMMARIZING This strategy is *not* optional. You need to summarize the work *briefly* and explain the passages or elements that prompted your response.

PARAPHRASING Restate passages in your own words. Your retelling can convey your point of view.

DESCRIBING Point out details of character, setting, atmosphere, and style in the text that affected you.

ANALYZING Explain *why* a passage affected you. Did a plot detail stir a memory? Did you find a character especially moving? Why? Did the atmosphere affect you? Why?

QUOTING You can quote from the work as well as from reference sources to help explain your response.

COMPARING AND CONTRASTING Connect the work to real life by comparing yourself or someone you know to a character or by pointing out something in the work that seems true to life.

MODEL

. . . Henry runs away from his first battle and pretends to be wounded. In a later battle, though, he stands his ground and fights. Although he hates the war, he decides he wants to be a good soldier. Henry's experiences reminded me that even if I never go to war, I, like everyone else, will have to face fear and deal with conflict.

HOW CAN I ORGANIZE MY RESPONSE?

A response to a literary work has three basic parts: an introduction, a body, and a conclusion. The **introduction** (one or more paragraphs) identifies the work, briefly describes it, and establishes the focus of the response. The **body** of the response explains and explores the response, giving examples and reasons that clarify reactions. The **conclusion** restates or sums up the response.

The outline on page 202 shows the organization of a response to Stephen Crane's novel:

For more on organizational plans, see p. 24.

Introduction Paragraphs 1 and 2	Title: The Red Badge of Courage Overall response: Stephen Crane's descriptions of warfare are so vivid that they appalled me. Summary: Henry joins army, runs from battle, and then fights courageously.
Body Paragraphs 3 and 4	Author information: Crane never saw warfare. Quoted passage: "The blue smoke-swallowed line curled and writhed like a snake stepped upon. It swung its ends to and fro in an agony of fear and rage." My response: The images repelled me.
Conclusion Paragraph 5	Crane's novel made me see the horror of war.

HOW DO I REVISE A RESPONSE TO LITERATURE?

When you reread your response to a work of literature, imagine that you have not read the book. Role-playing the part of your readers will help you clarify your response. In addition, you may want to ask yourself these questions:

CHECKPOINTS FOR REVISING

► Did I note the title, author, and genre?

► Did I summarize the work or passage(s) I explored in my response?

► Did I focus on the significant part(s) of the work?

► Did I express how I think and feel about the work?

► Did I analyze my response?

► Did I clarify my response with examples from the work?

WRITING FOR MUSIC

You may be asked to write a response to a piece of music in your music class. Like literature, a musical piece expresses a mood and elicits various feelings. The main difference is that the composer uses melody, rhythm, and lyrics to achieve an effect. Here are some questions to ask yourself as you respond to a piece of music:

- Is the beat strong or weak? Focus on the movements you feel like making when you listen to the music.
- What images does the melody suggest? Drawing some of them may help you formulate a response.
- What emotions does the music arouse in you?

When you write your response to music, you can use many of the strategies you would use in a response to literature. Describe the music, note its composer and genre, point out specific parts of the piece that affected you strongly, and analyze why they did so. Use appropriate words such as *rhythm, melody,* and *harmony* to discuss the musical elements that prompted your response.

For more on listening to music, see p. 455.

In the following response to literature, a writer uses examples from the story, information about the author, and personal reactions to illustrate the novel's powerful effect:

MODEL

What is it like to take part in a ground war? I hope I never have to find out. When I read Stephen Crane's classic novel, <u>The Red Badge of Courage</u>, however, I felt as if I were on the front line.

At first, I didn't think the story could have anything to do with my life. In the 1860's, Henry Fleming, a farm boy from New York, joins the Union Army to fight in the Civil War. Terrified by what he sees, Henry runs away from his first battle and pretends to be wounded. In a later battle, though, he stands his ground and fights. Although

A question draws the reader into the writer's response.

The writer identifies the work and states its major effect: to feel so involved in the action is frightening.

The writer briefly summarizes the story.

he hates the war, he decides he wants to be a good soldier. Henry's experiences reminded me that even if I never go to war, I, like everyone else, will have to face fear and deal with conflict.

What amazes me most, though, is that although Stephen Crane never fought in a battle, he wrote a novel that reads like an eyewitness account. Even Civil War veterans believed that Crane had fought alongside them. The truth, however, was that Crane was born ten years after the Civil War began and was twenty-one years old when he wrote the novel. What a phenomenal imagination he had to make an experience he never witnessed seem so awful.

Crane's descriptions of the war are incredibly detailed, which is what makes them so terrifying. For example, when describing a line of Union soldiers marching into battle, he writes, "The blue smoke-swallowed line curled and writhed like a snake stepped upon. It swung its ends to and fro in an agony of fear and rage." This vivid image repelled me because I have an innate fear of snakes.

I am sure that I'll never forget Crane's imagery of warfare. The horror of his images made such an indelible impression on me that I almost feel that Henry's experiences are my own. All I can say is I hope I'm never called on to fight a war.

WRITING ABOUT LITERATURE: INTERPRETING A WORK OF LITERATURE

47

How do I interpret a work of literature?

Have you ever gone to see a movie with a friend, and in talking it over afterward, wondered whether both of you had seen the same film? Maybe you've even said, "That thought never occurred to me," or "I didn't see it that way at all." Even though most people interpret or give personal (or subjective) meanings to a work, there are guidelines for making interpretations that can help you gain a more objective understanding.

> An **interpretation** of a work is an exploration of its meaning that is based on personal understanding.

GUIDELINES

An interpretation of a literary work

- ▶ identifies the work and its author and provides background.

- ▶ explains the meaning of a whole work or some part of it.

- ▶ provides support for the interpretation in the form of personal experience, examples from related works, and passages from the work itself.

- ▶ is organized clearly and logically.

WHAT ELEMENTS OF A WORK CAN I INTERPRET?

You can choose to interpret many different aspects of a work, from its title to its meaning as a whole. Many interpretations are explorations of the meanings of more than one element to gain a broader understanding of a subject, whether it is a film, a book, a work of art, a performance, or a piece of music. Here is a chart of elements and possible questions to ask about literary works:

Element	Questions
PLOT:	What is the central conflict of the work? Why does the conflict occur? What larger meaning is suggested by the way the conflict is resolved?
CHARACTERS:	Why do characters act as they do? What are their motives? Do the characters change? How?
SETTING/ATMOSPHERE:	How does the setting or atmosphere influence the work?
PURPOSE:	What is the author's main reason for writing: to inform, narrate, entertain, persuade, or express personal feeling?
POINT OF VIEW:	What is the point of view? Is it consistent? How does it affect your understanding of the work? Why did the author choose that point of view?
TONE:	How does the tone, or author's attitude, affect the work?
STYLE:	What stylistic devices does the author use? What effects do they have?
SYMBOLS:	What symbols does the work include? What do they mean? What do they suggest about the meaning of the work as a whole?
TITLE:	What does the title mean? How is its meaning illustrated or revealed in the work?
THESIS/THEME:	What central idea or insight into life does the work convey? How do other elements help illustrate or reveal this idea or insight?

COMPUTER TIP

If you enter the above chart into your glossary, leave space for your responses. Then you will be able to fill in the appropriate sections.

HOW DO I PLAN AN INTERPRETATION?

First, choose a work to interpret. The kind of work you choose will influence how you organize your interpretation. If you choose a novel or a biography, for example, you may wish to look at only one aspect of it. For a poem or a short story, you may choose to interpret the whole work.

1. Read and review the work. Read it once to get an overall impression. Jot down a summary of the work and any questions you have about the text. Note any elements that stood out for you during your first reading, and ask yourself questions from the chart above. When you review the work, expand your notes. Add quotations and details that affected you, and answer remaining questions.

2. Respond to the work personally. Write down how reading the text made you feel. Then look back to determine what prompted your feelings. Did the setting remind you of a place you know? What was your response to the author's tone and word choice?

3. Begin to formulate your interpretation. Remember that interpreting a work means giving meaning to it. Look over your notes. Asking yourself questions about your response to a character may spark further thoughts about his or her role.

HOW DO I WRITE MY INTERPRETATION?

Like most essays, an interpretation should have an introduction, a body, and a conclusion.

The **introduction** should provide the name of the work, the author, essential background, and a thesis statement that summarizes your interpretation. If you are interpreting only a section of a work, you may want to summarize what comes before and after that section. If your interpretation deals with one element, you will want to describe that element.

Here is an example of an introduction:

TRY THIS

Present an oral interpretation at the beginning and end of your exploration. Notice differences that reflect a deepening understanding of the work. Decide on an interpretation after exploring several possibilities. The challenge is to find an interpretation that you can support.

MODEL

"Through the Tunnel" by Doris Lessing is, on first reading, a suspenseful story of a young boy's dangerous swimming feat. On closer examination, however, it becomes clear that the tunnel through which the boy passes represents much more than a physical passageway. For Jerry, movement through the tunnel is a passage from the dependence and immaturity of boyhood to an independent, mature adulthood.

A brief summary of the work helps orient readers.

A thesis statement presents the writer's interpretation.

The **body** of your essay will be devoted to supporting your interpretation. You can use any or all of the following as support:

- examples, details, and quotations from the work
- summaries of the work
- comparisons and contrasts with other works
- personal responses to the work
- personal experience or knowledge

◆ WHEN YOU WRITE ◆

Begin your draft with the body, using the examples and quotations you gathered during the prewriting phase as a jumping-off point.

You can organize and present your support in a variety of ways, including moving from the most important to the least important element or proceeding chronologically, giving interpretations of the beginning, middle, and end of the work.

For more on organizational plans, see p. 24.

The **conclusion** of your essay should summarize your interpretation. You can refer to your strongest evidence but avoid repetition. Use the conclusion to reinforce the case that you have made for your interpretation of the work.

WRITING FOR ART

Interpreting a work of art involves focusing on a set of elements that are different from those of a written work. Nevertheless, you can apply many of the guidelines on page 205 to interpreting a work of art. Also, you can apply some of the following elements and questions as you interpret a work of art:

- **Color** How does the artist use color? How do the colors relate to the subject matter? How do they affect the mood of the work?
- **Line** What kind of line does the artist use? Is it bold or delicate? If the work is a sculpture, is the line well defined?
- **Shading** Does the artist use shading to suggest depth and shadow? How does the shading affect the mood of a painting or drawing?
- **Composition** How are the parts of the work of art put together? Is the arrangement symmetrical? What is the center of attention? What does the central focus suggest about the artist's purpose?

HOW DO I REVISE MY INTERPRETATION?

After you've written an interpretation, you may wish to share it with someone who knows the work. Ask your reader to tell you whether your interpretation is stated clearly and your support is presented convincingly. Then look at the terms you have used. Are they precise? Do they describe the methods that were used to create the work? Change any terms that are vague or general.

CHECKPOINTS FOR REVISING

▶ Do I identify the work and its author in my introduction? Do I include necessary background information?

▶ Do I present my interpretation clearly in a thesis statement?

▶ Do I support my interpretation with one or more of the following: quotations and examples from the work, references to other works, knowledge, and personal experience?

▶ Do I use literary terms correctly?

▶ Do I organize my interpretation clearly and logically?

▶ Do I conclude with a strong restatement of my interpretation?

Here are the body and conclusion of the essay on Lessing's story:

MODEL

As the story opens, the author refers to Jerry as "the boy," suggesting his state of relative immaturity. The other boys Jerry meets are bigger. His actions, both with his mother and with the French boys, reveal his immaturity. His behavior toward the boys appears to be a "desperate, nervous supplication," illustrating his childish insecurity. When the other boys swim through the rock tunnel, Jerry panics. His behavior becomes even sillier: ". . . he began splashing and kicking in the water like a foolish dog." This description reflects Jerry's perception of himself, and his desperation becomes intense when he sees the other

The writer uses quotations, details, and examples as support.

The placement of the quotations makes the essay flow smoothly.

The writer organizes the essay chronologically to show the action as it occurs in the narrative and then interprets it.

boys leave and imagines that they are fleeing from him. Because Jerry is the center of his own childish universe, he cannot understand that the other boys are not interested in him at all.

Jerry's initial attempts to swim through the tunnel are marked by his immaturity. He whines to his mother for goggles and boasts to her of his ability to hold his breath. As his efforts grow more serious, however, his motives change. Getting through the tunnel becomes a symbol for Jerry, as it is for the reader, of the movement from cowardice to bravery, from childhood to maturity. When at last he succeeds, he neither boasts of his efforts nor alarms his mother by telling her of his injuries. He has faced death, and his whole attitude has changed. He made the swim for himself, not for anyone else, and in doing so became his own person.

Most of us can identify with the character Jerry. Though our passages to adulthood may not take place in an underwater tunnel, we will probably perform certain feats that come to represent more than physical accomplishments to us. Perhaps our passages will involve reaching the summit of a mountain on a hiking trip or running three miles instead of two. We understand the story's theme because we also have struggled through our own long, dark tunnels, striving to draw a full breath on the other side.

The writer uses particular literary terms as appropriate.

In the conclusion, the writer restates the interpretation and gives it a universal meaning. The writer alludes to personal experience to help support the universal nature of the interpretation.

48

WRITING ABOUT LITERATURE: COMPARATIVE ANALYSIS

How can I discuss the similarities between items?

An essay of comparative analysis can provide a sharper and clearer look at items whose similarities are not immediately apparent. In writing an effective comparative analysis, you do more than explore similarities— you also make a point or draw a conclusion about the similarities you see.

> A **comparative analysis** examines and draws conclusions about the similarities between items.

GUIDELINES

A comparative analysis

▶ explores similarities in two or more related but different items.

▶ makes a point or draws a conclusion about the similarities.

▶ has one or more of the following purposes: to inform, to persuade, to evaluate, or to entertain.

▶ offers specific examples to support its conclusions.

▶ is organized clearly and consistently.

▶ uses transitions, such as *like, similarly, in the same way, both, too,* or *also,* to help readers follow the writer's reasoning.

WHAT KINDS OF ITEMS CAN I COMPARE?

Choose items whose similarities are not immediately obvious. There's not much point in explaining similarities that are already clear to your readers. Examine the sample topics that follow:

Science

• How is the structure of a carbon atom like the structure of the solar system?

• How is photosynthesis in plants similar to respiration in animals?

• What does the elephant have in common with its small, rodentlike relative, the hyrax?

Social Studies

• How were the rights of women in ancient Egypt like the rights of women in the United States today?

- How does the organization of the executive branch of the government resemble that of the judicial branch?
- What does England's Magna Carta have in common with the Bill of Rights in the United States Constitution?

Literature and the Arts

- What similarities are there between contemporary Latin American fiction and the painting of the European surrealist movement?
- How are song lyrics and poetry alike?
- How do the details of Edgar Allan Poe's life resemble events and characters in his poetry and prose?
- How are the narrative techniques of some twentieth-century fiction writers similar to techniques filmmakers use?

HOW DO I GATHER INFORMATION FOR MY ESSAY?

One good way to gather and organize information for a comparative analysis is to use a graphic organizer like the one shown here. After the numbers, write the characteristics your items have in common. After the letters, write examples of each characteristic for each item.

If you are developing a comparative analysis of two poems, short stories, essays, or plays, your examples will consist of words, phrases, and images from both works. (In your notes, include page numbers and line numbers of your examples so that you can find them again easily.)

For more on graphic organizers see p. 15.

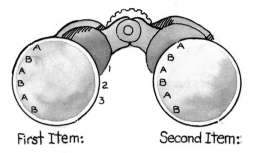

First Item: Second Item:

HOW DO I FORMULATE MY THESIS?

For more on writing a thesis statement, see p. 223.

Once you have examined the two items you are comparing, write a *thesis statement*, an overall point about the similarities you have found. Ask yourself questions like the following:

How would I sum up the similarities between these two items?

What is important about these similarities?

Write out your answers and keep revising them until you have one sentence that reflects the main point you want to present in your essay.

HOW DO I DRAFT MY ESSAY?

Your essay will have three main parts—an introduction, a body, and a conclusion—but you may draft them in whatever order you wish. Feel free, for example, to begin with the body of your essay. You may then find it easier to draft an effective introduction and conclusion.

THE INTRODUCTION Use your first paragraph to catch your readers' interest and to let them know what your essay will cover. For example, you might start your introductory paragraph with a surprising statement or an unusual image, then end the paragraph with your thesis statement.

Here is the introduction to an essay comparing the techniques of two poets:

MODEL

Imagine that a time machine has landed in eighteenth-century Japan, picked up poet Taniguchi Buson, and transported him to the twentieth century. Most of what Buson would find in the United States today would probably seem alien to him. However, if he opened a book of twentieth-century poetry and read William Carlos Williams's "The Red Wheelbarrow," Buson might start to feel at home. Williams's poetic techniques are similar in several ways to those Buson used in his haiku.

A surprising image captures readers' attention.

The paragraph ends with the thesis: The essay will explore similarities in the techniques of two poets from different cultures and time periods.

Haiku
Deep in a windless
wood, not one leaf dares
to move…
Something is afraid.
—*Buson*

The Red Wheel Barrow
so much depends
upon

a red wheel
barrow

glazed with rain
water

beside the white
chickens.
—*William Carlos Williams*

THE BODY You can organize the body of your essay in either of two ways. One approach is to compare your items feature by feature: You devote one paragraph to each feature your items have in common. The other approach is to discuss one item in its entirety; then discuss the other in its entirety, focusing on the similarities of the two. The following outlines show how each of the approaches could be used to compare the works of the two poets.

FEATURE BY FEATURE	ITEM BY ITEM
1. Introduction	1. Introduction
2. Vivid images, few words (Buson's haiku; Williams's poem)	2. Buson's haiku (vivid images, few words, understated emotions, invitation for reader participation)
3. Understated emotions (Buson's haiku; Williams's poem)	3. Williams's poem (vivid images, few words, understated emotions, invitation for reader participation)
4. Invitation for reader participation (Buson's haiku; Williams's poem)	4. Conclusion
5. Conclusion	

The key to organizing a comparative analysis is consistency. Don't start with a feature-by-feature paragraph and then go on to discuss one item in its entirety. This will confuse your readers. Choose one of the two approaches and stay with it.

WRITING FOR SCIENCE

Your examples for a scientific comparative analysis will consist of statistics, descriptions of scientific processes, and other factual information. Be sure to record this data accurately. Note your sources so that you can credit them; citing reputable sources is one way to lend weight to your statements.

THE CONCLUSION Just restating your main idea—your thesis—in your final paragraph is not enough. Let readers know why the similarities you have found are important or meaningful.

HOW DO I REVISE MY ESSAY?

As you revise your essay, check to be sure you have made your thought processes clear. If you are comparing two literary works, you may need to add quotations from both works to support your points. For other comparisons, ask yourself where you might add specific examples, descriptions, or data to illustrate your statements. Use appropriate transitions to clarify relationships among ideas in your comparative analysis, such as the following:

like	similarly	in the same way	both
too	also	as (or just as)	likewise

Use transitions between paragraphs to help readers see how each of your points relates to your thesis. Use transitions within paragraphs to help readers see how one idea relates to another.

CHECKPOINTS FOR REVISING

▶ Have I explored the similarities between two related but different items?

▶ Does my essay make a point or draw a conclusion based on similarities I found?

▶ Does the essay fulfill one or more of these purposes: to inform, to persuade, to evaluate, or to entertain?

▶ Does the essay contain specific examples that support my thesis?

▶ Is my essay organized clearly and consistently?

▶ Have I used transitions to help readers follow my line of thought?

The following model contains the body and conclusion of the essay comparing poems by Taniguchi Buson and William Carlos Williams:

MODEL

. . . For one thing, Buson and Williams both knew that a good poem does not need a lot of words. Buson's "Deep in a windless / wood, not one leaf dares to move . . . / Something is afraid." contains only fourteen words. Yet these few words

The transitions both and similarly alert readers to likenesses between the two poets.

allow the reader to imagine a thick forest, individual leaves on the trees, still air, and a frightening silence. Similarly, "The Red Wheel Barrow" has only sixteen words. Yet those words provide a concrete image of a wheelbarrow, its hard red sides shiny with water, contrasting with soft white-feathered chickens nearby.

The transitions *Both, Likewise,* and *like* help readers follow the writer's thinking.

Both Buson and Williams suggest emotions but leave them unexplained. In Buson's forest, "Something is afraid," but Buson does not say what or why. Likewise, in Williams's poem, "So much depends" on the wheelbarrow; yet Williams, like Buson, does not explain what depends on the wheelbarrow. These hints at ideas and feelings that are not stated constitute the most important similarity in the poets' techniques. They both rely on the reader to complete the picture.

The conclusion points out the importance of the poems' similarities.

In these ways, Buson's haiku and Williams's poem are related, although they were written two centuries—and half a world—apart. Because of the poets' similar techniques, these poems transcend their respective cultures, and even transcend time, to speak to readers from all eras.

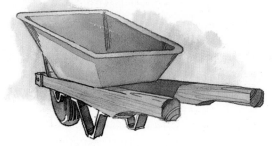

REPORTS: RESEARCH REPORT

49

How do I prepare a research report?

Preparing a research report is like using a telescope to find and examine a star. You need to focus carefully, search thoroughly, and think clearly about what you discover. Teachers assign research reports in the sciences, social studies, and the arts, as well as in English. Every research report involves locating and organizing information from a variety of sources.

> A **research report** is an in-depth, written examination of a topic, using information gathered from a variety of sources.

The Starry Night
1889, Vincent van Gogh
The Museum of Modern Art, New York

GUIDELINES

A research report

▶ presents factual information about a topic.

▶ brings together information from a variety of sources.

▶ develops a single thesis, or main idea.

▶ presents ideas and information in an organized way.

▶ has an introduction, a body, and a conclusion.

▶ correctly credits the sources consulted.

▶ includes a list of sources, the bibliography.

WHAT IS A GOOD TOPIC FOR RESEARCH?

A good topic is one that interests you and that you can cover thoroughly in the given time and space, using available resources. Some teachers ask you to find your own topic; others assign one. Even when a teacher assigns a topic, however, it is still up to you to choose the information you will present and how you will present it. The following chart indicates some ideas for finding a topic:

SCIENCE	SOCIAL STUDIES	ENGLISH OR THE ARTS
■ Visit a science museum.	■ Visit a history museum.	■ Visit an art museum.
■ Make notes of questions about science news.	■ Make notes of questions about current events.	■ Tour newspaper offices.
■ Browse through science references.	■ Consult newspapers and magazines from earlier decades.	■ Interview a technical writer.
■ Visit a zoo or botanical garden.	■ Attend an ethnic fair.	■ Attend a concert, play, musical, or opera.
■ Attend a planetarium show.	■ Interview an exchange student.	■ Check biographical references of authors and artists.
■ As you read for pleasure, jot down questions about science and nature.	■ As you read for pleasure, note questions about cultures and time periods.	■ Visit an art studio. ■ Be alert to your own ideas as you read for pleasure.

Here is an example of how reading for pleasure can suggest a research topic for an English class:

MODEL FROM LITERATURE

I remember my grandfather raising his hand and pointing to the swirl of the Milky Way which swept over us. Then he would whisper his favorite riddle . . .

Stars as silver coins—I like that! I wonder if people in different parts of the world have their own tales and images of stars and constellations.

There is a man with so much money
He cannot count it
A woman with a bedspread so large
She cannot fold it.

We knew the million stars were the coins of the Lord, and the heavens were the bedspread of his mother, and in our minds the sky was a million miles wide.

—Rudolfo A. Anaya, "In Commemoration: One Million Volumes"

In tracking down other cultures' tales about the stars, you might find a wealth of myths and legends. You might also find a research report topic: How myths of various cultures explain the Milky Way.

CHOOSING AND NARROWING YOUR TOPIC

When choosing a topic, be sure that you can find enough information about it to develop in your paper. As a rule of thumb, a search of your library's catalog and the *Readers' Guide to Periodical Literature* should yield at least five sources with information about your topic. If you find fewer, you will probably need to expand that topic.

When narrowing your topic, be sure you can cover it in the allotted space and time. If entire books have examined the topic you are planning for a ten-page paper, your focus is too broad. Use questions such as *when, where, who, what kind,* and *which one* to narrow your focus further, as in the following example:

COMPUTER TIP

Take advantage of online computer service networks; a bulletin-board service can put you in touch with experts. Also, explore online databases for information that your library may not have.

> **Possible topic:** Novas—exploding stars (What kind?)
> **Limited:** Supernovas (Which one?)
> **More limited:** The 1987 supernova (What about it?)
> **Manageable focus:** What did astronomers learn
> from the 1987 supernova?

HOW DO I ORGANIZE MY INFORMATION SEARCH?

A **primary source** is a firsthand account or document. A **secondary source** is an article written after the fact and is often based on research of primary sources. The astronomer Dr. Huerta would be a primary source if she witnessed the supernova herself; a secondary source, if she has used others' data. Both kinds of sources are useful.

Step 1: LIST POSSIBLE SOURCES.

Once you have limited your focus, recheck the library catalog and the *Readers' Guide*, and list the sources that fit your focus. At this point, you can include whole books, even though you will probably consult only the relevant parts of these longer works.

Step 2: EXAMINE AND EVALUATE YOUR SOURCES.

Briefly examine each book and article on your list, noting how much relevant information each offers. Skim book indexes and tables of contents; scan articles. For community resources, telephone to find out whether visits will provide useful information and if experts are available for interviews. Rate each source on your list as *most, very, somewhat,* or *not useful.*

TRY THIS

Use the Yellow Pages or Business section of the phone book. Look for headings that can lead to nonlibrary sources of information—places you can visit and experts you can interview.

Step 3: **MAKE SOURCE CARDS.**

Write one note card for each source you decide to use. This will help you locate the source again quickly. Source cards also make it easier for you to take notes and create the bibliography for your report.

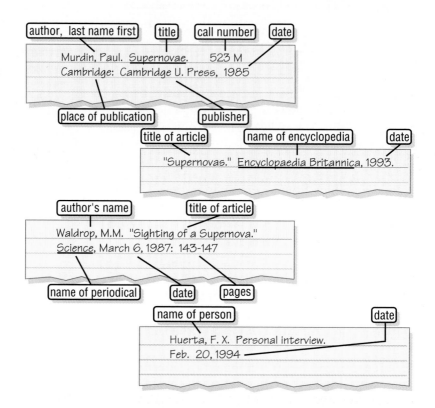

HOW SHOULD I TAKE NOTES FOR A REPORT?

When you are doing research, keep a stack of blank three-by-five cards with you to record your notes on. Later, you will use these notes to help you remember the information you have gathered and to draw conclusions about your findings.

- Use a separate card for each piece of information you record. When you are ready to write your paper, you can experiment with various ways of organizing it—just by changing the order of the cards.

- At the top of each note card, name the source of the information. Use an author or editor's last name or a key word from the title. Include the page number(s) where the information is located. This will make it easy to credit your sources later, when you are drafting your report and preparing the list of works cited.

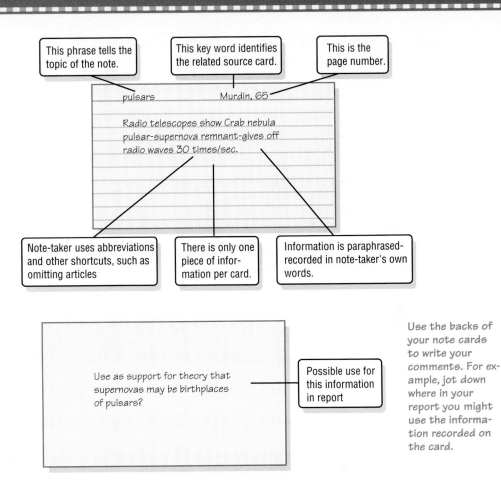

This phrase tells the topic of the note.

This key word identifies the related source card.

This is the page number.

pulsars   Murdin, 65

Radio telescopes show Crab nebula pulsar-supernova remnant-gives off radio waves 30 times/sec.

Note-taker uses abbreviations and other shortcuts, such as omitting articles

There is only one piece of information per card.

Information is paraphrased-recorded in note-taker's own words.

Use as support for theory that supernovas may be birthplaces of pulsars?

Possible use for this information in report

Use the backs of your note cards to write your comments. For example, jot down where in your report you might use the information recorded on the card.

WHAT EXACTLY SHOULD I INCLUDE IN MY NOTES?

Except for passages you plan to quote directly, your notes should always be in your own words. Be sure to record names, dates, facts, and figures accurately. It's fine to use abbreviations to save time, but keep a master list in case you forget what a particular abbreviation means. Here are some additional tips:

1. Write summaries of general ideas and main points. For a summary, you might condense a page into one or two sentences.

2. Write paraphrases of key material. A paraphrase, or rewording, is more detailed than a summary, and it helps you to understand your subject.

3. Record each quotation on a separate card. Copy quotations word for word and enclose them in quotation marks. Be sure to copy all punctuation accurately.

TRY THIS

Color code the tops of cards on which you record quotations or original ideas. This will help you to avoid plagiarism—the offense of presenting the words or ideas of others as your own.

HOW CAN I ORGANIZE MY INFORMATION?

It will be helpful to organize information before you begin writing.

GROUP YOUR NOTE CARDS. Arrange your note cards in piles according to subject matter, suggesting major headings to outline your report.

WRITE A THESIS STATEMENT. In one sentence, state your main idea. Keep revising this sentence until it reflects your findings accurately.

> **The 1987 supernova was an important astronomical event.**

Since this statement does not explain why the event was important, the student might revise the thesis as follows:

> **The 1987 supernova was an important astronomical event because scientists learned a lot from it.**

However, this statement is still too general. Therefore, the **final thesis statement** must focus on specific findings:

> **The 1987 supernova provided answers to certain cosmic mysteries that had puzzled astronomers for centuries.**

MAKE AN OUTLINE. Give each pile of note cards a label reflecting what they cover and arrange them in order. Use the labels as major topic headings in your outline, then sort each pile into smaller piles, and label subtopics. Include "introduction" and "conclusion" headings. This technique will help you to identify the main points of your paper.

MODEL

Roman numerals designate topic headings.

Capital letters designate subtopic headings. There must be at least two subtopics under a main topic—or none at all.

Arabic numerals and lowercase letters designate further subdivisions of a topic.

Supernova 1987

  I. Introduction

 II. Characteristics of supernovas

    A. Frequency of occurrence

    B. Behavior of supernovas

      1. Start as huge, dying stars

      2. Explode brightly

        a. Create cosmic dust clouds

        b. Tiny cores remain

III. Importance of 1987 supernova

The preceding example shows the beginning of a formal **phrase outline.** A formal **sentence outline** would begin in the following way:

For more on outlining, see p. 22.

> ### M O D E L
>
> I. Introduction
> II. Supernovas have several unusual characteristics.
>   A. Supernovas occur much more rarely than novas.
>   B. Supernovas exhibit unusual behavior.
>   1. They begin as unusually large, dying stars.
>   2. They explode with unusual brightness.
>   a. Explosions create cosmic dust clouds.
>   b. Only tiny cores remain after the explosions.

If you are asked to submit a formal outline with your report, use either phrases or complete sentences—not both—for all headings.

HOW DO I DRAFT MY RESEARCH REPORT?

Drafting your report means incorporating information from your note cards into sentences and paragraphs. Use your outline as a map, but be flexible. As you write the first draft, new approaches may occur to you. You are not obliged to stick to your original outline. The following tips can help you:

INTRODUCTION Focus your readers' attention with a surprising statistic, a strong quotation, or a dramatic anecdote that relates to your thesis. You may find that your thesis statement fits well at the end of your introductory paragraph.

BODY Though your research report may include complex ideas and a great deal of information, you can make your meaning clear by using

> **TRY THIS**
> Feel free to start your report by writing the body. It's usually easier to write the introduction after you know what is being introduced.

your own words. You cannot communicate anything unless you understand it first. When you do use the words of others, work these quotations smoothly into your sentences, as in the following example:

> Astronomers suspected that supernovas "might serve as stellar forges."

HOW DO I DOCUMENT MY SOURCES?

Remember to document each source you quote. Your teacher might ask you to use either the APA (American Psychological Association) style or the MLA (Modern Language Association) style for documentation within your report.

MODEL	
APA Parenthetical	Astronomers suspected that supernovas "might serve as stellar forges." (Murdin, 1985, p. 119)
MLA Parenthetical	Astronomers suspected that supernovas "might serve as stellar forges" (Murdin 119).

The following chart compares APA and MLA parenthetical styles of documentation.

APA PARENTHETICAL	MLA PARENTHETICAL
Each note appears in parentheses at end of relevant passage in research report.	Each note appears in parentheses at end of relevant passage in research report.
Note includes author's last name, date of publication, comma, the abbreviation p. or pp., and the page number(s).	Note includes author's last name and page number(s) where information was found.
Notes refer to "Reference List," a list of sources at end of paper.	Notes refer to "Works Cited," a list of sources at end of paper.

Whereas the APA style uses only parenthetical format, the MLA style offers two other choices of format: endnotes and footnotes.

M O D E L

<u>MLA</u>
<u>Endnote</u>

Astronomers suspected that supernovas "might serve as stellar forges."[1]

The raised arabic numeral indicates the passage the note refers to.

[at end of paper]

Notes

[1]Paul Murdin, <u>Supernovae</u> (Cambridge: Cambridge University Press, 1985), 119.

<u>MLA</u>
<u>Footnote</u>

Astronomers suspected that supernovas "might serve as stellar forges."[1]

[at bottom of page]

---

[1]Paul Murdin, <u>Supernovae</u> (Cambridge: Cambridge University Press, 1985), 119.

In the MLA endnote format, raised numbers at the ends of relevant passages refer to a list of notes at the end of the report. Each note includes an author's full name, the title of the source, publication data, and page numbers where the information was found. Formal rules, or conventions, govern the order, punctuation, and capitalization in these notes. The list of notes is followed by a "Works Cited" list.

In the MLA footnote format, notes appear at the bottom of each research report page instead of at the end of the report.

WHEN SHOULD I DOCUMENT MY SOURCES?

Document, or credit, your source when you are
- using another person's exact words.
- presenting an original idea that is not your own.
- reporting a fact available from just one source.

Do not document your source when you are reporting matters of common knowledge—information available from many sources, such as the fact that there are billions of stars in the universe.

AVOID PLAGIARISM

Plagiarism means presenting someone else's words or ideas as your own. It is a form of stealing and is a serious offense. You must credit your sources for any ideas you use that are not common knowledge and are not your own.

Proper documentation enables you to stress the validity of the information you are providing. It also enables your readers to evaluate your evidence. For example, a quotation from *Astronomy* magazine is likely to carry more weight than one from *Your Horoscope*.

CONCLUSION To wrap up your report, you might return to your thesis and offer some final thoughts about it. You might consider the significance of your research or pose possible questions for further investigation. An alternative is to refer to a quotation, anecdote, or statistic from your introduction, emphasizing its significance in light of the information you have presented.

WHAT SHOULD I LOOK FOR WHEN REVISING?

Check to see that the body of your report supports and develops the thesis you presented in the introduction. If there are points that have not been adequately developed, you may need to do further research and add this new material to your report. Also look for and eliminate any material not directly connected to your thesis.

CHECKPOINTS FOR REVISING

▶ Will my introduction catch readers' attention?

▶ Does my report develop a clear thesis stated at the beginning?

▶ Does the body of the report present material in an order that makes sense?

▶ Have I clarified the connections among ideas?

▶ Is the wording my own, except for direct quotations?

▶ Have I correctly documented the source of each quotation and of any original idea that is not my own?

▶ Does my report end effectively?

HOW DO I PREPARE MY BIBLIOGRAPHY?

The **bibliography** is the list of works cited that appears at the end of a research report. Write your bibliography after finishing the rest of your report. Include the sources of all the information and ideas you have used in your paper. Go back to your source cards for this data.

GUIDELINES

A bibliography

▶ lists the entries in alphabetical order by authors' last names.

▶ uses the first major word of the title, ignoring the articles *a, an,* and *the* for entries with no author.

▶ uses a long dash to replace the author's name in the second entry when more than one book by a writer is cited.

▶ indents all lines in each entry *except* the first line.

▶ uses a standard form for styling the entries.

Standard Form for Bibliographic Entries

book, one author:	Murdin, Paul. <u>Supernovae</u>. Cambridge: Cambridge University Press, 1985.
periodical article, two authors:	Marschall, L. A., and K. Brecher. "Will Supernova 1987A Shine Again?" <u>Astronomy</u> Fall 1992: 30–37.
periodical article, unidentified author:	"Supernova!" <u>Scientific American</u> May 1987: 54–55.
periodical article, one author:	Thomson, D. E. "Large Magellanic Explosion: Supernova 1987A." <u>Science News</u> Mar.1987: 40–43.
encyclopedia article:	"Supernovas." <u>Encyclopaedia Britannica</u>. 1993 ed.
interview:	Huerta, F. X. Personal interview. 28 Feb. 1994.

On the following page is an example of a final draft of the introduction and conclusion of a research report, along with examples from a Works Cited list.

Supernova 1987: Key to Cosmic Mysteries

Things were not going well for astronomer Ian Shelton on February 24, 1987. A bright blotch marred his nightly sky photo. Then he realized that the same bright blotch had not been there the night before. Shelton's camera had caught the birth of a supernova—a rare event that could hold a key to cosmic mysteries. . . . (Goldsmith 27)

The 1987 supernova is shedding light on the workings of the universe. Astronomers think that supernovas are birthplaces of pulsars and black holes. Supernova 1987 seems to prove at least part of this theory, for some astronomers detect faint radio waves—indicators of a pulsar—coming from the center of the dust cloud left after the explosion. (Marschall and Brecher 32)

Meanwhile, there is at least one other exciting possibility. Nearby supernovas seem to have occurred in pairs. The first two were less than 50 years apart (1006 and 1054), the second two less than 35 years apart (1572 and 1604). (Clark 28–29) Might another supernova explode in the next few years? Keep an eye on the sky!

Works Cited

Clark, David H. Superstars. New York: McGraw-Hill, 1984.

Goldsmith, Donald. Supernova! The Exploding Star of 1987. New York: St. Martin's Press, 1989.

Huerta, F. X. Personal interview. 28 Feb. 1994.

Marschall, L. A., and K. Brecher. "Will Supernova 1987A Shine Again?" Astronomy Fall 1992: 30–37.

An anecdote at the beginning catches readers' interest.

A thesis sentence appears at the end of the first paragraph. APA parenthetical style is used for documentation.

A restatement of the thesis keeps readers oriented.

A final question on the same topic leaves readers with food for thought.

How do I write a business letter?

One of the sneakers you bought a month ago has just lost a large piece of its sole. Surely sneakers ought to last more than a month! What can you do? You can write a business letter to the manufacturer. People write business letters for many reasons: to lodge complaints, to order products, to obtain forms, and to request information.

> A **business letter** is a formal letter written to an individual or organization for a specific, practical purpose.

GUIDELINES

An effective business letter

▶ states the writer's purpose clearly and briefly.

▶ uses a courteous tone and formal language.

▶ has six parts: heading, inside address, salutation, body, closing, and signature.

HOW DO I PREPARE A BUSINESS LETTER?

There are two styles for business letters. In modified block style, some parts begin near the right margin, and the first line of each paragraph is indented. In block style, all lines begin at the left margin.

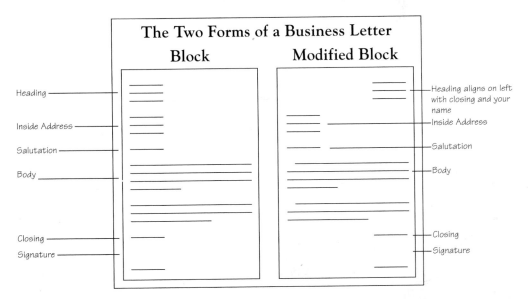

The Two Forms of a Business Letter

Block | Modified Block

Heading
Inside Address
Salutation
Body
Closing
Signature

Heading aligns on left with closing and your name
Inside Address
Salutation
Body
Closing
Signature

Heading: Your full address and the date.

34 Aspen Way
Pocatello, ID 83209
February 13, 19—

Inside Address: The name and address of the recipient. If possible, direct your letter to a particular person.

Manager, Customer Service
Ares Sport Shoe Company
2132 Dublin Road
Columbus, OH 43215

Salutation: A formal greeting like Dear Ms. (Name); To Whom It May Concern; or Dear Sir or Madam, followed by a colon.

Dear Sir or Madam:

Body: A clear, brief, courteous, formal statement of your reason for writing. Leave space between paragraphs.

I recently bought my fourth pair of Ares sneakers. I have always liked Ares shoes. However, this pair is unsatisfactory. Only a month after I bought them, a large piece of one sole fell off.

I would like to receive either a refund or a new pair of size 7-N black sneakers. I am enclosing the sales slip for your reference.

Thank you for your help.

Closing: Use a formal closing. Capitalize the first word. Use a comma after the last word.

Sincerely yours,

Signature: Leave four spaces. Then type or print your full name, and write your signature above it.

Sheila Watson

Sheila Watson

51

PRACTICAL AND TECHNICAL WRITING: RÉSUMÉ AND COVER LETTER

How do I write a résumé and cover letter?

The thought of applying for your first job can be a little frightening. You might wonder, "Why would anyone hire *me*? I have no experience, no qualifications. . ." That's not true, though. If you look carefully at your background and experience, you will discover that you already have skills and abilities you can bring to a job A résumé and cover letter are two ways you can communicate these qualifications to a prospective employer.

> A **résumé** is a written presentation of your educational background and job experience. A **cover letter** is the letter that accompanies a résumé when you apply for a job.

WHAT SHOULD I PUT ON A RÉSUMÉ?

A résumé should be divided into easy-to-read sections. All résumés should include the following information:

GUIDELINES

A résumé

▶ includes your name, address, and telephone number.

▶ describes your work experience.

▶ gives your educational background to date.

▶ states information about your references, recommendations by teachers or former employers.

▶ is usually one page long.

▶ does not use the pronoun *I*.

▶ is written in phrases, not complete sentences.

A résumé might also

▶ include a statement of your job objective if you are applying for a specific job.

▶ mention your qualifications for the job.

▶ list awards, prizes, or scholarships you have won.

▶ detail school activities, especially those that pertain to job skills.

▶ describe your interests, especially your career objective.

Personal information concerning your appearance, age, race, or religion is not necessary. In fact, it is illegal for an employer to consider these factors when hiring.

HOW SHOULD I WRITE MY RÉSUMÉ?

Type your résumé neatly. Put your name, address, and telephone number at the top. Organize the sections in order of importance, putting what is most impressive and relevant first. Proofread your résumé carefully to be sure it is free from errors. It is always a good idea to have someone else proofread it as well. When you send it out, send only originals, photocopies on bond paper, or offset copies.

CONTENTS OF A COVER LETTER

A cover letter usually accompanies a résumé and introduces you to the person in charge of interviewing candidates for a job. Here are some suggestions for writing an effective cover letter:

GUIDELINES

A cover letter

► is written in business letter form.

► uses formal language and does not include contractions, slang, or colloquialisms.

► addresses one specific person.

► includes your reason for writing by indicating the job for which you are applying and where you learned about it.

► explains why you want the job and why you are a good candidate.

► elaborates on any special skills that demonstrate your qualifications for the job.

► asks for an interview, and indicates when you will call to follow up your letter.

HOW SHOULD I WRITE MY COVER LETTER?

Use business letter form for a cover letter. Single-space the letter, unless it is very short. Double-space between paragraphs. Check your letter carefully for errors, and ask someone else to check it as well. Mistakes in a cover letter may lead an employer to conclude that you are routinely careless.

REVISING YOUR RÉSUMÉ AND COVER LETTER

After you've completed your résumé and cover letter, ask yourself these questions:

CHECKPOINTS FOR REVISING

▶ Is the factual information I have included—names, dates, addresses, and telephone numbers—accurate and complete?

▶ Is my résumé divided into clear sections?

▶ Is my résumé concise and easy to read?

▶ Does my cover letter stress my qualifications?

▶ Is my cover letter written in correct business letter form?

▶ Have I requested an interview and stated when I will be calling?

▶ Are my résumé and cover letter free from errors?

MODEL

Tamar Lesoinne
126 Claiborne Street
Philadelphia, PA 19143
215-555-5957

The writer centers her address and telephone number at the top.

OBJECTIVE: To become a library page

QUALIFICATIONS: Two years' volunteering at Thomas Jefferson High School Library
Complete knowledge of Dewey Decimal System and computerized checkout system

The writer lists the qualifications that pertain to her job objective.

WORK EXPERIENCE:
June 1993-Present. Part-time attendant, Tom's Sunoco, 11 Hall Street, Philadelphia
Responsible for filling tanks, checking oil, and working cash register
September 1992-Present. Volunteer librarian, Thomas Jefferson High School, Philadelphia
Responsible for shelving and repairing books, researching requests, and checking out materials

The writer includes her service station job, which shows that she is responsible and hard-working.

EDUCATION: Thomas Jefferson High School, Philadelphia, 1992-Present

AWARDS: National Merit Finalist, 1994

REFERENCES: Available on request

The writer lists an important award and indicates a willingness to send her references.

The applicant uses correct business letter form.

126 Claiborne Street
Philadelphia, PA 19143
May 2, 199-

The applicant addresses her letter to a specific person.

Mr. Robert Ngu
Children's Librarian
Norwood Public Library
665 Delft Street
Philadelphia, PA 19143

She points out where she heard of the job opening.

Dear Mr. Ngu:
I would like to apply for the job of children's room library page, advertised in this week's Neighborhood Advertiser. I have enclosed my résumé to give you an idea of my background.

The applicant elaborates on her experience, showing her specific skills.

I have worked in the Thomas Jefferson High School library for two years, shelving, repairing, and checking out library materials. I have also helped users find research materials.

The applicant states that her commitment to the job will be long term.

Because the advertised job is part time, I would hope to keep it though my senior year. After that, I plan to attend the community college, where I will take courses in library science. I would continue working at the Norwood library.

The applicant explains how she will follow up this letter.

I will call you in a few days to arrange for an interview.

Sincerely,

Tamar Lesoinne

Tamar Lesoinne

PRACTICAL AND TECHNICAL WRITING: TECHNICAL WRITING

52

How do I present technical information efficiently?

A scientist describes the progress of a reforestation program. A school principal announces a faculty meetings and defines the meeting's purpose. An astronomer reports the discovery of a star. A mountain climber details her new route to Mount Everest. What do all these activities have in common? They all involve the communication of technical information. Status reports, memoranda, and technical descriptions are examples of the kinds of documents that incorporate technical writing.

> **Technical writing** involves the clear and objective presentation of facts to a specific audience.

GUIDELINES

Technical writing

► presents the facts clearly and objectively.

► is usually directed to a specific audience.

► uses clear sentence structure and concise language.

► may document information with charts, tables, graphs, and statistics.

► has an impersonal, objective tone.

WRITING A STATUS REPORT

A **status report** describes the current state of an activity or project.

Suppose you were organizing a workshop and had to present a report on your progress. What would you write? Here are some guidelines for writing any type of status report:

• State the facts. Refresh your audience's memory by giving them a brief description of the project or event.

• Bring your audience up to date. Describe recent developments in your planning of the project: people you've contacted, decisions you've made, problems you've encountered.

• Ask for help if necessary. Point out specific areas in which you're looking for advice or assistance.

• Be clear and succinct. Don't take up time with unnecessary details.

When you present your status report, read it aloud or distribute copies of it so that others can read it on their own.

WRITING A MEMORANDUM

Suppose you wanted to remind the members of a local environmental group of a drive you have organized to raise money to clean graffiti from historic buildings in your town. One way to communicate with the members would be to send them a memo. Less formal than a business letter, a memo can be as succinct as a telegram and as terse as a military order. Here is an example of a memorandum:

MEMORANDUM

TO: EcoFreaks
FROM: Tanjou Green
SUBJECT: Antigraffiti Drive
DATE: May 5, 1995

A memo begins with a four-line header.

As you know, we've organized a drive to clean graffiti from three downtown landmarks. The cleanup will begin on August 1 if we raise the $2,000 we need for materials.

The writer explains the subject of the memo.

So far, we've raised $736. Most of our donations have come from local businesses. Less than $200 has been collected from consumers in the green containers we've placed in stores and supermarkets.

The writer reports the situation clearly and concisely.

Please let me know at the next meeting if you have any other ideas for raising money—especially from individuals.

The writer makes a request of the audience.

A memo does not have a formal closing.

WRITING A TECHNICAL DESCRIPTION

A **technical description** explains to a specific audience a process or event in clear, precise terms.

Suppose you made up a dance routine or you and your friends worked out an amazing basketball play. You want to record how it works, so that you won't forget it. Also, you want to share it with other people. To do this, you need to write a technical description. You would then be doing the same kind of writing that professional writers do when they write operating manuals, scientific reports, instructions for assembling products, and explanations of manufacturing procedures. To make your writing effective, you would use the following guidelines that technical writers follow:

- Break down the process into separate steps, and present those steps in chronological order. Use imperative sentences to describe the steps; for example, "Slide your right foot forward."

- Use precise vocabulary that is appropriate for your audience. Whenever possible, use comparisons or analogies to help your audience understand exactly what you mean.

- Use illustrations to clarify your description. To describe a dance routine or a basketball play, you would probably use diagrams to show the steps or how the players move. Other kinds of technical descriptions may require maps or flowcharts.

Contrary to common belief, a technical description doesn't have to be dense, dull, or confusing. Good technical writers present information clearly and logically, often using graphics or striking comparisons to get their points across.

Sometimes good technical writing can be worked into a piece of creative writing for special effect. Some of Ernest Hemingway's novels and short stories are filled with vivid, technically precise descriptions of fishing. In general, however, technical writing is primarily informative, as in the following model:

MODEL FROM TECHNICAL WRITING

WORD PROCESSING TERMS

Word processing programs give you two major capabilities: editing and formatting. *Editing* is the ability to enter text into the program, make corrections, save the text on disk, and later change the text. *Formatting* is the ability to specify how the text will look when you print it out. For example, formatting allows you to add special features to the printout, such as page numbers on each page, and to specify the width of the left and right margins.

In order to make a word processing program work, you give it *commands*, which are instructions that tell the program what you want it to do. . . . Give commands by using the mouse or by pressing the COMMAND key . . . and another key at the same time.

—Paul Hoffman, *Microsoft® Word Made Easy for the Macintosh™*

WRITING FOR MATH

If you work as a tutor, you might have to describe to other tutors your method for helping students understand a math subject like decimals. Here are some suggestions that may help you:

■ **Identify Your Audience.** You know that the audience for your written description will be math tutors, but you may not know which students will use your method. Will they be young children just developing a number sense? Will they be older students who need more work with decimals?

■ **Draw on Your Experience.** Try to remember when you were developing a number sense. How did you discover that 13 was 10 more than 3 and that 23 was 10 more than 13? Did you use counters or manipulatives to help you see the relationships?

■ **Try Out Your Ideas.** When you have an idea for teaching decimals, try it out. If it requires manipulatives—like counters or a number flip book—make rough prototypes. Once you have tried out your technique, you'll be able to describe it so that other tutors will be able to use it with their students.

Whether you are writing a status report, a memorandum, or some other form of technical description, you must consider these checkpoints as your review your draft:

CHECKPOINTS FOR REVISING

▶ Have I presented the facts clearly and objectively?

▶ Is my writing directed to a specific audience?

▶ Have I used vocabulary that is appropriate for my audience?

▶ Is my language clear and concise?

▶ Are my sentences straightforward and uncomplicated?

▶ If appropriate, have I documented my information with charts, tables, graphs, and statistics?

▶ Does my writing have an impersonal and objective tone?

How do I compose and deliver a speech?

In 1852 escaped slave Frederick Douglass was asked to give a speech in Rochester, New York, commemorating the Declaration of Independence. Here is a portion of his speech, which shocked the assembly.

> A **speech** is a talk delivered to a group, often for a persuasive purpose.

> Fellow citizens, pardon me, allow me to ask, why am I called upon to speak here today? What have I, or those I represent, to do with your national independence? Are the great principles of political freedom and of natural justice, embodied in the Declaration of Independence, extended to us? And am I, therefore, called upon to bring our humble offering to the national altar, and to confess the benefits and express devout gratitude for the blessings resulting from your independence to us?

Douglass's words were meant to be heard, not read. Once you realize that those words were spoken by a man who had become free only because he escaped from slavery, you can understand their impact.

When you write a speech, you want your words to have a dramatic impact on your audience. Here are some suggestions for writing an effective speech:

Frederick Douglass

GUIDELINES

An effective speech

▶ usually has one or more of these purposes: to inform, to persuade or inspire, to pay tribute, or to entertain.

▶ "hooks" listeners immediately by presenting an anecdote, an example, or a quotation or by posing a dramatic question.

▶ uses language appropriate for the occasion, audience, and purpose.

▶ uses rhythm, repetition, parallel structure, and sentence variety.

▶ is clearly organized and easy to follow.

▶ is presented to heighten its dramatic impact on the audience.

PLANNING YOUR SPEECH

Before you begin to write, determine your purpose or purposes for making the speech. If your teacher asks you to speak on an assigned topic or a topic that you choose and research yourself, you will probably decide that the main purpose of your speech is to inform your audience. If you want your classmates to vote for you for class president or to become more active in community service, the main purpose of your speech will be to persuade your audience. If you are asked to give a speech at graduation, your main purposes will probably be to inspire and to entertain your audience. If you are invited to speak at a social function honoring someone you know, your purposes will probably be to pay tribute, to entertain, or both.

Do any research that your speech requires. For some speeches, you may need to research a particular topic thoroughly; for others, you may need to find only a suitable quotation or two.

DRAFTING YOUR SPEECH

Once you begin to write your speech, follow these steps. Remember that your words will be heard, not read.

1. Using your audience and purpose to guide you, decide on your main idea and compose a thesis statement.

2. Organize your ideas. You can present them either chronologically or in order of importance. Focusing on your topic or purpose will help you select the method of organization.

3. Outline your speech on note cards.

4. Think about whether you will be more comfortable reading a written speech or working from note cards. If you choose to use note cards, write your main points in order along with facts, statistics, examples, and quotations.

5. Decide on an attention-grabbing opening. An amusing anecdote, a moving personal experience, a telling quotation, or a surprising question may serve to "hook" listeners. If appropriate to the audience and occasion, you might also consider opening with a humorous anecdote or a joke.

6. Use key speech-making strategies such as the following:

- **Rhythm** Use rhythm that sparks interest. Avoid a dull singsong beat that will bore your listeners or a choppy rhythm that may unnerve them.

- **Repetition** Repeat important words and phrases to make them stand out in listeners' minds.

- **Parallel structure** Put similar ideas in similar grammatical structures to emphasize them and make them memorable.
- **Sentence variety** Vary the lengths of your sentences, but rely on short sentences—even occasional fragments—to maintain the attention of your listeners.

WRITING FOR SCIENCE

In a science class you may have to make a speech that explains a process or an experiment. The following guidelines will help you write and deliver an effective speech:

- Do whatever research your subject requires.
- Use clear transitional words to indicate steps in the process or experiment.
- Use visual aids whenever possible. For example, if you are explaining a process, presenting a diagram or a series of graphics can be very helpful. If you are explaining a lab experiment, you might even demonstrate some or all of the steps in the experiment.
- As you practice your speech, make sure that you coordinate your visual aids with your presentation.
- Allow time for your audience's questions at the end of your speech and be prepared to answer those questions.

REVISING A SPEECH

Before you revise your speech, read it *aloud*. Listen to how your words sound. As you revise your speech, ask yourself these questions:

CHECKPOINTS FOR REVISING

▶ Are my ideas logically organized and clearly presented?

▶ Have I used key speech-making strategies to maintain my audience's interest?

▶ Are my anecdotes, examples, and language appropriate for my audience?

▶ Does my speech fulfill my purpose?

PRACTICING AND PRESENTING A SPEECH

Before you give your speech, practice it until you feel comfortable. Here are some tips for practicing:

- Tape yourself giving the speech. Listen to the tape, and jot down your immediate reactions on a copy of your script.

- Give your speech in front of a mirror. Indicate appropriate gestures on your note cards or script, but avoid making too many movements that will distract your audience.
- Ask a friend or relative to serve as your special audience and then to coach you.
- Time your speech. Because almost every speech must be given within a specific time period, you should time yours to ensure that it doesn't run long or short.

This graphic illustrates the steps you must take to deliver an effective speech.

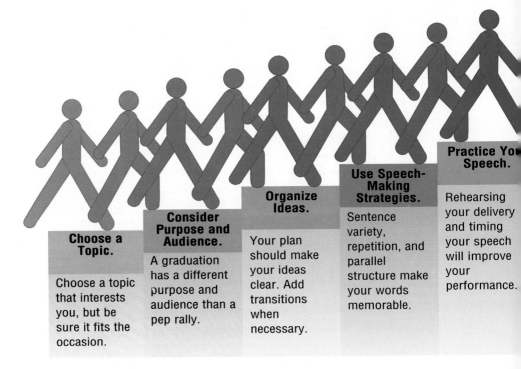

Choose a Topic.

Choose a topic that interests you, but be sure it fits the occasion.

Consider Purpose and Audience.

A graduation has a different purpose and audience than a pep rally.

Organize Ideas.

Your plan should make your ideas clear. Add transitions when necessary.

Use Speech-Making Strategies.

Sentence variety, repetition, and parallel structure make your words memorable.

Practice Your Speech.

Rehearsing your delivery and timing your speech will improve your performance.

Here are some tips for presenting a speech:

- Use your nervous energy to give a dynamic performance.
- Speak loudly and clearly but not too fast.
- Vary your pace and volume to create emphasis and drama.
- Use rhythm and repetition to move your audience emotionally.
- Maintain eye contact with your audience. Focus, in turn, on specific individuals for short periods of time. Avoid staring fixedly or glancing from one person to another.

LISTENING TO A SPEECH

Listening to a speech is almost as much an art as giving one. The following tips will help you become an attentive listener:

- Maintain a relaxed but attentive attitude.

- Determine the speaker's purposes and your own for listening.

- Think about what the speaker is saying, and identify the main ideas by focusing on organizational and transitional terms such as *the chief purpose, a second reason, another cause,* and *in summary.* These clues can help you sort out the information in the speech.

- Pay attention to changes in tone, facial expression, or gestures that usually signal key points of a speech. Visual aids such as charts and diagrams also usually signal important information.

- As you react to a speech, be aware of the setting. For example, cheering is appropriate at a political rally but out of place at a lecture.

- If appropriate, take notes highlighting important information. Organize your notes soon after the speech when the information is still fresh in your mind.

FROM A WRITER

66 *People who listen have different needs from people who read.* **99**

—Richard Lloyd-Jones

Here is part of the ending of Frederick Douglass's speech. Again, imagine this speech being delivered to a large audience on July 4, 1852.

MODEL FROM LITERATURE

At a time like this, scorching iron, not convincing argument, is needed. O! had I the ability, and could I reach the nation's ear, I would today pour out a fiery stream of biting ridicule, blasting reproach, withering sarcasm, and stern rebuke. For it is not light that is needed, but fire; it is not the gentle shower, but thunder. We need the storm, the whirlwind, and the earthquake. The feeling of the nation must be quickened; the conscience of the nation must be roused; the propriety of the nation must be startled; the hypocrisy of the nation must be exposed. . . .

—Frederick Douglass

The varied sentence structure creates interest.

The speaker uses parallel structure to emphasize his anger.

The parallel structure in the last sentence gives urgency to his call to action.

SPEAKING AND LISTENING PROJECTS: INTERVIEW

? *How do I conduct an interview?*

An **interview** is a process of gathering information on a topic by asking a person a series of questions.

What does it feel like to win a Nobel Prize for Literature? Talking to someone who has done just that can give you an insider's view. A personal perspective on an important event is just one example of the kind of information you can get from an interview. In addition, you can use an interview to get the following:

- technical information from an expert for a research paper.
- eyewitness testimony from a witness for a news story.
- personal information from a celebrity for a biographical profile.
- background information from a resident for a travel article.

Toni Morrison won the Nobel Prize for Literature in 1993.

An effective interview should meet these criteria:

GUIDELINES

An interview

- ▶ has one or more of the following purposes: informing, persuading, evaluating, and entertaining.

- ▶ has a clear focus.

- ▶ includes questions that fulfill the purpose and focus of the interview.

- ▶ follows either the question-and-answer or the narrative format.

- ▶ may be incorporated into many different types of writing such as research reports, newspaper or magazine articles, books, or oral history projects; an audio or videotaped version may also be played publicly or kept as documentation for the project.

HOW SHOULD I PREPARE FOR AN INTERVIEW?

Imagine you are writing a report on transportation in the twenty-first century. You have discovered that a city planner who specializes in urban transportation lives just down the block from you. You would really like her opinion on the future of your municipal transportation system. Before you set up an interview, though, think about your purpose and audience. What exactly do you want to find out about the system? Who will be reading your report—your teacher and classmates or a group of citizens interested in improving public transportation? These two groups might want to read about different aspects of the system. Once you've decided on your purpose and audience and narrowed your focus, follow these steps:

For more on focusing your topic, see p. 11.

- Write to the subject to ask for an interview, and explain what you want to talk about so that the person will have time to think about your topic. Follow up with a phone call in which you arrange when and where to meet.

- Find out as much as you can about the person and the topic you will be discussing.

- Write down the questions you will ask, keeping your purpose and focus in mind. To create questions that will spark a response, avoid beginning with the word *do* or *does* and instead start with *who, what, why, when, where,* and *how.* These questions cannot be answered with a *yes* or *no* answer.

    Poor Wording: Do you think our bus system will fail next year?

    Effective Wording: Based on your analysis of its most recent financial statement, what do you think will happen to our bus system next year?

- Arrange your questions in logical order on your notepad, leaving space for notes on the answer to each question.

- If you are planning to tape the interview, test the machine before the interview. Put in fresh, ready-to-record tape.

- Give yourself enough time to get to the place of the interview early, taking traffic and other potential delays into account.

COMPUTER TIP

If you have a laptop computer, you can type in notes on your subject's responses as he or she speaks. This will help you remember more details.

HOW CAN I CONDUCT A SUCCESSFUL INTERVIEW?

An interview is basically a live performance; you have to get it right the first time. Here are some tips to keep in mind:

- If you plan to tape the interview, ask permission first. Being taped makes some people nervous or uncomfortable.

- Begin with an opening question that is of special interest to your subject. Starting in this way may help your subject to relax.

- Invite your subject to express opinions and feelings and to provide anecdotes as well as facts and information. If you are doing a biographical profile, anecdotes can help reveal your subject's personality.

- Listen to your subject's answers. They will suggest follow-up questions that can help you explore the topic under discussion.

  > *Planned Question:* What technological innovation will contribute most to relieving automobile traffic in downtown areas?
  >
  > *Answer:* High-speed trains
  >
  > *Follow-Up Question:* Tell me more about these trains. How will they improve automobile traffic?

- Show your interest: Lean forward. Punctuate any pauses with interjections such as "I see" and "Yes."

- Let your subject speak. Avoid leading questions; don't put words in your subject's mouth.

- When the interview ends, ask permission to call back; you may need to double-check quotations or fill in missing facts. Offer to show your subject the completed interview.

HOW DO I WRITE UP THE INTERVIEW?

You will probably come out of the interview with a wealth of raw impressions and scribbled notes. Clean up and organize these notes while the memory of what was said is still fresh. If the interview was taped, transcribe or write down what was said on the tape. Also, jot down impressions of your subject and any descriptive details you noticed about his or her environment.

When you are ready to write up your interview, use one of the following two options for presenting it:

THE QUESTION-AND-ANSWER (Q-AND-A) FORMAT This is an edited version of the interview itself. It presents your questions and your subject's answers as spoken, though they may be shortened if necessary. Use ellipsis points to indicate places where material has been taken out or where there were pauses.

THE NARRATIVE ARTICLE This is an article in which you incorporate your subject's words. Similar to a newspaper article, it uses the information from your interview to create a profile of your subject.

HOW DO I REVISE MY INTERVIEW?

Whether you decide to use a Q-and-A format or write a narrative article, ask yourself these questions as you revise your first draft:

CHECKPOINTS FOR REVISING

▶ Do I give my audience enough background information to understand the purpose of the interview and the reason I chose my subject?

▶ Does my writing have a consistent focus? Do I need to sharpen or narrow the focus? Do I include unrelated material?

▶ Do I include information such as opinions, personal feelings, and anecdotes that reveals my subject's personality?

▶ Do I incorporate information from my interview into an appropriate written form such as a report or a biographical profile?

Here is an excerpt of an interview in a Q-and-A format:

MODEL

Q. Ms. Valdez, you have ridden some of the world's most famous trains such as the Orient Express. What do you enjoy about train travel?

A. I love train travel. I think it's a terrific way to relax.

The interview begins with a question that puts the subject at ease.

Q. Why did you decide to become a transportation expert? Did your love of trains influence you?

A. Yes, but I am also fascinated by the potential of high-tech developments such as electric cars, high-speed trains, and tram and sky rails.

The interview follows up with a question that reveals a personal note about the subject.

Q. Tell me a little about high-speed trains. How will they affect our municipal rail system?

A. They will alleviate some of the rush-hour congestion at our main rail terminals because rapid rides will encourage commuters to adopt flexible working schedules.

The interviewer relates the subject's interest in high-speed trains to the focus of the interview—the future of the municipal rail system.

Q. What do you see as the future of rail travel in our city?

A. I believe rail travel will increase in popularity as trains become quieter and, I hope, cleaner. . . .

The interviewer begins to ask questions that reflect the central focus.

55 MULTIMEDIA PROJECTS: DOCUMENTARY VIDEO

 How do I shoot a documentary video?

> A **documentary video** uses moving pictures to present information about a problem, situation, or event from real life.

Most television shows we watch are fictional. Some television programs, however, are documentaries. On television, documentary material might be presented as news, how-to programs, talk shows, nature shows, or analyses of history. Various businesses produce documentary videos to demonstrate products or services, train employees, or win the goodwill of the public. In addition, people make videos of family events.

GUIDELINES

An effective documentary video should

- ▶ fulfill its purpose.
- ▶ reflect the interests of the audience.
- ▶ be a faithful rendition of a written script.
- ▶ show varied, carefully edited, shots and angles.
- ▶ show subjects in motion where possible.
- ▶ make full use of sound.

PRODUCING A VIDEO

Before making a video, decide on your purpose and audience. Here are some ideas to help you:

AUDIENCE	PURPOSE
your classmates	to inform them about an event in history through a re-enactment
administrators of your school	to persuade them to restructure overcrowded lunch periods in the cafeteria
a sixth-grade class	to demonstrate a skill they can learn, such as cooking, carpentry, or laboratory work
the general public	to spark interest in an activity such as music

WRITING A SCRIPT

Even a video that contains no planned dialogue begins with a script. A good video script outlines everything that will be seen and heard.

The terms and format you use in writing a script are not as important as camera directions, settings, action, sounds, music, visual effects, and spoken narration or dialogue. Most video scripts are composed of two columns. The left column includes all the video—or visual—directions. The right column includes all the audio—or sound—directions. Video and audio directions that appear side by side in the script represent what will be seen and heard at the same time in your program.

The following is a list of technical terms that directors and camera operators use in shooting videos:

TRY THIS

Before deciding on a subject, try to visualize various topics. The more movement and visual images you can imagine, the better the topic will be for video.

Establishing shot: a view of a scene to show the audience where the action is going to take place

Long shot: a view from a distance, showing one or more people and the background

Medium shot: a view of one or more people from the waist up

Close-up: a view of a person from the shoulders up or of a single object

Pan: move the camera to the left or the right

Zoom: use a special lens that adjusts from a long shot to a close-up while shooting

Fade: increase or reduce the picture intensity to begin (fade in) or end (fade out) a scene

Cut: move directly from one shot to another

Audio dub: sound added to a videotape

Voice-over: comment or narration by an unseen person

The following is a partial script for a video production about the American poet Emily Dickinson:

1. Interior— medium shot: lace curtains blowing at an open window
Fade out

Voice-over (Emily): This is my letter to the world, / That never wrote to me,—

2. Fade in on exterior— medium shot: a leafy tree in a green field
Zoom in on close-up: a branch of the tree

Voice-over (Emily): The simple news that Nature told, / With tender majesty.

3. Cut to: photo (from book): the Dickinson house

Music (under): guitar
Voice-over (narrator): Emily Dickinson lived in the family home in Amherst, Massachusetts, until her death in 1886.

4. Cut to exterior— medium shot: woman in white dress seen dimly through the window

Voice-over (Emily): Her message is committed / To hands I cannot see;

5. Cut to interior— close-up: the woman inside the house at the window

Music: guitar solo ends
Voice-over (Emily): For love of her, sweet countrymen, / Judge tenderly of me!

6. Fade out

PREPARING TO SHOOT

After completing your script, decide what equipment you will use. Will you use a built-in or an external microphone? Will you set up lights or use natural light? Will you edit as you shoot or do it later?

SHOW YOUR SUBJECT IN MOTION. Making a video is different from taking still photographs. Show your subjects in motion.

VARY YOUR SHOTS AND CAMERA ANGLES. Try for a good balance of long shots, medium shots, pans, and close-ups. Try to use the zoom lens only between shots to change the viewpoint.

KEEP THE CAMERA STEADY. When you pan, move the camera on a tripod. Never walk with a camera while filming; let your subjects move.

EDITING AND SOUND

Editing is the way you assemble your shots for maximum effectiveness. To make the best selections, follow these guidelines:

- Review all your footage. Keeping your purpose in mind, select the shots you want, and arrange them in order on your final list.
- Look at the footage again, noting the exact counter numbers on your camera or VCR for the scenes selected.
- Copy your shots in the correct order after you have made clean edits or deletions. Use your list of counter numbers as a guide.
- Use your equipment to dub in voice-over narration, dialogue, comments by people interviewed, music, or sound effects.

CHECKPOINTS FOR EDITING

- ▶ Does my video achieve the purpose I set out to achieve?
- ▶ Is the video appropriate for my audience?
- ▶ Have I used a variety of camera shots and angles?
- ▶ Have I made full use of music and of sound in general?
- ▶ Is the dialogue—and the sound in general—of the best quality?
- ▶ Are my shots, after preliminary editing, still in the right order?

For more information, look for books like these:
Using Your Camcorder by Mandy Matson, © 1989, AMPHOTO.
Today's Video: Equipment, Setup, and Production, 2d edition, by Peter Utz, © 1992, Prentice-Hall, Inc.

MULTIMEDIA PROJECTS: MULTIMEDIA PRESENTATION

❓ *How can I put together a multimedia presentation?*

A **multimedia presentation** conveys information and ideas through the use of two or more media, or forms of communication.

The lights dim. You hear the sounds of waves crashing and men shouting orders. Onscreen you see a slide: a nineteenth-century painting of a whaling ship pursuing a huge breaching whale. The lights come up on a speaker standing behind a table covered with whale products. All the sounds, images, artifacts (objects), and spoken words communicate a historical fact: Many comforts of nineteenth-century life depended on the harvesting of whales. This is a multimedia presentation, a report in which several forms of communication convey thoughts on a subject.

GUIDELINES

A multimedia presentation

▶ conveys information and ideas about an engaging topic.

▶ presents its content through the interplay of two or more media.

▶ appeals to several senses.

▶ has a clear and unified focus.

▶ gives appropriate credit to sources.

WHAT MEDIA CAN I USE?

In a multimedia presentation you can use anything that your audience can understand through their senses. Here are some possibilities:

• audiotapes of music, sound effects, and speakers' words

• slides of people, places, paintings, and other subjects

• videotapes of interviews, films, and television programs

• printed articles, graphs, charts, and maps

• scale models and other objects that can be handled

• foods, plants, and other items that can be smelled or tasted

HOW DO I CHOOSE AN APPROPRIATE TOPIC?

The best topics are those that can be fully explored through images, sounds, and hands-on experience. Here are two topics and the notes a writer took in order to decide whether to write a report or give a multimedia presentation:

MODEL

Topics	Presentation or Report?
1. Heroism in <u>Hamlet</u>	could use videotapes or recordings of productions of the play, but I want to analyze Hamlet's language and character; better as a written report
2. Shakespeare's Globe Theatre	drawings of models of the theater would convey its appearance far better than words; also, a videotape or recording of a performance would help re-create the theatergoers' experience then and now; best as a multimedia presentation

HOW DO I GATHER INFORMATION AND MATERIALS?

First, reflect on your purpose for making the presentation. What aspects of your topic can your audience experience only through a multimedia approach? Then use a cluster to get ideas and identify the media to present them. Here is a cluster for a multimedia report on Shakespeare's Globe Theatre:

The following suggestions can help you focus your search for materials:

- Assemble a resource kit and start a notebook.
- Check the library for relevant books, periodicals, records, audio-tapes, videotapes, and computer databases.
- Check videotape stores for pertinent videotapes to rent.

- Investigate museums, historical soci-eties, and archives (places where papers and historical records and photos are kept). Also, business firms may have pertinent materials.
- Interview knowledgeable people.
- Keep a record of the source of each element that you discover.

Shakespeare's Globe Theatre

HOW SHOULD I PLAN MY PRESENTATION?

Outline the information you want to include in your presentation. Next to the headings, name your multimedia resources, as shown in the following outline for a multimedia presentation on the Globe Theatre.

MODEL	
The Globe	**Media Resources**
I. The Globe Theatre building	Henry V videotape
A. Location and dimensions	Scale model
B. Layout	Printed diagrams
1. audience gallery	as handouts
2. yard and main stage	
3. inner stage	
4. upper galleries	
II. Productions in Shakespeare's time	
A. Scenery	Paintings (slides)
B. Costumes	Drawings (slides)
C. Actors	Audiotape of scenes

Once you have written your outline, create a flowchart that shows what you or another student will be saying, doing, playing, or showing at each point during your presentation. Use the format of the following flowchart to develop a script for whatever topic you choose to present.

Flowchart for Multimedia Presentation:
The Globe Theatre in Shakespeare's Day

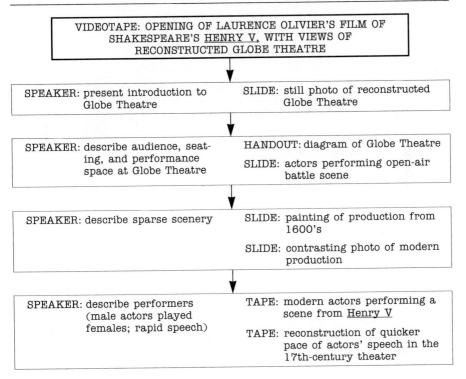

HOW WILL I PRESENT MY MULTIMEDIA REPORT?

Use your flowchart to create a script for your presentation. It should include the words you will say during the presentation, accompanied by directions, in capital letters, indicating when to introduce the multimedia elements. You may want to depart from your script during the presentation, but knowing you have it will give you confidence.

Presenting a multimedia report means giving a performance. Like any other performance, your presentation will be successful if you practice beforehand. Be sure to follow these steps:

- Rehearse with all the items and equipment you will use.

- If anyone will be helping you, he or she should rehearse with you.

- Before your audience arrives, make sure that all your equipment works and that all your materials are in the correct order.

Try to anticipate problems and solve them well before presentation time. Use the following tips for help:

1. To make sure that your audio material is heard in the correct order, edit it onto a single tape, leaving short gaps between items.

2. To prevent your script from getting out of order, number the pages and copy or paste them into a notebook or insert them into a ring binder.

3. Be ready in case something unexpected happens. If you have put your audience at ease, you can transform a mishap into a humorous incident.

4. To remain alert and sensitive to your audience's capacity to see and hear something you are presenting, be prepared to move about the room or ask the audience to move if necessary.

5. As with any presentation, speak loudly and clearly, and remember to vary your pace and tone. Your audience will be better able to pay attention if you make frequent eye contact with them.

WRITING FOR HEALTH

If you are planning a multimedia presentation about a health issue, in addition to using resources mentioned so far, you may want to consider demonstrating such techniques as first aid and the Heimlich Maneuver and discussing reflexes, respiration, and muscle action. If you plan to use a live demonstration, make sure that you carefully introduce and describe the subject matter.

Here is part of a multimedia presentation on the Globe Theatre:

MODEL

The directions are set off in capital letters and brackets.

[VIDEOTAPE: OPENING OF LAURENCE OLIVIER'S FILM OF <u>HENRY V</u> AS CAMERA PANS THAMES RIVER AND APPROACHES GLOBE THEATRE] [FREEZE FRAME ON VIEW OF GLOBE]

What you see on the screen is a reconstruction of Shakespeare's playhouse, the Globe, as it appeared in Laurence Olivier's film of Shakespeare's <u>Henry V</u>. Just as Olivier did in this film, I'd like to take you back to a theatrical production in Shakespeare's time. What you will experience is very different from today's Shakespearean productions.

The Globe sat on the banks of the Thames River, across from the city of London.

[HANDOUTS]

As you see from these diagrams, the Globe was eight-sided. Like many other buildings in Shakespeare's time, the Globe had a thatched roof.

[SLIDE OF ACTORS PERFORMING BATTLE SCENE]

The writer presents diagrams to give the audience a clear idea of what the Globe looked like.

Plays were put on in the afternoon, when there was natural light. None of the special lighting effects available today were available then.

What did a production in Shakespeare's day actually look and sound like?

In the late 1500's and early 1600's, there was very little scenery.

[SLIDE OF PAINTING OF EARLY PRODUCTION]

Contrast this nonrealistic scenery with the kinds of sets modern playgoers are used to.

[SLIDE FROM A CONTEMPORARY PLAY]

Shakespeare's actors also presented a great contrast to actors today. Shakespeare's women were played by young male actors. Also, because Shakespeare's plays were very long, and because the actors had to finish the play during daylight, they probably had to deliver their lines briskly. Listen to this tape of two modern actors performing a scene from Henry V.

[TAPE OF PRESENT-DAY ACTORS]

In addition to videotape, diagrams, and slides, the writer uses audiotape.

Listen to what the same scene would have sounded like at the faster pace spoken in Shakespeare's day.

[TAPE OF SAME SCENE WITH FASTER SPEECH]

GRAMMAR, USAGE, AND MECHANICS

■ ■ ■

Applying the Rules in Your Writing

The Window, 1925, Pierre Bonnard
Tate Gallery, London

Problem Solver

This Problem Solver gives examples of errors that student writers often make and tells you how to correct them. In each section of the Problem Solver, you will find one or more strategies to correct the error as well as sample revisions. To solve a problem quickly, use the following table of contents.

57

RUN–ON SENTENCES

57A **PROBLEM:** Two main clauses not separated by punctuation:

Error: Secretary of State William Seward bought Alaska from Russia the deal was mocked as "Seward's Folly."

Revision: Secretary of State William Seward bought Alaska from Russia. The deal was mocked as "Seward's Folly."

Revision: Secretary of State William Seward bought Alaska from Russia; the deal was mocked as "Seward's Folly."

Revision: Secretary of State William Seward bought Alaska from Russia, but the deal was mocked as "Seward's Folly."

Revision: When Secretary of State William Seward bought Alaska from Russia, the deal was mocked as "Seward's Folly."

Use an end mark and a capital letter to separate main clauses.

Use a semicolon between clauses.

Use a comma and a coordinating conjunction between clauses.

Introduce one clause with a subordinating conjunction and use a comma before the new main clause.

57B **PROBLEM:** Two main clauses separated only by a comma (comma splice):

Error: Seward's $7.2 million purchase proved a bargain, gold deposits were discovered three decades later.

Revision: Seward's $7.2 million purchase proved a bargain. Gold deposits were discovered three decades later.

Revision: Seward's $7.2 million purchase proved a bargain; gold deposits were discovered three decades later.

Revision: Seward's $7.2 million purchase proved a bargain, for gold deposits were discovered three decades later.

Revision: Seward's $7.2 million purchase proved a bargain when gold deposits were discovered three decades later.

Separate the two clauses with an end mark and a capital letter.

Change the comma to a semicolon.

Add a coordinating conjunction after the comma.

Introduce the second clause with a subordinating conjunction. No comma is needed.

58A **PROBLEM:** A fragment that lacks a subject:

Error: Prospectors first struck gold in Canadian territory. First found it in Alaska in 1886.

Add a subject to make the fragment a sentence.

Revision: Prospectors first struck gold in Canadian territory. They first found it in Alaska in 1886.

Revision: Prospectors first struck gold in Canadian territory and first found it in Alaska in 1886.

Combine the fragment with a sentence, rewording it if necessary.

58B **PROBLEM:** A fragment that lacks a verb:

Error: Trails to mining sites were extremely hazardous. Many lost prospectors dying in the cold.

Revision: Trails to mining sites were extremely hazardous. Many lost prospectors were dying in the cold.

Make the fragment a sentence by adding a helping verb.

Error: By 1896 the Gold Rush was in full swing. Mining camps all over eastern Alaska.

Revision: By 1896 the Gold Rush was in full swing. Mining camps flourished all over eastern Alaska.

Make the fragment a sentence by adding a verb.

Revision: By 1896 the Gold Rush was in full swing with mining camps flourishing all over eastern Alaska.

Join the fragment to a sentence, rewording it if necessary.

58C **PROBLEM:** A fragment that lacks a subject and verb:

Error: A second wave of the Gold Rush began in 1898. With the discovery of gold in western Alaska.

Combine the fragment with a sentence, rewording it if necessary.

Revision: A second wave of the Gold Rush began in 1898 with the discovery of gold in western Alaska.

58D **PROBLEM:** A fragment that is an isolated subordinate clause:

Error: After railways were completed in 1900. The dangers of the trail were substantially reduced.

Link the subordi-
nate clause to a
sentence. Make
the fragment a
sentence.

Revision: After railways were completed in 1900, the dangers of the trail were substantially reduced.

Revision: Railways were completed in 1900. The dangers of the trail were then substantially reduced.

59 LACK OF SUBJECT–VERB AGREEMENT

59A PROBLEM: Confusing the subject with the object of a preposition:

Make the verb
agree in number
with its subject.

Error: A strip of mountains cross Alaska.

Revision: A strip of mountains crosses Alaska.

59B PROBLEM: Using an incorrect verb with a compound subject joined by *and*:

If the parts of the
subject name
more than one
thing, use a plural
verb.

Error: The Bering Sea and Arctic Ocean borders Alaska on the west.

Revision: The Bering Sea and Arctic Ocean border Alaska on the west.

If the parts of the
subject refer to
the same thing,
use a singular
verb.

Error: The capital and third largest city are Juneau.

Revision: The capital and third largest city is Juneau.

59C PROBLEM: Using an incorrect verb with a compound subject joined by *or* or *nor*:

Make the verb
agree with the
compound subject
part closer to *or*
or *nor*.

Error: Neither Juneau nor Anchorage are as cold as Nome.

Revision: Neither Juneau nor Anchorage is as cold as Nome.

If *or* or *nor* links a
plural and a singu-
lar part, make the
second part plural
and use a plural
verb.

Error: Several highways or a railway go to Denali National Park.

Revision: A railway or several highways go to Denali National Park.

59D PROBLEM: Using an incorrect verb with a compound subject preceded by *many a, every,* or *each:*

Error: Every tourist and animal lover enjoy the whales on Alaska's coast.

Revision: Every tourist and animal lover enjoys the whales on Alaska's coast.

Use a singular verb.

59E PROBLEM: Using an incorrect verb with a subject separated from a verb:

Error: The sea otter as well as the sea lion inhabit coastal Alaska.

Revision: The sea otter as well as the sea lion inhabits coastal Alaska.

Make the verb agree with its subject. Ignore phrases like *as well as, in addition to,* and *together with.*

59F PROBLEM: Using an incorrect verb with a subject that differs in number from a subject complement:

Error: Scenic views is the main attraction in Glacier Bay National Park.

Revision: Scenic views are the main attraction in Glacier Bay National Park.

Make the verb agree with its subject.

59G PROBLEM: Using an incorrect verb with a subject that follows the verb (inverted order):

Error: On Alaska's Arctic coast lives several native peoples.

Revision: On Alaska's Arctic coast live several native peoples.

Make the verb agree with its subject. Ignore the words in opening phrases.

59H PROBLEM: Using an incorrect form of the verb *be* with a subject that follows *There* or *Here:*

Error: There is Inuit villages as far east as Prince William Sound.

Revision: There are Inuit villages as far east as Prince William Sound.

Make the verb agree with its subject.

59I PROBLEM: Using an incorrect verb with a singular subject that ends in *s*:

Error: The TV series *Northern Exposure* take place in Alaska.

Use a singular verb.

Revision: The TV series *Northern Exposure* takes place in Alaska.

59J PROBLEM: Using an incorrect verb with the title of a work as subject:

Error: *Arctic Dreams* describe author Barry Lopez's experiences in Alaska.

If the subject is a title, use a singular verb.

Revision: *Arctic Dreams* describes author Barry Lopez's experiences in Alaska.

59K PROBLEM: Using an incorrect verb with a noun naming an amount as subject:

Error: Six months of winter make life difficult above the Arctic Circle.

If the amount is a unit, use a singular verb.

Revision: Six months of winter makes life difficult above the Arctic Circle.

Error: The last few winters has been slightly warmer than usual.

If the subject is considered as separate units, use a plural verb.

Revision: The last few winters have been slightly warmer than usual.

59L PROBLEM: Using an incorrect verb with a collective noun as the subject:

Error: A group of Native Americans, the Tlingit, live in southern Alaska.

If the subject is considered as a whole group, use a singular verb.

Revision: A group of Native Americans, the Tlingit, lives in southern Alaska.

Error: The group offers different opinions on the best waters for fishing.

If the subject refers to each group member, use a plural verb.

Revision: The group offer different opinions on the best waters for fishing.

59M **PROBLEM:** Using an incorrect verb with *the number* or *a number* as the subject:

Error: The number of caribou apparently are decreasing.

Revision: The number of caribou apparently is decreasing.

If the *number* is preceded by *the*, use a singular verb.

Error: A number of unusual birds nests in Alaska.

Revision: A number of unusual birds nest in Alaska.

If a *number* is preceded by *a*, use a plural verb.

59N **PROBLEM:** Using an incorrect verb with an indefinite pronoun as the subject:

Error: Each of Alaska's main ports have a thriving fishing industry.

Revision: Each of Alaska's main ports has a thriving fishing industry.

If the pronoun is singular, use a singular verb.

Error: Some of the catch are sold to fish canneries.

Revision: Some of the catch is sold to fish canneries.

Use a singular verb when the pronoun refers to a singular noun.

Error: Some of the ports ships fish products overseas.

Revision: Some of the ports ship fish products overseas.

Use a plural verb when the pronoun refers to a plural noun.

60 VERB TENSES AND SHIFTS

60A **PROBLEM:** An incorrectly formed irregular verb:

Error: Susan Butcher winned the Iditarod dog-sled race several times.

Revision: Susan Butcher won the Iditarod dog-sled race several times.

Use the correct past form of irregular verbs. See the chart on p. 409, or consult a dictionary.

60B **PROBLEM:** Confusion between the past tense and the past participle:

Error: Many Alaskans have drove their dog sleds from Anchorage to Nome in the Iditarod.

Use the correct past participle of irregular verbs.

Add a helping verb.

Replace the past participle with the past form.

Revision: Many Alaskans have driven their dog sleds from Anchorage to Nome in the Iditarod.

60C PROBLEM: An incorrect use of the past participle:

Error: The dog-sled race begun in commemoration of a famous 1925 event.

Revision: The dog-sled race was begun in commemoration of a famous 1925 event.

Revision: The dog-sled race began in commemoration of a famous 1925 event.

60D PROBLEM: An incorrect shift in tense:

Error: When an epidemic swept Nome, a dog sled carries medical supplies the 1,049 miles from Anchorage.

When events occur at the same time, use the same verb tense.

Revision: When an epidemic swept Nome, a dog sled carried medical supplies the 1,049 miles from Anchorage.

60E PROBLEM: Failure to shift tense to show that one event preceded another:

Error: Many people died before the sled arrived from Anchorage.

Shift tenses to show the sequence of events.

Revision: Many people had died before the sled arrived from Anchorage.

61 PRONOUN SHIFTS AND PRONOUN REFERENCES

61A PROBLEM: An incorrect shift in gender when the antecedent can be male or female:

Error: Everyone has his favorite American writer.

Use male and female pronouns with _or_.

Revision: Everyone has his or her favorite American writer.

Eliminate the pronoun.

Revision: Everyone has a favorite American writer.

Error: The nature lover may find that Jack London's works interest him.

Revision: Nature lovers may find that Jack London's works interest them.

Make the antecedent and the pronoun plural.

61B   PROBLEM: An incorrect shift in person or number:

Error: The reader enjoys *The Call of the Wild* because we admire Buck.

Revision: We enjoy *The Call of the Wild* because we admire Buck.

Use an antecedent in the same person and number as the pronoun.

Error: Kay likes Jack London because you can learn about Alaska from his work.

Revision: Kay likes Jack London because she can learn about Alaska from his work.

Use a pronoun in the same person and number as the antecedent.

Revision: Kay likes Jack London because readers can learn about Alaska from his work.

Use a noun not a pronoun.

61C   PROBLEM: An incorrect shift in person when the antecedent is a singular indefinite pronoun:

Error: Each of the students reads "To Build a Fire" in their textbooks.

Revision: Each of the students reads "To Build a Fire" in his or her textbook.

Change the pronoun to a singular form.

Revision: All of the students read "To Build a Fire" in their textbooks.

Change the pronoun antecedent to a plural form.

Revision: The students read "To Build a Fire" in their textbooks.

Eliminate the indefinite pronoun antecedent.

61D   PROBLEM: A vague or weak pronoun reference:

Error: "To Build a Fire" is very suspenseful, which most readers enjoy.

Revision: "To Build a Fire" is filled with suspense, which most readers enjoy.

Reword the sentence to show a clear antecedent.

Error: The protagonist is inexperienced with the Arctic cold, and that causes his downfall.

Revision: The protagonist is inexperienced with the Arctic cold, and his inexperience causes his downfall.

61E **PROBLEM:** Indefinite use of *you* or *they*:

Error: In "To Build a Fire," they have vivid descriptions of Alaska.

Revision: "To Build a Fire" has vivid descriptions of Alaska.

Error: In Alaska's subzero temperatures, you need to build a fire.

Revision: In Alaska's subzero temperatures, the main character needs to build a fire.

61F **PROBLEM:** A pronoun that could refer to either antecedent:

Error: When an old timer meets the main character, he issues a warning.

Revision: When an old timer meets the main character, the older man issues a warning.

Revision: An old timer meets the main character and issues a warning.

62 MISPLACED OR DANGLING MODIFIERS

62A **PROBLEM:** Misplacing the adverb *only*:

Error: The normal January temperature in Fairbanks, Alaska, only reaches thirteen degrees below zero.

Revision: The normal January temperature in Fairbanks, Alaska, reaches only thirteen degrees below zero.

62B PROBLEM: A misplaced modifier:

Error: Nome is warmer than Fairbanks with a normal January temperature of nine degrees above zero.

Revision: Nome, with a normal January temperature of nine degrees above zero, is warmer than Fairbanks.

Move the modifier as close as possible to the word or phrase it modifies.

Error: Anchorage is also milder than Fairbanks, warmed by coastal waters.

Revision: Warmed by coastal waters, Anchorage is also milder than Fairbanks.

62C PROBLEM: A dangling modifier:

Error: Located in southern Alaska, Juneau's climate is rather moderate.

Revision: Located in southern Alaska, Juneau has a rather moderate climate.

Reword the sentence to include the word or phrase modified.

Error: Having an ice-free port, winter does not close down shipping.

Revision: Having an ice-free port, Juneau does not close down shipping in winter.

MISSING OR MISPLACED POSSESSIVE APOSTROPHES

63A PROBLEM: Missing apostrophes; singular nouns:

Error: Alaskas animal life is part of our biology classes studies.

Revision: Alaska's animal life is part of our biology class's studies.

Use an apostrophe and s to form the possessive of every singular noun.

63B PROBLEM: Missing apostrophes; plural nouns ending in s:

Error: The student's reports were very interesting.

Revision: The students' reports were very interesting.

With a plural noun ending in s, use an apostrophe after the s.

With plural nouns not ending in s, use an apostrophe and s.

Error: Jan reported on wolves habits and habitats.

Revision: Jan reported on wolves' habits and habitats.

63C **PROBLEM:** Missing apostrophes; plural nouns not ending in *s*:

Error: The savagery of wolves is exaggerated in some peoples minds.

Revision: The savagery of wolves is exaggerated in some people's minds.

63D **PROBLEM:** Incorrectly adding an apostrophe to make a plural noun:

Do not use an apostrophe.

Error: Farmer's fear these legendary beast's will kill all their livestock.

Revision: Farmers fear these legendary beasts will kill all their livestock.

63E **PROBLEM:** Missing or misused apostrophes; possessive forms of pronouns:

Use an apostrophe and s to form the possessive of a singular indefinite pronoun.

Error: Everyones negative view of wolves is not really fair.

Revision: Everyone's negative view of wolves is not really fair.

Do not use an apostrophe to form the possessive of a personal pronoun.

Error: Because wolves affect animal population, their's is an important duty.

Revision: Because wolves affect animal population, theirs is an important duty.

63F **PROBLEM:** Confusion between *its* and *it's*:

Do not use an apostrophe in the possessive personal pronoun its.

Error: A deer eating it's way through a field of crops is a problem.

Revision: A deer eating its way through a field of crops is a problem.

Error: Its the role of wolves to limit deer populations.

Revision: It's the role of wolves to limit deer populations.

Use an apostrophe in the contraction of it is or it has.

MISSING COMMAS

64A **PROBLEM:** Missing commas in a series:

Error: Wolves are found in Alaska Canada and Minnesota.

Revision: Wolves are found in Alaska, Canada, and Minnesota.

Use a comma to separate words in a series. Use a comma before the conjunction.

64B **PROBLEM:** Missing commas in compound sentences:

Error: Wolves once ranged throughout North America but human activity has limited their habitat.

Revision: Wolves once ranged throughout North America, but human activity has limited their habitat.

Use a comma between the main clauses unless they are very short.

64C **PROBLEM:** Missing or misplaced commas; adjectives:

Error: Years of being hunted have made them elusive wary creatures.

Revision: Years of being hunted have made them elusive, wary creatures.

Error: They have many, clever ways of surviving.

Revision: They have many clever ways of surviving.

If adjectives are equal, separate them with a comma.

Do not use a comma to separate adjectives that must be in a specific order.

64D **PROBLEM:** Missing commas; nonessential phrases:

Error: Wolves in pairs or sometimes in packs hunt animals such as deer and caribou.

Revision: Wolves, in pairs or sometimes in packs, hunt animals such as deer and caribou.

If a phrase adds nonessential information, set it off with commas.

Error: The wolves moving with great speed may chase such prey for hours.

Revision: The wolves, moving with great speed, may chase such prey for hours.

Use a comma after introductory words.

Error: To be sure they also eat smaller animals.

Revision: To be sure, they also eat smaller animals.

Do not set off a phrase that is essential to the meaning.

Error: Animals, falling into this category, include rodents and rabbits.

Revision: Animals falling into this category include rodents and rabbits.

64E **PROBLEM:** Missing commas; nonessential clauses:

Error: Wolves which usually kill weak or unhealthy animals help control the populations on which they prey.

If a clause adds information not essential to the meaning of a sentence, set it off with commas.

Revision: Wolves, which usually kill weak or unhealthy animals, help control the populations on which they prey.

Error: The wolf, that is found in Alaska, is called the gray wolf.

Do not set off a clause that is essential.

Revision: The wolf that is found in Alaska is called the gray wolf.

64F **PROBLEM:** Missing commas; nonessential appositives:

Error: The gray wolf a wild species of dog is also called the timber wolf.

If an appositive adds information not essential to the meaning of a sentence, set it off with commas.

Revision: The gray wolf, a wild species of dog, is also called the timber wolf.

Error: The writer, Farley Mowat, describes its habits in several books.

Do not set off an appositive that is essential to the meaning of a sentence.

Revision: The writer Farley Mowat describes its habits in several books.

Alphabetized Terms and Lessons

The Alphabetized Terms and Lessons listed here provide definitions of grammatical elements and examples of usage. Follow the cross-references after each definition to see more detailed information on a topic and to find related sections in the Problem Solver.

ABBREVIATIONS

65

A period after a letter or a word usually indicates an abbreviation; however, some abbreviated words do not use periods. If you are unsure of the spelling or meaning of an abbreviation, consult a dictionary. Most dictionaries list abbreviations alphabetically along with other entry words.

> **Abbreviations** are shortened forms of words.

ABBREVIATIONS OF PROPER NOUNS

In general, use a capital letter to begin abbreviations of proper nouns.

1. Use capital letters and periods for people's initials. Put a space between two initials. Do not put extra space between more than two initials.

For more on proper nouns, see p. 341.

E. F. Hutton   **F.W.B.** Lewis   **T. S.** Eliot

When using initials in place of a full name, do not use spaces or periods.

FDR (Franklin Delano Roosevelt)
JFK (John Fitzgerald Kennedy)

2. Use an opening capital letter and a period for each word in the abbreviation of a title or degree that accompanies a name.

Mr. and **Mrs.** John Okura   Joycelyn Edlers, **M.D.**
Rev. Billy Graham   Luis Rios, **Ph.D.**
Sen. Barbara Boxer   Martin Luther King, **Jr.**

The title *Miss* is not considered an abbreviation and has no period. On the other hand, *Ms.*, though it does not represent a longer word, is treated as an abbreviation and does end in a period.

Miss Jane Pittman   **Ms.** Susan Kwan

3. Use opening capital letters and periods in the abbreviations that come at the ends of the proper names of companies and other organizations.

Prentice-Hall, **Inc.**   Campbell Soup **Co.**
Harlem Girls **Assn.**

When the entire name of a company or an organization is abbreviated, use all capital letters and no periods in most cases.

GE (General Electric)
NOW (National Organization for Women)

4. Do not abbreviate the names of days or months in running text.

INCORRECT: It was the last **Mon.** in **Mar.**

CORRECT: It was the last **Monday** in **March.**

5. Use opening capital letters and periods in each abbreviated word of a street address. Abbreviate *Northeast, Northwest, Southeast,* and *Southwest* as **N.E., N.W., S.E.,** and **S.W.**

21 **E.** 42nd **St.**   33 Pennsylvania **Ave., N.E.**
4 Shore **Blvd.**

Use all capital letters and no periods in official post office abbreviations of states that precede a ZIP Code. Use post office abbreviations only in addresses with ZIP Codes. Use standard abbreviations in other situations.

OFFICIAL POST OFFICE ABBREVIATIONS

Alabama **AL**	Louisiana **LA**	Ohio **OH**
Alaska **AK**	Maine **ME**	Oklahoma **OK**
Arizona **AZ**	Maryland **MD**	Oregon **OR**
Arkansas **AR**	Massachusetts **MA**	Pennsylvania **PA**
California **CA**	Michigan **MI**	Rhode Island **RI**
Colorado **CO**	Minnesota **MN**	South Carolina **SC**
Connecticut **CT**	Mississippi **MS**	South Dakota **SD**
Delaware **DE**	Missouri **MO**	Tennessee **TN**
Florida **FL**	Montana **MT**	Texas **TX**
Georgia **GA**	Nebraska **NB**	Utah **UT**
Hawaii **HI**	Nevada **NV**	Vermont **VT**
Idaho **ID**	New Hampshire **NH**	Virginia **VA**
Illinois **IL**	New Jersey **NJ**	Washington **WA**
Indiana **IN**	New Mexico **NM**	West Virginia **WV**
Iowa **IA**	New York **NY**	Wisconsin **WI**
Kansas **KS**	North Carolina **NC**	Wyoming **WY**
Kentucky **KY**	North Dakota **ND**	District of Columbia **DC**

Do not abbreviate names of locations in running text.

For more on common nouns, see p. 341.

INCORRECT: We live at 4 Rose **Rd.** in **L.A., CA.**

CORRECT: We live at 4 Rose **Road** in **Los Angeles, California.**

ABBREVIATIONS OF COMMON NOUNS

Use lowercase letters to begin abbreviations of some common nouns. When in doubt, check a dictionary.

6. Use lowercase letters and periods in abbreviations of English units of measure.

ft. (foot)   **gal.** (gallon)   **lb.** (pound)   **tsp.** (teaspoon)

Do not use periods in abbreviations of metric units.

cm (centimeter)   **kg** (kilogram)
l (liter)   **mm** (millimeter)

7. Use opening capital letters and no periods in the abbreviations of chemical elements used alone or in compounds. Do not use these abbreviations in running text except in scientific writing.

He (helium)   **K** (potassium)   **NaCl** (sodium chloride)

8. Use full or small capital letters and periods for the abbreviations B.C., A.D., A.M., and P.M. Put A.D. before the date and B.C. after it.

500 **B.C.**   **A.D.** 1066   7:30 **A.M.**   4:30 **P. M.**

A.D. goes before the date because it means *anno Domini,* Latin for "in the year of the Lord"; A.D. 1066 means "in the year of the Lord 1066." B.C. stands for "before Christ."

9. Use lowercase letters and periods in most Latin abbreviations. Common Latin abbreviations use no italics.

i.e. (*id est,* "that is")

The people feared a tsunami—**i.e.,** a huge sea wave.

e.g. (*exempli gratia,* "for example")

Many famous films (**e.g.,** *Citizen Kane* and *Schindler's List*) were shot in black and white.

etc. (*et cetera,* "and the rest")

She listed each planet in order—Mercury, Venus, **etc.**

66

ABSOLUTE PHRASES

IDENTIFYING ABSOLUTE PHRASES

An **absolute phrase** consists of a noun or pronoun modified by a participle or participial phrase.

An **absolute phrase** is sometimes called a nominative absolute. It has no grammatical relationship to the rest of the sentence; instead, it stands absolutely by itself and is not considered part of either the subject or the predicate. Absolute phrases may open, interrupt, or conclude sentences and are always set off with commas.

For more on participles and participial phrases, see p. 399.

Her face brushed by the wind, the athlete stood at attention. She stood, **her eyes blinking,** as another anthem was played. She had won the silver, **the gold going to another skater. All considered,** she was pleased to come in second.

In some absolute phrases, the participle *being* is omitted as understood.

The Olympics [being] over, she returned to a hometown parade. She waved joyfully at the crowd, **her smile [being] broad.**

DEVELOPING YOUR STYLE: ABSOLUTE PHRASES

Absolute phrases are useful when you want to combine related ideas into a single, concise sentence.

ORIGINAL SENTENCES: The parade marched. The crowd yelled.

COMBINED WITH ABSOLUTE: The parade marched, **the crowd yelling.**

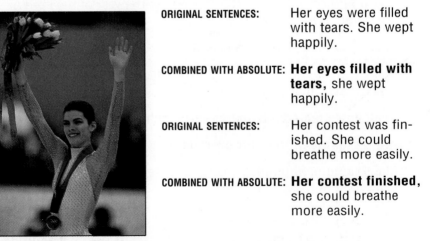

ORIGINAL SENTENCES: Her eyes were filled with tears. She wept happily.

COMBINED WITH ABSOLUTE: **Her eyes filled with tears,** she wept happily.

ORIGINAL SENTENCES: Her contest was finished. She could breathe more easily.

COMBINED WITH ABSOLUTE: **Her contest finished,** she could breathe more easily.

Nancy Kerrigan in the 1994 Olympics

ABSTRACT NOUN: a noun that names something that
cannot be perceived by any of the five senses　　[See **Nouns.**]

67

ACTION VERB: a verb that expresses physical or mental action
[See **Verbs.**]

68

ACTIVE VOICE: any verb form indicating that the subject
performs the action　　[See **Verbs.**]

69

ADDRESSES

70

　　When an address appears in running text, use a comma
between each part but not before the ZIP Code (or a postal
code used in a foreign country). Do not use abbreviations.

For more on state and
other abbreviations, see
p. 274.

ADJECTIVE CLAUSE: a subordinate clause that modifies a noun or a pronoun　　[See **Clauses.**]

71

ADJECTIVE PHRASE: a prepositional phrase that modifies a noun or a pronoun　　[See **Prepositions.**]

72

ADJECTIVES

73

IDENTIFYING ADJECTIVES

　　Adjectives make nouns and pronouns more vivid
and precise by telling *what kind, which one,* or *how many.*

HOW MANY?	WHICH ONE?	WHAT KIND?

Two people crossed **that desert** on a very **hot
day**.

> An **adjective** is a
> word that modifies
> a noun or a
> pronoun.

For more on nouns and
pronouns, see p. 340
and p. 358.

For more on exclamatory
sentences, see p. 387.
For more on predicate
adjectives and linking
verbs, see p. 353 and
p. 398.

POSITIONS OF ADJECTIVES

　　An adjective may occupy one of several positions in relation to the word it modifies.

BEFORE THE MODIFIED WORD:　　An **odd** lizard startled them.

BEFORE THE WORD IN AN EXCLAMATION:　How **odd** the lizard was!

SET OFF AFTER THE MODIFIED WORD:　　A lizard, **odd** and **ugly,** startled them.

PREDICATE ADJECTIVE [AFTER A LINKING VERB]:　The lizard was **odd**.

TYPES OF ADJECTIVES

DETERMINERS: ARTICLES AND DEMONSTRATIVE ADJECTIVES

Adjectives that tell *which one* or *how many* are sometimes called **determiners**. They include the three articles—*the, a,* and *an*—and the four **demonstrative adjectives**—*this, that, these,* and *those.*

ARTICLES

	Type and Function	Use	Example
the	**DEFINITE ARTICLE:** indicates specific person, place, or thing	modifies singular or plural noun	***The*** **travelers** crossed ***the*** **desert.**
a	**INDEFINITE ARTICLE:** indicates someone or something in general	modifies singular noun; precedes consonant sound	It was ***a*** hot **day.**
an	**INDEFINITE ARTICLE:** indicates someone or something in general	modifies singular noun; precedes vowel sound	***An*** **iguana** crossed their path.

Hint: An article signals that a noun is coming soon.

DEMONSTRATIVE ADJECTIVES

	Function	Use	Example
this	points out someone or something close	modifies singular noun or pronoun	***This*** **cactus** is quite large.
that	points out someone or something more distant	modifies singular noun or pronoun	***That*** **one** is even larger.
these	points out someone or something close	modifies plural noun or pronoun	***These*** **lizards** are ugly.
those	points out someone or something more distant	modifies plural noun or pronoun	***Those*** **lizards** are even uglier.

Hint: If a demonstrative adjective is not followed by a noun or pronoun, it is a demonstrative pronoun.

PROPER ADJECTIVES

A **proper adjective** is formed from a proper noun and begins with a capital letter.

For more on proper nouns, see p. 341.

America → **American** deserts   Jefferson → **Jeffersonian** democracy

COMMON ADJECTIVES

A **common adjective** does not begin with a capital letter unless it is the first word of a sentence.

red sand   **desert** people

COMPOUND ADJECTIVES

An adjective in which two or more words are joined together, usually by hyphens, is called a **compound adjective**.

three-day-long journey   **well-worn** shoes

Adjectives linked by a conjunction such as *and* or *or* may also be called **compound adjectives**. However, in such a structure each adjective keeps its separate identity: the **long** and **tiresome** journey.

NOUN, PRONOUN, OR ADJECTIVE?

Words that we usually think of as nouns become adjectives when we use them to modify another noun or a pronoun.

NOUN: the barren **desert**   ADJECTIVE: the **desert** travelers

Possessive forms of nouns and pronouns also may serve as adjectives, modifying nouns or pronouns. When they do, they are sometimes called **possessive adjectives**.

For more on possessive forms, see p. 350.

POSSESSIVE ADJECTIVE: **Abdul's** journey was a tiring one.

POSSESSIVE ADJECTIVE: **His** trek was hot and tiresome.

Many other words are adjectives when they modify a noun or another pronoun but are pronouns when they stand alone, replacing a noun.

DEMONSTRATIVE ADJECTIVE: **That** cactus has sharp thorns.

DEMONSTRATIVE PRONOUN: **That** has sharp thorns.

INDEFINITE ADJECTIVE: **Each** cactus can hold a lot of water.

INDEFINITE PRONOUN: **Each** can hold a lot of water.

COMPARATIVE AND SUPERLATIVE FORMS

Most adjectives have a basic or **positive form**, a **comparative form** for comparing two items, and a **superlative form** for comparing more than two items. Almost all one-syllable adjectives and some two-syllable adjectives use *-er* to form the comparative and *-est* to form the superlative. Other adjectives use the words *more* and *most*, respectively, for the comparative and superlative forms.

Positive Form	Comparative Form	Superlative Form
slow	slower	slowest
sunny	sunnier	sunniest
arid	more arid	most arid
terrible	more terrible	most terrible

Negative comparisons use *less* and *least*.

Positive Form	Negative Comparative	Negative Superlative
slow	less slow	least slow
sunny	less sunny	least sunny
convincing	less convincing	least convincing

A few adjectives have irregular comparative and superlative forms.

Positive Form	Comparative Form	Superlative Form
good *or* well (health)	better	best
bad *or* ill	worse	worst
little	less	least
much *or* many	more	most
far	farther (distance) further (degree)	farthest (distance) furthest (degree)

When in doubt about how to form the comparative or superlative, check a dictionary. A dictionary lists any acceptable *-er* and *-est* forms in the entry for the positive form; if none are listed, use *more* and *most*.

COMMON USAGE PROBLEMS

CORRECT USE OF DEMONSTRATIVE ADJECTIVES

Do not insert the words *here* or *there* after *this, that, these,* or *those.*

For the use of adjectives versus adverbs, see p. 287.

> ***That*** ~~there~~ cactus is called a saguaro.

Do not modify singular nouns with *these* or *those.*

> INCORRECT: ***These* kind** of plants are found in many deserts.
>
> CORRECT: ***These* kinds** of plants are found in many deserts.

Do not use the pronoun *them* in place of the demonstrative adjective *those.*

> INCORRECT: **Them** lizards really are strange creatures.
>
> CORRECT: **Those** lizards really are strange creatures.

CORRECT USE OF COMPARATIVE AND SUPERLATIVE FORMS

Remember to use the comparative when comparing two things and the superlative when comparing more than two. Examine the following paired examples:

> INCORRECT: Which is **hottest**, a desert or a jungle?
>
> CORRECT: Which is **hotter**, a desert or a jungle?
>
> INCORRECT: Among the Sahara, Gobi, or Kalahari, which is **larger?**
>
> CORRECT: Among the Sahara, Gobi, or Kalahari, which is **largest?**

Avoid double comparisons that use *-er* or *-est* as well as *more* or *most.*

> A jungle is ~~more~~ **rainier** than a desert.

> That desert is the ~~most~~ **driest** place in the world.

Do not use comparative or superlative forms of adjectives that are already absolute, such as *perfect*, *ideal*, and *unique*.

| INCORRECT: | That was **the most perfect** desert description. |
| CORRECT: | That was **a perfect** desert description. |

When you compare a member of a group to one or more members, do not make an incomplete comparison that omits *other* or *else*.

INCOMPLETE:	The Gobi Desert is higher than any desert.
COMPLETE:	The Gobi Desert is higher than any **other** desert.
INCOMPLETE:	Death Valley is lower than anywhere in America.
COMPLETE:	Death Valley is lower than anywhere **else** in America.

Make sure your comparisons are between like things.

UNLIKE THINGS:	The thorns on that cactus are sharper than a rose.
LIKE THINGS:	The thorns on that cactus are sharper than a rose's **thorns**.
OR:	The thorns on that cactus are sharper than **those on** a rose.

Use *fewer*, not *less*, to refer to plural nouns.

INCORRECT:	Some deserts have **less *people*** than camels.
CORRECT:	Some deserts have **fewer *people*** than camels.
CORRECT:	It took **less** than ***two days*** to reach the oasis. [*Two days* is considered as a single time period.]

DEVELOPING YOUR STYLE: ADJECTIVES

AVOIDING EMPTY ADJECTIVES

Precise adjectives can help make writing vivid. However, overused empty adjectives, like *awful*, *cute*, *interesting*, and *nice*, do nothing to make meanings stronger or clearer.

| EMPTY: | That cactus has **nice** flowers with an **interesting** texture. |
| PRECISE: | That cactus has **pink** flowers with a **waxy** texture. |

USING ADJECTIVES AS QUALIFIERS

Whenever a generalization has at least one exception, make sure the statement is accurate by using an adjective like *most* or *many* as a **qualifier**, or limiting word.

UNQUALIFIED: Cactuses take years to bloom.

QUALIFIED: **Many** cactuses take years to bloom.

In the following description, notice how the writer replaces empty adjectives with precise ones and adds qualifying adjectives to generalizations.

MODEL

Hardy Cactuses

^Many People who relish the desert Southwest take pleasure in the ~~interesting~~ ^colorful plant life. They often try to grow ~~cute~~ ^small cactuses at home. However, in our ~~awful~~ ^frigid Wisconsin winters, cactuses are ~~not~~ ^few hardy enough to survive from year to year outdoors. An exception is the ~~nice~~ ^adaptable cactus Opuntia, which includes the prickly pear cactus. ^Many Members of the Opuntia, simply lay their ~~funny~~ ^thorny little arms down on the ground for the winter and let the ~~awful~~ ^icy weather blow over them. In summer, if they get ~~good~~ ^direct sun and ~~good~~ ^adequate moisture, ~~the~~ ^most Opuntia will produce ~~great~~ ^big, colorful flowers. Each flower stays open for just one day.

The writer inserts the qualifiers many, few, and most to make the generalizations more accurate.

The writer replaces the empty adjectives interesting, cute, awful, nice, funny, good, and great with more precise adjectives to give clearer pictures of what he is describing.

ADVERB CLAUSE: a subordinate clause that modifies a verb, an adjective, or an adverb   [See **Clauses.**]   74

ADVERB PHRASE: a prepositional phrase that modifies a verb, an adjective, or an adverb   [See **Prepositions.**]   75

ADVERBS

Adverbs satisfy our curiosity to know more. They answer the questions *how, when, where,* and *to what extent* about verbs and the question *to what extent* about adjectives and other adverbs.

IDENTIFYING ADVERBS

This chart shows questions that adverbs answer:

Adverbs Modifying Verbs

HOW?	Football players **benefit** amazingly from ballet training.
WHEN?	Ballet practice **usually** keeps the defense on their toes.
WHERE?	At first some hulks **panic** here in the tiny studio.
TO WHAT EXTENT?	Yet they **hardly** notice pain that would sideline others.

Adverb Modifying an Adjective

TO WHAT EXTENT?	These ballet beginners are **very** dedicated.

Adverb Modifying Another Adverb

TO WHAT EXTENT?	Used to grueling training, they **hardly** ever miss a lesson.

An adverb that modifies an adjective or another adverb and that answers the question *to what extent* is called an **intensifier.**

ADVERBS FORMED FROM ADJECTIVES

Many adverbs are formed by adding *-ly* to an adjective. Sometimes the spelling of the adjective changes when this suffix is added. Study the chart that follows:

Adjective	Adverb	Adjective	Adverb
quick + *-ly*	quickly	gentle + *-ly*	gently
hungry + *-ly*	hungrily	clumsy + *-ly*	clumsily

Note that when *-ly* is added to a base word that ends with a consonant plus *y*, the final *y* changes to *i*.

Remember that not all words ending in *-ly* are adjectives. For example, the words *lonely, costly, homely,* and *prickly* are adjectives, not adverbs. The word *rely* is a verb. The word *early* is often an adverb, but it can also be used as an adjective.

ADJECTIVE: Most pros were playing football at an **early** age.

ADVERB: They should not be expected to be graceful too **early**!

OTHER TYPES OF ADVERBS

The **negative words** *not* (and its contraction *n't*), *never, nowhere, hardly, barely,* and *scarcely* are adverbs.

For information on avoiding double negatives, see p. 331.

Ballet strains muscles that linebackers **hardly** knew they had.

They **aren't** expected to learn without external support.

Conjunctive adverbs are used to connect ideas between clauses. Examples of such adverbs are *consequently, hence, however, indeed, meanwhile, moreover, nevertheless,* and *therefore.* A conjunctive adverb is usually preceded by a semicolon and followed by a comma.

The players practice at the *barre;* **indeed,** they could not work without it!

Feet take a beating in ballet; **hence,** even size 13 shoes must fit perfectly.

If the words *when, where, why, before,* and *since* introduce adjective clauses, then they are usually called **relative adverbs.**

The date **when** all players need to be ready was approaching.

They have their reasons **why** they work together so carefully.

ADVERB OR PREPOSITION?

Words that show position or direction such as *in, out, up, down,* and *around* can be used as both adverbs and prepositions. They are prepositions when they are followed by noun or pronoun objects (O). As prepositions, they connect the objects to the rest of the sentence. When they are functioning as adverbs, they answer the question *where* about the verbs.

ADVERB: Stocky tackles cannot always hold their stomachs **in**.

PREPOSITION: Quarterbacks move gracefully **in** the air.

PLACEMENT OF ADVERBS IN SENTENCES

An adverb that modifies a verb can usually appear in various positions in a sentence without changing the meaning.

Position your feet **correctly. Correctly** position your feet.

Some adverbs that tell *to what extent* have to be placed carefully next to the words they modify or the meaning of the sentences will change. These adverbs include *only, nearly, almost, scarcely,* and *merely.*

Like a perfect pass, all ballet lifts depend on **nearly** perfect timing. [This sentence says the timing need not be absolutely perfect.]

Like a perfect pass, **nearly** all ballet lifts depend on perfect timing. [This sentence says most lifts, but not all, require perfect timing.]

COMPARATIVE AND SUPERLATIVE FORMS OF ADVERBS

Like adjectives, most adverbs have comparative and superlative forms. For one-syllable adverbs and a few two-syllable adverbs, form the comparative by adding *-er* and the superlative by adding *-est.* Use *more* and *most* (or *less* and *least*) to make the comparative and superlative forms of most two-syllable adverbs and all longer adverbs.

Adverb	Comparative	Superlative
low	lower	lowest
late	later	latest
early	earlier	earliest
seldom	more seldom	most seldom
rudely	more rudely	most rudely
politely	more politely	most politely

A few adverbs have irregular comparative and superlative forms.

Adverb	Comparative	Superlative
well	better	best
badly	worse	worst
far	farther (distance)	farthest (distance)
	further (degree)	furthest (degree)
little	less	least
much	more	most

If you are uncertain about which adverb form to use, check a dictionary. The dictionary lists acceptable *-er* and *-est* forms under the entry for the base form of the adverb. When such forms are not listed, use *more* and *most* (or *less* and *least*) to form the comparative and superlative.

For more on comparative and superlative forms of adjectives, see p. 279.

COMMON USAGE PROBLEMS

ADVERB VERSUS ADJECTIVE

Do not confuse an adjective with the adverb that is formed from it. Remember to use an adverb, not an adjective, to modify a verb.

INCORRECT: Lee lunged **desperate** to keep from dropping his partner. [*Desperate* is an adjective.]

CORRECT: Lee lunged **desperately** to keep from dropping his partner. [*Desperately* is an adverb.]

Use a predicate adjective (PA) after a linking verb (LV) such as a form of *be*. The predicate adjective modifies the subject of the sentence, not the verb.

                LV   **PA**

CORRECT: Lee was **desperate** to keep from dropping his partner.

GOOD OR WELL? BAD OR BADLY?

Good and *bad* are always adjectives. *Well* and *badly* are adverbs; *well* may also be used as an adjective to describe someone's health. Remember to use *good* as a predicate adjective after a linking verb when health is not involved. Also, use *bad* as a predicate adjective after a linking verb.

                                    LV

INCORRECT: Our quarterback's jumps look **well**.

CORRECT: Our quarterback's jumps look **good**.

                         LV

INCORRECT: Our halfback looks **badly** in comparison.

For more on predicate adjectives and linking verbs, see p. 353 and p. 398.

CORRECT: Our halfback looks **bad** in comparison.

Use *well* and *badly* to modify action verbs (AV).

                                                AV

INCORRECT: Gridiron greats and prima ballerinas dance **good**.

CORRECT: Gridiron greats and prima ballerinas dance **well**.

             AV

INCORRECT: P.J. needs more practice **bad**.

CORRECT: P.J. needs more practice **badly**.

USE OF <u>HOPEFULLY</u>

Do not use this adverb loosely to modify an entire sentence. Be sure that it modifies a specific verb, or reword the sentence, using the verb *hope*.

AWKWARD: **Hopefully,** the halfback will catch his partner in time.

BETTER: The halfback **hopefully** stretched out his arms.

BETTER: **We hope** the halfback will stretch out his arms.

DEVELOPING YOUR STYLE: ADVERBS

USING STRONG ADVERBS

Improve your style by using strong adverbs to describe actions clearly and concisely and to indicate precise degrees of certain qualities or conditions. Adverbs can also be useful as transitions, making your writing more coherent. Take care, however, not to overuse certain adverbs. Also, avoid repeating weak adverbs like *actually, truly,* or *really.*

Almost qualifies a generalization; truly is omitted; badly replaces bad after an action verb; a semicolon and a conjunctive adverb connect two simple sentences; enthusiastic replaces enthusiastically after a linking verb; a run-on is broken into two sentences, avoiding hopefully; seriously replaces serious after an action verb; and only moves in front of the word it modifies.

M O D E L

almost
Backstage had never been as busy as it was on opening night of our ballet recital. I was ~~truly~~ amazed at how nervous our football heroes were despite all their practice. The advertising for the
badly; nevertheless,
event had been handled ~~bad.~~ The crowd looked
enthusiastic.
~~enthusiastically~~. More than half the audience had
. We hoped
never seen a ballet before~~, hopefully,~~ they would
seriously
take our efforts ~~serious~~. Of course, only the most satisfying tribute comes when a first-timer wants to learn more about ballet. In this case, three athletic-looking members of the audience signed up for ballet lessons.

By using adverbs precisely, you can improve your style and make your meaning clearer to your readers.

AGREEMENT: making a subject and verb match in number or a pronoun and its antecedent match in number, gender, or person

[See **Pronouns, Verbs, Problem Solver.**]

77

ANTECEDENT: the noun or pronoun to which a pronoun refers

[See **Pronouns.**]

78

ANTITHETICAL ELEMENT: part of a sentence that is similar in structure, but opposite in meaning, to another part

[See **Comma.**]

79

APOSTROPHE

80

IDENTIFYING APOSTROPHES

An **apostrophe** (') is a punctuation mark used to show possession and contraction. In a few cases it is also used to form the plural.

For more on possessive forms, see p. 350. For more on nouns and their number, see p. 342.

APOSTROPHES TO SHOW CONTRACTION

1. Use an apostrophe to show where one or more letters have been omitted in a contraction.

she + is *or* has → **she's**	does + not → **doesn't**	*For more on contrac-tions, see p. 328.*
of + the + clock → **o'clock**	madam → **ma'am**	

Note: Use only one apostrophe—in place of the missing *o*—in *won't* and *shan't*.

will + not → **won't**   shall + not → **shan't**

2. Use an apostrophe to show the omission of one or more letters from slang or dialect.

a-goin' home   **'ard** luck

3. Use an apostrophe to show the omission of the first two numbers from a year. Do not use this construction in formal writing or in a span that contains a dash (*1941–1952*).

My parents were married in the summer of '**75.**

OTHER USES OF APOSTROPHES

1. Use an apostrophe to form the plurals of letters, numbers, symbols, and words used as words.

For the use of underlining and italics, see p. 397.

two *t*'s	many **YMCA's**
two ***6***'s	two **&**'s
four ***but*'s	

2. Use an apostrophe for the plurals of years.

the **1500's**   the **1990's**

APPOSITIVES

IDENTIFYING APPOSITIVES

> An **appositive** is a noun or pronoun placed near another noun or pronoun to provide more information about it.

In this example, the noun *Mahmoud* is said to be in apposition to the noun *friend* because it tells something about the friend.

My ***friend* Mahmoud** was born in Cairo.

Appositives often appear in **appositive phrases** along with other words that modify them. Appositive phrases may come before or after the noun or pronoun they provide more information about.

Cairo, **a large and crowded city,** is the capital of Egypt.

A large and crowded city, Cairo is the capital of Egypt.

A **restrictive** appositive or appositive phrase is essential to the meaning of the sentence and is not set off with commas.

The writer **Naguib Mahfouz** sets most of his fiction in Egypt.

A **nonrestrictive** appositive or appositive phrase interrupts a sentence. It is not essential to the sentence's meaning and is set off with commas.

Naguib Mahfouz, **Mahmoud's favorite writer,** won a Nobel Prize.

COMMON USAGE PROBLEMS

PRONOUNS AND APPOSITIVES

When a pronoun is in apposition to a subject (S) or a subject complement (SC), use the subject form of the pronoun.

$\overset{\text{S}}{\text{My new friends,}}$ **he** and Hana, speak fluent Arabic.

$\overset{\text{SC}}{\text{My newest friends}}$ are two classmates from Egypt, Mahmoud and **she.**

For more on subject forms of pronouns, see p. 359. For more on subjects and subject complements, see p. 380 and p. 384.

When a pronoun is in apposition to a direct object (DO), an indirect object (IO), or an object of a preposition (OP), use the object form of the pronoun.

$\overset{\text{DO}}{\text{I met Hana's neighbors,}}$ Mrs. Soong and **him,** at Hana's party.

$\overset{\text{IO}}{\text{Mrs. Soong gave two people,}}$ Jan and **me,** a lift home.

$\overset{\text{OP}}{\text{We said goodbye to the last guests,}}$ Eric and **them.**

For more on object forms of pronouns, see p. 359. For more on direct and indirect objects, see p. 383. For more on objects of prepositions, see p. 354.

When a pronoun is followed by an appositive, use the form of the pronoun that would be correct if the appositive were omitted.

$\overset{\text{S}}{\textbf{We students}}$ cannot stay up too late on a week night.

$\overset{\text{OP}}{\text{The school day begins early for}}$ **us students.**

DEVELOPING YOUR STYLE: APPOSITIVES

Appositives are useful when you want to add or clarify information without adding too many words. Often you can combine short sentences by using appositives or appositive phrases.

TWO SHORT SENTENCES:	Arabic is spoken in many lands. It is the main language of Egypt.
COMBINED:	Arabic, **the main language of Egypt,** is spoken in many lands.

Also, opening a sentence with an appositive can help add variety.

The main language of Egypt, Arabic is spoken in many lands.

ARTICLE: the adjective *the, a,* or *an*   [See **Adjectives.**]   82

BASE FORM: the basic form of a word before prefixes or suffixes are added or other changes are made to show a different number, tense, and so on.   [See **Verbs.**]   83

USING CAPITAL LETTERS

In deciding what to capitalize, observe the following guidelines:

Capitalization helps signal where ideas begin. It also indicates which ideas are important.

WORDS THAT MARK BEGINNINGS

1. Capitalize the first word of every sentence.

Television today is changing rapidly.

For more on sentences and sentence fragments, see p. 380 and p. 261.

2. Capitalize the first word of a direct quotation that can stand alone as a complete sentence.

Lamar said, "Change doesn't always mean improvement."

If the quotation is not a complete sentence, do not capitalize the first word except when it introduces a sentence fragment in informal conversation.

This informative article promises "hundreds of brand-new TV channels."

Lamar said, "Six hundred channels of bad TV shows!"

In a divided quotation, capitalize the first word of the second part only when that word begins a new sentence.

"That's right, Lamar," Jo added. "Don't be such a skeptic."

For more on quotations, see p. 374.

"The information superhighway," said Cara, "will include TV."

3. Capitalize the first word in a sentence in parentheses only if the sentence stands by itself.

Most schools and libraries will be linked to the information superhighway. (Hospitals should have free hookups.)

For more on parentheses, see p. 346.

Many libraries (ours is one) look forward to being hooked up.

For more on colons, see p. 303.

4. Capitalize the first word of a complete sentence after a colon.

The new superhighway will move quickly: A whole encyclopedia of information will be sent from coast to coast in a few minutes.

5. In an outline, capitalize the first word in each line and also the letters before major subtopics. For more on outlines, see p. 22.

I. Information superhighway

    A. Public access

    B. Private access

II. Interactive television

6. Capitalize all important words in the greeting of a letter but only the first word of the closing.

Dear **S**ir or **M**adam: **V**ery truly **y**ours,

7. Generally capitalize the first word of a line of poetry.

Then a new wind blew, and a new voice
Rode its wings with quiet urgency,
Strong, determined, sure.
        —Naomi Long Madgett, "Alabama Centennial"

Modern poetry, however, often ignores traditional capitalization rules.

PROPER NOUNS

A **proper noun** names a specific person, place, thing, or idea; a **common noun** names something general. A proper noun should begin with a capital letter. If it consists of more than one word, capitalize all the important words (everything except articles, coordinating conjunctions, and prepositions of fewer than five letters).

Proper Noun	**Common Noun**
Amy **T**an	writer
Tomb of the **U**nknown **S**oldier	landmark

Tomb of the Unknown Soldier

Names and Titles of People

For more on proper nouns, see p. 341.

1. Capitalize people's names, initials, and nicknames.

Linda Ronstadt   N. Scott Momaday   Wilt the Stilt

2. Capitalize titles used before a name and abbreviations of titles used before or after a name. If the abbreviation consists of more than one word, capitalize each part.

Governor Ann Richards   General Anderson   Dr. Okara

Martin Luther King, Jr.   Ana Lopez, M.D.   Marc Wu, Ph.D.

For more on direct address, see p. 331.

Capitalize titles that are used alone or that come after a name only in direct address or to show respect for a current high officeholder.

May I speak, Your Honor?

Both the President and the Vice President met with the Queen.

Do not capitalize titles that refer to a general class or type.

When was he elected president?   She is a colonel.

3. Capitalize family titles used before or in place of a name.

Aunt Mabel   Where is Mom?   How are you, Grandpa?

For more on possessive forms, see p. 350.

Do not capitalize family titles that express general relationships. These titles often follow *a, an,* or a possessive form.

A mother can also be a friend.   Have you met my aunt?

His wife's father visited them.   Her dad is a good cook.

4. Capitalize the pronoun *I.*

For more on pronouns, see p. 358.

Someday I hope to be a writer.

5. Capitalize the names of races, nationalities, tribes, ethnic groups, religious groups, political groups, and their members.

a Caucasian   the Egyptians   the Iroquois   Greek Americans

a Muslim   Episcopalians   a Democrat   Young Republicans

6. Capitalize proper adjectives, which are adjectives formed from proper nouns.

Victoria—Victorian art   Algonquin—Algonquian languages

Do not capitalize most words that originated from people's names. When in doubt, check a dictionary.

braille   **p**asteurization   **s**andwich   **w**att

Names of Places

1. Capitalize the names of villages, cities, states, countries, provinces, and continents.

Hope, **A**rkansas   **B**uenos **A**ires, **A**rgentina   **N**orth **A**merica

2. Capitalize the names of geographic features.

Lake **S**uperior   **B**lue **R**idge **M**ountains   **G**obi **D**esert

3. Capitalize the names of streets, highways, bridges, and parks.

Elm **S**treet   **R**oute 66   **Y**osemite **N**ational **P**ark

4. Capitalize the names of landmarks, buildings, and monuments.

the **W**hite **H**ouse   the **E**iffel **T**ower   the **W**ailing **W**all

5. Do not capitalize plurals such as *rivers* and *streets* when they are used after more than one name.

Elm and **O**ak **s**treets   **R**ocky and **O**zark **m**ountains

6. Capitalize the names of most heavenly bodies.

Mars   the **M**ilky **W**ay   the **B**ig **D**ipper

Do not capitalize *sun* and *moon*. The word *earth* is only capitalized when it appears with the proper names of other planets. It is never capitalized when it follows *the*.

The **s**un blocked the **m**oon.   It's the best show on **e**arth.

The rocket left the **e**arth.   We went from **E**arth to **V**enus.

7. Capitalize the names of geographical areas.

Arizona is in the **S**outhwest.   Did you visit the **F**ar **E**ast?

Do not capitalize *east*, *west*, and other words when they show direction only.

Go **w**est two blocks.   The plane flew **n**ortheast to Boston.

8. Capitalize adjectives formed from the proper names of places. Do not capitalize adjectives that simply show direction.

Spain—**S**panish music   a **w**estern wind

Titles

1. Capitalize the first word, the last word, and all important words in a title of a literary work, a musical composition, a work of art, a movie, or a TV show.

For more on underlining/italics, see p. 397.

A *Separate Peace* "**C**asey at the **B**at" "**L**ean on **M**e"

Guernica ***The Sound of Music*** ***The Tonight Show***

2. Capitalize the titles of newspapers and magazines. Do not capitalize *the* or *magazine* unless it is part of the title.

The New York Times **the *Reader's Digest***
Time Magazine

3. Capitalize the titles of documents and sacred works.

the **D**eclaration of **I**ndependence   the **B**ible   the **K**oran

Other Words and Terms

1. Capitalize the names of languages and dialects.

Hebrew   **A**rabic   **M**iddle **E**nglish   **G**ullah

2. Capitalize the names of specific school courses. Do not capitalize the names of general subjects other than languages.

History 101   **B**iology 2A   geometry   **S**panish

3. Capitalize the names of religions and the various terms for the deity.

Buddhism **R**oman **C**atholicism **G**od the **L**ord **A**llah

4. Capitalize the days of the week, the months of the year, and names of holidays. Do not capitalize the names of the seasons.

Friday   **M**arch   **M**emorial **D**ay   **P**assover   spring

5. Capitalize the names of historical periods and events. Do not capitalize the names of centuries.

the **B**ronze **A**ge   **W**orld **W**ar II   the **t**wentieth **c**entury

6. Capitalize the names of awards, prizes, and special events.

an **A**cademy **A**ward   the **N**obel **P**rize   the **S**uper **B**owl

7. Capitalize brand names but not any common nouns that follow them.

a **B**lazer   **W**heaties   **H**einz **k**etchup   **C**rest **t**oothpaste

8. Capitalize the names of ships, spacecrafts, and other vehicles.

the *Pinta*   *Apollo I*   *Air Force One*   the *Nautilus*

For more on underlining/italics, see p. 397.

9. Capitalize the names of businesses, organizations, schools, government agencies, and political parties.

Ford **M**otor **C**ompany   the **R**otary **C**lub   **D**uke **U**niversity

the **L**ibrary of **C**ongress   the **D**emocratic **P**arty

Do not capitalize common nouns such as *university* and *museum* when they are not part of a specific name.

The **m**useum is closed Mondays. The **c**lub meets on Tuesdays.

10. Capitalize *act* and *law* in bills that have become law.

the **S**herman **A**ntitrust **A**ct   the **V**olstead **A**ct

11. Capitalize most abbreviations of words that are capitalized.

For more on abbreviations, see p. 273.

United Kingdom—**U.K.**   Federal Bureau of Investigation—**FBI**

February—**Feb.**   Columbia Broadcasting System—**CBS**

Use capital letters for the abbreviations B.C., A.D., A.M., and P.M.

CASE: any form indicating whether a pronoun is a subject or an object   [See **Pronouns.**]

`85`

CHOPPY SENTENCES: a series of short sentences that create an abrupt, jerking rhythm   [See **Sentence Combining, Sentence Problems** in Section Two.]

`86`

CLAUSES

`87`

IDENTIFYING CLAUSES

Some people like being by themselves; others choose to be part of a group. Similarly, some clauses can stand alone (as sentences), and other clauses team up with others.

A **clause** is a group of words that contains a subject and a verb.

TYPES OF CLAUSES

The two major types of clauses are **main clauses** and **subordinate clauses.**

	Description	Examples
MAIN CLAUSE:	A main clause can stand alone as a sentence.	**Our school started a community service program.**
	A sentence can contain more than one main clause.	**The program is voluntary,** but **many students have joined.**
SUBORDINATE CLAUSE:	A subordinate clause cannot stand alone. It must be linked to a main clause.	Students volunteer **because they want to help others.**

TYPES OF SUBORDINATE CLAUSES

There are three kinds of subordinate clauses: **noun clauses, adjective clauses,** and **adverb clauses.**

	Description	Examples
NOUN CLAUSE:	A **noun clause** is used as a noun in a sentence.	
	Noun clause as subject	**What one does** is up to the individual.
	Noun clause as direct object	Nguyen says **that he likes working at the hospital.**
	Noun clause as indirect object	LaKisha tells **whoever will listen** about her work at the nursing home.
	Noun clause as predicate noun (subject complement)	A job helping out at a soup kitchen was **what Amitai wanted.**
	Noun clause as object of preposition	The school offers course credit to **whoever participates.**

Some common words that introduce noun clauses are

that	what	whoever
which	who	when
whomever	whose	why
how	whether	
where	whatever	

	Description	**Examples**
ADJECTIVE CLAUSE:	An **adjective clause** is used as an adjective to modify a noun or pronoun in the main clause.	Winona, **who is an intern at City Hall,** wants to go into politics. Kent enjoys the hours **that he spends working at the public library.** Ms. Rodriguez was the teacher **who designed the program.** All the places **where students work** are very interesting.

Some common words that introduce adjective clauses are

RELATIVE PRONOUNS:	that	which	what	whom
	whose	whoever	who	

RELATIVE ADVERBS:	where	when

An adjective clause is also called a **relative clause** because it is introduced by a relative pronoun or a relative adverb. The relative pronoun *that* is sometimes omitted at the beginning of this type of clause:

Reading to the blind was the job [*that*] Jill enjoyed most.

Restrictive Versus Nonrestrictive Adjective Clauses

Some adjective clauses are necessary to complete the meaning of the noun or pronoun they modify. Do not use commas to set off these **restrictive,** or essential, clauses from the rest of the sentence.

The student **who helps most with Little League** is Thurman.

The team **that Thurman coaches** is on a winning streak.

The relative pronoun *who* introduces restrictive clauses when the antecedent is a person. The relative pronoun *that* introduces restrictive clauses when the antecedent is not a person.

Some adjective clauses add unnecessary information about the noun or pronoun they modify. These **nonrestrictive clauses** are set off by commas from the rest of the sentence.

Hwang, **who works with the Parks Department,** wants to be a landscape architect.

Vanessa volunteers two hours a week at the museum, **which is located on Peachtree Street.**

Use *who* to introduce nonrestrictive clauses when the antecedent is a person. Use *which* to introduce this type of clause when the antecedent is not a person.

	Description	Examples
ADVERB CLAUSE:	An **adverb clause** is used as an adverb in a sentence.	
	Adverb clauses tell	
	how: ——————→	Volunteers work as hard **as if they had salaried jobs.**
	when: ——————→	**Before the program began,** some people criticized the plan as impractical.
	where: ——————→	The first volunteer group earned praise **wherever they worked.**
	why: ——————→	**Because the early results have been so favorable,** the program has grown.
	under what circumstances: —→	**Although students are not paid,** they are rewarded in many other ways.

The following are some common words that introduce adverb clauses:

RELATIONSHIP EXPRESSED:	SUBORDINATING CONJUNCTIONS:
Time: $\longrightarrow$	after, as, as soon as, before, until, when, whenever, while
Place: $\longrightarrow$	where, wherever
Reason, Cause/Effect: $\longrightarrow$	because, so that
Condition: $\longrightarrow$	although, unless
Manner: $\longrightarrow$	as, as if, as though

◆ WHEN YOU WRITE ◆

When you use an adverb clause to begin a sentence, you should separate it from the main clause with a comma to avoid confusion.

COMMON USAGE PROBLEMS

AVOIDING FAULTY SUBORDINATION

A subordinate clause is called *subordinate* because the idea it expresses is not as important as the idea in the main clause. If you mistakenly place your main idea in a subordinate clause, your sentence will have **faulty subordination.** The main clause should contain the main idea, and the subordinate clause should contain ideas of lesser importance. In the sentences below, the main idea is in bold type. Note where it appears in the correct sentences.

FAULTY: Because **I took an internship with Consumer Affairs,** I was interested in retailing.

CORRECT: Because I was interested in retailing, **I took an internship with Consumer Affairs.**

FAULTY: Rena's work at the zoo was exhausting, although **she found it very satisfying.**

CORRECT: Although Rena's work at the zoo was exhausting, **she found it very satisfying.**

For more on subordinate clauses, see Problem Solver, p. 268.

To tell whether a sentence has faulty subordination, follow these steps:

1. Determine the main idea in the sentence.

2. Identify the subordinate clause and the main clause.

3. Make sure the main idea is in the main clause. If it is not, restructure the sentence.

DEVELOPING YOUR STYLE: CLAUSES

ACHIEVING SENTENCE VARIETY

To achieve a variety of sentence lengths when you are revising a piece of writing, look for short, simple sentences that can be subordinated to main clauses in other sentences. Look also for long sentences with strings of clauses that can be separated into shorter sentences with fewer clauses. The writer of the following essay made both these kinds of revisions:

MODEL

When
I decided to volunteer as a reading assistant at our public library∧ I didn't know what to expect. I thought I'd be simply helping little kids find books they'd enjoy reading∧. Instead, but, as it turned out, I had to become a walking encyclopedia to answer the questions I was bombarded with.

It's true that the kids did ask me where they could find books on certain subjects∧. However, but those were the easy questions. It was much more challenging to answer questions <u>about</u> what they had read. How do they get the same drawing into more than one copy of a book? Can dinosaurs really be recreated from an insect preserved in amber? Who invented the refrigerator? What makes a balloon float? What did King Tut die from?

Because

Questions like these sometimes drove me nuts, I
often had to sneak out and take a break. However,
I have to admit that it was a good feeling to be
able to answer each question or to show the kids
how to find the answer. *Although* Teaching little kids isn't
easy, ~~It~~ it can be a lot of fun.

COLLECTIVE NOUN: a noun that refers to a group

88

It can be singular or plural, depending on whether the group is viewed
as a unit or as a collection of individuals. **[See Nouns.]**

COLON

89

A **colon (:)** often serves as a signal to anticipate certain sentence
elements. It also separates groups of numbers in specific situations.

1. Use a colon to introduce a list, especially if the list follows
words such as *these*, *the following*, or *as follows*.

> The recipe calls for these spices: salt, pepper, and cumin.

> The cooking procedure has the following three steps:
>
> 1. Boil and drain the cabbage.
>
> 2. Heat the butter and cumin and pour over
>   the cabbage.
>
> 3. Sprinkle with salt and pepper to taste.

For more on verbs and their objects, see p. 405. For more on prepositions and their objects, see p. 354.

Do not use a colon between a preposition or a verb and
the rest of the predicate.

> The recipe calls **for** cabbage, butter, and
> spices.

> The spices **are** salt, pepper, and
> cumin.

2. Use a colon to introduce material that clarifies, restates, or illustrates
the preceding material.

the following :

Substituting olive oil for butter is beneficial: The olive oil has less cholesterol.

The cuisines of many nations use cumin: It is a staple of Mexican cooking and a main ingredient in the food of India.

◆ WHEN YOU WRITE ◆

Capitalize the first word following a colon when it begins a complete sentence.

A colon is often used between a label and an example or clarification.

INTERROGATIVE SENTENCE: Did you enjoy the meal?

3. Use a colon before a long or formal quotation.

Julio Cortázar opens his story "Axolotl" as follows:

There was a time when I thought a great deal about the axolotls. I went to see them in the aquarium at the Jardin des Plantes and stayed for hours watching them, observing their immobility, their faint movements. Now I am an axolotl.

Use a colon to introduce a quotation that lacks explanatory words such as *he said* or *she asked.*

Ginevra's response was enthusiastic: "I loved the story."

A colon may also be used in a play or script to separate the name of a character from his or her lines.

Lady Macbeth: Out, damned spot! Out, I say!

4. Use a colon after the greeting of a business letter.

Dear M & M Auto Shop:
Dear Sir or Madam:

For more on business letters, see p. 229.

5.   Use a colon (with no space around it) between the hour and the minute in numerical expressions of time.

The bell rings at 8:45 A.M.

6. Use a colon (with no space around it) between the chapter and the verse or verses in biblical references.

Genesis 1:10   Matthew 4:2–4

COMMA

90

Omitting commas creates confusion, but using too many commas makes writing choppy and hard to read. As you examine the following guidelines, keep in mind that the main purpose of a comma is to prevent misreading.

> A **comma** indicates a pause or a change in thought and helps to clarify writing.

SERIES AND COMPOUND STRUCTURES

1. Use commas to separate three or more words, phrases, or other elements in a series. Include a comma before the final conjunction.

For more on conjunctions, see p. 322.

Jazz, blues, rhythm and blues, gospel, **and** country music all played a part in the birth of rock-and-roll.

Early fans enjoyed rock on the radio, at concerts, **and** on records.

The music emerged in the fifties, took on new energy in the sixties, **and** remains a major force on the pop music scene.

Rock histories examine when the music arose, how it has changed, **and** who its greatest stars have been.

Do not use commas if each item is separated by a conjunction.

Chuck Berry and Dinah Washington and Clyde McPhatter successfully moved from rhythm and blues to rock-and-roll.

2. Place a comma before a coordinating conjunction that joins the main clauses in a compound sentence.

For more on main clauses and compound sentences, see p. 298 and p. 388.

Elvis Presley and Buddy Holly came from the world of country music, **but** they won fame in rock-and-roll.

If the clauses are short, you can omit the comma unless it is needed for clarity.

Mom loves fifties music and I also like it. [clear]

Mom loved Elvis, and Dad also liked him. [comma prevents mis-reading]

For more on predicates, see p. 380. Do not use a comma between the parts of a compound predicate.

A tragic plane crash **cut short Buddy Holly's career and claimed the lives of several other rock stars.**

To avoid a run-on sentence, use a semicolon, not a comma, between two main clauses when no coordinating For more on run-on sentences, see p. 260. conjunction comes between them.

Richie Valens died in that same crash; the Big Bopper also perished.

SUBORDINATE CLAUSES

1. Use commas to set off nonrestrictive adjective clauses. A nonrestrictive clause interrupts a sentence to add details that are not necessary to the sentence's meaning.

Chuck Berry, **who had studied to be a hairdresser,** had an early hit called "Maybelline."

Do not set off restrictive adjective clauses. A **restrictive** For more on clauses, see p. 297. **clause** limits the meaning of the term it modifies and is necessary to the sentence's meaning.

The rock singer **who first recorded "La Bamba"** was Richie Valens.

2. Use a comma to set off an introductory adverb clause.

When a film was made about Valens, Los Lobos redid "La Bamba."

Set off an internal adverb clause that interrupts the flow of a sentence.

> Bill Haley, after his 1955 movie *Rock Around the Clock* appeared, became one of rock-and-roll's earliest stars.

Do not set off a final adverb clause unless it is clearly nonessential and interrupts the flow of the sentence.

> Little Richard won fame **after he recorded "Tutti Frutti."**

> "Blue Suede Shoes" made Carl Perkins famous, although Elvis Presley's later recording of the song was an even bigger hit.

3. Do not use commas to set off noun clauses serving as subjects, objects, or subject complements (predicate nouns).

> People agree that **rock-and-roll was born in Cleveland.**

> **What they debate** is **if "Sh-Boom" was the first rock-and-roll song.**

For more on subjects, objects, and complements, see p. 380 and p. 383.

APPOSITIVES, VERBALS, AND PHRASES

1. Use commas to set off a **nonessential** or **nonrestrictive appositive,** which interrupts a sentence to add information and is not necessary to the sentence's meaning.

> The Chords, **an African American group**, recorded "Sh-Boom" in 1954.

Do not set off an **essential** or **restrictive appositive,** which limits the meaning of the noun it clarifies and is necessary to the sentence's meaning.

> The Canadian group **the Crew Cuts** redid the song two months later.

For more on appositives, see p. 290.

2. Use a comma after a long introductory prepositional phrase or a string of introductory prepositional phrases.

> **For both the Chords and the Crew Cuts,** "Sh-Boom" was a huge hit and a big seller.

> **By the end of the summer of 1954,** a phenomenon had swept America.

After a short introductory prepositional phrase, a comma is not necessary unless it is needed for clarity.

To teenagers the new music was fresh and exciting. [clear]

In Cleveland, disc jockey Alan Freed began calling the music rock-and-roll. [comma avoids misreading]

For more on preposition-al phrases, see p. 355. Do not set off an internal or final prepositional phrase unless it clearly interrupts the sentence.

Freed may have borrowed the term **from a song** recorded **in 1934.**

Freed, in Cleveland first and then in New York City, was one of rock-and-roll's earliest champions.

3. Set off nonessential or nonrestrictive participles, infinitives, and their phrases. Remember that a **nonessential** or **nonrestrictive** element interrupts a sentence and is not necessary to its overall meaning.

Fats Domino, **playing piano,** was another early rocker.

To entertain fans, pianist Jerry Lee Lewis gyrated flamboyantly.

Use a comma after both an introductory participle and a participial phrase.

Twisting and swiveling, Elvis Presley became the biggest star of rock-and-roll.

Recorded in 1956, "Heartbreak Hotel" was Elvis Presley's first Number 1 hit.

Do not set off essential or restrictive participles, infinitives, and their phrases. Remember that an **essential** or **restrictive element** is essential to a sentence's meaning.

One of the first couples **to sing a rock hit** was Mickey and Sylvia.

For more on participles and infinitives, see p. 399 and p. 400.

Another duo **singing hits in the fifties** was Shirley and Lee.

4. Use commas to set off absolute phrases. These phrases are made up of a subject and a participle. They do not modify a word or phrase but the whole sentence.

The Drifters, **their members changing from record to record,**
stayed at the top of the charts.

For more on absolute phrases, see p. 276.

Their recordings filled with humor, the Coasters
were favorites of millions.

ADJECTIVES

1. Use a comma between **coordinate adjectives,** adjectives of
equal rank that separately modify the noun they precede.

Harmonious, tuneful songs were a trademark of doo-wop.

Do not use a comma if the adjectives are not coordinate.

Doo-wop groups like the Platters redid **great old** songs like
"Smoke Gets in Your Eyes."

2. Set off adjectives that come after the word they modify if they
clearly interrupt the flow of the sentence.

The Chordettes, **skillful and glamorous,** started as a female
barbershop quartet.

For more on adjectives, see p. 277.

Adjectives that come before a noun are coordinate if
their order can be reversed.

CONJUNCTIVE ADVERBS AND INTERRUPTERS

1. Use a comma after a conjunctive adverb that introduces a clause or a sentence.

For more on conjunctive adverbs, see p. 285.

Doo-wop was an urban phenomenon; **meanwhile,** the Everly
Brothers introduced country harmonies to rock-and-roll.

Additionally, Roy Orbison brought country keening to rock.

Set off internal or final conjunctive adverbs only when they
interrupt the flow of the sentence.

Gospel, **however,** probably trained even more rock crooners.

Gospel was **indeed** influential in shaping the styles of popular
singers like Sam Cooke and Ray Charles.

2. Use commas after clarifying expressions such as *that is* and *for
example* or their Latin abbreviations, *i.e.* and *e.g.*

Motown—**that is,** songs produced by Motown Records in
Detroit—helped popularize soul music in the sixties.

Female groups (**e.g.,** the Shirelles and the Supremes) were also on the rise in the new decade.

3. Use commas to set off parenthetical expressions like *by the way* and *on the other hand* that have a fairly close relationship to the rest of the sentence.

By the way, Diana Ross first won fame with the Supremes.

Connie Francis, **on the other hand,** got her start on a television talent show.

Use parentheses or dashes rather than commas when the parenthetical material is interruptive or only loosely related to the rest of the sentence.

California surfing songs also made waves **(pun intended)** in the early sixties.

For more on parentheses and dashes, see p. 346 and p. 329.

Stars of soul music—**the term is related to gospel—** included Aretha Franklin and Otis Redding.

4. Use commas to set off mild interjections not set off by exclamation points.

For more on interjections, see p. 338.

Yes, Bob Dylan helped pioneer folk rock.

And, **wow,** I almost forgot to mention the British Invasion!

5. Use commas to set off terms of **direct address,** interrupters that clearly indicate to whom (or sometimes to what) the speaker or writer is talking.

Aunt Bet, did you like the Beatles better than the Rolling Stones?

I'd say, **Kevin,** that I liked them both.

6. Use a comma to set off a **tag question** such as *didn't I?* or *have you?* that suggests an answer to the statement that precedes it.

You also liked Motown a lot, **didn't you?**

ANTITHETICAL AND OTHER PARALLEL ELEMENTS

1. Use commas to set off an antithetical element that interrupts the flow of a sentence. An **antithetical element** contrasts with or expresses the opposite of an adjacent element.

The Beatles were the best known, **if not the finest,** British group.

They, **unlike many other groups,** wrote their own material.

Their rhythmic, **though at the same time harmonious,** early hits showed the influence of Chuck Berry and the Everly Brothers.

Asian Indian, **not Native American,** music was a later influence.

2. In general, use a clarifying comma to separate identical words.

Whatever the Beatles **had, had** conquered America.

Soon other British groups poured **in, in** droves.

Do not separate the verb phrase *had had* or two *that's*.

For more on verb phrases, see p. 405.

The Rolling Stones **had had** much interest in the blues.

British groups recognized **that that** form of African American music deserved more attention.

3. Use a comma to indicate words in parallel structures that are omitted because they are understood.

The Beatles were Number 1 with many fans; **the Stones, with others.**

QUOTATION MARKS AND QUOTATIONS

1. Always place a comma before a final quotation mark.

"She Loves You," an early Beatles tune, broke all British sales records.

2. Use a colon to set off a longer direct quotation.

3. Use commas to set off shorter direct quotations.

"My favorite album is *The White Album,*" said a fan.

"Yesterday," crooned the Beatles, "all my troubles seemed so far away."

Do not set off quotations that serve as subjects, direct objects, or subject complements.

For more on quotation marks, see p. 372.

For more on quotations, see p. 374. For more on colons, see p. 303.

"I love the Beatles" was written on the face of each cheering fan.

OTHER USES

1. Use a comma after the greeting of a friendly letter and after the closing of any letter.

Dear Yoko,   **Sincerely yours,**

2. Use commas to separate the parts of a place name or of an address.

Liverpool, England, was the home of the Mersey sound.

Detroit, Michigan, was the home of Motown.

A catalog of music is available from **Rhino Records, 2225 Colorado Avenue, Santa Monica, California 90404.**

Do not put a comma between the state and ZIP Code.

When you write an address on separate lines (as you do in the inside address of a letter or on an envelope), do not include commas at the ends of the lines.

For more on letter form, see p. 229.

Rhino Records
2225 Colorado Avenue
Santa Monica, CA 90404

3. In general, use commas to separate the parts of a date.

Friday, February 7, 1964, marks the Beatles' landing in New York.

No comma is needed if only the month and day or month and year are given.

That **February 7** was a crazy day in New York City.

February 1964 was the beginning of the so-called British Invasion.

If the date is on a line by itself (as it is near the top of a letter), do not put a comma at the end.

Monday, February 7, 1964   **December 15, 1995**

4. Use commas to set off the parts of a reference to a source.

Turn to ***The Encyclopedia of Rock,*** **page 654,** for more about *soul.*

We rehearsed **Act II, scene i,** of the rock musical.

5. In numerals of more than three digits, generally use a comma with no space after every third digit from the right.

20,000   **1,246,321**

Do not use a comma in years, house numbers, phone numbers, ZIP Codes, and other code numbers.

That recording company's ZIP Code is **10022.**

Use a comma between two groups of numerals to prevent misreading.

In 1964, 123 people from my hometown went to see the Beatles.

COMMON ADJECTIVE: an adjective that ordinarily begins with a lowercase letter, as opposed to a proper adjective

[See **Adjectives.**]

91

COMMONLY CONFUSED OR MISUSED WORDS

92

The following items include words that are often confused because they sound alike, look alike, or have related (though different) meanings.

accept, except *Accept* is a verb meaning "to receive" or "to agree with." *Except* is usually a preposition meaning "not including" but is sometimes a verb meaning "to leave out."

Have any writers **except** Sartre refused to **accept** a Nobel Prize?

If you **except** Whitman, few poets a century ago **accepted** the use of free verse.

adapt, adopt *Adapt* means "to change for a different use." *Adopt* means "to take as one's own."

When I **adapt** a book as a film, I **adopt** a new way of imagining the story.

adverse, averse *Adverse* means "unfavorable." *Averse* means "showing reluctance."

Despite **adverse** weather, I am not **averse** to visiting Brontë country.

advice, advise *Advice* is a noun meaning "a helpful suggestion." *Advise* is a verb meaning "to offer helpful suggestions."

As a new writer, I need **advice.** Please **advise** me about publishers.

affect, effect *Affect* is a verb meaning "to influence." *Effect* is a noun meaning "result" or a verb meaning "to bring about; to cause."

Will new technology **affect** book sales? What will the **effect** be?

New technology will surely **effect** a change in how we do research.

all right, alright *All right* is always two words. Do not write *alright.*

Is it **all right** to listen to the assigned book on audiocassette?

allude, elude *Allude* means "to refer to." *Elude* means "to avoid; to escape detection or notice."

Maya Angelou's remark **alludes** to a poem whose title **eludes** me.

allusion, illusion *Allusion* means "an indirect reference." *Illusion* means "an unreal impression."

The title *The Mirror Crack'd* is an **allusion** to a Tennyson poem.

The story "The Bet" suggests that freedom may be an **illusion.**

a lot, alot *A lot* is always two words. Do not write *alot.* Use *a lot* sparingly, especially in formal writing.

I met **a lot** of young writers at the workshop.

already, all ready *Already* is an adverb meaning "previously" or "by now." *All ready* means "completely ready."

I have **already** finished the final draft of my research paper. It is **all ready** to type.

altogether, all together *Altogether* is an adverb meaning "completely; in all; on the whole." *All together* means "in a group."

> Emily Dickinson published only seven poems **altogether.**

> She gathered her other poems **all together** and tied them with ribbon.

awhile, a while *Awhile* is used only as an adverb. *A while* is usually preceded by *in* or *for* to form part of a prepositional phrase.

> Wait **awhile,** and we'll leave. The poetry reading begins in **a while.**

borrow, lend, loan *Borrow,* a verb, means "to take temporarily." *Lend,* also a verb, means the opposite, "to give temporarily." *Loan,* a noun, means "a temporary gift."

> I **borrow** most books from the library, but my friends **lend** me some.

> I occasionally obtain a book through an interlibrary **loan.**

breath, breathe *Breath,* with a short *e* sound, is a noun. *Breathe,* with a long *e* sound, is a verb.

> Do you hold your **breath** or use a snorkel to **breathe** underwater?

bring, take *Bring* suggests motion toward the speaker or writer. *Take* suggests motion away from the speaker or writer.

> I **bring** home a library book each week and **take** it back the next.

can, may Use *can* to show the ability to do something. Use *may* to show permission for doing something or the possibility of doing something.

> I know you **can** speed-read, but you **may** not do so in my class.

capital, Capitol *Capitol,* when it refers to the building where Congress meets, is a proper noun. The word *capitol* is a common noun when it means "a building where state lawmakers meet." For a city that is "the seat of government" and all meanings other than legislative buildings, use *capital.*

The **Capitol** is a building in Washington, our nation's **capital.**

In it, Congress debates **capital** punishment and a **capital** gains tax.

cloths, clothes *Cloths*, with a short *o*, means "fabrics." *Clothes*, with a long *o*, means "garments."

Sometimes I cut up my old **clothes** for use as dust **cloths.**

complement, compliment *Complement* means "to complete or bring to perfection" or "that which completes or brings to perfection." *Compliment* means "to praise" or "a remark of praise."

"Those lovely shoes **complement** your suit," he **complimented** her.

She was pleased with his **compliment.**

continual, continuous Use *continual* for an action repeated with pauses. Use *continuous* for an action with no interruptions.

The faucet's drip was **continual;** the radio's blare, **continuous.**

council, counsel *Council* means "a group that discusses or legislates." *Counsel* means "advice," "a lawyer or adviser," or "to advise."

The Town **Council** hired legal **counsel** to **counsel** its members.

desert, dessert A *desert* [DEZert] is "a dry area"; *desert* [dezERT] means "to abandon." A *dessert* [dezERT] is "a sweet last dish at a meal."

If you **desert** me in the **desert,** do it after we eat **dessert.**

discreet, discrete *Discreet* means "prudent"; *discrete*, "separate."

A **discreet** spy master organizes spies into **discrete** cells.

disinterested, uninterested *Disinterested* means "impartial." *Uninterested* means "showing no interest; bored."

An effective, independent prosecutor must be a **disinterested** party.

Frankly, I'm **uninterested** in all of these political shenanigans.

emigrate, immigrate To *emigrate* is "to leave one country for another." To *immigrate* is "to enter a country and settle there."

Of those now **immigrating** to America, many **emigrate** from Asia.

eminent, immanent, imminent *Eminent* means "outstanding." *Immanent* means "remaining within; inherent." *Imminent* means "about to happen."

The **eminent** philosopher said that human decency is an **immanent** characteristic that is not in **imminent** danger of disappearing.

farther, further Use *farther* to refer to physical distance. Use *further* to mean "additional" or to refer to intensity or degree.

Further study may reveal a planet **farther** away from the sun than Pluto.

formally, formerly *Formally* means "politely" or "according to rule or custom." *Formerly* means "previously."

Formerly, authors wrote more **formally** than they do today.

healthful, healthy Use *healthful* to mean "promoting good health." Use *healthy* to mean "having good health."

A **healthy** person eats a **healthful** diet.

historic, historical Use *historic* for an important occurrence. Use *historical* for anything related to the past.

Historical records describe the **historic** landing of the Pilgrims.

imply, infer To *imply* is "to hint or suggest." To *infer* is "to understand a hint or suggestion."

> Authors usually **imply** a theme that we must **infer** from story details.

indigenous, indigent *Indigenous* means "native." *Indigent* means "poor."

> Is the **indigenous** population **indigent** or relatively wealthy?

ingenious, ingenuous *Ingenious* means "clever"; *ingenuous*, "naive."

> She talks like an **ingenuous** youngster, but her inventions are **ingenious.**

lay, lie *Lay*, "to set something down," has a direct object. *Lie*, "to place oneself down or stay in a horizontal position," has no object.

> **Lay** down the beach blanket so that we can all **lie** on it.

lead, led *Lead* is a noun meaning "a heavy metal" or a verb meaning "to show the way." *Led* is the past tense of the verb lead.

> I told the miner, "**Lead** me to the **lead** pile." He **led** me there.

learn, teach *Learn* means "to gain knowledge"; *teach*, "to instruct."

> When good instructors **teach,** good students **learn.**

leave, let To *leave* is "to go away." To *let* is "to allow" or, together with *alone (let alone)*, "to refrain from bothering."

> Let's **leave** before those idiots **let** the lion out of its cage.

literally Use *literally* to mean "actually," not as a figure of speech.

> CORRECT: Because of the drought, the nomads were **literally** starving to death.
>
> INCORRECT: We were literally starving to death. [If the intention of the person making this statement is to call attention to his or her hunger by exaggerating it, then the person is not *literally*, or actually, starving and is using the word incorrectly.]

loose, lose *Loose* means "not tight." *Lose* means "to misplace."

> That bracelet is so **loose** that you're likely to **lose** it.

oral, aural, verbal *Oral* refers to speech or the mouth. *Aural* refers to hearing. *Verbal* refers to skill with language.

> Pills are **oral** medication; a hearing aid is an **aural** device.

> The **oral** verse of illiterate people may display great **verbal** skills.

passed, past *Passed*, the past tense of *pass*, means "went or gone by." *Past* is a noun meaning "a former time" or a preposition meaning "beyond."

> After going **past** a park, we **passed** the local history museum. Outside were many artifacts from America's **past.**

personal, personnel *Personal* means "private." *Personnel* means "staff."

> Company **personnel** should not make **personal** phone calls when at work.

precede, proceed *Precede* means "to come before." *Proceed* means "to move along" or "to continue."

> A meal will **precede** the show; later, the show can **proceed.**

principal, principle *Principal* means "of chief importance," "a chief person such as a school's head," or "an amount on which interest is computed." *Principle*, always a noun, means "a basic rule or truth."

> Our **principal** follows strict **principles** in running our school. What **principal** factors affect the interest I earn on my **principal?**

raise, rise *Raise*, meaning "to lift up" or "to rear," has a direct object. *Rise*, meaning "to go up" or "to get up," has no object.

> The soldiers **rise** early to **raise** the flag.

real, really *Real* is an adjective; *really,* an adverb.

> It is **really** possible to see a **real,** live unicorn?

regardless, irregardless Always use *regardless*. *Irregardless* is nonstandard English.

> Will she be convicted **regardless** of the facts?

respectfully, respectively *Respectfully* means "with polite regard." *Respectively* means "in the order given."

> We listened **respectfully** to the governor and mayor, **respectively**.

set, sit *Set*, "to place" or "to put down," has an object except when referring to the sun. *Sit*, "to occupy a seat," usually has no object.

> **Set** your groceries down, and **sit** in that chair to watch the sun **set**.

stationary, stationery *Stationary* is an adjective meaning "in one place" or "fixed" or "still." *Stationery* is a noun meaning "letter paper."

> The **stationary**, not portable, typewriter held a sheet of **stationery**.

than, then *Than* introduces the second part of a comparison. *Then* means "next" or "after that."

> After they were washed my new slippers seemed softer **than** cotton, and **then** they fell apart.

weather, whether *Weather*, a noun, refers to atmospheric conditions such as rain or cold. *Whether*, a conjunction, indicates a choice or alternative.

> I don't know **whether** the **weather** will be sunny or cloudy today.

---

93   **COMMON NOUN:** a noun that does not refer to a specific person, place, thing, or idea and that usually begins with a lowercase letter   [See **Nouns**.]

94   **COMPARATIVE FORM:** an adjective or adverb form used to compare two things, usually created by adding *-er* to the base form or using *more*   [See **Adjectives, Adverbs**.]

COMPLEMENT: a word in the predicate that completes the meaning of the verb   [See **Sentences: Structures and Types.**]   95

COMPLETE PREDICATE: in a sentence or a clause, the verb along with any of its complements and/or modifiers   [See **Sentences: Structures and Types.**]   96

COMPLETE SUBJECT: in a sentence or a clause, the simple subject along with any of its modifiers   [See **Sentences: Structures and Types.**]   97

COMPLEX SENTENCE: a sentence that contains one main clause and one or more subordinate clauses   [See **Sentences: Structures and Types.**]   98

COMPOUND: [Subject, Predicate, Direct Object, Subject Complement, etc.] two or more equal structures linked by a coordinating conjunction   99

COMPOUND-COMPLEX SENTENCE: a sentence that contains at least two main clauses and one or more subordinate clauses   [See **Sentences: Structures and Types.**]   100

COMPOUND NOUN: a noun made up of more than one word   [See **Nouns.**]   101

COMPOUND PREPOSITION: a preposition of more than one word   [See **Prepositions.**]   102

COMPOUND SENTENCE: a sentence containing two or more main clauses and no subordinate clauses   [See **Sentences: Structures and Types.**]   103

CONCRETE NOUN: a noun that names something that can be perceived by one or more of the five senses   [See **Nouns.**]   104

CONJUNCTIONS

IDENTIFYING CONJUNCTIONS

A **conjunction** is a word that links two or more words or groups of words.

Based on how they are used in sentences, conjunctions fall into four categories: **coordinating conjunctions, correlative conjunctions, subordinating conjunctions,** and **conjunctive adverbs.**

COORDINATING CONJUNCTIONS

A **coordinating conjunction** links two or more words or groups of words of equal importance. Use a comma before the coordinating conjunction in a series of more than two items or if the conjunction links two or more main clauses.

Chess, checkers, **and** backgammon are games with long histories. [links three subjects]

Chess arose in **or** near India. [links two prepositions]

It is a fascinating game of strategy **but** requires great patience. [links two predicates]

Checkers is simpler **yet** equally popular. [links two predicate adjectives]

Checkers was played in ancient Egypt **and** by Greeks in Homer's day. [links two prepositional phrases]

Backgammon may be older, **for** a backgammon board from 3000 B.C. has been found. [links two main clauses]

Coordinating Conjunctions

and	but	or	nor	for	yet	so

For more on subjects and predicates, see p. 380. For more on prepositions and prepositional phrases, see p. 354. For more on predicate adjectives, see p. 353. For more on clauses, see p. 297.

CORRELATIVE CONJUNCTIONS

Correlative conjunctions work in pairs to link two words or groups of words of equal importance. If the correlative conjunctions link two main clauses, put a comma before the second conjunction in the pair.

> **Both** chess **and** checkers use the same board. [links subjects]

> Backgammon uses **not only** a board **but also** dice.
> [links direct objects]

> **Just as** checkers cross a checkerboard, **so too** do
> backgammon disks cross a board. [links main clauses]

For more on direct objects, see p. 383.

Correlative Conjunctions

both . . . and	just as . . . so (too)	not only . . . but (also)
either . . . or	neither . . . nor	whether . . . or

SUBORDINATING CONJUNCTIONS

A **subordinating conjunction** makes a clause subordinate (less important or lower in rank), and it links the subordinate clause to the rest of the sentence. Use commas to set off a subordinate clause only if it introduces a sentence or comes in the middle of it.

> **After** the doubling rule was introduced in the 1920's, backgammon became more popular.

> The new rule increased popularity **because** it made the game go faster.

> America, **as soon as** the rule was introduced, enjoyed a backgammon craze.

Common Subordinating Conjunctions

after	as though	in order that	until
although	because	provided that	when
as	before	since	whenever
as far as	considering that	so that	where
as if	even though	than	whereas
as long as	if	though	wherever
as soon as	inasmuch as	unless	while

CONJUNCTIVE ADVERBS

A **conjunctive adverb** links main clauses and clarifies their relationship; it also serves as an adverb in the clause in which it appears.

> Backgammon boards need not be ornately decorated; **in fact,** the basic board is quite simple.

> Romans called backgammon the twelve-lined game; **also,** in Chaucer's day it was known as tables.

When conjunctive adverbs do not link clauses but merely make transitions, or connections, between ideas clearer and smoother, they are often called **transitional adverbs** or transitional expressions. When a conjunctive adverb links clauses, as in the two sample sentences above, put a semicolon before it and a comma after it. Otherwise, set it off with commas if it interrupts the flow of the sentence.

> The French, **on the other hand,** called the game *trictrac* in reference to the sound of the dice.

For more on adverbs, see p. 284.

> **Similarly,** one version of the game is known as *ticktack.*

Common Conjunctive Adverbs

accordingly	equally	in addition	nevertheless
additionally	finally	indeed	on the other hand
also	for example	in fact	otherwise
as a result	for instance	instead	similarly
at the same time	furthermore	likewise	still
besides	hence	meanwhile	therefore
consequently	however	moreover	thus

CONJUNCTION OR PREPOSITION?

Many words used as subordinating conjunctions can also be used as prepositions. To determine which of the two a word is, consider what sentence element the word introduces. If the word introduces a phrase that ends with a noun or pronoun object (OP), it is a preposition. If the word introduces a clause, which contains both a subject (S) and a verb (V), it is a subordinating conjunction.

PREPOSITION:	The chess tournament grew exciting **OP** **after** several hours.
SUBORDINATING CONJUNCTION:	The chess champ was interviewed **S** **V** **after** she won.

COMMON USAGE PROBLEMS

USING <u>LIKE</u>, <u>AS</u>, AND <u>AS IF</u>

Like, meaning "similar to," is a preposition, not a subordinating conjunction. Use *like* to introduce a prepositional phrase; use the subordinating conjunction *as* or *as if* to introduce a subordinate clause. Keep in mind that *as* sometimes introduces **elliptical** clauses in which all or part of the verb is omitted but understood. In the third example below, the omitted part of the verb is shown in brackets.

PREPOSITION:	Pachisi is an Indian game **like** backgammon.
SUBORDINATING CONJUNCTION:	as if **S** **V** Jon plays backgammon ~~like~~ he has played for years.
SUBORDINATING CONJUNCTION:	as **S** **V** He plays ~~like~~ a good player should [play].

USING <u>SO</u>

So is acceptable as a coordinating conjunction in informal English, but in formal writing this usage is discouraged.

AVOID: She had moved her pawn hastily, **so** I captured her queen.

BETTER: **Because** she had moved her pawn hastily, I captured her queen.

OR: She had moved her pawn hastily; **as a result**, I captured her queen.

Also discouraged in formal English is the use of *so* for the subordinating conjunction *so that*. In general, replace *so* with *so that* whenever *so that* makes sense in a sentence.

AVOID: I watched them play chess **so** I could learn to play better.

BETTER: I watched them play chess **so that** I could learn to play better.

USING <u>BUT</u>

In formal English, avoid an unnecessary *but* after *doubt* or *help*.

AVOID:	I have no doubt **but that** I will beat my computer at checkers.
BETTER:	I have no doubt **that** I will beat my computer at checkers.
AVOID:	I can't help **but think** that someday I will win.
BETTER:	I can't help **thinking** that someday I will win.

USING CORRELATIVE CONJUNCTIONS

In general, structures joined by correlative conjunctions should be parallel.

AVOID:	Neither my sister nor brother can play backgammon.
BETTER:	Neither my sister nor **my** brother can play backgammon.

STARTING SENTENCES WITH COORDINATING CONJUNCTIONS

In the past, starting a sentence with a coordinating conjunction was discouraged in formal writing. Today, however, many established writers begin sentences with coordinating conjunctions to create transitions, achieve a dramatic effect, or make dialogue more realistic.

FOR A TRANSITION:	I was winning. **And** then, suddenly, he took my queen.
FOR A DRAMATIC EFFECT:	I tried several moves. **But** it was too late.
IN DIALOGUE:	"**But** I'll never win the game now," I whispered sadly.

DEVELOPING YOUR STYLE: CONJUNCTIONS

CHOOSING CONJUNCTIONS TO COMBINE SENTENCES

Instead of using short, choppy sentences or stringing together several sentences with coordinating conjunctions, good writers use a variety of conjunctions to combine related sentences. The following chart lists common relationships that different conjunctions can express:

For more on avoiding choppy and stringy sentences, see p. 71–72 and p. 76.

Relationship	**Addition:** One thing is added to another.
COORDINATING CONJUNCTIONS:	and
CORRELATIVE CONJUNCTIONS:	both . . . and
CONJUNCTIVE ADVERBS:	additionally, also, besides, furthermore, in addition, moreover

Relationship	**Equality:** One thing is the same as another.
COORDINATING CONJUNCTIONS:	and
CORRELATIVE CONJUNCTIONS:	both . . . and, just as . . . so (too)
CONJUNCTIVE ADVERBS:	equally, likewise, similarly

Relationship	**Alternative:** One thing or another
COORDINATING CONJUNCTIONS:	or, nor
CORRELATIVE CONJUNCTIONS:	either . . . or, neither . . . nor
SUBORDINATING CONJUNCTIONS:	unless
CONJUNCTIVE ADVERBS:	otherwise, on the other hand

Relationship	**Contrast:** One thing is different from another.
COORDINATING CONJUNCTIONS:	but, yet
CORRELATIVE CONJUNCTIONS:	not only . . . but (also)
SUBORDINATING CONJUNCTIONS:	although, even though, though, while
CONJUNCTIVE ADVERBS:	however, on the other hand, still, nevertheless, instead

Relationship	**Reason or Consequence:** One thing results from another.
COORDINATING CONJUNCTIONS:	for, so
SUBORDINATING CONJUNCTIONS:	as, because, considering that, if, in order that, provided that, since, so that
CONJUNCTIVE ADVERBS:	accordingly, as a result, consequently, hence, thus, therefore

Relationship	**Time:** One thing occurs before or after another.
COORDINATING CONJUNCTIONS:	and
SUBORDINATING CONJUNCTIONS:	after, as, as long as, as soon as, before, when, whenever, since, until, while
CONJUNCTIVE ADVERBS:	finally, at the same time, meanwhile

You can usually use two or three different kinds of conjunctions to express the same relationship. In choosing among them, remember that a subordinating conjunction makes the clause it introduces less important than the main clause. In each of the first two sample sentences below, the two clauses are of equal importance; in the last sample sentence, the main clause, *Mom prefers chess*, gets more emphasis.

Relationship	Contrast
COORDINATING CONJUNCTION:	Dad loves checkers, **but** Mom prefers chess.
CONJUNCTIVE ADVERB:	Dad loves checkers; **however,** Mom prefers chess.
SUBORDINATING CONJUNCTION:	**Although** Dad loves checkers, Mom prefers chess.

As you read this passage, note the variety of conjunctions used to combine sentences:

MODEL

After clarifies a time relationship.

Combining with both . . . and avoids repetition.

In fact creates a smooth transition.

But and while show contrast. While subordinates a clause and thus stresses the importance of the last clause.

After enjoyable
~~I enjoyed~~ reading Amy Tan's book The Joy Luck
both ∧ and
Club͵ I became interested in chess. ~~I also became~~
∧
~~interested in~~ mah-jongg. The two games play
⌒; in fact,
prominent roles in Tan's book͵ The Joy Luck Club
of the title is a mah-jongg club at which the older
characters meet. Only one main character plays
⌒, but
chess͵ ~~T~~he excitement of her championship play
While
reawakened my interest in that game. I had
⌒, ∧
played chess years ago͵ Mah-jongg was something
totally new to me.

106 **CONJUNCTIVE ADVERB:** a word that serves both as a conjunction linking main clauses and also as an adverb in the clause it introduces   [See **Conjunctions**.]

107 **CONTRACTION:** a word in which an apostrophe indicates the omission of one or more letters

[See **Pronouns, Verbs, Adverbs, Nouns**.]

COORDINATE ADJECTIVES: adjectives of equal rank that separately modify the noun they precede
[See **Adjectives, Comma.**]

108

COORDINATING CONJUNCTION: a conjunction that works alone to link words or groups of words of equal rank
[See **Conjunctions.**]

109

COORDINATION: the joining of words, phrases, or clauses of equal rank   [See **Conjunctions, Clauses, Semicolon, Sentences: Structures and Types.**]

110

CORRELATIVE CONJUNCTIONS: a pair of conjunctions that work together to link words or groups of words of equal rank
[See **Conjunctions.**]

111

DANGLING MODIFIER: the incorrect use of a prepositional phrase, a verbal phrase, a subordinate clause, or another modifier without the word it modifies   [See **Verbals, Problem Solver #62C.**]

112

DANGLING PARTICIPLE: the incorrect use of a participle or participial phrase without the word it modifies
[See **Verbals.**]

113

DASH

114

IDENTIFYING DASHES

A **dash** (—) is a punctuation mark that creates a longer, more emphatic pause than a comma and usually shows an abrupt change in thought. On a typewriter or a printer that does not have a dash, use two hyphens to indicate a dash.

1. Use dashes to set off one sentence that interrupts another.

An Academy Award—Oscar is only a nickname—is very valuable.

2. Use dashes to set off and emphasize other interrupters that show an abrupt change in thought.

The Academy of Motion Picture Arts and Sciences awarded its first statue—soon to be nicknamed Oscar—in 1927.

115 DATES

1. Capitalize the names of months and days of the week.

January   **M**ay   **T**hursday   **S**aturday

2. When a date includes a month, day, and year, use a comma to separate the day from the year. Use another comma between a date and any words that follow it in a sentence.

July 4, 1776

January 1, 2000, will call for special celebrations.

3. Do not use a comma between a month and year.

July 1776   January 2000 is nearer than you may realize.

4. Use capital letters and periods with initials to refer to dates.

According to tradition, ancient Rome was founded in 753 **B.C.** [before Christ]

The last Roman emperor was deposed in **A.D.** 476. (*Anno Domini*—"in the year of the Lord")

753 **B.C.**   476   1776   2000

116 DECLARATIVE SENTENCE: a sentence that makes a statement and ends with a period

[See **Sentences: Structures and Types.**]

117 DEFINITE ARTICLE: the adjective *the*

[See **Adjectives.**]

118 DEMONSTRATIVE ADJECTIVE: The word *this, that, these,* or *those* when used to modify a noun or a pronoun

[See **Adjectives.**]

DEMONSTRATIVE PRONOUN: The word *this,* *that, these,* or *those* when it stands alone in place of a noun

[See **Pronouns.**]

119

DETERMINER: an article, a demonstrative adjective, or any other adjective that tells *which one?* or *how many?* [See **Adjectives.**]

120

DIRECT ADDRESS: the name, title, or descriptive phrase used when speaking directly to someone or something, set off from the rest of the sentence by one or two commas [See **Comma.**]

121

DIRECT OBJECT: a noun or pronoun that receives the action of a verb in the active voice and that answers the question *whom?* or *what?* after the verb

[See **Sentences: Structures and Types, Verbs.**]

122

DIRECT QUOTATION: a restatement of someone's exact words placed within quotation marks or set off on separate lines

[See **Quotations.**]

123

DOUBLE COMPARISON: the incorrect use of both *more* and the *-er* ending to create the comparative form or of both *most* and the *-est* ending to create the superlative form of an adjective or adverb [See **Adjectives.**]

124

DOUBLE NEGATIVES

125

Avoid using a **double negative**—two negative words—when only one is correct. Here is a list of commonly used negative words. Pay special attention to the four in the far right column; it is easy to forget that they are negative words.

For more on contractions, see p. 328.

For more on adverbs, see p. 284.

no	not (and its contraction, *n't*)	neither
none	no one	barely
never	nothing	scarcely
nobody	nowhere	hardly

NONSTANDARD:	I **couldn't scarcely** afford to buy gas.
STANDARD:	I **could scarcely** afford to buy gas.

NONSTANDARD:	After 20 miles, we had **hardly no** gas left.
STANDARD:	After 20 miles, we had **hardly any** gas left.

NONSTANDARD:	We **didn't** want **no one** to push our car.
STANDARD:	We **didn't** want **anyone** to push our car.

NONSTANDARD:	The bad weather **didn't** do **nothing** to help.
STANDARD:	The bad weather **didn't** do **anything** to help.

126 **DOUBLE POSSESSIVE:** the use of both the possessive form and *of* to show possession

This usage is correct when the thing possessed is one of several such things belonging to the possessor.   [See **Possessive Forms.**]

127 **DOUBLE SUBJECT:** the incorrect use of a subject followed by a pronoun that repeats it

[See **Sentences: Structures and Types.**]

128 **ELLIPSES**

1. Use **ellipsis points (. . .)** to show an interruption in dialogue.

"Was Mark Twain . . . a writer or was he a painter?" the embarrassed student asked.

2. Use ellipsis points to identify an incomplete quotation or other incomplete thoughts.

My sister tried to tell me she writes like Mark Twain. I said there probably were similarities: She sits at a desk when she writes, and so did Twain; then, of course, each of them . . . but she didn't let me finish.

◆ WHEN YOU WRITE ◆

In humorous writing, you might try using this device to call attention to your reluctance to put a certain thought into words.

When ellipsis points fall at the end of a sentence, they are either preceded by a period or followed by another end mark: a question mark or exclamation point.

Mark Twain once wrote that the best letters he ever received were from children seven or eight years of age: "They write simply and naturally and without straining for effect. . . ."

ELLIPTICAL CLAUSE: a clause in which one or more words are omitted because they are understood

`129`

[See **Conjunctions, Prepositions.**]

EMPTY SENTENCE: a sentence that provides too little information, either because it simply repeats an idea or because it makes an unsupported claim. [See **Sentences: Structures and Types, Sentence Problems** in Section Two.]

`130`

EXCLAMATION POINT

`131`

IDENTIFYING EXCLAMATION POINTS

1. Use an **exclamation point** (!) at the end of a strong command or any other sentence that expresses strong feeling.

Don't let any light into this darkroom!

I simply *must* develop these pictures before the guests arrive!

2. Use an exclamation point after an interjection meant to show strong feeling.

For more on interjections, see p. 338.

No! Don't you *dare* touch those prints before they dry!

Ugh! Have you ever seen such muddy color in a photo?

Use exclamation points sparingly. Instead, get into the habit of using expressive words and phrases to show strong feelings. The overuse of exclamation points lessens their impact.

132 **EXCLAMATORY SENTENCE:** a sentence that expresses strong emotion and ends with an exclamation point
[See **Sentences: Structures and Types.**]

133 **EXPLETIVE:** a word that has no grammatical role other than to fill out a sentence [See **Sentences: Structures and Types.**]

134 **FAULTY PARALLELISM:** the incorrect use of dissimilar grammatical structures to express similar ideas
[See **Sentence Problems** in Section Two.]

135 **FAULTY SUBORDINATION:** the incorrect placement of the main idea in a subordinate clause [See **Clauses.**]

136 **FIRST PERSON:** the person speaking or writing
The first-person pronouns are *I, me, my, mine, myself, we, us, our, ours,* and *ourselves.* [See **Pronouns.**]

137 **FRAGMENT:** an incomplete thought incorrectly punctuated and capitalized as a sentence [See **Problem Solver #58.**]

138 **FUTURE TENSE:** a verb form showing an action or a condition that has not yet occurred, formed by using the helping verb *will* or *shall* plus the base form of the main verb [See **Verbs.**]

139 **GENDER**
Gender as a grammatical concept indicates the sex of someone or something named by a noun or pronoun. In English, nouns and any personal pronouns referring to them have three genders.

masculine *(he, him, his)* → male persons/some male animals

feminine *(she, her, hers)* → female persons/some female animals

neuter *(it, its)* → things/ideas/some animals

Third-person singular pronouns (*he*, *she*, *it*) must agree in gender with their antecedents.

In the past, when an indefinite pronoun antecedent indicated both masculine and feminine persons, some writers avoided the awkwardness of *his or her* by using a masculine pronoun only.

> **Anyone** who hopes to produce a potential blockbuster should plan **his** documentary with great care.

Writers now consider this practice sexist. They use plural subjects or rephrase the sentence in some other way.

> **Filmmakers** who hope to produce potential blockbusters should plan **their** documentaries with great care.

For more on indefinite pronouns, see p. 363.

> If **you** want to produce a potential blockbuster, plan **your** documentary with great care.

GERUND: a verbal that ends in *-ing* and is used as a noun
[See **Verbals.**]

140

GERUND PHRASE: a group of words serving as a noun
and consisting of a gerund and its complements and/or modifiers
[See **Verbals.**]

141

GRAMMAR: the set of rules governing the forms of words and
their arrangement in phrases, clauses, and sentences

142

HELPING VERB: a verb that works with the main verb in a
verb phrase
[See **Verbs.**]

143

HYPHEN

144

1. A **hyphen** (-) separates the parts of some compound nouns and adjectives.

> When the **red-hot** embers fell on the lifeguard's foot, he hopped along the waterfront like a **jack-in-the-box.**

Notice that not all compound words are written with hyphens.

2. When you use a phrase of two or more words to modify a noun, you may need to create a temporary compound adjective to keep readers from getting confused.

> The **well-built** Treviño house can stand up to any storm. [The hyphen shows that two words make up one modifier.]

> A **well built** by Julio Treviño stands near the barn. [No hyphen is used when the words do not form a unit and can't be misread.]

Exceptions
- Do not hyphenate a compound modifier that follows a linking verb and modifies a subject noun or pronoun.

> A house is not **well built** if substandard lumber has been used.

- Do not use a hyphen between an adverb ending in *-ly* and the adjective or participle that the adverb modifies.

> Julio's family was proud of their **carefully constructed** house.

3. Use hyphens in compound cardinal numbers from twenty-one through ninety-nine, in their ordinal forms, and in fractions used as modifiers.

> Cardinal number: **twenty-one**

> Ordinal number: **twenty-first**

> Fraction: **one-half** teaspoon

4. Use a hyphen after the prefixes *ex-*, *self-*, *all-*, and *great-* and before the suffixes *-free* and *-elect*.

> The **ex-governor** and the **governor-elect** praised my **great-grandmother** for her **all-consuming** dedication to working her farm. She gave her children a good deal of **self-esteem** and managed to be as **debt-free** as possible.

5. Use a hyphen to separate any prefix from a proper noun or a proper adjective.

For more on prefixes and suffixes, see p. 392.

> **post-Depression** America   **non-European** nations

6.   Use a hyphen to divide a word between syllables at the end of a line. Do not leave a one-letter syllable standing alone at the end or beginning of a line. Check correct syllabification by looking up the word in a dictionary.

IMPERATIVE MOOD: any verb form that gives a command or makes a request   [See **Verbs.**]   `145`

IMPERATIVE SENTENCE: a command or request, whose subject, *you*, is usually omitted but understood   [See **Sentences: Structures and Types.**]   `146`

INDEFINITE ADJECTIVE: a term sometimes applied to a word used as an adjective that in other instances is used as an indefinite pronoun   [See **Adjectives, Pronouns.**]   `147`

INDEFINITE ARTICLE: the adjective *a* or *an*   [See **Adjectives.**]   `148`

INDEFINITE PRONOUN: a pronoun that does not refer to a specific noun   [See **Pronouns.**]   `149`

INDICATIVE MOOD: any verb form making a statement or asking a question   [See **Verbs.**]   `150`

INDIRECT OBJECT: a noun or a pronoun that answers the questions *to whom*, *for whom*, *to what*, or *for what* after an action verb   [See **Sentences: Structures and Types.**]   `151`

INDIRECT QUESTION: an interrogative sentence reworded as a noun clause within another sentence   [See **Question Mark.**]   `152`

INDIRECT QUOTATION: someone's words restated as a noun clause   [See **Quotations.**]   `153`

INFINITIVE: the base form of a verb, usually preceded by *to*, used as a noun, an adjective, or an adverb   [See **Verbals.**]   `154`

INFINITIVE PHRASE: a group of words consisting of an infinitive plus its complements and/or modifiers that serves as a noun, an adjective, or an adverb   [See **Verbals.**]   `155`

156   **INITIAL:** a one-letter abbreviation for a name or other word
Initials are capitalized but are not always followed by periods.
[See **Abbreviations, Addresses, Dates.**]

157   **INTENSIFIER:** an adverb that answers the question *to what extent?* and modifies an adjective or another adverb   [See **Adverbs.**]

158   **INTENSIVE PRONOUN:** a pronoun, usually ending in *-self* or *-selves,* that merely emphasizes its antecedent and could be dropped without changing the meaning of a sentence [See **Pronouns.**]

159   **INTERJECTIONS**

An **interjection** is a word or phrase used to express emotion (either strong or mild). It has no grammatical relation to the other

words in a sentence. Use a comma after an interjection that expresses mild emotion; use an exclamation point after one that expresses strong feeling.

Yes, I would like more soup right now.

Hey! I don't like the soup well enough to wear it.

◆ **WHEN YOU WRITE** ◆

Limit your use of interjections, even in dialogue. Their overuse creates a dull, choppy, or forced effect.

160   **INTERROGATIVE PRONOUN:** a pronoun used to ask a question   [See **Pronouns.**]

161   **INTERROGATIVE SENTENCE:** a sentence that asks a question and ends with a question mark
[See **Sentences: Structures and Types.**]

162   **INTERRUPTER:** a phrase or a clause that interrupts a sentence to add information not essential to a sentence's meaning
[See **Comma, Problem Solver #64D.**]

INTRANSITIVE VERB: a verb that does not have an
object   [See **Verbs.**]

163

INVERTED SENTENCE: a sentence in which the
subject follows the verb
    [See **Sentences: Structures and Types, Problem Solver #59G.**]

164

IRREGULAR VERB: a verb whose past and past participle
are not formed by adding *-ed* or *-d* to the present form   [See **Verbs.**]

165

ITALICS: slanted type used in printed material to indicate the
titles of full-length books, movies, words used as words, and so on
                                        [See **Underlining/Italics.**]

166

LINKING VERB: a verb that expresses a state of being
rather than action and links the subject to a noun, pronoun, or adjective
in the predicate   [See **Verbs.**]

167

MAIN CLAUSE: a clause that can stand alone as a sentence
                                        [See **Clauses.**]

168

MISPLACED MODIFIER: a phrase, a clause, or
another modifier incorrectly placed so far from the term it modifies that
it seems to modify something else [See **Verbals, Problem Solver #62B.**]

169

MODIFIER: any word, phrase, or clause serving as an adjective
or adverb to describe or limit the meaning of another word, phrase, or
clause   [See **Adjectives, Adverbs, Clauses, Prepositions, Verbals.**]

170

MOOD: the aspect of a verb that shows the speaker's attitude
toward the idea expressed; for example, verbs in the subjunctive mood
indicate possibility, supposition, or desire   [See **Verbs.**]

171

NAMES: See **Capitalization, Initials, Nouns.**

172

NEGATIVE: a word, word part, or expression that denies or
means "no"   [See **Double Negatives.**]

173

174 **NEGATIVE COMPARISON:** a comparative or superlative form indicating less than the positive form indicates and usually using *less* or *least*   [See **Adjectives.**]

175 **NONRESTRICTIVE APPOSITIVE:** an appositive or appositive phrase that interrupts a sentence to add information not essential to the sentence's meaning   [See **Appositives, Comma.**]

176 **NONRESTRICTIVE CLAUSE:** a clause that interrupts a sentence to add information not essential to the sentence's meaning   [See **Clauses, Comma.**]

177 **NONRESTRICTIVE PHRASE:** a phrase that interrupts a sentence to add information not essential to the sentence's meaning   [See **Comma.**]

178 **NOUN CLAUSE:** a subordinate clause that functions in a sentence as a subject, object, or predicate noun   [See **Clauses.**]

179 **NOUNS**

IDENTIFYING NOUNS

A **noun** names a person, place, thing, or idea.

What's the first word most infants try to say— *Mama? Dada?* Chances are that the word is a noun. Nouns are naming words, words that tell *who* or *what.* They give names to everything we encounter in life— and to things we can only imagine. In the following passage, the nouns are in bold type:

The word *the* always signals that a noun is coming soon.

The nouns name unfamiliar things —a bird called an *ibis* and flowers called *ironweeds* and *phlox.*

> ### MODEL FROM LITERATURE
>
> It was in the **clove** of **seasons, summer** was dead but **autumn** had not yet been born, that the **ibis** lit in the bleeding **tree.** The flower **garden** was stained with rotting brown magnolia **petals** and **ironweeds** grew rank amid the purple **phlox.**
>
> —James Hurst, "The Scarlet Ibis"

TYPES OF NOUNS

Concrete and Abstract Nouns

A **concrete noun** names something physical that can be perceived by one or more of the five senses. An **abstract noun** names something that cannot be seen, heard, smelled, tasted, or touched.

CONCRETE NOUNS:	elephant, violin, perfume, chocolate, silk
ABSTRACT NOUNS:	love, faith, friendliness, prosperity, democracy

Proper and Common Nouns

A **proper noun** names a particular person, place, thing, or idea. A **common noun** names a person, place, thing, or idea in a nonspecific, general way. Proper nouns begin with capital letters; common nouns do not.

	Common Nouns	**Proper Nouns**
PERSON:	girl	Diana Tallchief
PLACE:	city	Seattle
THING:	poem	"The Raven"
IDEA:	religion	Buddhism

Compound Nouns

Nouns that consist of more than one word are called **compound nouns.** In some cases the words in compound nouns are written as separate words. In other cases they are written as one word, or they are joined with a hyphen.

MORE THAN ONE WORD:	Abraham Lincoln, Newport Savings Bank, home run
HYPHENATED:	sister-in-law, jack-of-all-trades, well-wisher
ONE WORD:	blueberry, horsefly, cornerstone

Consult a dictionary if you are unsure of how to write a compound noun.

SINGULAR AND PLURAL NOUNS

A **singular noun** refers to one of something; a **plural noun,** to more than one. Most nouns have singular and plural forms.

SINGULAR: The bird calls.

PLURAL: The birds call.

The following chart summarizes the rules for forming plural nouns. If you are uncertain about a plural form, consult a dictionary. Dictionary entries usually indicate plurals not formed by just adding *-s* or *-es*.

RULES FOR PLURAL NOUNS	EXAMPLES
To form the plural of most nouns, add *s*.	school → school**s**
If a noun ends in *ch, s, sh, x,* or *z*, add *es.*	beach → beach**es**
If a noun ends in a vowel + *y*, add *s*.	monkey → monkey**s**
If a noun ends in a consonant + *y*, change *y* to *i* and add *es.*	fly → fl**ies** enemy → enem**ies**
If a noun ends in *fe*, usually change *f* to *v* before adding *s*.	knife → kni**ves** wife → wi**ves**
If a noun ends in *lf,* change *f* to *v* and add *es.*	calf → cal**ves**
If a noun ends in *f* not preceded by *l*, usually add *s* but sometimes change *f* to *v* and add *es*.	chief → chief**s** *but* leaf → lea**ves**
If a noun ends in a vowel + *o*, add *s*.	patio → patio**s**
If a noun ends in a consonant + *o,* usually add *es* but sometimes add just *s*.	potato → potato**es** *but* silo → silo**s**
To form the plural of one-word compound nouns or of measurements ending in *-ful,* follow the preceding rules for plurals.	butterfly → butterfl**ies** cupful → cupful**s**
To form the plural of compound or hyphenated words, make the most important word plural.	mother-in-law → mother**s**-in-law attorney general → attorney**s** general
To form the plural of people's names, add *s* or *es* according to the first two rules above. Do not make any other spelling changes.	Kennedy → Kennedy**s** Lopez → Lopez**es** Wolf → Wolf**s**

RULES FOR PLURAL NOUNS	EXAMPLES
Some nouns use the same form in the singular and the plural.	sheep → sheep series → series
Some nouns from foreign languages form their plurals as they do in their original languages.	datum → da**ta** crisis → cris**es**
Some nouns have irregular plurals that do not follow any of the preceding rules.	child → child**ren** foot → **fee**t

COLLECTIVE NOUNS

A **collective noun** names a group. It is singular when it refers to the the group as a whole; it is plural when it refers to individual group members.

SINGULAR: The club goes birdwatching.

PLURAL: The club argue about the birds' names.

Most collective nouns also have plurals that refer to more than one group. Plural collective nouns are formed in the same way as other plural nouns.

PLURAL: Clubs meet all over the city.

POSSESSIVE FORMS OF NOUNS

Most nouns have **possessive forms** that show ownership or possession. The following chart summarizes the rules for forming these possessives:

For more on possessive forms of nouns, see possessive forms, p. 350.

RULES FOR POSSESSIVE FORMS OF NOUNS	EXAMPLES
To form the possessive of singular nouns, add an apostrophe and **s.**	school → the school**'s** rules James → James**'s** book
To form the possessive of plural nouns that end in **s,** add just an apostrophe.	shoes → the shoe**s'** price lawyers → the lawyer**s'** club
To form the possessive of plural nouns that do not end in **s,** add an apostrophe and **s.**	women → women**'s** rights teeth → her teeth**'s** enamel sheep → the sheep**'s** fleeces

NOUN OR ADJECTIVE?

Many words used as nouns can also be used as adjectives. The word is a noun when it tells *who* or *what* and functions as a subject, object, or complement. It functions as an adjective when it modifies or describes a noun by telling *what kind* or *how many*.

NOUN: I recently bought a computer. [direct object; tells *what*]

ADJECTIVE: I need new computer software. [tells *what kind*]

Note that the noun is often preceded by the article *a*, *an*, or *the*.

DEVELOPING YOUR STYLE

USING SPECIFIC CONCRETE NOUNS

Good writers usually avoid general, abstract nouns and instead choose specific, concrete nouns that make their writing clearer and more interesting. On the following word lines, notice how vague and dull the more general words are:

GENERAL ──────────────────→ SPECIFIC

animal → mammal → horse → stallions

appliance → stove → oven → microwave

Notice how a writer revises the following passage from an editorial for a school paper to make the nouns more specific and concrete:

M O D E L

The writer changes general nouns into concrete nouns.

Publications is vague; specific magazine titles are more precise.

Specific names avoid repetition and vagueness.

       mailbox
  Lately our ~~place~~ is filled with all sorts of useless
catalogs and flyers.   brochures
~~mail.~~ Shiny four-color ~~papers~~ advertise sales at
    supermarkets.
local ~~places.~~ Publishers urge us to subscribe to
Yuppie Home Journal and TV Philosophy.
~~their publications.~~ All of this junk mail goes

straight from the mailbox to the garbage. As I dis-
      pines and spruces
card it, I think about all the ~~trees~~ that were cut
      trash.
down to make paper for this ~~stuff.~~ Wouldn't we be

better off with the trees?

NUMBER: a change in form to show whether one or more than one is meant

180

For example, the singular noun *proverb* shows one in number; the plural noun *proverbs* shows more than one.

[See **Nouns, Pronouns, Verbs.**]

NUMBERS

181

There are two kinds of numbers, cardinal and ordinal. **Cardinal** numbers tell how many: *two, 202, 200 billion.* **Ordinal** numbers rank items in a series: *second, 202nd, billionth.*

In general, spell out numbers from *one* to *one hundred.* Use numerals for numbers *101* and above. Note that most newspapers use numerals for everything over ten.

We live **fourteen** miles from the nearest hospital.

The hospital employs **234** workers.

1. Use numerals plus *million, billion,* or *trillion* for large numbers. Spell out round numbers that can be expressed in one or two words.

Do more than **8.4 million** Americans work in the health industry?

I believe over **eight million** are employed.

2. If related numbers appear in the same passage and any of them should be written as numerals, use numerals throughout the passage.

The hospital has **85** part-time and **149** full-time employees.

3. Spell out a number at the beginning of a sentence. You can also rewrite so that the numeral comes later in the sentence.

One hundred forty-nine of our employees work full time.

Or: Our full-time employees number **149.**

4. Use numerals and symbols for amounts of money unless the amount can be expressed in one or two words.

He earns **$12.50** an hour.

The newspaper costs **seventy-five** cents.

5. Use numerals for decimals and percentages.

The jar holds **1.5** liters.

Interest rates are now under **9** percent.

6. Use numerals for page, chapter, scene, act, and similar numbers.

Turn to page **21.**

Read chapter **4** of section **3.**

7. Use numerals to express quantities or amounts in scientific, statistical, mathematical, or other technical writing.

Heat **3** cubic liters to **65°** F.

182 **OBJECT:** a noun or a pronoun that receives the action, directly or indirectly, of an action verb or verbal or that a preposition relates to the rest of the sentence
[See **Prepositions, Sentences: Structures and Types, Verbals, Verbs.**]

183 **OBJECT COMPLEMENT:** a noun, a pronoun, or an adjective that identifies or describes a direct object
[See **Sentences: Structures and Types.**]

184 **OBJECT FORM OF A PRONOUN:** the form of a pronoun used as a direct object, an indirect object, an object of a preposition, or any other object
[See **Pronouns.**]

185 **OBJECT OF A PREPOSITION:** the noun or pronoun that a preposition relates to the rest of the sentence
[See **Prepositions.**]

186 **PARALLEL STRUCTURE:** expressing similar ideas in similar grammatical structures
[See **Sentence Problems** in Section Two of the book.]

187 **PARENTHESES AND BRACKETS**
Parentheses ( ) and **brackets** [ ] are used to enclose extra information.

1. Use parentheses to set off information that does not rate special attention but is relevant enough to be included.

The traffic jam **(a result of holiday shopping)** kept us from getting to the movie theater on time.

A sentence in parentheses that occurs *within* another sentence should not be capitalized or have its own end mark.

Frustrated and angry **(the traffic wasn't moving)**, we were almost tempted to walk away from the car.

If a sentence requires a comma or a semicolon, put that punctuation mark outside the closing parentheses.

When Nguyen, Lita, and I got to the theater **(totally out of breath)**, there was a long line.

I enjoyed the movie **(in spite of all the trouble we had)**; but I'm still wondering what we missed.

A separate sentence in parentheses that follows another sentence should begin with a capital letter and conclude with an end mark in the usual way.

At least we found a safe place to leave the car. **(There is a parking garage not far away.)**

◆ WHEN YOU WRITE ◆

Use dashes when you want to call attention to extra information. Unlike parentheses, dashes signal that this information deserves immediate attention.

Being late for a hit movie—something I can't stand—can be worse than not getting there at all. I have to keep this complaint to myself—or risk losing some of my slower-moving friends.

2. Use brackets to set off information that clarifies, explains, or otherwise alters a detail in *quoted* material.

The review of the movie we saw said, "**[Humphrey]** Bogart defined the character as no other actor of his time could have."

"**[Bogart]** went on to play a series of other characters who had a lot in common with Rick Blaine in *Casablanca*." (The sentence being quoted actually begins with the pronoun *he*.)

188 PARTICIPIAL PHRASE: a group of words that serves as an adjective [See **Verbals**.]

189 PARTICIPLE: a verb form, usually ending in -ed or -ing, that is sometimes used as an adjective and sometimes as the main verb after a form of the helping verb have or be [See **Verbals, Verbs**.]

190 PASSIVE VOICE: a verb form in which the subject receives the action, created by using a form of the helping verb be plus the past participle of the main verb [See **Verbs**.]

191 PAST PARTICIPLE: a verb form, usually ending in -ed, that is sometimes used as an adjective and sometimes as the main verb after a form of the helping verb have (creating a perfect tense) or be (creating the passive voice) [See **Verbals, Verbs**.]

192 PAST TENSE: a verb form showing an action or a condition that began and ended at a given time in the past, usually created by adding -ed or -d to the base form of the verb [See **Verbs**.]

193 PERFECT TENSE: one of three verb forms showing an action or a condition completed when another begins or one that began in the past and continues into the present.

This tense is created by using a form of the helping verb have and the past participle of the main verb. [See **Verbs**.]

194 PERIOD

A **period (.)** indicates the end of a sentence, shows that an initial or an abbreviation is being used, marks decimals, or separates dollars from cents.

1. Use a period to end a declarative sentence (one that makes a statement), an imperative sentence (one that gives a command or that makes a request), or a sentence that ends with an indirect quotation.

For more on types of sentences, see p. 380.

For more on quotations, see p. 374.

My parents have several videotapes of me as a child.

Please don't show those tapes when I'm around.

Hiroko asked whether I would show her the tapes.

2. Use periods to indicate initials and other abbreviations.

K. C. Jones   Mr.   Ms.   Tues.   M.D.
Capt. Kidd   Mrs.   U.S.A.   Apr. 17   A.D. 450

Use only one period following a sentence that ends with an abbreviation.

Those tapes look as if they date from 12 B.C.

Some abbreviations do not include periods. Abbreviated names of many organizations consist of only capital letters. Many dictionaries show abbreviations among the main alphabetized entries; others have separate lists in the back.

For more on abbreviations, see p. 273.

NBA National Basketball Association
UPS United Parcel Service

For more on punctuating direct quotations, see p. 372.

3. Use a period *inside* the closing quotation marks to end a direct quotation that comes at the end of a sentence. No additional period is needed.

My mother said, "I'd really like to show those videotapes."

I begged, "Please spare me that, Mom."

4. Use a period to show decimals and to separate dollar amounts from cents.

At an interest rate of 7.5 percent, savings double in 9.6 years.

A deposit of $19.95 would increase to $39.90.

PERSON: a property of nouns and pronouns that indicates who is speaking or writing (*first person*), who is being addressed (*second person*), and who or what is being discussed (*third person*)

195

All nouns are in the third person; personal pronouns change form to indicate person, and some verbs change form to agree with their subjects: *I am, you are, he/she/it is,* and so on.   [See **Pronouns, Verbs.**]

PERSONAL PRONOUN: one of the pronouns in which the form indicates the person speaking or writing (*first person*), the person being addressed (*second person*), or the person or thing being discussed (*third person*)

196

[See **Pronouns.**]

197   PHRASE: a group of words that usually serves as a single part of speech, such as a noun, an adjective, or an adverb, and that does not contain both a subject and its verb

[See **Absolute Phrases, Appositives, Prepositions, Verbals.**]

198   PLURAL: indicating more than one

Nouns, verbs, pronouns, and a few adjectives change form to indicate the plural.   [See **Nouns, Pronouns, Verbs.**]

199   PLURAL NOUN: a noun that indicates more than one person, place, thing, or idea and usually ends in *s*   [See **Nouns.**]

200   POSITIVE FORM: the basic form of an adjective or an adverb, as opposed to its comparative and superlative forms

[See **Adjectives.**]

201   POSSESSIVE FORMS

IDENTIFYING POSSESSIVE FORMS

The **possessive form** of a noun or pronoun shows ownership, belonging, or another close relationship.

Keep in mind that possessive forms do not always show true possession. For example, while *Kimba's teeth* means "the teeth that Kimba possesses," *Kimba's dentist* merely means "the dentist that Kimba visits regularly."

POSSESSIVE NOUNS

Most singular nouns form the possessive by adding an apostrophe and *s*:

dentist → the dentist**'s** drill   drill → the drill**'s** noises

Singular nouns ending in *s* form the possessive in the same way:

Marcos → Marcos**'s** glass   glass → the glass**'s** contents

Plural nouns ending in *s* add just an apostrophe to form the possessive:

dentists → dentists**'** convention   glasses → glasses**'** cases

Plural nouns not ending in *s* form the possessive by adding an apostrophe and *s*:

teeth → teeth**'s** shine   children → children**'s** teeth

Compound nouns form the possessive after the last word, regardless of how they form their plurals.

For more on compound nouns, see p. 341.

runner-up → runner-up**'s** prize   sit-ups → sit-ups**'** value

The possessive form of a noun is the same whether it comes before the word it possesses or stands alone.

My **dentist's** sign has a big tooth on it.

The sign with the big tooth on it is my **dentist's**.

POSSESSIVE PRONOUNS

Personal pronouns have possessive forms that do not use apostrophes. In addition, most have two possible forms, depending on whether the possessive comes before the word it possesses or stands alone.

For more on personal pronouns, see p. 359.

	Pronoun → Possessive	Sample Sentences
FIRST PERSON SINGULAR:	I → **my** [before] → **mine** [alone]	**My** dentist has a light touch. That dentist isn't **mine**.
FIRST PERSON PLURAL:	we → **our** [before] → **ours** [alone]	**Our** dentist is Dr. Painless. The nickname is **ours**.
SECOND PERSON SINGULAR OR PLURAL:	you → **your** [before] → **yours** [alone]	Is **your** dentist painless? Is that dentist **yours**?
THIRD PERSON SINGULAR MASCULINE:	he → **his** [before and alone]	**His** tooth fell out. The missing tooth is **his**.
THIRD PERSON SINGULAR FEMININE:	she → **her** [before] → **hers** [alone]	She got **her** tooth capped. That new cap is **hers**.
THIRD PERSON SINGULAR NEUTER:	it → **its** [before] [can't stand alone]	This molar has **its** problems.
THIRD PERSON PLURAL:	they → **their** [before] → **theirs** [alone]	**Their** gums need work. That huge bill is **theirs**.

The interrogative and relative pronoun *who* also has a possessive form that does not use an apostrophe: *whose*. It has the same form whether or not it stands alone.

For more on interrogative and relative pronouns, see p. 361 and p. 362. For more on indefinite pronouns, see p. 363.

INTEROGATIVE: **Whose** tooth is it? **Whose** is it?

RELATIVE: I know **whose** tooth it is. I know **whose** it is.

Indefinite pronouns form the possessive by adding an apostrophe and *s* and use the same forms whether or not they stand alone.

Is this anybody**'s** tooth? Is this tooth anybody**'s**?

POSSESSIVES AS ADJECTIVES

For more on adjectives, see p. 277.

When a possessive noun or pronoun modifies another noun or pronoun, it may also be called a **possessive adjective**.

POSSESSIVE NOUN OR ADJECTIVE: **Paul's** tooth was loose.

POSSESSIVE PRONOUN OR ADJECTIVE: **His** tooth fell out.

COMMON USAGE PROBLEMS

JOINT VERSUS SEPARATE POSSESSION

If two or more nouns jointly possess the same thing, use the possessive form only for the last one:

The toothbrush and toothpaste**'s** manufacturer is Cleanorama.

If two or more nouns possess separate things, use the possessive form for each:

The dentist**'s** and hygienist**'s** treatments have different prices.

DOUBLE POSSESSIVES

For more on prepositional phrases, see p. 355.

The possessive form can often be replaced with a prepositional phrase beginning with *of*. Both wordings are called the **single possessive**.

Kimba's teeth → the teeth **of Kimba**

When the thing possessed is only one of several such things belonging to the possessor, use both the possessive form and *of*. This usage is called the **double possessive**.

that tooth of Kimba**'s**   a patient of my dentist**'s**

POSSESSIVES VERSUS CONTRACTIONS

For more on contractions versus possessives, see p. 367.

Remember that the possessive forms of personal pronouns and *who* do not use apostrophes. Do not confuse them with similar-sounding contractions of pronouns plus verbs.

POSSESSIVE PRONOUN: **Whose** X-rays are these?

CONTRACTION: **Who's** [Who is] the next patient?

DEVELOPING YOUR STYLE: POSSESSIVE FORMS

STREAMLINING SENTENCES WITH POSSESSIVES

Possessive forms can help streamline sentences, saving the reader's time, avoiding repetition, and making the message clearer.

M O D E L

That dentist's
~~The~~ nickname ~~of that dentist~~ is Dr. Painless.
his
Outside ~~the~~ office ~~he owns~~ is a sign showing a
my
large tooth. According to ~~a~~ younger sister ~~of mine,~~
Dr. Painless's
~~the~~ motto ~~of Dr. Painless~~ should be "the tooth, the
whole tooth, and nothing but the tooth."

Using possessive forms shortens sentences and makes them more direct.

POSSESSIVE NOUN: a noun form that shows owner-ship or belonging and ends in an apostrophe or an apostrophe plus *s*
[See **Nouns, Possessive Forms**.]

202

POSSESSIVE PRONOUN: a pronoun form that shows ownership or belonging   [See **Possessive Forms, Pronouns**.]

203

PREDICATE: the part of a sentence that tells what the subject does or is   [See **Sentences: Structures and Types**.]

204

PREDICATE ADJECTIVE: an adjective that follows a linking verb and modifies the subject
[See **Adjectives, Sentences: Structures and Types**.]

205

PREDICATE NOUN: a noun that follows a linking verb and further identifies the subject
[See **Nouns, Sentences: Structures and Types**.]

206

PREDICATE PRONOUN: a pronoun that follows a link-ing verb and further identifies the subject
[See **Sentences: Structures and Types**.]

207

208 **PREFIX:** a word part added to the beginning of a base word

For example, *sub-* is a prefix meaning "under," as in *sublevel* and *submarine*. [See **Spelling.**]

209 **PREPOSITIONAL PHRASE:** a phrase that serves as an adjective or an adverb and that consists of a preposition (at the beginning), its object (usually at the end), and any words that modify the object [See **Prepositions.**]

210 **PREPOSITIONS**

IDENTIFYING PREPOSITIONS

A **preposition** relates a noun or pronoun to another word in the sentence.

Like conjunctions, prepositions help connect key words in a sentence. The **object of the preposition (OP)** is the noun or pronoun that the preposition (PREP) relates to another word in the sentence.

           PREP   OP
The **price *of*** the **coat** was reduced. [*Of* relates *coat* to *price*.]
                       PREP   OP
The store **reduced** the price ***on* Monday**. [*On* relates *Monday* to *reduced*.]

Many prepositions are single words, but some, called **compound prepositions**, consist of more than one word.

Common Prepositions

about	below	in front of	over
above	beneath	in place of	past
according to	beside	inside	since
across	besides	in spite of	through
after	between	instead of	throughout
against	beyond	into	to
ahead of	but ("except")	like	toward
along	by	near	under
amid	by means of	next to	underneath
among	despite	of	until
around	down	off	unto
as ("in the capacity of")	during	on	up
aside from	except	on top of	upon
at	for	onto	with
because of	from	out	within
before	in	out of	without
behind	in addition to	outside	

PREPOSITIONAL PHRASES

A group of words that begins with a preposition and includes its object is called a **prepositional phrase**. The phrase may also include one or more words, such as *the* and *green* below, that modify the object of the preposition.

For more on nouns, see p. 340. For pronouns, see p. 358.

PREP ⌐   ⌐   ↓↓ OP
The coat **with the green stripes** was a real bargain.

The entire prepositional phrase acts as a modifier. An **adjective phrase** is a prepositional phrase that, like an adjective, modifies a noun or a pronoun. An **adverb phrase** is a prepositional phrase that, like an adverb, modifies a verb, an adjective, or another adverb.

For more on phrases, see p. 355. For more on adjectives, see p. 277. For more on adverbs, see p. 284. For more on verbs, see p. 403.

ADJECTIVE PHRASE: The coat **with the green stripes** was also incredibly ugly. [modifies the noun *coat*]

ADJECTIVE PHRASE: Everyone **in the store** avoided that coat. [modifies the pronoun *everyone*]

ADVERB PHRASE: **For slightly more money,** I bought a much nicer coat. [modifies the verb *bought*]

ADVERB PHRASE: The green stripes were unsuitable **for daily wear**. [modifies the adjective *unsuitable*]

ADVERB PHRASE: Everyone pushed the ugly coat off **to the side**. [modifies the adverb *off*]

PREPOSITION, SUBORDINATING CONJUNCTION, OR ADVERB?

Many words used as prepositions can also be used as subordinating conjunctions or as adverbs. Remember that a preposition introduces a phrase that includes its object (OP), usually a noun or a pronoun. A **subordinating conjunction** introduces a clause that contains a subject (S) and a verb (V). An **adverb** works alone to modify a verb, an adjective, or another adverb.

OP
PREPOSITION: Many bargain hunters arrived ***before* noon**.

S   V
SUBORDINATING CONJUNCTION: Some arrived ***before* the store opened**.

V
ADVERB: Some had never **shopped** there ***before***.

COMMON USAGE PROBLEMS

AVOIDING UNNECESSARY PREPOSITIONS

Do not use the preposition *at* or *to* without an object when the sentence makes perfect sense without the preposition.

Where's the coat section **at**?

What time is the store opening **at**?

Where did that manager go **to**?

Do not use two prepositions when one will do.

That ugly striped coat fell **off of** the rack.

Inside of the coat was a puce lining.

USING PREPOSITIONS CORRECTLY

Be careful not to confuse *beside* and *besides*. *Beside* is a preposition that means "next to." *Besides* is sometimes a preposition meaning "in addition to" and sometimes an adverb meaning "too."

PREPOSITION: Green stripes look especially bad **beside** puce.

PREPOSITION: Many shoppers **besides** me grimaced at the ugly coat.

ADVERB: I bought a different coat and two blouses **besides**.

Use *between* to show a relationship between two items at a time. Use *among* to show a relationship among more than two items at one time.

While in the long checkout line, I stood **between** two angry shoppers.

I was **among** the many customers who left with a headache.

Use *from* to open a prepositional phrase; use *than* to open a clause. Remember that a prepositional phrase usually ends with a noun or a pronoun, the object of the preposition (OP). A clause contains both a subject (S) and a verb (V).

                                         OP

Big sales days are different **from** other **days.**

                                        S V

The store becomes a different place **than it was** before.

Be careful to use *from* before a prepositional phrase even when the phrase is *followed* by an elliptical clause. An **elliptical clause** is one from

which words have been omitted because they are understood.
In the following example, the omitted word is in brackets:

For more on clauses, see
p. 297.

It becomes a different place **from** the one [that] I know.

PREPOSITIONS AT THE ENDS OF SENTENCES

Traditionally, ending a sentence with a preposition has been discouraged in formal English.

INFORMAL: What credit card are you paying **with**?

FORMAL: **With** what credit card are you paying?

However, English speakers and writers disregard this rule so often that many sentences now sound more awkward when the prepositions are moved from the end.

INFORMAL: Which coat are you talking **about**?

FORMAL BUT AWKWARD: **About** which coat are you talking?

A good way to avoid the dilemma is to reword the sentence:

REWORDED: Which coat are you **discussing**?

DEVELOPING YOUR STYLE: PREPOSITIONS

USING PREPOSITIONAL PHRASES TO ADD DETAILS

Like adjectives and adverbs, prepositional phrases add descriptive details that make your writing more precise, clear, and vivid. In addition, occasionally opening sentences with a prepositional phrase is one way to vary sentence beginnings. In the following passage, notice how the writer revises by adding prepositional phrases:

M O D E L

for bargains   *At the mall,*
Shopping has become a popular leisure activity. A
                           of thrifty shoppers.
big coat sale last week drew huge crowds. The
                 with wide green stripes.
biggest bargain was a very ugly coat. Even the most
avid bargain hunters avoided this monstrosity.

The prepositional phrases for bargains, at the mall, and with wide green stripes make the message more precise and add sentence variety.

PRESENT PARTICIPLE: a verb form ending in *-ing*
that is sometimes used as an adjective and sometimes as the main verb
after a form of the helping verb *be* (creating a progressive form)

[See **Verbals, Verbs.**]

211

212 PRESENT TENSE: a verb form showing an action or a condition that exists at the present time, usually consisting of the base form of the verb except when *-s* or *-es* is added to agree with a third-person singular subject   [See **Verbs.**]

213 PRINCIPAL PARTS OF A VERB: the four main forms of a verb, from which all other tenses and forms are created   [See **Verbs.**]

214 PROGRESSIVE FORM: one of six verb forms showing an ongoing action or condition, created by using a form of the helping verb *be* plus the present participle of the main verb   [See **Verbs.**]

215 PRONOUN-ANTECEDENT AGREEMENT: using a pronoun of the same gender, person, and number as its antecedent   [See **Pronouns, Problem Solver #61.**]

216 PRONOUNS

IDENTIFYING PRONOUNS

Most pronouns replace words that have already been used and thus help avoid repetition. The word or group of words to which the pronoun refers is called the **antecedent (ANT)**.

ANT   *she*   *her*
Faye studies tuba, but ~~Faye~~ is afraid ~~Faye's~~ playing lacks soul.

ANT   *him*
Luke writes tuba melodies. A friend introduces ~~Luke~~ to Faye.

TYPES OF PRONOUNS

There are four pronoun types: personal pronouns, interrogative pronouns, demonstrative pronouns, and indefinite pronouns. Each type has a specific function.

Personal Pronouns

A personal pronoun refers to a specific person, place, thing, or idea by indicating if it is (1) the person or persons speaking or writing, called the **first person;** (2) the person or persons being addressed, called the **second person;** or (3) the person(s) or thing(s) being discussed, called the **third person.**

Personal pronouns have different forms depending on their **number**—singular or plural—and their **gender**—masculine, feminine, or neuter (neither masculine nor feminine). Most personal pronouns also have different subject and object forms, or **cases,** which reflect how they are used in the sentence.

Personal Pronouns

	Singular		Plural	
	Subject	Object	Subject	Object
FIRST PERSON:	I	me	we	us
SECOND PERSON:	you	you	you	you
THIRD PERSON:	*Masc.* he	him	they	them
	Fem. she	her		
	Neut. it	it		

The **subject form,** or **subjective case,** is used when a personal pronoun serves as a subject or as a subject complement (predicate noun) after a linking verb.

SUBJECT: Faye tries Luke's compositions. **She** is delighted.

SUBJECT COMPLEMENT: Faye plays Luke's soulful "Tuba Concerto in D" for a local talent show. The first-prize winner is **she**!

For more on subjects, see p. 380. For subject complements and linking verbs, see p. 384. For direct objects, see p. 383. For indirect objects, see p. 384. For prepositions and their objects, see p. 354. For verbals and their objects, see p. 399.

The **object form,** or **objective case,** is used when a personal pronoun serves as an object of any kind.

DIRECT OBJECT:	Mr. Ono, Faye's tuba teacher, applauds **her**.
INDIRECT OBJECT:	The audience gives **her** a standing ovation.
OBJECT OF A PREPOSITION:	Luke takes a bow with **her**.
OBJECT OF A VERBAL:	Hearing **her**, seventeen members of the audience decide to take up the tuba.

Possessive Forms of Personal Pronouns

For more on possessive forms, see p. 350.

Personal pronouns also have possessive forms that show ownership or belonging. Notice that these forms are spelled without apostrophes.

Possessive Forms of Personal Pronouns

	Singular		Plural	
	Before Noun	Stands Alone	Before Noun	Stands Alone
FIRST PERSON:	my	mine	our	ours
SECOND PERSON:	your	yours	your	yours
THIRD PERSON:	*Masc.* his	his	their	theirs
	Fem. her	hers		
	Neut. its	its		

The possessive form usually changes depending on whether it is used before a noun or stands alone.

| BEFORE A NOUN: | Faye is not always on key during **her** lessons. |
| STANDING ALONE: | **Hers** is a powerful but unpolished talent. |

Reflexive and Intensive Pronouns

Reflexive and **intensive pronouns** are both formed by adding *-self* or *-selves* to object or possessive forms of personal pronouns.

Reflexive and Intensive Pronouns		
Person	**Singular**	**Plural**
FIRST PERSON:	myself	ourselves
SECOND PERSON:	yourself	yourselves
THIRD PERSON:	*Masc.* himself	themselves
	Fem. herself	
	Neut. itself	

Despite their similar forms, reflexive and intensive pronouns have different functions. A reflexive pronoun refers to the subject and is necessary to complete the meaning of the sentence.

> REFLEXIVE: After each lesson, Faye burbles, "I outdid **myself** that time!" Mr. Ono has resigned **himself** to Faye's style.

An intensive pronoun merely emphasizes a noun or pronoun mentioned earlier. It can be dropped without changing the meaning of the sentence.

> INTENSIVE: Mr. Ono **himself** dreams of joining the Foreign Legion. Faye occasionally hears him murmur, *"En garde!"* though he is not aware of it **himself**.

Interrogative Pronouns

Interrogative pronouns are used to form questions.

Interrogative Pronouns

Pronoun	Function	Example
who whoever	subject; refers to a person	**Whoever** is that masked woman? **Who** knows? Could it be the Pronoun Crusader?
whom whomever	object; refers to a person	**Whomever** is she seeking? For **whom** has she come?
whose	possessive; refers to a person	**Whose** knowledge of pronouns is not up to snuff?
what whatever	refers to a thing or an idea	**What** is her mission? **Whatever** does she do with those she apprehends?
which	usually refers to a thing; shows a choice	**Which** is worse: a week's detention or the wrath of the Pronoun Crusader?

Notice that some relative pronouns have intensive forms, made by adding -*ever* to the pronoun. These forms add emphasis to the question being asked. However, they do not change the meaning of the sentence.

INTENSIVE: **Whoever** is that masked woman?

REGULAR: **Who** is that masked woman?

Relative Pronouns

For more on adjective and noun clauses, see p. 299 and p. 298.

Relative Pronouns introduce adjective or noun clauses and usually serve as subjects, objects, or subject complements in those clauses.

Relative Pronouns

Pronoun	Function	Example
who, whoever	subject; refers to a person	Les, **who** has never understood pronouns, sidles toward the door.
whom, whomever	object; refers to a person	Even Kenyatta, **whom** we consider a grammar whiz, looks uneasy.
whose	possessive; refers to a person	The Pronoun Crusader, **whose** satchel bristles with red arrows, strides to the front of the room.
what, whatever, which, whichever	refers to a thing	"Ask **whatever** you want," challenges Kenyatta. Her brave words, **which** surprise the Crusader, echo ominously.
that	refers to a person or thing	The Crusader wonders if ours is a class **that** can defeat her.

Demonstrative Pronouns

Demonstrative pronouns point out specific people or things.

Demonstrative Pronouns

Pronoun	Number	Example
this, that	singular	**"This** may be a difficult encounter," muses the Crusader.
these, those	plural	**"Those** appear to be unusually confident students."

Indefinite Pronouns

Indefinite pronouns refer to nouns or pronouns that are not specifically named.

Indefinite Pronouns

Pronoun	Number	Example
another, anybody, anyone, anything, each, either, everybody, everyone, everything, much, neither, no one, nothing, one, other, somebody, someone, something	singular	**Everyone** pales as the Crusader commands, "Les, name a relative pronoun!" When Les stammers, "Um, what?" **nobody** breathes. **Something** clicks in Kenyatta's mind. "He's right!" she shouts.
both, few, several, many others	plural	**Many** have faced the Crusader, but **few** have bested her.
all, any, most, none, some	plural or singular	**All** of us were relieved. We had feared that **all** was lost.

PRONOUN OR ADJECTIVE?

Many words used as demonstrative, interrogative, and indefinite pronouns are also used as adjectives. They are pronouns when they stand alone and replace nouns or other pronouns. They are adjectives when they modify nouns or other pronouns.

For more on adjectives, see p. 277.

DEMONSTRATIVE ADJECTIVE:	The Crusader met her match **that** day.
DEMONSTRATIVE PRONOUN:	**That** was the day the Crusader retired.
ADJECTIVE:	On **which** plane did she leave?
INTERROGATIVE PRONOUN:	**Which** flew directly to Hawaii?
ADJECTIVE:	**Some** people say she has taken up surfing.
INDEFINITE PRONOUN:	**Some** say she shouts "Cowabunga!" every morning and heads for the waves.

Possessive forms of pronouns also may function as adjectives. In such cases they are called either **possessive pronouns** or **possessive adjectives.**

POSSESSIVE PRONOUN/ADJECTIVE:	**Her** surfboard is neon orange.
POSSESSIVE PRONOUN ONLY:	**Hers** is a neon orange surfboard.
POSSESSIVE PRONOUN ADJECTIVE:	**Her** surfing instructor, **whose** name is Wally, plays the bass ukulele.

COMMON USAGE PROBLEMS

SUBJECT FORMS AFTER LINKING VERBS

In informal speech it is sometimes acceptable to use an object pronoun after a linking verb, but this usage should be avoided in formal speech or writing.

INFORMAL: Which one's Wally? That's **him.**

FORMAL: Which of those gentlemen is Wally? That is **he.**

PRONOUNS IN COMPOUND STRUCTURES

Choose the correct case of personal pronouns in **compound structures,** structures linked by conjunctions such as *and* or *or.*

COMPOUND SUBJECT:	That madcap Crusader! <u>She</u> **~~Her~~ and Wally** entered a surfing contest.
COMPOUND SUBJECT COMPLEMENT:	The winner was neither **Wally** <u>she</u> **nor ~~her~~**.
COMPOUND DIRECT OBJECT:	Still, competing thrilled **Wally** <u>her</u> **and ~~she~~**.
COMPOUND INDIRECT OBJECT:	The judges awarded **Wally and** <u>her</u> ~~**she**~~ the "Mr. and Ms. Congeniality" trophies.
COMPOUND OBJECT OF A VERBAL:	Watching **Wally and ~~she~~** <u>her</u> hang ten must have been quite an experience.
COMPOUND OBJECT OF A PREPOSITION:	Between **you and ~~I~~**, <u>me</u> the Crusader seems happier surfing than crusading.

◆ WHEN YOU WRITE ◆

If in doubt about which case to use, drop the other parts of the compound.

> Here is a postcard from the Crusader and (he? him?).
> Here is a postcard from . . . **him.**

In a compound structure, put any first-person singular pronoun last.

AWKWARD: **I and Les** read it together. It surprised **me and him.**

PREFERRED: **Les and I** read it together. It surprised **him and me.**

PRONOUNS WITH GERUNDS AND PRESENT PARTICIPLES

For more on gerunds and participles, see p. 400 and p. 399.

Use the possessive form before a **gerund,** an *-ing* verbal used as a noun. Use the object form before a **present participle,** an *-ing* verbal used as an adjective.

BEFORE A GERUND: We appreciated ~~them~~ _their_ thinking of us.

BEFORE A PRESENT PARTICIPLE: We imagined ~~their~~ _them_ basking on warm Hawaiian sands.

PRONOUNS USED WITH AND AS APPOSITIVES

For more on appositives, see p. 290.

Use the subject form of a pronoun when it appears in apposition to a subject (S) or a subject complement (SC).

> **S**   **I**
> The class officers—**Les, Kenyatta, and ~~me~~**—decided to write to the Crusader.

> **SC**   _she_
> Our heroes were now those two supersurfers, **Wally and ~~her~~.**

Use the object form if the pronoun appears in apposition to a direct object (DO), an object of a preposition (OP), or any other object.

> **OP**   _her_
> We wrote to our idols, **Wally and ~~she~~,** in Honolulu.

When a pronoun is followed by an appositive, use the form of the pronoun that would be correct if the appositive were omitted.

> _We_
> ~~Us~~ **students** weren't prepared for what happened next.

> _us_
> The Crusader and Wally sent ~~we~~ **students** thirty gardenia leis.

PRONOUNS AFTER **THAN** AND **AS**

Than and *as* often introduce elliptical (incomplete) adverb clauses from which words have been omitted. In such clauses, use the case of the pronoun that would be correct if the omitted words were present.

In the following examples, the omitted words are shown in brackets.

For more on adverb clauses, see p. 300.

Very few people are as generous as ~~them~~ *they* [are].

No class ever smelled more fragrant than ~~us~~ *we* [smelled].

Our friends noticed no one more than [they noticed] ~~we~~ *us*.

CORRECT USE OF POSSESSIVE FORMS

Do not use apostrophes in possessive forms of personal pronouns. Be especially careful not to confuse the possessive form *its* with *it's*, a contraction of the pronoun *it* and the verb *is* or *has*.

Is this lei ~~your's~~ *yours*? No, ~~its~~ *it's (it is)* mine. Careful—~~it's~~ *its* scent attracts bees.

CORRECT USE OF REFLEXIVE AND INTENSIVE PRONOUNS

Do not use a pronoun that ends in *-self* or *-selves* when a personal pronoun is all that is necessary.

Many students gave their leis to Kenyatta and ~~myself.~~ *me*.

End plural reflexive or intensive pronouns with *-selves*, not *-self*.

We soon found ~~ourself~~ *ourselves* up to our eyebrows in flowers.

Avoid the nonstandard words *hisself* and *theirselves*.

Les didn't recognize us, and so he introduced ~~hisself~~ *himself*.

Our friends laughed so hard that they almost hurt ~~theirselves~~ *themselves*.

CORRECT USE OF DEMONSTRATIVE PRONOUNS AND ADJECTIVES

Do not insert *here* or *there* after *this*, *that*, *these*, or *those*.

That ~~there~~ package came yesterday. These ~~here~~ came today.

Do not use the personal pronoun *them* in place of *those*.

What do they contain—more of ~~them~~ *those* delightful leis?

CORRECT USE OF INTERROGATIVE AND RELATIVE PRONOUNS

Do not confuse *whose*, a pronoun or adjective that shows possession, with *who's*, a contraction of the pronoun *who* and the verb *is* or *has*.

~~Who's~~ ~Whose~ idea was this correspondence? ~~Whose~~ ~Who's (who is)~ willing to accept delivery of thirty bass ukuleles?

For more on restrictive and nonrestrictive clauses, see p. 299. For more on subordinate clauses, see p. 298.

Begin an adjective clause with *that* only if the clause is restrictive or essential to the meaning of the sentence. Begin an adjective clause with *which* only if the clause is nonrestrictive and modifies a thing.

The ukulele ***that* Wally plays** was handmade by his Cousin Philbert.

The ukulele, ***which* Wally plays so well**, resembles a small guitar.

In an interrogative sentence or a subordinate clause, use *who* or *whoever* as the subject (S) of the verb (V).

   S   V
Who taught Wally that moving rendition of "Three Blind Mice"?

        S   V
The one **who** taught him was Cousin Philbert.

Be sure to use *who* or *whoever* even if another clause comes between the subject and verb of the main clause in an interrogative sentence.

   S   V
Who do you think is learning to play ukulele now?

In an interrogative sentence or a subordinate clause with a linking verb (LV), use *who* or *whoever* as the subject complement (SC). The complement will precede the subject (S) and verb (V) of the sentence or clause.

          SC   LV   S LV
Let me guess. **Who** could it be?

                        SC   S LV
I know where to find thirty instruments for **whoever** it is.

Use *whom* or *whomever* as a direct object (DO), an object of a preposition (OP), or any other object. In both interrogative sentences and subordinate clauses, the object usually precedes the subject of the sentence or clause.

     DO   **V**   **S**   **V**   **DO**   **S**   **V**
Whom should we thank for this bounty? **Whomever** we thank, let us be prompt and sincere.

     OP   **V**   **S**   **V**
To **whom** might we donate these ukuleles?

                                  OP   **S**   **V**   **V**   **DO**
Kenyatta knows a musician of **whom** we could ask advice.

AGREEMENT WITH INDEFINITE PRONOUNS
Make verbs agree with indefinite pronouns used as subjects.

Each of the ukuleles *comes* with an embossed carrying case.

Many of the ukuleles *come* with instruction booklets, too.

When an indefinite pronoun is used as an antecedent, make sure the pronoun that refers to it agrees with it in number and gender.

Each of the ukuleles has *its* own special touches.

Everyone in the class chooses *his or her* favorite.

Several of the ukuleles are prized for *their* amplifier jacks.

Remember that *all, any, most, none,* and *some* may be singular or plural. They are singular when they indicate something taken as a whole and plural when they indicate individual people or things.

Some of my classmates *are* now members of a ukulele marching band.

Some of their music *is* fairly unusual.

AGREEMENT WITH COMPOUND ANTECEDENTS LINKED BY OR
When the antecedent is a compound structure linked by *or,* use a singular pronoun unless the last part of the compound is plural.

Either Les or Leroy will bring *his* camera to the big parade.

Will **Les or his friends** cheer for *their* musical schoolmates?

AGREEMENT IN PERSON
Be sure pronouns agree in person with their antecedents.

                                           she
Kenyatta has chosen a college where ~~you~~ can study the ukulele.

                                         their
Her **teachers** say that her strumming brings tears to ~~your~~ eyes.

DEVELOPING YOUR STYLE: USING PRONOUNS

Pronouns are useful writing tools that help you avoid repetition while tying ideas together.

It's important to keep the meaning of a pronoun clear. Avoid using *this, that, which,* and *it* without a clear antecedent. If necessary, rewrite the sentence.

VAGUE:	Parade day was a warm, clear Sunday, **which** was perfect.
VAGUE:	Parade day was a warm, clear Sunday. **This** was perfect.
CLEAR:	Parade day was a warm, clear Sunday. **This** *weather* was perfect.

Rewrite to avoid using *you* or *they* with no definite meaning.

VAGUE:	At parades, **they** expect to be entertained.
CLEAR:	At parades, **the onlookers** expect to be entertained.

If a pronoun refers to more than one antecedent, rewrite the sentence to make the exact meaning clear.

VAGUE:	When people applauded the ukulele players, **they** leaped and whistled.
CLEAR:	People leaped and whistled while applauding the ukulele players.

In the following model, notice how pronouns are used to combine sentences and create transitions:

M O D E L

The relative pronoun *who* combines sentences.

Personal pronouns act as transitions.

Since *this* has no clear antecedent, the writer rewords the sentence.

The verb *remember* becomes singular to agree in number with *nobody.*

The ukulele was named after a ~~certain~~ man [the] who made ~~the ukulele~~ [it] famous. ~~The man was~~ [He] Edward Putvis, [a] ~~Putvis was~~ British officer stationed in Hawaii in the 1800's. ~~Putvis~~ [He] must have given lively performances, ~~Evidence of this is that~~ [for] the Hawaiians nicknamed ~~the man~~ [him] uku lele, or "flea jumping." Today nobody remember[s] Putvis, but ~~Putvis's~~ [his] nickname lives on in the sprightly little instrument ~~the man~~ [he] played.

PROPER ADJECTIVE: an adjective that is formed from a proper noun and begins with a capital letter

[See **Adjectives, Capitalization.**]

217

PROPER NOUN: a noun that names one specific person, place, thing, or idea and begins with a capital letter

[See **Capitalization, Nouns.**]

218

PUNCTUATION: the standardized marks used to separate sentences, sentence parts, and word parts

[See entries for individual punctuation marks.]

219

QUALIFIER: a modifier, an indefinite pronoun, or anything else that limits the meaning of a generalization   [See **Adjectives.**]

220

QUESTION MARK

221

A **question mark (?)** indicates that a sentence is interrogative, one that expresses a query.

1. Use a question mark to end a direct question.

Has anybody seen a yellow submarine**?**

2. When someone's question is being quoted directly, use a question mark inside the closing quotation marks.

She asked, "Has anybody seen a yellow submarine**?**"

"Has anybody seen a yellow submarine**?**" she asked.

3. Sometimes a sentence that is a question contains a statement in quotation marks. Place the question mark at the end of the sentence outside the closing quotation marks.

Did she say, "I've seen a yellow submarine"**?**

4. When a sentence contains a question that is quoted only indirectly, do not use a question mark.

She asked whether anyone had seen a yellow submarine.

The question is not being quoted word for word within quotation marks.

For more on punctuating quotations, see page 372.

"Has anybody seen a yellow submarine?"

USING QUOTATION MARKS

Quotation marks ("/") are marks of punctuation that set off a speaker's or writer's exact words, indicate the titles of short works, or set off special words or phrases such as nicknames, slang expressions, or terms used in an ironic sense.

Use quotation marks to show where a direct quotation begins and ends.

1. When a statement or command comes before the identification of the speaker (the speaker tag) in a sentence, use a comma inside the closing quotation marks. When a question is quoted before the speaker tag, use a question mark inside the closing quotation marks.

> "I've decided to be a standup comic," my brother announced.

> "Wouldn't you say I could make anybody laugh?" he asked confidently.

2. When a quoted statement or question comes after the speaker tag, use a comma before the opening quotation marks and a period or question mark inside the closing quotation marks.

For more information on dialogue, see p. 97.

> He added nonchalantly, "It can't be too difficult to make up jokes."

> Then he asked, "Will you help me write something funny?"

3. When a speaker tag interrupts a direct quotation, use commas to set off the two parts of the quotation from the speaker tag.

> "Thinking up funny material," I said, "is probably easier than getting an audience to laugh at it."

4. When a question mark or exclamation point relates to a sentence as a whole rather than a quotation within the sentence, put the end mark outside the closing quotation marks.

> Then he floored me. He actually said, "I can't do it without you"!

> Did *my brother* actually say, "I can't do it without you"?

5. When a quoted passage is more than one paragraph long, omit the closing quotation marks at the end of all but the very last quoted paragraph. Use an opening quotation mark to begin each new paragraph.

> "What makes people laugh?" a book about humor asks. The author goes on to say, "Many people have tried to answer that question. Some have written books about it.

"There is no simple answer to the question. People laugh for many different reasons.

"Sometimes we laugh at something that includes a sudden surprise. A story might make us think of a certain subject. Then the punch line of the joke will suddenly make us think of something else."

6. Don't use quotation marks with an indirect quotation, which is a restatement of someone else's words.

The writer said that every American should be an environmental activist.

OTHER USES OF QUOTATION MARKS

7. Use quotation marks to enclose the titles of short works.

SHORT STORY:	"The Lottery"
SHORT PLAY:	"Trifles"
POEMS:	"Jade Flower Palace"
CHAPTER OF A BOOK:	"A Warning" (Chapter One of *A Tale of Two Cities*)
SONG:	"Hawaiian Wedding Song"
ESSAY:	"Politics and the English Language"

8. Use quotation marks to call attention to words or phrases used in a special sense.

Jennifer "The Clown" Bronski was eager to do her comedy act. [The quotation marks indicate a nickname that is not part of her real name.]

The comic told about his uncle, who was always afraid his friends would call him "square." [The quotation marks show that the word is to be understood in its slang sense.]

The "genius" who wrote that comedy routine should get into a different line of work. [The quotation marks show that the word is being used ironically rather than sincerely].

IDENTIFYING QUOTATIONS

Whenever you do research for a report, you read or listen to other people's ideas about the topic you plan to write about. When you put your report together, those ideas will play an important part in what you write. To avoid **plagiarism,** using other people's words or ideas without crediting them, you must be careful to represent others' ideas accurately and to identify your sources.

For more on research reports, see p. 217.

DIRECT QUOTATIONS

The surest way to avoid plagiarism is to use direct quotations and to identify them as such. A **direct quotation** is a word-for-word repetition of what someone said or wrote.

For more on quotation marks, see p. 372.

Here, from a report on dramatic acting, are examples of two different ways to set off, or identify, direct quotations:

MODEL

In *The Actor's Scenebook,* editors Michael Schulman and Eva Mekler say that stage fright is not a problem only for beginning actors. "Virtually every actor, no matter how skilled or confident, has had to confront stage fright."

The editors go on to explain that stage fright does not take the same form with all actors, illustrating their point in this way:

On stage, different actors experience anxiety over different things. Some are embarrassed about expressing anger or sorrow; some are self-conscious about their laughs or smiles, or their faces when they cry. Others are afraid of being overwhelmed by an emotion once it gets started. The one thing common to every actor's fear is that it undermines his or her concentration. When fear comes, concentration goes, and vice versa. Since fear and concentration are antagonists, the first step in learning to overcome stage fright is to learn *how to concentrate.*

When a direct quotation is short, set it off with quotation marks, as was done with the first quotation from *The Actor's Scenebook*. For quotations of four lines or more, use the method shown for the second quotation: Precede the quotation with a colon, start the quotation on a new line, and write or type the quoted material to a narrower measure than that used in the rest of the report.

INDIRECT QUOTATIONS

Sometimes a writer restates, or paraphrases, someone else's words instead of quoting them directly, word-for-word. This restatement is called an **indirect quotation** and should *not* be put in quotation marks. However, the source of an indirect quotation must be acknowledged in a report, even though the original wording is not being reproduced. Here is an example of an indirect quotation from the same report excerpted above:

M O D E L

All the actors who spoke to our class emphasized a single point: The ability to concentrate is absolutely vital to good acting. Fred Russo, the first actor to talk to us, said that he had some simple techniques for helping himself focus on the part he had to play. One of these techniques involved standing on his head for five minutes. He said that this helped him forget everything that was happening in his personal life. He couldn't explain why, but he thought it had something to do with flooding the brain with blood.

USING QUOTATIONS

Direct and indirect quotations can add substance and authority to an essay or a report that might otherwise be little more than a string of personal opinions. When you use quotations in a report or an essay, follow these guidelines:

When using quotations in a report or essay

- remember that not everything in print is reliable; make sure the person you are quoting is very knowledgeable about your topic.
- use only quotations that illustrate or support the point you want to make; irrelevant quotations make your report seem padded.
- make sure you have recorded exactly what your source said or wrote if you are using a direct quotation.
- compare your paraphrase against the original source to make sure you haven't changed the meaning if you are using an indirect quotation.
- identify the speaker or writer of every quotation and give the book or other source from which you obtained it.

WRITING DIALOGUE

Dialogue is a conversation between two or more people. Plays, most stories, and some nonfiction include dialogue.

When you write dialogue, follow these guidelines:

GUIDELINES

When writing dialogue in a story or an essay

- punctuate each speaker's words the same way you would any other direct quotation.
- reidentify the speakers in a lengthy dialogue to keep readers from becoming confused.
- begin a paragraph each time the speaker changes.

Read the following narrative to see how these guidelines have been applied to written dialogue:

MODEL

"We've been holding auditions for three days!" the director exclaimed wearily. "I don't know if we'll ever find anyone who is right for this role."

"We'll find someone," the producer snapped. "We have to. We're opening in less than a month."

The stage manager called out, "Next!"

A burly young man plodded to the center of the stage and looked out over the orchestra pit.

"Too brawny," the director muttered. "We are not casting a boxing movie."

"We'll listen to him . . . and break for lunch," the producer announced. Then she called out, "Read from the top of the page, please."

The smooth, deep tones that came from the actor's mouth caused everyone in the theater to freeze. He might look like a boxer, but this man's voice had the sound of a harp played with gloved hands.

"His voice is magnificent!" the producer declared.

"Yes," the director agreed. "He's not the type I had in mind, but. . . ."

"Maybe," the producer suggested, "the playwright would do a few revisions."

"What kind of revisions?"

"Well, do you think he'd consider turning it into a radio play?"

DEVELOPING YOUR STYLE: QUOTATIONS

When using direct quotations in your reports or essays, try to vary the way you integrate them into your text. For example, it would probably not be a good idea to have two long, set-off quotations back to back. Try to separate the longer quotations with your own ideas and analyses, with indirect quotations, or with short quotations that can be embedded, or included, in the running prose.

Another way to achieve variety is to use different methods of embedding quotations in your running text. Sometimes quoting only part of a statement can make your sentences flow more smoothly. Here's an example:

> **GOOD:** The director said, "In my opinion, good actors are the ones who know their lines and don't knock over the stage furniture."

> **BETTER:** The director said he admired actors "who know their lines and don't knock over the stage furniture."

224 **REFLEXIVE PRONOUN:** a pronoun ending in *-self* or *-selves* that refers to an earlier noun or pronoun and is essential to a sentence's meaning   [See **Pronouns.**]

225 **REGULAR VERB:** a verb whose past and past participle are formed by adding *-ed* or *-d* to the present form   [See **Verbs.**]

226 **RELATIVE ADVERB:** a word that introduces an adjective clause and also serves as an adverb in the clause   [See **Clauses.**]

227 **RELATIVE CLAUSE:** another term for **Adjective Clause**

228 **RELATIVE PRONOUN:** a word that introduces a subordinate clause and also stands in for a noun, often serving as a subject or object in the subordinate clause   [See **Pronouns.**]

229 **RESTRICTIVE APPOSITIVE:** an appositive that limits the meaning of the word it modifies and is essential to a sentence's meaning   [See **Appositives, Comma.**]

230 **RESTRICTIVE CLAUSE:** a clause that limits the meaning of the word it modifies and is essential to a sentence's meaning   [See **Clauses, Comma.**]

231 **RESTRICTIVE PHRASE:** a phrase that limits the meaning of the word it modifies and is essential to a sentence's meaning   [See **Comma.**]

RUN-ON SENTENCE: two or more sentences incorrectly punctuated as one

[See **Problem Solver #57.**]

SECOND PERSON: the person addressed

The second-person pronouns are *you, your, yours, yourself,* and *yourselves.*

[See **Pronouns.**]

SEMICOLON

A **semicolon** is like a period and a comma combined. It shows more finality than a comma but less than a period.

1. Use a semicolon between two main clauses in a compound sentence when the clauses are not connected by a coordinating conjunction.

> That new company with the amusing name is doing quite well; its name is Everything Including the Kitchen Sink.

For more on coordinating conjunctions, see p. 322.

2. Use a semicolon before a conjunctive adverb that joins two clauses. (Usually a comma appears after the adverb.)

For more on conjunctive adverbs, see p. 324.

> The company had a clever ad campaign; therefore, most consumers are now aware of its products and prices.

3. Use semicolons to separate items in a series when the items already contain commas.

> That company manufactures soups and other foods; shoes, boots, and other footwear; and kitchen sinks.

For more on the use of commas in a series, see p. 305.

> Their products are sold in department stores, especially in footwear departments; at supermarkets, including the Food-o-rama chain; at shoe stores; and at hardware stores.

SENTENCE FRAGMENT: an incomplete thought
incorrectly capitalized and punctuated as a sentence

[See **Problem Solver #58.**]

SENTENCES: STRUCTURES AND TYPES

IDENTIFYING SENTENCES

A **sentence** is a group of words that expresses a complete thought.

Every sentence contains a subject and a predicate. The **subject** tells whom or what the sentence is about. The **predicate** tells what the subject does or is. Usually the subject comes before the predicate, as in these sample sentences:

Subject	Predicate
Silkworms	are caterpillars of certain moths.
The best silk producers	are mulberry silkworms.
They	feed on the leaves of mulberry trees.
The development of the silk industry	took place in ancient China.
Japan and India	also became famous for silkworms.

COMPLETE AND SIMPLE SUBJECTS

The **complete subject** usually consists of a noun or pronoun and any words that describe it. This main noun or pronoun is called the **simple subject,** or sometimes just the subject. In the complete subjects of the following sentences, the simple subjects are in bold type. Notice that sometimes, as in the last sentence, the simple subject is the only word in the complete subject.

For more on nouns and pronouns, see p. 340 and p. 358.

Complete Subject	Complete Predicate
Ancient Chinese **royalty**	raised silkworms.
The **art** of producing silk	was a closely guarded secret.
Everything about it	was unknown outside China.
Japan	finally learned the art from four Chinese women.

Chinese silkworm

Sometimes the simple subject is a **compound noun** of more than one word. Proper nouns, in particular, are often compound nouns.

For more on compound nouns, see p. 341.

Complete Subject	Complete Predicate
The **Byzantine Empire**	smuggled silkworms from China.
Marco Polo	visited China in the fifteenth century.

Sometimes the subject consists of two or more nouns or pronouns linked by a coordinating conjunction such as *and* or *or*. These nouns or pronouns make up a **compound subject.**

For more on conjunctions, see p. 322.

Complete Subject	Complete Predicate
An **emperor** and his **wife**	founded China's silk industry.
He or **she**	made silkworms fashionable.
Myths, legends, and **poetry**	praise the couple.

Sometimes the complete subject contains a phrase or clause that serves as an adjective describing the simple subject. Do not confuse any nouns or pronouns in these phrases or clauses with the simple subject. In the following sentences, the simple subjects are in bold type:

For more on phrases, see p. 350. For more on clauses, see p. 297.

SENTENCES: STRUCTURES AND TYPES

Complete Subject	Complete Predicate
Legends about silkworms	abound.
A Chinese **princess** marrying in India	supposedly smuggled in silk-worm eggs.
The **bride**, who wanted silk clothing,	hid the eggs in her headdress.

COMPLETE AND SIMPLE PREDICATES

A **complete predicate** usually consists of a verb and any words that modify it or complete its meaning. The verb is called the **simple predicate** or, more often, the **verb;** the complete predicate is usually called just the **predicate.** In the predicates of the following sentences, the verbs are in bold type. Notice that sometimes, as in the first sentence, a verb may be the only word in the complete predicate.

Complete Subject	Complete Predicate
Monarch butterflies	**migrate.**
They	**fly** great distances every year.
These orange and black butterflies	usually **travel** in large groups.

For more on verbs and verb phrases, see p. 403 and p. 405.

The verb, or simple predicate, may also be a **verb phrase,** a main verb with one or more helping verbs. Notice that other words in the predicate may interrupt a verb phrase.

Complete Subject	Complete Predicate
Monarchs	**may journey** from Canada to Mexico.
Thousands	**are** often **seen** heading south in August.

A modifier that is part of the complete predicate can sometimes be shifted to an opening position in a sentence.

Part of Complete Predicate	Complete Subject	Part of Complete Predicate
Often	thousands	are seen heading south in August.
In August	thousands	are often seen heading south.

Sometimes the complete predicate contains two or more verbs joined by a coordinating conjunction such as *and, but,* or *or.* These verbs make up a **compound verb.**

Complete Subject	Complete Predicate
Monarchs	**pirouette, dip,** and **soar.** [compound verb]
They	**rest** or **feed** in clusters. [compound verb]
Birds	**dislike** their taste and usually **ignore** them. [compound verb]

OBJECTS AND OTHER COMPLEMENTS

A **complement** is a word in the predicate that completes the meaning of a verb. Only some verbs require complements. There are four kinds of complements: **direct objects, indirect objects, object complements,** and **subject complements.** In all cases, coordinating conjunctions can be used to create a compound form.

1. A **direct object** answers the question *what* or *whom* after an action verb. It is usually a noun or a pronoun.

Viceroy butterflies resemble **monarchs.**

For that reason, birds usually ignore **them.**

Birds chase **fritillaries** and **swallowtails** instead. [compound]

Monarch butterflies

2. An **indirect object (IO)** is a noun or pronoun that answers the questions *to what, for what, to whom,* or *for whom* after an action verb.

For more on action verbs, see p. 404. For more on adjectives, see p. 277.
Almost all sentences with indirect objects also have direct objects (DO). The indirect object comes between the verb and the direct object.

                         V   **IO**   **DO**
McAnn's Butterfly Park **gives** *visitors* their money's **worth.**

                    V   **IO**   **DO**
The park's keeper **showed** *us* several rare **butterflies.**

             V   **IO**   **IO**   **DO**
She **showed** *Malcolm* and *me* an African **specimen.**
[compound]

3. An **object complement (OC)** is a noun, pronoun, or adjective that identifies or describes a direct object. Sentences with object complements must have direct objects.

                              DO   **OC**
Tourists have made the butterfly **park** a major *attraction.*

                            DO   **OC**
Local volunteers at the park consider the **honor** *theirs.*

                     DO **OC**   **OC**
Weekend visitors find the **park** *busy* but *lovely.* [compound]

4. A **subject complement (SC)** follows a linking verb (LV) and identifies or describes the subject. It may be a noun, called a **predicate noun;** a pronoun, called a **predicate pronoun;** or an adjective, called a **predicate adjective.**

For more on linking verbs, see p. 404.

The term *predicate nominative* is sometimes used for both predicate nouns and predicate pronouns.

PREDICATE NOUN:	The butterfly park is a giant **greenhouse.**
PREDICATE PRONOUN:	The head gardener's job is **hers.**
[COMPOUND] PREDICATE ADJECTIVE:	The flowers always seem **lush** and **beautiful.**

Dryadula phaetusa, a Costa Rican butterfly

SENTENCE PATTERNS

By definition, a sentence must express a complete thought. In order to do that, it needs a subject, a verb, and any complements that the verb requires. The subject, the verb, and complements form the basic elements of a sentence. When only these elements are considered, sentences often fall into one of the five patterns shown on this chart.

Common Sentence Pattern	Sample Sentence
1. subject—action verb (S + V)	S V Locusts attack.
2. subject—action verb—direct object (S + V + DO)	S V DO Locusts attack farms.
3. subject—action verb—indirect object—direct object (S + V + IO + DO)	S V IO Locusts bring farms **DO** misfortune.
4. subject—action verb—direct object—object complement (S + V + DO + OC)	S V Locusts make **DO** **OC** farmers miserable.
5. subject—linking verb—subject complement (S + LV + SC)	S LV SC Locusts are deadly.

By adding modifiers to the basic elements, you can expand sentences while still maintaining the same pattern. For example, both of the following sentences, despite their differences in length, have the same *S + V + DO* pattern.

ORIGINAL: Locusts attack farms.

EXPANDED: Eating their way across the African veldt, deadly **locusts** in their seven-year cycle of destruction **attack** several **farms** in Doris Lessing's short story "A Mild Attack of Locusts."

INVERTED ORDER

As the five basic sentence patterns indicate, the subject usually precedes the verb. Some sentences, however, are written in **inverted order,** that is, the subject follows the verb. Inverted order can be used to build suspense and to create a poetic effect.

REGULAR ORDER:
                 S   V
A **swarm** of bees **swept** over the field.

INVERTED ORDER:
                        V   S
Over the field **swept** a **swarm** of bees.

Many sentences using inverted order open with the word *here* or *there*. In such sentences, *here* or *there* can function as an adverb or an **expletive**, a word that has no grammatical role other than to get a sentence started.

For more on adverbs, see p. 284.

	V	S
ADVERB:	*Here* **lies** another **victim** of killer bees.	

	LV	S
EXPLETIVE:	*There* **are** several **kinds** of swarming insects.	

MODEL FROM LITERATURE

LV   S

. . . for miles in every direction there **was nothing** but a black, glittering multitude, a multitude of rested, sated, but none the less voracious ants.

—Carl Stephenson, "Leiningen Versus the Ants"

SENTENCE TYPES

Sentences may be classified into one of four types: **declarative, interrogative, imperative,** or **exclamatory.**

1. A **declarative sentence** makes a statement and ends with a period. It is the most common type of sentence. It uses regular subject-verb order or sometimes inverted order, in which the subject follows the verb.

S   V
A hive of bees drones in the morning air.

V   S
In the morning air drones a hive of bees.

TRY THIS

To identify the subject, mentally turn the sentence into a declarative one: *You are afraid of honeybees.*

2. An **interrogative sentence** asks a question and ends with a question mark. The subject usually comes after the verb or after a helping verb (HV) in a verb phrase. The subject may also come before the verb, especially in informal English.

LV   S
Why are you afraid of honeybees?

HV   S   V
Do they ever sting without provocation?

S   V
The beekeeper said what? [informal]

3. An **imperative sentence** makes a request or gives a command and ends with a period. The subject *you* is usually dropped.

    S   V
[You] Just ignore the bees.

    S HV   V
[You] Do not swat them.

4. An **exclamatory sentence** expresses strong feeling and ends with an exclamation point. Often it begins with *How* or *What,* and any direct object, object complement, or subject complement may come before the subject and verb.

TRY THIS
To identify the subject and complement, mentally turn the sentence into a declarative one: *The hive produces much honey.*

        DO   S   V
What honey the hive produces!

      OC   S   V
How heavy the beekeeper finds her protective

  DO
outfit!

    SC   S V
How hot the protective veil is!

      S   V
How the beekeeper works! [no complement]

A declarative, interrogative, or imperative sentence becomes exclamatory when it expresses strong emotion. To indicate such emotion, end the sentence with an exclamation point.

Beekeeping is certainly a lot of work!

Do you believe the noise a hive makes!

Don't annoy the bees!

SENTENCE STRUCTURES AND CLAUSES

A **clause** is a group of words that contains a subject and its verb. A **main** (or **independent**) **clause** can stand alone as a sentence. A **subordinate** (or **dependent**) **clause** cannot stand alone because it does not express a complete thought.

                         S   LV
MAIN CLAUSE: Several kinds of bees are social creatures.

                               S   V
SUBORDINATE CLAUSE: Although many bee species make solitary nests

The structure of a sentence is determined by the number and kind of clauses it contains. There are four sentence structures: **simple, compound, complex,** and **compound-complex.**

1. A **simple sentence** is a main clause that stands alone.

S   V
Bees depend only on flowers for food.

2. A **compound sentence** contains two or more main clauses, or simple sentences, separated by a semicolon or linked by a comma and a coordinating conjunction such as *and, but, or, for, nor, so,* or *yet.*

S   V   S   HV   V
Bees live on pollen and nectar; they may convert the nectar to honey.

S   V   S   V
Bees obtain food from flowers, **but** wasps usually eat small insects.

Hint: Do not confuse compound sentences with simple sentences that have compound subjects or predicates.

COMPOUND SUBJECT: All **ants** and some **bees** are social insects.

COMPOUND VERB: Social insects **nest** together and **divide** labor.

3. A **complex sentence** contains one main clause and one or more subordinate clauses. In the following sentences, the subordinate clauses are in bold type. Notice that a subordinate clause may interrupt a main clause.

S   S   V   V
Honeybees, **which beekeepers raise**, live mainly in human-made hives.

S   LV   S   LV
Although their honey is valuable, honeybees are even more valuable as pollinators.

S   V   S   V
They inadvertently spread pollen **as they move from flower to flower.**

For more on relative pronouns, see p. 378.

Hint: The relative pronoun that begins some subordinate clauses may be the subject of the clause.

S   S   V   V
Farmers **who need crop pollination** often use honeybees.

4. A **compound-complex sentence** contains at least one subordinate clause and at least two main clauses.

S   V   S   V
When a honeybee finds flowers, it communicates in a kind of

S   V
dance, and fellow bees learn the location of the tasty treats.

COMMON USAGE PROBLEMS

DOUBLE SUBJECTS

Do not follow a subject with a pronoun that repeats it.

INCORRECT: **Joellen she** has an ant farm.

CORRECT: **Joellen** has an ant farm.

SUBJECT-VERB AGREEMENT

A verb should agree with its subject in number.

For more on subject-verb agreement, see Problem Solver #59, p. 262.

SINGULAR: An **ant belongs** to a highly organized social structure.

PLURAL: **Ants belong** to a highly organized social structure.

Ant farm

DEVELOPING YOUR STYLE: SENTENCES

SENTENCE VARIETY

By varying sentence lengths, structures, types, and openings, you can make your writing more lively. In the following passage from a report, notice the variety of sentence lengths, structures, types, and beginnings.

For more on sentence variety, see p. 82.

MODEL

Do you think of spiders as disgusting creatures that make cobwebs in hard-to-reach corners? Think again. Most spiders benefit humans by controlling the insect population. Spiders themselves are not insects, but they are close cousins. While insects have six legs, spi-

The opening interrogative sentence captures attention; a short, punchy imperative sentence follows.

ders have eight. In addition, insects' bodies have three main segments; spiders' bodies have only two. Inside those bodies are special silk-producing glands. The fluid from these glands solidifies into a silken thread as soon as air reaches it, and then spiders use the thread for cocoons, webs, and other purposes. Webs, which only some spiders make, come in many shapes and sizes. Many have intricate geometrical patterns, which glisten with dew in the morning sun. To insects, they are deathtraps.

---

237 **SERIES:** three or more words, phrases, or clauses in a row, separated by commas and usually with a conjunction before the last item
[See **Comma, Semicolon.**]

238 **SIMPLE PREDICATE:** the verb or verbs constituting the key word or words in the complete predicate
[See **Sentences: Structures and Types.**]

239 **SIMPLE SENTENCE:** a sentence that consists of just one main clause   [See **Sentences: Structures and Types.**]

240 **SIMPLE SUBJECT:** the one or more nouns or pronouns constituting the key word or words in the complete subject
[See **Sentences: Structures and Types.**]

241 **SINGULAR:** indicating one
Nouns, verbs, pronouns, and a few adjectives change form to indicate whether they refer to one or more than one.
[See **Nouns, Pronouns, Verbs.**]

242 **SINGULAR NOUN:** a noun that indicates one person, place, thing, or idea   [See **Nouns.**]

HOW CAN I IMPROVE MY SPELLING?

Some of the world's smartest people are bad spellers, but that's no defense against the bad impression that poor spelling can create. To avoid the distracting effect of spelling errors in your writing, follow these strategies:

STRATEGIES FOR IMPROVED SPELLING

1. Keep a list of words you often misspell, and try learning one a day—or take your daily word from the list of commonly misspelled words at the end of this lesson.

2. When learning to spell a word, use as many of your senses as possible. Say the word aloud, exaggerating each sound—including any silent letters. Visualize the word, and use your finger to trace it in the air or on a flat surface. Write the word, using, first, a pencil and then ink. If possible, type the word on a typewriter or computer.

3. Create a memory device to remember the word's spelling. For example, to remind yourself that *gerbil* begins with a *g*, not a *j*, you might say "A *gerbil* is not a *jay*." The sillier the device, the more likely you are to remember it.

4. Proofread everything you write, and take the time to check spellings in a dictionary. When writing a first draft, mark tricky words for checking later. If you work on a computer, use any spell-checking features.

As the following examples show, the same sounds are often spelled differently in English:

/b/ = **b**eauty, **b**uild

/g/ = **gh**ost, **g**overnor, **g**uard

/k/ = **c**afeteria, **ch**orus, **k**ayak, **qu**iche

/n/ = **gn**at, **kn**ife, **mn**emonic, **n**ecessary, **pn**eumonia

/s/ = **c**ider, **sc**issors, **s**uccess

/sk/ = **sc**allop, **sch**edule, **sk**etch

/z/ = **x**ylophone, **z**ucchini

/f/ = **f**oreign, **ph**armacy

/j/ = **g**el, **j**ewel

/l/ = **l**eisure, **ll**ama

/r/ = **r**ecipe, **rh**yme, **wr**itten

/sh/ = **ch**ampagne, **sh**eathe

/w, hw/ = **w**eight, **wh**im

FROM A WRITER

❝I'm not very good at it myself, but the first rule about spelling is that there is only one z in is.❞

—George S. Kaufman

TRY THIS

If you want to find a word in a dictionary but are unsure of its spelling, guess at the spelling of its first syllable and scan the appropriate section of the dictionary. If the word isn't there, consider other spellings of the first syllable.

ADDING PREFIXES AND SUFFIXES

A **prefix** is a word part added to the beginning of a word; a **suffix** is a word part added to the end. The form of the word without any prefixes or suffixes is called the **base form** of the word.

1. When adding a prefix to the base form of a word, do not drop any letters.

dis- + satisfied → dissatisfied   mis- + spell → misspell

2. When adding a suffix other than *-like* to the base form of a word ending in a consonant and y, change y to *i* unless the suffix begins with *i*.

baby + -like → babylike   cry + -ed → cried
beauty + -fy → beautify   cry + -ing → crying

EXCEPTIONS: dryness, shyly, shyness

3. When adding a suffix to the base form of a word ending in a vowel and y, keep the y.

coy + -ness → coyness   joy + -ous → joyous

EXCEPTIONS: daily, gaily

4. When adding a suffix that begins with a consonant other than y to the base form of a word ending in silent *e*, keep the *e*.

care + -less → careless   manage + -ment → management

EXCEPTIONS: argument, awful, judgment, truly, wisdom

5. When adding a suffix that begins with a vowel or y to the base form of a word ending in silent *e*, drop the *e*.

desire + -able → desirable   rose + -y → rosy

Do not drop the *e* if the base form of a word ends in *ce* or *ge* and *e* is needed to retain the soft /c/ or /g/ sound.

notice + -able → noticeable   advantage + -ous → advantageous

Do not drop the *e* if the base form of a word ends in *ee* or *oe*.

agree + -able → agreeable   hoe + -ing → hoeing

If the word ends in *ie*, change the *ie* to y before adding *-ing*.

die + -ing → dying   lie + -ing → lying

6. When adding a suffix that begins with a vowel to the base form of a word ending in a single vowel and a single consonant (other than x, y, or w), double the final consonant if the word is as follows:

- one syllable long: slug + -ish → sluggish
- a one-syllable word with a prefix: recap + -ing → recapping
- stressed on the last syllable, and the stress does not shift when the suffix is added:

    prefer + -ing → preferring   regret + -able → regrettable

    Do not double the final consonant if

- the stress shifts: prefer + -ence → preference
- the stress is not on the last syllable: open + -er → opener
- two vowels precede the final consonant: ruin + -ing → ruining
- a consonant precedes the final consonant: mend + -ed → mended
- the suffix begins with a consonant: commit + -ment → commitment

7. When adding -ly to a word ending in a single l, keep both l's. If the word ends in double l, drop one l.

    cool + -ly → coolly   dull + -ly → dully

8. When adding -ness to a word ending in n, keep both n's.

    stubborn + -ness → stubbornness
    sudden + -ness → suddenness

OTHER SPELLING RULES

1. Use this rhyme to remember the order of i and e:

Use *i* before *e*   → achieve, hieroglyphic, lien, niece
except after *c*   → ceiling, conceive, deceit, receipt
or when sounded as /ā/   → eighth, freight, weight
as in *neighbor* and *weigh*. → reign, sleigh, veil

EXCEPTIONS: caffeine, either, foreign, forfeit, height, heirloom, leisure, neither, protein, seize, sheik, species, weird

2. Use -cede to spell the sound /sēd/.

concede   intercede   precede   recede

EXCEPTIONS: exceed, proceed, succeed, supersede

3. Use -sion when the syllable is pronounced /zhən/ (as in *persuasion*) or after l or s; otherwise, use -tion.

explosion   revulsion   passion   ambition   motion

4. To spell an unstressed vowel sound, see if you can spell another form of the word in which the syllable containing the vowel sound is stressed. Then use the same vowel in the unstressed syllable.

Unknown Spelling	Clue Word	Correct Spelling
lab?r	la**bor**ious	la**bor**
mor?l	mo**ral**ity	mo**ral**
reb?l	re**bel**lion	re**bel**

SPELLING HOMOPHONES

Homophones, words with the same sounds but different spellings and meanings, are a frequent source of spelling errors and need careful proofreading. Even though we are aware of the differences among common homophones like *to, too,* and *two,* we often write the wrong word when we are writing quickly. The following are some examples of less common homophones:

altar: religious platform **alter:** to change	**base:** bottom; main; dishonorable **bass:** low musical range or instrument
aural: of the ear **oral:** spoken	**complement:** to complete or balance **compliment:** to praise
discreet: tactful **discrete:** distinct	**foul:** unpleasant; bad; against the rules **fowl:** poultry
gorilla: type of ape **guerrilla:** irregular soldier	**idle:** not working **idol:** religious image; admired figure

COMMONLY MISSPELLED WORDS

The following hundred words are often misspelled. To improve your spelling, you might try learning one of these words a day, using the strategies presented earlier in this lesson.

absence	conscious	laboratory	phenomenon
accidentally	defendant	license	playwright
accommodate	definite	lieutenant	predictable
accumulate	descendant	lightning	prevalence
acknowledgment	discipline	liquefy	privilege
adolescent	ecstasy	maintenance	psychology
adviser	eighth	maneuver	recommendation
all right	elementary	marshal	reference
answer	eligible	medieval	relevant
apparatus	embarrass	memento	reminisce
arctic	environment	millionaire	resurrect
ascend	existence	miscellaneous	rhythm
assassinate	February	mischievous	righteous
attendant	forty	moccasin	separately
bankruptcy	genius	muscle	sergeant
beggar	government	nickel	siege
biscuit	guarantee	ninety	silhouette
bouillon	gyp	nuclear	sincerely
calendar	harass	occasion	tournament
cemetery	hemorrhage	occurrence	truly
changeable	hygiene	parallel	unanimous
chauffeur	hypocrisy	paralyze	unnecessary
choir	immediately	paraphernalia	vacuum
colonel	inauguration	parliament	versatile
committee	incidentally	pastime	warranty
conscience	inoculate	perseverance	Wednesday
conscientious	jewelry	persistence	weird

SPLIT INFINITIVE: the use, avoided in formal English, of an infinitive interrupted by one or more words between the *to* and the base form of the verb
[See **Verbals.**]

244

STRINGY SENTENCE: a sentence containing too many ideas connected by *and, so, then, and so,* or *and then*
[See **Sentence Problems** from Section Two.]

245

SUBJECT: the part of a sentence that tells what or whom the sentence is about; also, the key word or words in that part, called the simple subject
[See **Sentences: Structures and Types.**]

246

SUBJECT COMPLEMENT: a noun, a pronoun, or an adjective that follows a linking verb and identifies or describes the subject
[See **Sentences: Structures and Types.**]

247

248 **SUBJECT FORM OF A PRONOUN:** the form of a pronoun used as a subject or as a predicate pronoun after a linking verb [See **Pronouns.**]

249 **SUBJECT–VERB AGREEMENT:** using a verb with the same number as its subject [See **Problem Solver #59.**]

250 **SUBJUNCTIVE MOOD:** any verb form indicating possibility, supposition, or desire [See **Verbs.**]

251 **SUBORDINATE CLAUSE:** a clause that serves as an adjective, an adverb, or a noun and that cannot stand alone as a complete sentence [See **Clauses.**]

252 **SUBORDINATING CONJUNCTION:** a conjunction that introduces a subordinate clause and also links or relates the clause to the rest of the sentence [See **Clauses, Conjunctions.**]

253 **SUBORDINATION:** the joining of two clauses in a way that makes one of lesser rank or importance than the other [See **Clauses, Conjunctions.**]

254 **SUFFIX:** a word part added to the base form of a word
For example, *-or* is a suffix meaning "one who does," as in *actor* and *inventor*. [See **Spelling.**]

255 **SUPERLATIVE FORM:** an adjective or adverb form used to compare more than two things, usually created by adding *-est* or using *most* [See **Adjectives, Adverbs.**]

256 **TENSE:** one of six verb forms indicating time [See **Verbs.**]

257 **THIRD PERSON:** the person or thing spoken about
The third person pronouns are *he, him, his, himself, she, her, hers, herself, it, its, itself, they, them, their, theirs,* and *themselves.* All demonstrative, interrogative, relative, and indefinite pronouns and all nouns are in the third person. [See **Pronouns.**]

TRANSITIVE VERB: an action verb with a direct object　259
[See **Verbs.**]

UNDERLINING/ITALICS　260

When writing or typing, underline any words that would be printed in **italics**, type in which the printed letters slant upward to the right. (Letters that do not slant in this way are roman type.)

I enjoyed reading *The Great Gatsby* by F. Scott Fitzgerald.

Some word processors and computers allow you to generate italic type.

1. Use underlining or italics for the following kinds of titles:

BOOK:	*The Joy Luck Club*
FULL-LENGTH PLAY:	*Death of a Salesman*
LONG POEM:	*The Epic of Gilgamesh*
MOVIE:	*Glory*
TELEVISION SERIES:	*The Fresh Prince of Bel-Air*
LONG MUSICAL WORK:	*Miss Saigon*
WORK OF ART:	*Sugar Cane*
NEWSPAPER:	*The New York Times*
MAGAZINE:	*Ebony*
SHIP:	*U.S.S. George Washington*
TRAIN:	*Orient Express*
AIRCRAFT:	*Spirit of St. Louis*
SPACECRAFT:	*Explorer*

2. Use underlining or italics for foreign words and phrases.

Huckleberry Finn lacks *savoir-faire,* or tact, but is a decent person.

3. Use underlining or italics when referring to a particular word, letter, or number.

Twain misspells *civilize* to show how Huck might spell it.

Does he use an *a* instead of an *i* ?

261 **USAGE:** the customary way in which words and phrases are written or spoken **[See Commonly Confused or Misused Words.]**

262 **VERBAL PHRASE:** a group of words that contains a participle, gerund, or infinitive along with its complements and/or modifiers and is used in a sentence as an adjective, an adverb, or a noun

[See Verbals.]

263 **VERBALS**

IDENTIFYING VERBALS

A **verbal** is a verb form used as a part of speech other than a verb.

Do you enjoy *masquerading* on Halloween? Do you like *to dress* as someone else, or do you prefer *being* yourself? The words in italics are examples of verbals: They look like verbs, but they function as other parts of speech. The three kinds of verbals are **participles, gerunds,** and **infinitives.** All three can act alone or can be expanded into **verbal phrases**.

TYPES OF VERBALS
Participles and Participial Phrases

A **participle** is a verb form that can be used as an adjective to modify a noun (N) or pronoun. There are two kinds of participles, **present** and **past.** A participle may occupy one of several positions in a sentence. However, it must be near the noun or pronoun that it modifies.

For more on verbs, see p. 403.

For more on adjectives, see p. 277.

For more on the past participles of irregular verbs, see p. 409.

Type	Form	Participles Serving as Adjectives
PRESENT PARTICIPLE:	ends in *-ing*	Herve is an **entertaining** speaker.
PAST PARTICIPLE:	usually ends in *-ed* or *-d* but may be irregular	He gave an **inspired** speech on water awareness. He blends **known** facts with new information when he writes a speech.

Position	Examples
AT THE START OF A SENTENCE OR CLAUSE:	**Coughing**, the next student began his speech.
JUST BEFORE THE WORD IT MODIFIES:	The **coughing** student was Herve Villar.
AFTER THE WORD IT MODIFIES:	"It's Water Awareness Week," said Herve, **coughing**.

A participle may occur in a **participial phrase**, which consists of the participle plus any complements or modifiers. The entire participial phrase then serves as an adjective to modify a noun or a pronoun (PRO).

Suddenly stopping his speech, Herve took a large gulp of water.

"You see? It works!" he announced, **clearing his throat.**

The audience, **breaking into laughter**, applauded his joke.

A participle can also be used as a main verb (V) along with one or more helping verbs (HV) as part of a verb phrase. In such a case, it is not a verbal.

For more on verb phrases, see p. 405.

PARTICIPLE AS ADJECTIVE (VERBAL):	**Laughing**, we enjoyed Herve's joke.
	HV V
PARTICIPLE AS VERB:	We **were laughing** at Herve's joke.

Gerunds and Gerund Phrases

For more on nouns, see p. 340.

A **gerund** is a verb form that is used as a noun. Gerunds always end in -ing. Like nouns, they function in sentences as subjects, as complements (such as direct objects and subject complements), and as objects of prepositions.

For more on subjects and complements, see p. 380 and p. 384.

For more on prepositions, see p. 354.

Noun Function	Examples
SUBJECT:	**Joking** relaxed Herve's audience.
DIRECT OBJECT:	Herve enjoyed **speaking.**
SUBJECT COMPLEMENT:	His favorite activity is **talking.**
OBJECT OF A PREPOSITION:	He is gifted in the art of **communicating.**

A gerund may occur in a **gerund phrase,** which consists of the gerund plus any complements or modifiers.

Speaking in public is torture for some people.

Herve, however, enjoys **communicating his ideas to an audience**.

Don't confuse gerunds and present participles, which both end in -ing. Remember that gerunds function as nouns, which serve as subjects (S), subject complements (SC), or objects of prepositions. Present participles function as adjectives, which describe nouns or pronouns, or as the main verbs with helping verbs in verb phrases, which express the action the subject performs.

	S SC
GERUND:	His favorite activity is **talking**.

	S HV V
PRESENT PARTICIPLE:	He **is talking** about clean water.

Infinitives and Infinitive Phrases

For more on adverbs, see p. 284.

An **infinitive** is the base form of a verb, usually preceded by *to*; it can be used as a noun, an adjective, or an adverb. When used as nouns, infinitives may function as subjects or complements.

Function	Examples
SUBJECT (NOUN):	**To act** is now Herve's burning ambition.
DIRECT OBJECT (NOUN):	He longs **to perform**.
SUBJECT COMPLEMENT (NOUN):	His goal is **to star**.
ADJECTIVE:	He has the talent **to succeed**.
ADVERB:	He doesn't find the lines hard **to remember**.

An infinitive may occur in an **infinitive phrase**, which consists of the infinitive plus any complements or modifiers. Like an infinitive, an infinitive phrase can function as a noun, an adjective, or an adverb.

Function	Examples
SUBJECT (NOUN):	**To act on stage** is now Herve's burning ambition.
DIRECT OBJECT (NOUN):	He longs **to perform famous roles brilliantly.**
SUBJECT COMPLEMENT (NOUN):	His goal is **to star in a Shakespeare play.**
ADJECTIVE:	He has the talent **to succeed as an actor.**
ADVERB:	**To evaluate his work,** he uses a video recorder.

Don't confuse infinitives with prepositional phrases that begin with *to*. Remember that an infinitive combines *to* with the base form of a verb; the preposition *to* (P) links a noun or pronoun, called the object of the preposition (OP), to the rest of the sentence.

For more on prepositions, see p. 354.

INFINITIVE:	Herve loves **to perform.**
	P OP
PREPOSITIONAL PHRASE:	At every opportunity he takes **to the stage.**

COMMON USAGE PROBLEMS

AVOIDING MISPLACED AND DANGLING PARTICIPLES

A participle or participial phrase is **misplaced** when it is not located near the noun or pronoun it modifies and it seems to modify another word. To avoid the problem, place participles and participial phrases as close as possible to the words they modify.

For more on misplaced and dangling modifiers, see p. 268.

MISPLACED:	Herve finished his speech, **bowing to the crowd.** [Who is bowing to the crowd—Herve or his speech?]
CORRECT:	**Bowing to the crowd,** Herve finished his speech.

Also avoid a **dangling participle,** a participle or participial phrase that seems to modify the wrong word because the word it really modifies is missing from the sentence.

DANGLING:	**Enjoying the speech,** the applause was enthusiastic. [Who is enjoying the speech—the applause?]
CORRECT:	**Enjoying the speech,** we applauded enthusiastically.

AVOIDING SPLIT INFINITIVES

A **split infinitive**, in which a modifier is placed between *to* and the base form of the verb, is discouraged in formal English. In your school reports and other formal writing, avoid this problem by changing word order.

AVOID:	He was ready **to quickly leave** the stage.
BETTER:	He was ready **to leave** the stage **quickly.**

DEVELOPING YOUR STYLE: VERBALS

By using verbals to combine sentences, you can vary sentence lengths and structures to make your writing more interesting. Verbals can also help make your writing clearer and less wordy. Here's a draft of the review of Herve's speech that a classmate later published in the school newspaper. Notice how she revised with verbals to improve her style.

Water Awareness Week Not All Wet

~~Herve Villar~~ *Kicking* ~~kicked~~ off Water Awareness Week at Jefferson High School. ⌢ *, Herve Villar* ~~He~~ gave a speech on the importance of ~~the preservation of~~ *preserving* our water supply. The first moments of his speech caught everyone's attention. ~~He realized~~ *Realizing* the need for an effective opening. ~~It would~~ *to* stress his point. ⌢ *, he* ~~He~~ dramatically took a gulp ~~of water after~~ *to stop* a cough. He told the assembly that without clean, fresh water, he might have been forced ~~into a cancella-~~ *to cancel* ~~tion of~~ his speech. The audience ~~clapped and~~ ⌢ *, clapping and laughing,* ~~laughed. They~~ were in the palm of his hand, ready ~~for participation~~ *to participate* in the Water Awareness activities his committee has planned. ~~Volunteer service~~ *Volunteering* begins today.

To link her ideas more strongly, Carrie turns her first sentence into a participial phrase and links it to the second sentence.

She links short, choppy sentences by using an infinitive phrase and uses participles to improve *The audience clapped and laughed.*

Awkward, wordy phrases are replaced with more precise gerunds and infinitives.

VERB PHRASE: a main verb and all its helping verbs

[See **Verbs.**]

264

VERBS

265

IDENTIFYING VERBS

Every clause or sentence must contain a verb. The verb tells what the subject does or is. In the following passage, the verbs are in bold type.

A **verb** is a word that expresses an action, a condition, or the fact that something exists.

A single knoll **rises** out of the plain in Oklahoma, north and west of the Wichita Range. . . . The hardest weather in the world **is** there. Winter **brings** blizzards, hot tornadic winds **arise** in the spring, and in summer the prairie **is** an anvil's edge.

—N. Scott Momaday, *The Way to Rainy Mountain*

ACTION VERBS AND LINKING VERBS

The two main categories of verbs are **action verbs (V)** and **linking verbs (LV)**.

|

For more on subjects see p. 395.

Action Verb	An **action verb** expresses physical or mental action and tells what the subject (S) does.	

The second sample sentence has a compound verb, two separate verbs joined by a conjunction such as *and*.

SAMPLE SENTENCES:	S V The tornado **rolls** down the prairie. [physical action] S V V Everyone **dreads** and **fears** the deadly funnel. [mental actions]

For more on conjunctions, see p. 322.

Linking Verb	A **linking verb** expresses state of being and tells what the subject is by linking it to one or more words in the predicate that describe or further identify it.
SAMPLE SENTENCES:	S LV Snowstorms **seem** gentler. [links *snowstorms* with *gentler*, which describes *snowstorms*] S LV Yet they **are** also a menace. [links *they* with *menace*, which further identifies *they*]

Only a handful of verbs can be used as linking verbs.

Common Linking Verbs

Common linking verbs include the following: *become, seem, appear, feel, look, taste, smell, sound, stay, remain, grow,* and *be* (including the forms *am, is, are, was,* and *were*).

Some of these verbs also can be used as action verbs. If you can re-. place the verb with a form of *be* and the sentence still makes sense, the verb is probably a linking verb.

ACTION VERB: People in six states **felt** the earthquake.

LINKING VERB: The quake **felt** like the big one. [Replacing *felt* with *was* makes sense: The quake was like the big one.]

TRANSITIVE VERBS AND INTRANSITIVE VERBS
Action verbs are either **transitive** or **intransitive.**

For more on objects, see p. 346.

Transitive Verb	A **transitive verb** has a direct object (DO), the receiver of the action the subject performs.
	S V DO
SAMPLE SENTENCE:	A fierce hurricane **hit** the coast. [*Coast* receives the action.]

Intransitive Verb	An **intransitive verb** does not have a direct object.
	S V
SAMPLE SENTENCE:	The hurricane **hit** at two in the morning.

MAIN VERBS AND HELPING VERBS
Sometimes two or more verbs work together in a **verb phrase.** The most important verb in the phrase is called the **main verb (V).** The other verb or verbs are called **helping verbs (HV)** or **auxiliary verbs.**

              HV   V
Natural disasters **may strike** any part of the United States.

      HV   HV   V
We **have been getting** some real doozies this year.

The main verb and any helping verbs may be separated by words or contractions that are not part of the verb phrase.

          HV   V
The Midwest **had** never **experienced** a flood as bad as the flood of 1993.

          HV   V
The Northeast **wasn't used** to temperatures as cold as those of 1994.

HV   V
Did the L.A. earthquake **cause** more damage than Hurricane Andrew?

Common Helping Verbs

FORMS OF *HAVE:*	has, have, having, had
FORMS OF *BE:*	am, is, are, was, were, be, being, been
OTHER HELPING VERBS:	do, does, did, may, might, must, can, could, will, would, shall, should

VERB FORMS, NUMBER, AND PERSON

Verbs may change form to agree with a subject in **number** and **person.** In the **first person,** the subject is the speaker (or writer). In the **second person,** the subject is the person spoken to. In the **third person,** the subject is the person or thing spoken about.

	Singular	Plural
FIRST PERSON:	I **swelter**	we **swelter**
SECOND PERSON:	you **swelter**	you **swelter**
THIRD PERSON:	he, she, it [or any singular noun] **swelters**	they [or any plural noun] **swelter**

VERB TENSES AND PRINCIPAL PARTS

Verbs also change form to show time. The six main forms that show time are called the **tenses** of the verb. Four **principal parts** of the verb help to create these tenses. The following chart shows principal parts formed in the regular way; you'll learn about irregular ones later in the lesson:

Principal Part	Examples	Description
BASE FORM:	shiver, quake, drown	basic form of the verb
PAST FORM:	shivered, quaked, drowned	adds *-ed* or *-d*
PRESENT PARTICIPLE:	shivering, quaking, drowning	adds *-ing*
PAST PARTICIPLE:	shivered, quaked, drowned	adds *-ed* or *-d*

The principal parts are used, sometimes along with helping verbs, to form the main six tenses of the verb.

1. present tense
2. past tense
3. future tense
4. present perfect tense
5. past perfect tense
6. future perfect tense

You can also express a present action or condition by using a form of *be* plus the present participle: *I am shivering.*

See progressive form on p. 358.

1. The **present tense** shows an action or condition that exists at the present time. It uses the base form of the verb without any helping verbs and adds *-s* or *-es* to agree with a third-person singular subject. Two exceptions are the verbs *have* and *be*.

Present Tense [Regular]

FIRST PERSON:	I **shiver**	we **shiver**
SECOND PERSON:	you **shiver**	you **shiver**
THIRD PERSON:	he, she, it [or any singular noun] **shivers**	they [or any plural noun] **shiver**

Present Tense of the Verb *Have* [Irregular]

FIRST PERSON:	I **have**	we **have**
SECOND PERSON:	you **have**	you **have**
THIRD PERSON:	he, she, it [or any singular noun] **has**	they [or any plural noun] **have**

Present Tense of the Verb *Be* [Irregular]

FIRST PERSON:	I **am**	we **are**
SECOND PERSON:	you **are**	you **are**
THIRD PERSON:	he, she, it [or any singular noun] **is**	they [or any plural noun] **are**

---

2. The **past tense** shows an action or condition that began and ended at a given time in the past. It uses the past form of the verb without any helping verbs. Unlike the present tense, it usually does not change form to agree with its subject; the only exception is the verb *be*.

Past Tense [Regular]

FIRST PERSON:	I **shivered**	we **shivered**
SECOND PERSON:	you **shivered**	you **shivered**
THIRD PERSON:	he, she, it [or any singular noun] **shivered**	they [or any plural noun] **shivered**

Past Tense of the Verb *Be* [Irregular]

FIRST PERSON:	I **was**	we **were**
SECOND PERSON:	you **were**	you **were**
THIRD PERSON:	he, she, it [or any singular noun] **was**	they [or any plural noun] **were**

You can also express future time by using a form of be plus going or about plus the infinitive: I am going to shiver; I am about to shiver.

3. The **future tense** shows an action or condition that has not yet occurred. It is formed by using the helping verb *will* (or sometimes *shall*) before the base form of the main verb.

Future Tense

FIRST PERSON:	I **will shiver**	we **will shiver**
SECOND PERSON:	you **will shiver**	you **will shiver**
THIRD PERSON:	he, she, it [or any singular noun] **will shiver**	they [or any plural noun] **will shiver**

For more on infinitives, see p. 400.

4. The **present perfect tense** shows an action or condition that occurred at an unnamed, indefinite time in the past or one that began in the past and has continued into the present. It is formed by using the helping verb *have* or *has* before the past participle of the main verb.

Present Perfect Tense

FIRST PERSON:	I **have shivered**	we **have shivered**
SECOND PERSON:	you **have shivered**	you **have shivered**
THIRD PERSON:	he, she, it [or any singular noun] **has shivered**	they [or any plural noun] **have shivered**

Sometimes the helping verb *have* or *has* is contracted to 've or 's: *I've shivered, she's shivered,* and so on.

For more on contractions, see p. 328.

Irregular Verbs

Regular verbs such as *shiver* form past tense and past participles by adding *-ed* or *-d*. **Irregular verbs,** like those below, form past tense or past participles or both in different ways.

Common Irregular Verbs

BASE	PAST	PAST PARTICIPLE	BASE	PAST	PAST PARTICIPLE
be	was, were	been	hung	hung or hanged	hung or hanged
beat	beat	beaten			
become	became	become	hurt	hurt	hurt
begin	began	begun	keep	kept	kept
bite	bit	bitten	know	knew	known
blow	blew	blown	lay	laid	laid
break	broke	broken	lead	led	led
bring	brought	brought	leave	left	left
burst	burst	burst	lend	lent	lent
buy	bought	bought	let	let	let
catch	caught	caught	lie	lay	lain
choose	chose	chosen	lose	lost	lost
come	came	come	make	made	made
cost	cost	cost	pay	paid	paid
cut	cut	cut	put	put	put
do	did	done	ride	rode	ridden
draw	drew	drawn	ring	rang	rung
drink	drank	drunk	rise	rose	risen
drive	drove	driven	run	ran	run
eat	ate	eaten	say	said	said
fall	fell	fallen	see	saw	seen
feel	felt	felt	set	set	set
fight	fought	fought	shake	shook	shaken
find	found	found	shrink	shrank or shrunk	shrunk or shrunken
fling	flung	flung			
fly	flew	flown	sing	sang	sung
freeze	froze	frozen	sink	sank or sunk	sunk
get	got	got or gotten	sit	sat	sat
give	gave	given	speak	spoke	spoken
go	went	gone	split	split	split
grow	grew	grown	steal	stole	stolen
have	had	had	sting	stung	stung
hear	heard	heard	swim	swam	swum
hit	hit	hit	take	took	taken

BASE	PAST	PAST PARTICIPLE	BASE	PAST	PAST PARTICIPLE
teach	taught	taught	throw	threw	thrown
tear	tore	torn	wear	wore	worn
tell	told	told	win	won	won
think	thought	thought	write	wrote	written

5. The **past perfect tense** shows a past action or condition that ended before another past action began. It is formed by using the helping verb *had* before the past participle of the main verb.

Sometimes the helping verb *had* is contracted to *'d:* **I'd shivered,** he**'d shivered,** we**'d shivered,** and so on.

Past Perfect Tense

FIRST PERSON:	I **had shivered**	we **had shivered**
SECOND PERSON:	you **had shivered**	you **had shivered**
THIRD PERSON:	he, she, it [or any singular noun] **had shivered**	they [or any plural noun] **had shivered**

---

6. The **future perfect tense** shows a future action or condition that will have ended before another begins. It is formed by using the helping verbs *will* (or sometimes *shall*) and *have* before the past participle of the main verb.

Future Perfect Tense

FIRST PERSON:	I **will have shivered**	we **will have shivered**
SECOND PERSON:	you **will have shivered**	you **will have shivered**
THIRD PERSON:	he, she, it [or any singular noun] **will have shivered**	they [or any plural noun] **will have shivered**

Progressive and Emphatic Forms

Each of the six tenses had a **progressive** form that is often used to show an action or condition in progress. It uses a form of the helping verb *be* plus the present participle of the main verb.

PRESENT PROGRESSIVE:	They **are shivering.**
PAST PROGRESSIVE:	They **were shivering.**
FUTURE PROGRESSIVE:	They **will be shivering.**
PRESENT PERFECT PROGRESSIVE:	They **have been shivering.**
PAST PERFECT PROGRESSIVE:	They **had been shivering.**
FUTURE PERFECT PROGRESSIVE:	They **will have been shivering.**

In common practice, the present progressive form is widely used to show a single action in progress now, at the present time. The simple present tense is more often used for an action that occurs in general in the present.

PRESENT PROGRESSIVE:	The crossing guard **is shivering.** [in progress now]
PRESENT:	Outdoor workers **shiver** during cold spells. [in general]

To show force or emphasis, the present and past tenses also have **emphatic** forms that use a form of the helping verb *do* plus the base form of the main verb.

PRESENT EMPHATIC:	Mail carriers certainly **do shiver** in cold weather.
PAST EMPHATIC:	How that lumberjack **did shiver** last January!

The same forms are used in interrogative and negative sentences, although in those cases they do not show special force.

INTERROGATIVE:	Does a walrus **shiver** in the cold water?
NEGATIVE:	The walruses at the zoo **didn't shiver** last winter.

Active and Passive Voice

Action verbs also change form to indicate **voice.** A verb is in the **active voice** when the subject (S) of the sentence performs the action. It is in the **passive voice** when the subject receives the action—that is, has something done to it. The passive voice uses a form of the helping verb *be* (HV) before the past participle of the main verb (V).

                       S   V

ACTIVE VOICE: Hurricanes **destroy** many homes each year.

                               S   HV   V

PASSIVE VOICE: Each year many homes **are destroyed** by hurricanes.

The passive voice can conceal the performer of the action or be used when the performer is uncertain.

                                        S   HV   V

PERFORMER CONCEALED: The trailer camp **was** completely **destroyed.**

                                         S   HV V

PERFORMER UNCERTAIN: That storm **was named** Hurricane Iniki.

The passive voice can be used in the perfect and future tenses and with other helping verbs.

                                         S   HV   HV   V

PRESENT PERFECT PASSIVE: The hurricane's progress **has been monitored.**

                                  S HV   HV   V

PAST PERFECT PASSIVE: It **had been spotted** at sea.

                                      S   HV HV   V

FUTURE PASSIVE: Its future path **will be considered.**

                                      S   HV HV   V

OTHER HELPING VERBS: Hurricanes **can be predicted.**

Indicative, Imperative, and Subjunctive Mood

In the margin: *In imperative sentences, the subject, always you, is usually omitted because it is understood: [You] Go to the nearest hurricane shelter.*

In addition to tense and voice, verbs also express **mood.** A verb is in the **indicative mood** when it is used to make a statement or ask a question. A verb is in the **imperative mood** when it is used to give a direct command or make a direct request.

INDICATIVE MOOD: Before a hurricane, most people **go** inland.

IMPERATIVE MOOD: **Go** to the nearest hurricane shelter.

A verb is in the **subjunctive mood** when it is used for one of the purposes shown on the following chart:

Subjunctive Mood

PURPOSE: to express indirectly a demand, suggestion, or statement of necessity

FORM: base form of the verb, regardless of subject

SAMPLE SENTENCES: The police demanded that I **go** to an inland location.

    The Red Cross urged that she **go** to the nearest shelter.

    They recommend that everyone **listen** to radio bulletins.

    It is necessary that we **be** ready at a moment's notice.

Subjunctive Mood

PURPOSE: to state a wish or a condition contrary to fact

FORM: usual verb form except for the past of *be,* which uses *were,* not *was,* regardless of subject

SAMPLE SENTENCES: The Red Cross treated me as if I **were** a guest.

One boy wished that he **had** his own radio.

If he **were** smart, he would have brought it.

I wish that I **were** insured against hurricanes.

For this purpose, the indicative mood often replaces the subjunctive mood in informal English: The Red Cross treated me as if I was a guest.

COMMON USAGE PROBLEMS

USING PRINCIPAL PARTS AND HELPING VERBS CORRECTLY

Remember that irregular verbs do not form past tenses or past participles in the usual way.

INCORRECT: The earthquake **splitted** this building in two.

CORRECT: The earthquake **split** this building in two.

When you use irregular verbs in perfect tenses after forms of the helping verb *have*, remember to use their past participles.

INCORRECT: The quake **has shook** that house off its foundation.

CORRECT: The quake **has shaken** that house off its foundation.

Be especially alert to the use of the contractions *'ve* for the helping verb *have*, *'s* for the helping verb *has*, and *'d* for the helping verb *had*.

INCORRECT: We**'ve saw** the site where the building**'s fell.**

CORRECT: We**'ve seen** the site where the building**'s fallen.**

When you write, be careful not to use the preposition *of* for the helping verb *have* or its contraction, *'ve*.

For more on prepositions, see p. 354.

INCORRECT: We would **of** seen more, but TV cameras blocked our view.

CORRECT: We would **have** [or would**'ve**] seen more, but TV cameras blocked our view.

KEEPING TENSES COMPATIBLE

Avoid changing tenses when events occur at the same time.

INCORRECT: TV cameras **filmed** the earthquake victims, who **ask** for help.

CORRECT: TV cameras **filmed** the earthquake victims, who **asked** for help.

On the other hand, change tenses when you want to show that events did not occur at the same time. For example, to show that one event in the past finished before another event in the past began, use the past perfect tense for the first event and the past tense for the second.

INCORRECT: TV cameras **filmed** earthquake victims, many of whom **lost** everything in the quake.

CORRECT: TV cameras **filmed** earthquake victims, many of whom **had lost** everything in the quake.

DEVELOPING YOUR STYLE: VERBS

CHOOSING THE ACTIVE VOICE

Excessive use of the passive voice makes writing flat, wordy, and hard to follow. The active voice is generally more lively, concise, and easier to understand. Therefore, choose the active voice in most cases.

AVOID: Midwestern farmlands **were devastated** by the 1993 flood.

BETTER: The 1993 flood **devastated** Midwestern farmlands.

Use the passive voice only if the performer of the action is unclear, unimportant, or too complicated or obvious to mention.

AWKWARD: Record keepers and local residents **described** the disaster as a five-hundred-year flood.

BETTER: The disaster **was described** as a five-hundred-year flood. [The performers of the action are unimportant and too complicated and obvious to be worth mentioning.]

USING STRONG AND PRECISE VERBS

Strong, precise verbs make writing lively and imaginative by appealing to the senses. Such verbs can also cut down on wordiness by replacing duller verbs and their modifiers. The following revision shows the effectiveness of strong and precise verbs.

streaked

Just a few months after deadly wildfires ~~moved swiftly~~ down the hills near Malibu, a major earth-

rocked

quake ~~hit~~ the Los Angeles area. The quake, which

measured   struck

~~was~~ 6.6 on the Richter scale, ~~occurred with sud-

terrified

denness~~ in early morning and really ~~scared~~ me ~~a-

suffered

lot~~. Yet, a few weeks later, the Northeast ~~had~~ a

record-breaking cold spell in which more people

perished

~~died tragically~~ than in the earthquake. Our warm

bestows

California climate ~~kindly offers~~ benefits, even if

endure

we must ~~live through~~ a fire or earthquake now

and then.

Measured and suffered are more precise than the general verbs was and had.

The writer replaces weaker verbs and their modifiers with strong verbs such as streaked, struck, terrified, perished, bestows, and endure.

VOICE: any verb form indicating whether the subject performs the action (*active voice*) or has the action performed on it (*passive voice*)

[See **Verbs.**]

266

WORDY SENTENCE: a sentence containing words that do not add to its meaning   [See **Sentence Problems** in Section Two.]

267

GUIDE TO LEARNING

■ ■ ■

Taking Charge of How You Learn

Libraries Are Appreciated, 1943, Jacob Lawrence
Philadelphia Museum of Art

RESEARCH:
LIBRARY RESOURCES

How can the library help me with my writing assignments?

Do any of these comments seem familiar?

"You're off to a good start—now add more specific details."
"Can you elaborate on this?"
"Your topic is too broad. Narrow it to a more manageable size."
"Your statement needs support. How about some more facts and statistics?"

Whenever you need ideas, details, or information, a library can help. The following diagram shows how one student used different library resources to find information for a specific writing assignment:

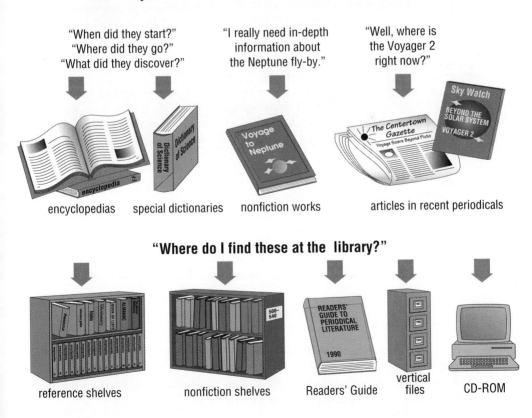

Assignment: Essay about Space Exploration
Idea: "Maybe I could write about the Voyager space probes."

"When did they start?"
"Where did they go?"
"What did they discover?"

"I really need in-depth information about the Neptune fly-by."

"Well, where is the Voyager 2 right now?"

encyclopedias   special dictionaries   nonfiction works   articles in recent periodicals

"Where do I find these at the library?"

reference shelves   nonfiction shelves   Readers' Guide   vertical files   CD-ROM

WHERE CAN I FIND WHAT I NEED IN THE LIBRARY?

Libraries vary, but most include five main areas: fiction, nonfiction, biography, reference, and periodicals (magazines and newspapers). Knowing which materials are kept in each of these areas can help you find what you need among the open shelves or in the stacks (additional shelves, not always open to the public). For extra help, ask at the librarian's desk.

The library offers a variety of information sources that can be used for many different writing tasks from magazine articles to music reviews, as shown in the chart that follows:

ASSIGNMENT	▶ INFORMATION SOURCES IN THE LIBRARY
essay about a famous person	biographies and autobiographies, encyclopedias and almanacs, periodical articles, biographical dictionaries, interviews on video
comparison and contrast of characters in novels	fiction, literary criticism in periodicals, literary reference work
research report about a scientific discovery	encyclopedias and special dictionaries, nonfiction books, articles in periodicals, almanacs, vertical file, documentaries on video
short story set in an ancient culture	nonfiction books about the culture, historical atlases, encyclopedias, slides of ancient art and architecture
essay about the origin of a word	specialized dictionaries, books about language history
review of a music group's new compact disk	periodicals, CD and listening equipment, music encyclopedias

TOOLS FOR USING THE LIBRARY

Libraries use special shelving systems to organize their materials so they can be located easily. A library catalog is the key to these shelving systems.

Library Catalogs

The library catalog lists every book in the library and gives you the information you need to locate it. You can look for a book in the catalog by its title, author, or subject. If it doesn't appear under any of these categories, the library does not have it. In some libraries, you will use a card catalog—a set of index cards filed in drawers. In other libraries, you will find the same information in book form or on microfiche (small film cards that contain a number of reduced entries), or you can access the catalog by computer.

THE CARD CATALOG The drawers in a card catalog are arranged alphabetically, top to bottom and left to right. Each index card in the drawers lists a book you can find in the library. On the top line of each card is a call number telling where to locate the book on the open shelves or in the stacks. On the next line is the title, author, or subject, depending on the type of card.

TRY THIS

Browse through the subject cards in the catalog when you want to explore a topic. The librarian can tell you which heading your topic is listed under.

You would find this **subject card** under S for *Space*.

523.46 C	call number
Space probes	subject
Cooper, Henry S.	author
Imaging Saturn: The Voyager Flights to Saturn,	title
New York: Holt, Rinehart and Winston,	publisher
1983	
248 p.; ill; 24 cm.	number of pages, size of book

You are likely to find many cards under each subject heading. Note that a subject card tells the date of publication, whether the book is illustrated, and how many pages it contains. Some subject cards also briefly describe the books' contents.

This is an **author card**. You would find it under C for *Cooper*.

523.46 C
Cooper, Henry S.
Imaging Saturn: The Voyager Flights to Saturn,
New York: Holt, Rinehart and Winston, 1983
248 p.; ill; 24 cm.

You might find several cards under the same author's name, each listing a different title. Scanning these listings can give you clues to an author's areas of expertise.

This is a **title card**. You would find it under *I* for *Imaging*.

523.46 C

Imaging Saturn: The Voyager Flights to Saturn,

Henry S. Cooper
New York: Holt, Rinehart and Winston, 1983
248 p.; ill; 24 cm.

If your library has its catalogs on microfiche, look for stands holding microfiche cards in alphabetical order.

THE COMPUTER CATALOG Like a card catalog, a computer catalog lists books by subject, by author, or by title. Using a computer, however, can simplify your search since the computer can locate a title even if you do not remember it correctly or recall only part of it. The computer can locate an author even if you misspell the name, and it can suggest other subject headings for the topics you are investigating.

This is a typical **computer-catalog search** query screen:

```
26 FEB 94          CENTRAL LIBRARY          4:00 pm

         FOR ASSISTANCE ASK ANY STAFF MEMBER
              Select one of the options below:

              1. Look for TITLE
              2. Look for WORD(s) in TITLE
              3. Look for AUTHOR or NAME
              4. Look for WORD(s) in NAME
              5. Look for SUBJECTS
              6. Look for WORD(s) in SUBJECTS

       Enter your selection (1-6) and press<RETURN>: 5
```

A computer list of options, **a menu**, lets you choose your means of search: title, author, or subject. If you wanted this computer to do a subject search, you would press the numeral 5 and then the <RETURN> key.

This is a typical **subject-search** query screen:

```
26 FEB 94          CENTRAL LIBRARY              4:01 pm

            FOR ASSISTANCE ASK ANY STAFF MEMBER

   SUBJECT SEARCH   Enter the subject you are inter-
                    ested in. Then press <RETURN>.
                    Proper capitalization and
                    punctuation are NOT required.

       EXAMPLES:    history american
                    IMPRESSIONISM in Art

      Enter SUBJECT:  VOYAGER SPACE PROBES
```

If you don't know the subject heading, type relevant key words. With each screen, your search narrows toward the book you want.

This is a typical screen for a **single book:**

```
26 FEB 94          CENTRAL LIBRARY              4:05 pm

Call Number        523.46 C              Status: available

AUTHOR             Cooper, Henry S.

TITLE              Imaging Saturn: the Voyager flights
                   to Saturn/Henry S. Cooper

PUBLISHER          New York: Holt, Rinehart Winston, 1983

DESCRIPTION        248 p.; ill; 24 cm.
```

The status of a book shows whether the book is currently in the library. This information is not obtainable from card or book catalogs.

HOW CAN I FIND A BOOK FROM THE SHELVES?

Knowing your library's numerical classification system can help you go from the catalog right to the place where the book is kept.

CLASSIFICATION SYSTEMS

There are two library classification systems: Dewey Decimal and Library of Congress. Most school and public libraries use the Dewey Decimal System. University libraries and other large libraries use the Library of Congress System.

The Dewey Decimal System organizes nonfiction books by general content into ten numerical categories. (Fiction books are generally shelved separately in alphabetical order by the author's last name.) These ten categories are then divided into subcategories. Categories and their subcategories have related numbers. For example, 700 indicates the broad category of art; under it, 730 is the subcategory for sculpture. All nonfiction books about sculpture have call numbers in the 730's. In the area where the 730's are shelved, books with the same call number are alphabetized by author.

The Library of Congress (LC) System uses twenty-one major categories indicated by letters of the alphabet. Subcategories are shown by secondary letters and numbers so that no two books have the same call number. For example, *P* is the major category of language and literature. *PS* is American literature, and *Collected Works* by the early American poet Phillis Wheatley is PS 866.W5.

In the Dewey Decimal System	In the Library of Congress System
• fiction is separate from nonfiction.	• an author's fictional works are shelved along with nonfiction books about that author's life and work.
• biographies are shelved alphabetically by the last name of the person the book is about. For example, biographies of astronaut Sally Ride are shelved under *R*.	• biographies are shelved in the category in which the person earned a reputation. Biographies of astronaut Sally Ride are shelved with other books about space flight.

USING CALL NUMBERS

Call numbers identify individual books. In each catalog listing, the call number is in the upper right corner of the card or computer screen. The same call number is also on the spine of each book. This number signals the area of the library where the book is located.

HOW CAN I FIND SMALL BITS OF INFORMATION?

THE REFERENCE SHELVES

You probably know that the reference area houses dictionaries, encyclopedias, atlases, almanacs, and other information sources. Some of these resources will be available in book form, some on CD-ROM, and some in both formats. The chart that follows lists some very useful reference works that you can find in many library reference sections:

TYPE OF SOURCE	EXAMPLES
Dictionaries	■ Oxford English Dictionary (20 volumes) ■ Random House Unabridged Dictionary, Newly Revised and Updated, 1993
Specialized Dictionaries	■ Grove's Dictionary of Music ■ Roget's International Thesaurus ■ The Slang Dictionary
Encyclopedias	■ Encyclopaedia Britannica ■ The World Book Encyclopedia ■ Encarta (on CD-ROM)
Specialized Encyclopedias	■ Encyclopedia of Science and Technology ■ Larousse Encyclopedia of Mythology ■ Cassell's Encyclopedia of World Literature
Biographical and Other Literary References	■ Contemporary Authors ■ Dictionary of American Biography ■ The International Who's Who ■ Webster's Biographical Dictionary ■ The Oxford Companion to American Literature ■ Bartlett's Familiar Quotations ■ Granger's Index to Poetry (available on CD-ROM)
Almanacs and Atlases	■ Information Please Almanac ■ World Almanac and Book of Facts ■ Hammond Ambassador World Atlas ■ Cambridge Atlas of Astronomy

TRY THIS

Try creating a word web with your subject at the center. This brainstorming strategy may help you find the heading you need.

VERTICAL FILES

Vertical files are cabinets containing short, current items such as magazine and newspaper clippings, pamphlets, and brochures. Because their irregular shapes make them difficult to shelve, these items are kept in file folders alphabetized by subject. When consulting these files, be creative in your pursuit of subject headings. For example, information about recycling programs in schools may be under ecology, environment, or schools. The more headings you look under, the better your chances of finding material on your topic.

PERIODICALS: MAGAZINES AND NEWSPAPERS

Periodicals are sources of new information from around the world. They are usually more up-to-date than books. If you want the latest research on cholesterol, a periodical article, not a book, is where to find it. At the same time, back issues of periodicals are like windows on history. They show what daily life was like years ago and how what we know and use has changed and evolved. If you wonder what the first computers looked like, for example, look at photographs in the back issues of magazines from the 1950's.

Periodical Indexes

Specialized periodical indexes give you lists of articles in particular subject areas. For example, the *MLA* (Modern Language Association) *Index* itemizes thousands of articles on literature and languages, and the *General Science Index* gives articles from more than one hundred science periodicals. *The New York Times Index*, which goes back over a century, and the *Wall Street Journal Index* list articles from those newspapers.

The Readers' Guide The *Readers' Guide to Periodical Literature*, a multivolume work updated every two weeks, lists articles from about 250 magazines and is the most widely used periodical index. As in most other periodical indexes, articles are listed by subject or by author.

This is a **subject entry:**

subject heading

article, author, illustrated magazine, magazine title, volume number, page numbers, month, year

SPACE FLIGHT
See also
Voyager flights

To the edge. K. Croswell. il *Astronomy* 20:34–41 My '92

Notice the *See also* reference included in the subject entry. Under this additional heading, you may find other relevant articles.

VOYAGER FLIGHTS

Coreless Uranus and Neptune [Voyager 2 data: work of William B. Hubbard] il *Sky and Telescope* 83:251 Mr '92

Neptune's arcs ring true [analysis of Voyager 2 data by Carolyn C. Porco] il *Sky and Telescope* 83:127 F '92

Bracketed material summarizes article.

This is an **author entry:**

LEAVY, WALTER 1940–

Lt. Col. Guion S. Bluford Jr. takes a historic step into outer space. il pors *Ebony* 39:162–4+ N '83

author

article title, illustrated portraits, title of periodical, volume number, page numbers, + shows article continues on later pages, issue date

Notice that *Readers' Guide* entries use abbreviations to save space. The following abbreviations stand for the months of the year: Ja, F, Mr, Ap, My, Je, Jl, Ag, S, O, N, D.

How to Find an Article Listed in the *Readers' Guide* First, find out if your library carries the periodical that contains the article by consulting your library's periodical catalog. Like the book catalog, this listing may be computerized, on microfiche, or on cards. If your library does have the periodical, you may find recent issues shelved in the periodical area.

Back issues of periodicals may be bound by volume or recorded on microfilm and kept in storage areas. If they are on microfilm, you will be directed to a microfilm reader, which magnifies the film and shows it on a viewing screen. If you need to copy an article, some microfilm readers have built-in copying mechanisms.

If your library does not have a periodical you need, the librarian may be able to order a copy of the article through an interlibrary loan service.

AUDIOVISUAL MATERIALS

The audiovisual section of the library may contain filmstrips, slides, videos, photographs, fine art prints, audiocassette tapes, recordings, and CDs.

TRY THIS

Before you request a magazine issue through interlibrary loan, check to see if the article is not available on disk. Most libraries also have large circulating collections of videos, many of them on nonfiction subjects.

For more information about library audiovisual materials, see p. 426.

269

RESEARCH:
TECHNOLOGICAL RESOURCES

How can technology help me find and use information?

How would you like to see inside a living human body? What would an orchestra have sounded like in Mozart's time? How would you like to watch the birth and death of a mountain range, a star, or a hurricane—all in a minute's time? With the appropriate information and technology, you can do all these things right now. The following chart shows some of the resources available to researchers and writers today:

Audio Resources These include audiocassette tapes, compact disks (CDs), and records.	Examples include recordings of live concerts; speeches; instructions for learning foreign languages; and stories and music from cultures around the world.
Visual Resources These include photos and prints, slides, and filmstrips.	Examples include fine art prints of masterpieces from museums and slides of cells, molecules, and atoms photographed through microscopes.
Audiovisual Resources These include films and videotapes.	Examples include filmstrips on scientific and historical topics; videotapes of plays; and videotapes of authors reading their works.
Microform Resources These include **microfilm** (a strip of film) and **microfiche** (card-shaped pieces of film) with reduced images of pages from newspapers, magazines, catalogs, and indexes.	Examples include newspapers, magazines, catalogs, and indexes.
Computer Resources These include **software** (sets of electronic codes that direct computers to do tasks), **online services** (a network for computer users that offers information and search services), and **CD-ROM** (compact disks that can hold whole **databases**—collections of information).	Examples include writing, graphics, and educational computer programs; online encyclopedias and reference works; and interactive, multimedia CD-ROM programs.

Schools and libraries have many technological resources. Ask a librarian to show you what is available. Many students will also do some research at home. Whole libraries can now be accessed with a simple voice command or the touch of a finger.

USING COMPUTERS AND COMPUTER SOFTWARE

The computers you're most likely to use are **personal computers:** portable or semiportable units with a **keyboard** and a **monitor** (the screen on which words and graphics are displayed). Some portable computers are also equipped with a **mouse** (a hand-held selector for giving the computer commands), a **printer** (for creating a paper printout, or **hard copy,** of whatever is input into the computer), and a **modem** (a device that connects one computer to others via telephone lines).

Computers operate by using software that tells the computer what to do. Here are some types of software:

WORD PROCESSING Word processing programs are powerful writing tools that allow you to key in your work and then edit it, moving around or deleting words, sentences, and paragraphs. You can also create different versions of your work, print them in several formats, and keep what you wish on a **floppy disk,** a $3\frac{1}{2}$ or $5\frac{1}{4}$ inch square magnetic device for storing data. Some programs can help check spelling and grammar, choose a synonym, or verify a word definition.

GRAPHICS As monitors improve in color and detail, and graphics programs become more sophisticated, you will be able to use increasingly complex graphic images on a computer. At present, graphics software is available, for example, to explore the inner workings of the human heart, design a new subway system, or create animated cartoons.

DESKTOP PUBLISHING With these programs you can "publish" your own professional-quality material, creating posters, newsletters, and brochures, and designing books and magazines.

EDUCATIONAL PURPOSES New software programs can teach you just about anything. Many programs display several "windows" of information (text, graphics, and an index, for instance) at the same time; they also define unfamiliar words and point you to related books and articles.

REFERENCE Programs for dictionaries, encyclopedias, and almanacs are easy and fun to use. For instance, if you don't know how to spell a word but know what it means, you can call it up by its definition.

USING CD-ROM RESOURCES

Compact disks—the small plastic disks that make music sound clean and crisp—are also useful for storing information. By converting digitized information into minute patterns of ridges and grooves, one CD-ROM disk can store up to 275,000 double-spaced typed pages!

CD-ROM These disks are similar to the floppy disks you insert in a personal computer, with one important exception: You can't add or delete information stored on many CD-ROM disks. (CD-ROM stands for Compact Disk-Read Only Memory, which means you can only read information on a CD-ROM; you can't change it.) Programs on CD-ROM are versatile, offering a sophisticated mix of text, graphics, sound, and motion pictures. One program, for instance, might explore the Brazilian rain forest through maps, text, recordings of bird calls, and moving color images of rare and endangered species.

Here is a sample of the types of materials now available on CD-ROM: *Facts on File News Digest* contains information about current events in the United States from 1980 to the present; *USA Factbook* is a computerized almanac of the United States, with state-by-state information about population, geography, and politics; *County and City Statistics Compendium* contains the most recent census data; *Consumers Reference Disc* contains evaluations of American-made products and information and advice about travel, jobs, food, and health; *Image Gallery* contains graphics in a variety of categories, including sports, travel, fashion, and people; and *Languages of the World* contains translations and definitions of words in more than a dozen languages.

USING ONLINE RESOURCES

By using a modem to link your personal computer to data stored in more powerful computers elsewhere, you can vastly increase your access to information. This type of data access is called **"online,"** as you are using telephone lines to link two computers.

If your library subscribes to online services, you can tap into **databases** (computerized information banks containing reference materials, newspaper and magazine articles, and information on weather, travel, and entertainment). Online services at home enable you to access special message systems called **electronic mail** (or **E-mail**) to communicate directly with others across the country. These informal networking systems are a good way to make friends and trade information.

Most online services charge a fee, and you must also pay for the time you spend on the phone. Your local library may also charge a fee; however, the charge may be as low as a few dollars.

Here is what you can access with three popular online services:

CompuServe:	news, weather, sports, games, entertainment, and travel, as well as E-mail and "discussion groups" about hobbies and special interests
Prodigy:	"bank-by-computer," online shopping services, information about travel and education, E-mail, and public "bulletin boards" about topics such as food, money, and travel
America Online:	shopping, news, computer games with color displays and sound, education information, "discussion groups," and E-mail

◆ WHEN YOU SEARCH ◆

If you decide to try an online search, the right strategy can save you time—and money. Follow these tips:

■ **Narrow your topic.** Instead of starting out with a broad category like "endangered species," narrow it to a specific topic line like "white tigers in Tibet and Nepal."

■ **Pick your key words and phrases carefully.** For example, if you want information about teenagers who run their own businesses, you might need to search under "young entrepreneurs" rather than "teenage business owners."

■ **Select the right database.** Ask your librarian to find you a description of the database you would like to use. For instance, if you're searching for articles about turn-of-the-century baseball teams, it would be a waste of time to consult a sports database specializing in current information.

ELECTRONIC NEWSPAPERS

Try to imagine it: no more ink on your hands, no papers piling up in your living room, no early-morning thump outside your door or brisk walk to the newsstand. Newspapers are going online. Several national online services offer up-to-date editions of national papers like the *Chicago Tribune*, and many smaller newspapers have their own online services delivering electronic papers to subscribers.

Electronic newspapers offer options that standard papers cannot. For example, articles on a specific topic are easier to find: Just enter a key word or phrase, such as "Chicago Cubs," hit the search key, and, presto, the article appears! You may also be able to find related stories that ran in earlier editions simply by punching in a command. Some services also let you send electronic messages to reporters and editors.

WHAT'S IN STORE FOR THE FUTURE?

Computer technology is changing so quickly that it's impossible to keep up with all the new developments. Not many years ago compact disks didn't even exist, and now it's hard to find a record in a music store. Likewise CD-ROMs are evolving so rapidly that even your library may be hard-pressed to keep up with what's available.

It's always risky to predict which innovations will last and which will be replaced. However, here's a list of new technological resources that seem—at least for the moment—to have a promising future:

INTERACTIVE TV By combining computers, video, and storage technology such as CD-ROMs, TV is being transformed into a tool for active learning. Soon you may be able to sit in your living room and participate in an electronic roundtable about, for example, the problems of health care, or the intricacies of composing a poem. Rather than sitting back and passively taking in information, you'll become an active participant, stopping to ask questions, probing for a deeper level of meaning, pausing to watch films or flip through charts or photographs related to your subject.

THREE-DIMENSIONAL DISPLAYS Some companies are marketing CD-ROM graphics that can be seen in three dimensions with the aid of special glasses. The technology has practical applications; anatomy students, for instance, can study three-dimensional renderings of the human body that are far more realistic than the typical two-dimensional illustrations in textbooks.

VIRTUAL REALITY Developed to aid pilots and astronauts in navigating their craft, virtual-reality technology has educational applications. By donning special masks or gloves, students can "enter" scenes on a video screen and "walk around" as if they were actually transported to the place they see. For example, students studying the culture of the Mayas could "roam through" an archeological dig of an ancient temple.

The future is sure to bring new technologies that will make it easier for you to communicate with others around the world. Having grown up with technology, you will be in a position to use these new resources wisely and efficiently.

270

STUDY SKILLS: GENERAL STUDY SKILLS

How can I study more effectively?

Do you remember how, when you were younger, time seemed to go on forever? As you get older, time appears to shrink. To fit your studying into your "shrinking" time, you need to develop effective study habits. There are four factors you should consider when you evaluate your study habits: time, place, materials, and techniques.

TIME

When you get an assignment that is due in a month, the deadline may seem far away. However, without a plan, days may go by without progress. To prevent last-minute panic, try to develop a useful study plan based on your own habits and the schedule. Begin by discovering how you actually spend your time .

1. Keep a journal or log for a week, including the weekend, to record how you use your time. Look for periods of time when you were doing nothing useful or enjoyable that could become study time.

2. Determine the time of day that you study most effectively. Are you most alert early in the day or late in the evening? Try to arrange to study during your strongest hours.

3. Decide whether you prefer to study in short spurts or long blocks of time. If your deadlines permit a choice, often you can choose to do assignments in several short periods or one long study session.

4. Use the information you've compiled to make a study schedule. You can use a daily planner or notebook. As you finish each assignment, write down the date completed.

MODEL

Tuesday February 3

7 a.m. Study hall: finish preparation for history test

8 a.m. History test

9 a.m. Memorize verbs for Spanish

10 a.m. Begin research paper on medicines from the Amazon

11 a.m. Math homework

You can also use or create a monthly or weekly calendar in which you record assignments, due dates, and test dates. That way, you will be able to plan your study time in advance.

MODEL

Monday, February 2
Due: Science paper, Mar. 6

Tuesday, February 3
History test

Wednesday, February 4
Math quiz

Thursday, February 5
Present music project

Friday, February 6
Due: English paper, Mar. 8

Saturday, February 7

Sunday, February 8

PLACE

Where you study often matters as much as when you study. Some people can shut out the world when they open a book; others need absolute quiet to concentrate. Determine your study needs by asking yourself these questions:

- **Do I need quiet to focus on my work?** If so, find a secluded area, a room or a table, at home, in study hall, or at the library.

- **How much space do I need?** If you need several books or supplies for an assignment, arrange to work in a space where you can spread out. Planning ahead will help you have on hand what you need.

- **How can I study comfortably?** Sitting in a chair at a desk or table allows easy access to books and materials. If you are reading a longer work that doesn't require much note-taking, try an armchair.

MATERIALS

Supplies you'll need for studying include the following:

NOTEBOOK OR PLANNER These help keep track of assignments.

WRITING TOOLS Use a pencil for work that may need to be erased or changed. Use a pen for formal drafts, unless your teacher requires typewritten work. Typewriters, word processors, and personal computers are useful tools for writing, but they are not essential.

PAPER Keep lined paper for written assignments and note-taking. Use unlined paper for making sketches and for typing. If you use note cards in research projects, have a supply on hand.

BOOKS The following books are helpful resources: a dictionary, for looking up unfamiliar words; a thesaurus, for finding synonyms and antonyms; encyclopedias, for doing research.

ADEQUATE LIGHT Poor lighting is hard on the eyes and makes it difficult to concentrate. A desk lamp focuses light where needed.

CLOCK A clock or watch will help you keep track of the time you spend on assignments.

MISCELLANEOUS ITEMS These items may be useful: pocket calculator, ruler, highlighting marker, pencil sharpener, eraser, correction fluid, paper clips, stapler, tape, scissors. If you find it useful and your teacher allows it, you might use a tape recorder to tape lectures.

Two items you *don't* need while studying are a telephone and a television.

TECHNIQUES

Here are several techniques that can streamline studying:

CLARIFY THE SCOPE AND PURPOSE OF ASSIGNMENTS. Make sure you know what to do and when it must be done. If you have questions or doubts, discuss them with your teacher.

PRIORITIZE ASSIGNMENTS. Consider doing the most challenging work first, while you are most alert. However, be sure you leave time to get to assignments that are due the next day.

DETERMINE YOUR STUDY STYLE. If you retain information better by visualizing it, use graphic aids such as maps, timelines, charts, and graphs to help you study. If you remember best when you hear information, use tape-recorded lectures and listen to your tapes to refresh your memory.

GATHER YOUR MATERIALS. Before you sit down for an uninterrupted study session, gather everything you will need. It will break your concentration if you have to get up for a pen or a book.

TAKE OCCASIONAL BREAKS. Studying too long without a break is tiring. Get up and move around for a while—but set a definite time limit for your breaks.

WORK WITH OTHERS. It may be helpful to set up a study group for some assignments. You can also have a friend or family member ask you questions, listen to summaries of what you've learned, or read and react to your drafts.

271

STUDY SKILLS: READING SKILLS

How can I better understand what I read?

If you find yourself faced with a weekend of heavy-duty assignments that require a lot of reading, you may feel like the mythological Greek character Sisyphus who pushed a huge boulder up a mountain over and over, only to see it roll back down again each time. Knowing the most effective way to approach each reading assignment can make your task much easier. Unlike Sisyphus, you can get to the top of a mountain of schoolwork—and stay there.

READING TECHNIQUES

Before you begin reading any material, consider your purpose for reading. If you need to read quickly, there are two techniques you can use: **skimming** and **scanning**. For a thorough understanding, you can use the **in-depth, sustained reading** technique.

SKIMMING When you skim a text, you look it over quickly to get a sense of its contents. Look for highlighted or bold type, headings, and topic sentences. For example, you might skim a biography to see whether it includes information you need for a biographical sketch.

SCANNING When you scan a text, you look it over to find specific information. Look for words related to your topic or purpose for reading. You might scan a science textbook, for instance, to find information on arthropods for a research paper.

IN-DEPTH, SUSTAINED READING When you use this technique, you ask yourself questions about the material and read for the answers. As you read, evaluate and respond to the ideas in the text. This is the technique you would use to read a story, novel, or poem as you prepare to write a response-to-literature essay.

READING NONFICTION

Much of the reading you do—except the literature you read for English class and for your own pleasure—is nonfiction. Everything from encyclopedias to car repair manuals to your science and social studies textbooks falls into the category of nonfiction. There are two helpful strategies for reading nonfiction: **KWL** and **SQ3R.**

KWL This stands for *What I Know, What I Want to Know, What I Have Learned*. To use this technique, create a chart like the one shown here.

Fill in the *What I Know* and *What I Want to Know* sections before you begin to read. The information you list in both columns will show you the gaps in your knowledge and help you focus your reading. After you finish reading, write what you have learned in the third column.

PATAGONIA

What I Know	What I Want to Know	What I Have Learned
It's located somewhere in South America.	Where exactly is it, and what are the terrain and climate like?	It's part of both Argentina and Chile. It's a dry, cold, windy plateau.
It's sparsely populated.	Who lives there?	Some of the original inhabitants were known as the Patagonian Giants. Later it was settled by Argentines and Chileans.

SQ3R This stands for *Survey, Question, Read, Record, Review*. This technique is especially useful if you are reading about an unfamiliar topic or if you are researching a specific topic. Follow these steps in SQ3R:

    1. Survey. Skim and scan your text to familiarize yourself with its contents. Notice titles, headings, and any highlighting such as bold type, colored print, or large type. Read the table of contents and scan the index for entries related to your topic.

    2. Question. Ask questions about the material. If a chapter lists questions at the end, preview them. Look at any graphic aids such as charts, graphs, or maps and chapter and section titles. Use all of these features to develop questions about your topic. If you are making a KWL chart, list your questions under *What I Want to Know*.

    3. Read. Read carefully and look for information that answers your questions. Notice key terms, main ideas, and important relationships.

For more information on taking notes, see p. 217 and p. 417.

4. Record. Take notes on main ideas, key terms, and definitions. Copy important dates and names. Write answers to your questions. On a KWL chart, write the answers under *What I Have Learned.*

5. Review. Look over your notes to be sure they are complete. Fill in any gaps by scanning the material for specific information. Summarize what you have learned from the material. This process will help you understand and retain the information.

With some reading assignments, you can take SQ3R a step further. You can make inferences, or educated guesses, about what you have read. For example, if you read in a history text that the original inhabitants of Patagonia were Native Americans and later learned that the present-day inhabitants of Patagonia are predominately Chileans and Argentines of European descent, you might infer that the European settlers deliberately displaced the original inhabitants.

TRY THIS

Organizing information visually can help you understand relationships among ideas in a text. Try using graphic aids such as a timeline to track the chronology of events, a cause-and-effect chart to relate causes and effects, a classification frame to identify categories, or a compare-and-contrast chart to analyze what you read.

READING FICTION AND POETRY

Reading fiction and poetry involves using your imagination and responding to the work on a personal level. Using the following six techniques will help you to broaden your understanding and enhance your appreciation of the work. Use the techniques that work best for you.

PREDICT. As you read fiction, think about what might happen next and why the events you predict might occur. Then check your predictions against actual events.

VISUALIZE. Try to picture the characters, setting, and action of a fictional work as if you were watching a movie in your mind.

MAKE PERSONAL CONNECTIONS. Your own experience can help you understand what you are reading. Look for connections between people and events in your own life and those in the poem or fictional work.

READ ALOUD. This technique is especially valuable for poetry, which depends on sound and rhythm for its effects. However, you might also try reading aloud passages from fiction to get a better sense of the dialogue or the author's voice.

ANALYZE. Look closely at the choices the author has made. Think about why he or she chose a particular poetic form or a certain setting and plot. Then think about the effect each choice has on the work.

RESPOND. As you read, probe your feelings about the characters and their actions. Afterward, think about what the work means to you and how it has affected you. Analyze your responses to be sure you understand the work's effect on you and the reasons for that effect.

For more on responding to literature, see p. 198.

DETECTING LOGICAL FALLACIES

An important reading and listening skill is the ability to detect **logical fallacies,** statements that sound reasonable but really aren't. Here are the main types of logical fallacies.

OVERGENERALIZATION An **overgeneralization** is an all-inclusive statement that can't be true. The following words often indicate that an overgeneralization is being made: *everybody, nobody, always, never.*

Example: "But everybody is going to the party!"

What's wrong? This statement is an overgeneralization because obviously not *everyone* is going to the party. Someone, somewhere, is doing something else.

CIRCULAR REASONING **Circular reasoning** is the attempt to support an argument by restating it in other words.

Example: Passenger-side airbags in cars are necessary because it is important to have an airbag on the passenger's side.

What's wrong? The reason does not prove the argument—it simply echoes it, resulting in a circular argument.

EITHER/OR ARGUMENT An **either/or argument** is an extreme statement that allows for only two possibilities.

Example: Either I get the lead role, or I might as well forget about an acting career.

What's wrong? There are usually other possibilities. An either/or statement is usually too extreme.

QUESTIONABLE CAUSE-AND-EFFECT STATEMENT A **questionable cause-and-effect statement** gives a cause that did not necessarily result in the stated effect.

Example: My opponent voted to raise the minimum wage. Because of this, your taxes went up five percent!

What's wrong? The effect of raised taxes could have resulted from a number of other causes; it was not necessarily a result of the increase in the minimum wage.

STUDY SKILLS:
READING GRAPHIC AIDS

 How do I interpret information in graphic aids?

A **graphic aid** is a picture that presents organized information.

You'll find most graphic aids in nonfiction sources—reference books, newspapers, magazines, and textbooks. If you know how to create and interpret these graphic tools, you'll be able to select and incorporate appropriate information into your own writing. Follow these steps when reading any graphic aid:

IDENTIFY THE FORM. Is it a chart, a graph, a timeline, or a flow-chart? When you recognize the form, you will be able to interpret the information easily and quickly.

READ THE TITLES AND SUBTITLES. The title will tell you what information the graphic aid is presenting. The subtitles or subheads label the categories of information and the relationships among these categories.

DECODE SYMBOLS. Usually a key or footnote explains the meaning of each symbol.

INTERPRET THE INFORMATION. Once you understand the form, topic, and symbols in a graphic aid, you can use this knowledge to compare and contrast, make predictions, see parts of a whole, understand a process, or interpret an event or series of events.

READING A CHART OR TABLE

Tables and **charts** present information in several categories. They are organized into columns and rows that are clearly labeled. Look down the side column or across the top row until you find the label you need.

Vitamin Sources and Functions

Vitamin	Source	Function	Deficiency Disease
A	green and yellow vegetables, milk	promotes bone growth and vision	night blindness
B₁	grains, liver, legumes	metabolizes carbohydrates	beriberi
C	citrus fruits, potatoes, tomatoes	aids immunity, helps connective tissue growth	scurvy
D	milk, yeast	regulates bone formation	rickets, bowlegs

READING A GRAPH

A **graph** presents facts and figures, usually in numerical form. You can use graphs to compare and contrast, to predict trends, and to show changes over time. There are four main types of **graphs: circle graphs (or pie charts), line graphs, bar graphs,** and **picture graphs.**

CIRCLE GRAPHS A circle graph shows parts of a whole, represented by a circle which is divided into sections. Each section represents a percentage of the whole, 100 percent. To read a circle graph, look at each portion of the circle and compare it to other portions. This circle graph shows projected income from the 1996 Olympic games.

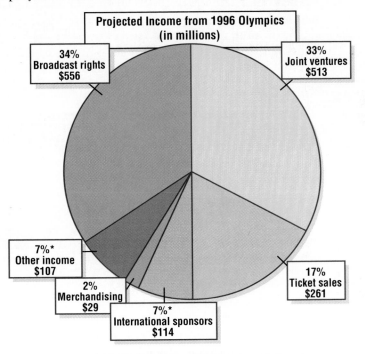

Projected Income from 1996 Olympics (in millions)

34% Broadcast rights $556

33% Joint ventures $513

7%* Other income $107

2% Merchandising $29

7%* International sponsors $114

17% Ticket sales $261

*Percentages have been rounded to the nearest whole number.

LINE GRAPHS Line graphs show change or movement over time. They are divided into a vertical (up-and-down) axis and a horizontal (side-to-side) axis. The vertical axis usually shows the **dependent variable**—the information that is being measured. The horizontal axis usually shows the **independent variable**—often a measurement of time. When you want to find specific information on a line graph, note where the two variables intersect. To read a trend or movement, look at the direction the line takes. An upward direction indicates an increase; a downward direction, a decrease. After looking at the graph on p. 440, what can you say about the child mortality rate in developing nations?

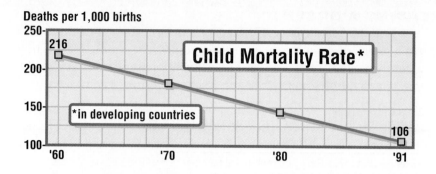

Deaths per 1,000 births

Child Mortality Rate*

*in developing countries

216 ... 106

'60 '70 '80 '91

BAR GRAPHS A bar graph shows changes over time or compares and contrasts information. Like a line graph, a bar graph is formed along a vertical axis and a horizontal axis. One axis shows the subjects being measured. The other axis lists numbers. Look at the height or length of each bar. Compare these heights or lengths to reveal differences and similarities among subjects or to see changes over time. This bar graph contrasts the profits of original movies with the profits of their sequels.

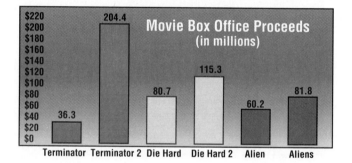

Movie Box Office Proceeds
(in millions)

$220 $200 $180 $160 $140 $120 $100 $80 $60 $40 $20 $0

204.4 115.3 80.7 60.2 81.8 36.3

Terminator Terminator 2 Die Hard Die Hard 2 Alien Aliens

PICTURE GRAPHS Like a bar graph, line graph, or circle graph, a picture graph presents information. However, in a picture graph, pictures replace bars, lines, or sections of the circle. Picture graphs are interesting to look at and easy to read. This picture graph shows why people spy.

What makes people spy?

Money	52.2%
Ideology	18.3%
Anger/Revenge	14.8%
Pleasing Someone	8.7%
Blackmail	3.5%
Thrills/Self-Importance	2.6%

READING A TIMELINE

A **timeline** is a line on which points, representing dates, have been placed in chronological order. A timeline can represent millennia, centuries, decades, or even a single day. Look to the left of the line for the earliest event. Then read from left to right. To find a specific event on the line, read until you locate the information you seek. This time-line shows record times for the mile run from 1864 to 1979.

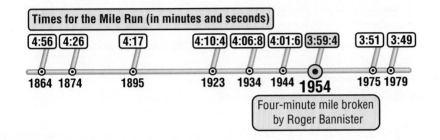

READING A FLOWCHART

A **flowchart** is a diagram that illustrates the steps in a process. Instructions or steps are written in boxes or circles. They are linked with arrows that show the direction in which the process flows. Arrows also can indicate alternate steps or directions the process includes. To read a flowchart, locate the start of the process. Then follow the arrows from one step to the next. This flowchart shows the process of making and recycling paper.

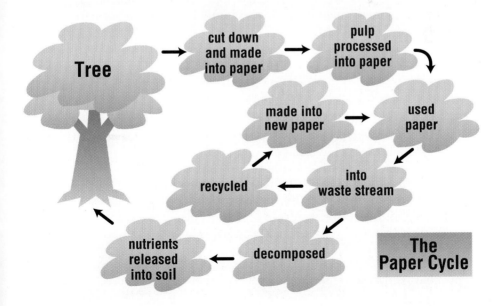

? *How can I improve my performance on tests?*

When you hear the word *test,* do you freeze like the person in this cartoon, panicked into forgetting everything you ever knew? It doesn't have to be that way. Just as you have learned how to meet other challenges in your life—like sports competitions, auditions, or job interviews—you can learn how to take tests. (By the way, the answers to the questions in the cartoon are 10.9444444, Lincoln, and William Henry Harrison.)

GLASBERGEN

The following is a test from the Emergency Broadcasting System: What is 197 divided by 18? What is the capital of Nebraska? Who was the ninth President of the United States?

TAKING CLASSROOM TESTS

Teachers use classroom tests to assess your knowledge of the subject matter covered in your school courses. The following strategies will help you perform better on classroom tests, whether they call for a choice among given items, a short written answer, or a multiparagraph essay.

1. Allow yourself several days to study for the test. Trying to cover everything the night before the test will only hurt your performance by robbing you of sleep.

2. Predict what will be asked on the test. List the main topics, concepts, events, and so on, that the teacher has covered. Write some practice questions and answers for these topics. If you're working with a partner, read and discuss each other's practice questions and answers.

3. Identify key facts, dates, terms, and formulas. Write them down or repeat them until you have them memorized.

4. Review the test and then budget your time. Decide which sections of the test count for more points and spend more time on those. Do the easiest parts of the test first.

OBJECTIVE TESTS

Objective tests require a single, brief answer to each question. This chart shows strategies for answering types of objective questions:

QUESTION TYPE AND STRATEGY	EXAMPLE

True-False

Note all-inclusive words such as *always, every, all,* and *never,* which can make statements false by ignoring exceptions.

1. T(F)Since 1960 every presidential campaign has included debates. (False: There were no debates in 1964, 1968, or 1972.)

Look for qualifying words such as *many* and *sometimes,* which can make statements true by acknowledging exceptions.

2.(T)F Most successful presidential candidates once held elective office . (True: Not all presidential candidates held elected positions, but most did.)

Sentence Completion

The grammatical structure of the test item may give you a clue about the part of speech and form of the word to fill in.

1. *Personification* is a figure of speech that gives human attributes to nonhuman things. (The singular verb *is* suggests that a singular noun is needed.)

Multiple Choice

Look at every choice, since you may not pick the best one if you stop reading.

1. Which of the following elements can be found in all proteins?
A) oxygen   B) hydrogen
C) nitrogen   (D) all of these
(A is correct; so are B and C. Therefore, the best answer is D.)

Narrow your choices by eliminating answers that are obviously incorrect.

2. Every acid contains
(A) hydrogen   B) salt
C) a base   D) sulphur
(C and D are clearly wrong; B is also wrong. Only A is correct.)

Short Answer

Know exactly what is required— a phrase, a list, a sentence, a formula.

1. Name the countries of Hispaniola. (Just the names are required: Haiti and the Dominican Republic.)

ESSAY QUESTIONS

In answering essay questions, you need to compress your usual writing process. The following suggestions will help you answer questions in a limited period of time:

1. Budget time for each essay question on a test and for each stage of the writing process: prewriting/planning, writing, and revising/proofreading.

2. Be sure you understand exactly what is being asked of you. Underline key terms in the essay question such as *causes* or *effects*, *compare* or *contrast*, *define*, or *trace the process*.

- Are you analyzing a topic with several parts? Make sure you don't leave any part out.

- Have you been asked to explain how something developed over time? Make sure you cover the process from beginning to end.

- Are you comparing items? Devote equal space to each one.

Each type of essay question requires a different thought process, a different organization, even different transitional words.

3. Before you write, jot down any key information you need to remember: names, dates, and other facts. Make an outline to guide your writing.

4. As you write, consult your notes and follow your outline. Use transitional words that suit your purpose (for example, words like *at first*, *then*, and *finally* for tracing a process or tracking change).

5. Leave time for revising and proofreading. Add necessary information and improve your grammar, punctuation, and spelling.

TAKING STANDARDIZED TESTS

In any large bookstore you will see many books designed to help you do better on standardized tests, from the SSATs for admission to certain secondary schools up through GREs and CATs for entrance to graduate and medical schools. Whereas classroom tests assess your *specific* knowledge, standardized tests measure your *general* knowledge.

You may be preparing to take a standardized college entrance examination—perhaps the SAT (Scholastic Aptitude Test), which focuses on verbal and mathematical abilities or the ACT (American College Test), which focuses on English, mathematics, social studies, and natural science. To do better on standardized tests, use some of the techniques covered in this lesson, particularly tips for responding to multiple-choice and essay questions. Also, familiarize yourself with the format by reviewing previous tests.

READING-COMPREHENSION QUESTIONS

These questions require you to read a short passage and then answer questions about its content. The questions assess such reading skills as identifying the main idea, locating details, making inferences (informed guesses), and drawing conclusions.

Tips for Answering Reading-Comprehension Questions

1. Preview the questions before you read the passage.
2. As you read, mark the passage for important ideas and details.
3. Check the passage to confirm the accuracy of your answers.

Sample Reading-Comprehension Questions

Read this paragraph carefully. Then answer the questions.

William Shakespeare is England's greatest playwright; many believe that he is the foremost writer in English literature. However, even though he was famous in his own time, much of his early life is entirely unknown to us. His educational background is murky, and for a whole period of his life, about eight years, he disappeared from the public record. He left his home in Stratford and at some point became involved in the theater, for he surfaced years later as a well-established member of an acting company based in London. But how he got there—and why—has remained a mystery for almost four centuries.

1. The paragraph is mostly about
A. Shakespeare's greatness
B. the English theater
C. literature
D. Shakespeare's early life

2. From Shakespeare's disappearance, you can infer that during this time he
A. was banished
B. did little to attract attention
C. did not know how to read
D. was in France or Italy

VOCABULARY QUESTIONS

These questions assess your understanding of word meanings. You will usually be given a word and then asked to identify, from several choices, its closest **synonym** (word similar in meaning) or **antonym** (word opposite in meaning).

- Read the directions to determine whether a word similar or opposite in meaning is required. Often standardized tests include among their "trick" choices a synonym when an antonym is called for—and vice versa.

- Even if you don't recognize a word, use your knowledge of prefixes, suffixes, and roots to deduce its meaning.

Choose the word closest in meaning to the underlined word.

1. a <u>cerulean</u> cape
A. beautiful   Ⓑ blue
C. warm   D. old-fashioned

Choose the word opposite in meaning to the underlined word.

2. He was especially skillful at <u>prevaricating</u>.
A. writing   Ⓑ telling the truth
C. lying   D. public speaking

SENTENCE-COMPLETION QUESTIONS

Sometimes standardized vocabulary tests ask you to fill in blanks.

Tips for Sentence-Completion Items

- Use context clues—the meanings of the words around the missing words—to help you choose the missing word.
- Use grammatical structure to help you narrow choices: Is a singular or plural word called for? A noun or an adjective?

Sample Sentence-Completion Question

1. She had a difficult time _____ the _____ success of her first film.
     A. overcoming...fearful   B. recapture...surprising
     Ⓒ repeating...remarkable   D. undoing...prodigy

ANALOGY QUESTIONS

Analogies are comparisons that show relationships between ideas. An analogy question usually requires you to complete a sentence or equation based on two pairs of words.

Sample Analogy Questions

Here are three ways of posing the same analogy question.
Kiwi is to fruit as sedan is to <u>automobile</u>.
Kiwi→fruit : sedan→ <u>automobile</u>
Kiwi : fruit :: sedan : <u>automobile</u>
The question includes a pair of related terms, *kiwi* and *fruit*; a third term, *sedan*; and a blank. You must decide on the relationship between the first two terms and then find an answer that creates the same relationship with the third term. In this case, kiwi is a specific kind of fruit; a sedan is a specific kind of automobile.

Here are some relationships expressed in analogy questions:

- specific :: general (*Kiwi* is to *fruit* as *sedan* is to *automobile.*)
- performer :: action (*Chef* is to *cook* as *sculptor* is to *carve.*)
- part :: whole (*Keyboard* is to *computer* as *blade* is to *ax.*)
- time sequence (*Appetizer* is to *dessert* as *toddler* is to *adult.*)
- cause :: effect (*Tidal wave* is to *flood* as *bacteria* is to *infection.*)
- synonyms (*Congenial* is to *friendly* as *respectful* is to *polite.*)
- antonyms (*Penurious* is to *generosity* as *vindictive* is to *mercy.*)

Note that the words in the second pair must be the same parts of speech as their counterparts in the first pair, as in the last example:

Penurious (adjective) is to *generosity* (noun) as *vindictive* (adjective) is to *mercy* (noun).

GRAMMAR, USAGE, AND MECHANICS QUESTIONS

These items assess your knowledge of standard English by asking you to identify which underlined section of a passage contains errors.

- Look for mistakes in capitalization, punctuation, and spelling, as well as errors such as dangling modifiers or incorrect verb forms.
- Remember that some items are error-free. Before choosing the "No error" answer, however, read the passage several times.

WRITING ASSESSMENTS

Standardized writing assessments measure your ability to compose a paragraph or essay within a strict time limit in response to a writing prompt. The instructions usually ask you to write about your own experiences and observations rather than about facts and information. Most of the techniques for answering essay questions (page 443) apply here. In addition, keep the following strategies in mind:

1. Restate the topic, purpose, and audience specified in the instructions. If no audience is identified, assume that you are writing for the teachers who will be reading your response.

2. Put your prewriting notes on your answer sheet. If you do not finish your essay, the evaluators may be able to assess your response.

3. Wherever possible, use concrete, specific details that show exactly what you mean.

4. Remember that your writing will be evaluated according to the criteria on page 448.

- clear sense of purpose and audience

- strong personal voice

- coherent, easy-to-follow organization

- fluent sentence structure

- concrete, specific language

- command of standard English grammar, usage, and mechanics

Sample Writing Prompt

You have 50 minutes to write a response to the following prompt: Imagine that you are a screenwriter describing characters in a movie about your life. Choose someone important to you, and write a character sketch detailing that person's appearance and personality.

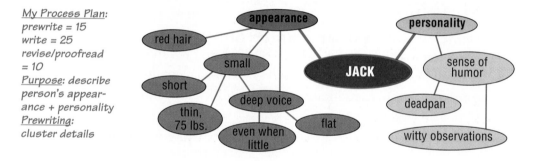

My Process Plan:
prewrite = 15
write = 25
revise/proofread
= 10
Purpose: describe
person's appear-
ance + personality
Prewriting:
cluster details

PORTFOLIO ASSESSMENT

Sometimes your writing progress will be evaluated on the basis of your **writing portfolio**, a collection of work you have done throughout the year. Prepare for portfolio assessment in the following way:

- After you finish each assignment, write your own evaluation, indicating what you thought was especially difficult, what you think you did best, what you'd change if you could revise the piece further.

- Choose what you consider your most successful piece of writing. Analyze what contributed to its success.

Note where you improved your writing. At assessment time, offer writing samples that show your progress.

- Ask classmates to help you select papers for evaluation.

- Do final revisions of these assignments.

- Plan to discuss your goals and achievements for each assignment.

PERFORMANCE ASSESSMENT

A performance assessment evaluates your work on an extended project. Here are tips for each step in the process:

1. Be clear about the requirements and goal of your performance task.

- Understand the rubric that will be used to assess your project.
- Envision the outcomes that will repesent the successful comletion of your project.

2. Locate resources in your home, school, and community.

- Do specific library research.
- Interview people who have special knowledge.
- Use computer online services to do further research.
- Contact the media to locate audiovisual resources.

3. Integrate your knowledge of various subjects to add depth to and evoke interest in your project.

- Math skills can help you analyze findings and create charts and graphs.
- Use social studies skills to create maps and timelines.
- Consider writing a story or drama to illustrate what you have learned.

4. Choose the most effective method of presenting your project.

- Enliven your presentation by using art and music. Use visual aids in an oral project.
- Include other people in your presentation; for example, you could arrange for your class to witness a panel discussion.

> *How do I apply to college?*

DEFINING YOUR COLLEGE GOALS

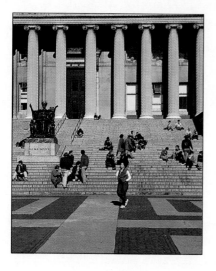

Do you want to attend a college within an hour's drive of your home, or one in another state? Do you think you'd fit in best at a small college with small discussion classes or a big university campus where lecture classes contain hundreds of undergraduates? What is the main field of your academic interest? These are just three of the many questions a high school student considering college must ask in order to narrow down the possibilities from among thousands of American colleges and universities. When beginning your search, read college guidebooks, such as *Barron's*, *Lovejoy's*, or *Peterson's*, which provide a broad overview of colleges. Make an appointment with your guidance counselor to match your interests and your school record with the most likely college choices. Draw up a list of about half a dozen colleges, and write a letter to the admissions office at each one, requesting a catalog and an application form.

VISITING A COLLEGE CAMPUS

After deciding which colleges you're most interested in, consider visiting their campuses. This will give you the clearest possible picture of a school's geography, buildings, and atmosphere. You can take guided tours of the college and speak to students, professors, and townspeople. You can also have an admissions interview—a chance for you to present yourself well, and a chance for the college to convince you that it's the place where you'll want to spend the next four years of your life.

HAVING A SUCCESSFUL INTERVIEW

1. Schedule the interview in advance so you'll have time to prepare.

2. Expect questions about your in-school and extracurricular interests and activities, your strengths and weaknesses (both academic and personal), and what makes you a good candidate for admission. Practice talking about these subjects with a person you trust.

3. Arrive at the interview on time, neatly dressed and groomed. Courteously greet the interviewer at the beginning of the interview, and thank him or her at the end. Even if you feel "butterflies," speak in a clear, confident manner and maintain a good posture.

4. Emphasize the positive in your answers. Be enthusiastic in presenting yourself as a candidate who wants to go to this particular college.

5. Take your time answering questions, to make sure you answer completely and say what you really think. A few seconds of silent thought, or a polite "Let me think about that for a minute," will probably make a better impression than a hasty, incomplete answer.

6. The interview is your chance to ask questions about the college, and asking good ones will favorably impress the interviewer. Make a list beforehand of questions that the college catalog has not answered, on topics such as courses, intramural sports, faculty, and social life.

WHAT THEY MIGHT ASK YOU

- Why are you applying to this college?
- What field do you think you might major in? Why?
- What books have you read this year? Tell me about one of them.
- What are your goals?
- How would your best friend describe you?
- What do you think makes a person successful in life?
- What do you see yourself doing five years from now? Ten?
- What would you like us to know about you?

COMPLETING AN APPLICATION FOR COLLEGE

College applications will probably look intimidating to you when you first try to grapple with them. Remember that they look intimidating to everyone else, too. Take your time reading all the instructions carefully. In the process, you'll begin to feel more comfortable with the form. Most applications consist of informational questions and a personal essay. Here are some tips for filling out a college application:

- First photocopy the blank application. Write rough drafts on photocopies, and save the original for your final draft.
- Provide accurate, concise information about factual matters such as your family and your school record.
- State your interests, experience, and achievements in a concrete, positive way—don't be vague, and don't fudge!

THE APPLICATION ESSAY

You'll want your essay to stay in the reader's mind. Being yourself—a unique individual—will achieve that in the right way. (Being gimmicky, pretentious, or cute will achieve it in the wrong way.) The first step in writing the essay is to determine what the instructions ask. The instructions might be as general as "Tell us about yourself" or as specific as "Describe the most important experience of your past year." They might ask you to assess yourself, to express an opinion on world events, or to respond to an imaginary situation. Use whatever prewriting techniques work best for you and write as many drafts as you need to. Write using your own personal voice rather than a stuffy "official" voice. Here's the first paragraph of an essay that answers the instruction "Tell us about an extracurricular activity you've participated in."

> ### MODEL
>
> "Good morning, ma'am, are you registered to vote?" I've asked that question hundreds, perhaps thousands of times during the past year while I was working for our county's voter-registration drive. I've sat at a table at the weekly farmer's market, handing out leaflets and signing people up. I've rung doorbells and made telephone calls. A year ago, I pictured myself diving into a swimming pool all summer and tossing a football all autumn—recreations I still enjoy, but ones that have taken second place to my new-found interest in politics.

The applicant went on to discuss how her work helped the voter registration drive, and how the experience helped her.

TESTING

As a prospective college student, you'll probably take one or more standardized college-entrance exams such as the Scholastic Aptitude Test (SAT) or the test of the American College Testing Program (ACT). Your first step in preparing for such tests should be to read the booklets sent by the test companies.

For more on preparing for standardized tests, see p. 444.

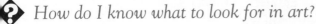
How do I know what to look for in art?

When you look at paintings in a museum or the graphics in advertisements, you probably respond to five key elements of the visual arts: content, medium, color, line, and composition. The chart below explains these elements, and the text that follows shows how to apply this information to a specific work, Jacob Lawrence's *The Studio*:

ELEMENT	EXPLANATION	QUESTIONS TO ASK
Content	the subject matter of a work of art	■ What is the subject of the work? Is it realistic? Abstract? What does it suggest about the artist's purpose?
Medium	the materials and technique used to create a work of art	■ What materials and techniques has the artist used? How do they contribute to the purpose?
Color	Colors can be grouped according to the feelings they tend to evoke. Neutral: black, white, gray Cool: blues, greens Warm: reds, oranges, yellows, some browns	■ What mood do the colors evoke? Are they from the same group? How might they reflect the artist's feelings about the content?
Line	the marks—horizontal, vertical, diagonal, curved, long, or short—that outline objects or indicate direction in a work of art	■ What kinds of lines does the artist emphasize? Do they lead the eye in a particular direction? Do they form a pattern?
Composition	the arrangement of lines, colors, and space in a work of art	■ How does the artist's composition indicate a center of interest? How does this center of interest relate to the artist's purpose?

The Studio, 1977, Jacob Lawrence
Seattle Art Museum

In Jacob Lawrence's *The Studio*, the subject, or content, is the artist himself as he enters his working space. Although the subject can be easily identified, the bold geometric lines of the work suggest an abstract painting. This striking treatment further suggests that Lawrence felt confident about portraying himself at work.

The medium, oil on canvas, allows Lawrence to use strong colors as well as light tints (colors mixed with white) and subtle shades (colors mixed with black). Warm colors predominate: the red stairwell railing, the sunny gold of the walls, and the paler tan of the floor. Lawrence offsets these warm colors with the blue in his shirt, the paintings on the walls, and the sky framed in the window. This use of warm and cool colors suggests Lawrence's balanced feelings about his art.

Lawrence depicts himself with bold vertical and diagonal lines so that he seems to be moving energetically up the stairs. The format of the painting is also vertical, emphasizing the feeling of energy and confidence.

Lawrence's composition has two centers of interest: the artist and the window. The stairwell railing leads the viewer's eye to these focal points. The artist's left hand frames the window scene, a crowded city neighborhood. In this way, Lawrence connects the artist to the outer world he depicts.

HUMANITIES: LISTENING TO MUSIC

How do I know what to listen for in music?

Our early ancestors may have turned stones or bones into percussion instruments to beat out rhythms around the campfire. Today, the stones and bones have been replaced by drums, cymbals, and other intricate and beautiful musical instruments. Nevertheless, the basic elements of music-making have remained the same. Understanding what makes music "musical" and learning what to listen for can add to your enjoyment.

This chart presents an overview of basic musical elements:

ELEMENT	QUESTIONS TO ASK
Rhythm: a pattern of strong and weak stresses, or **beats,** and their speed, or **tempo.**	Is the rhythm regular, or changeable? Is the tempo fast or slow? How does the rhythm make me feel?
Melody: tune; a pattern of higher and lower sounds, or tones. A **theme** is a brief melody that is repeated, usually with **variations**.	What patterns do I hear in the rising and falling tones? What feelings does the melody evoke in me?
Harmony: the pleasing combination of two or more tones. **Dissonance** is a deliberately jarring combination of tones.	What harmonies do I hear? Are there any examples of dissonance? What effect does the harmony or dissonance create?
Key: a system of related notes. Music composed in a major key, such as C-major, sounds upbeat and vigorous. Music in a minor key, such as A-minor, sounds plaintive.	Is the melody written in a major key or in a minor one? What is the emotional effect of the main melody, or theme of the music?
Form: the structure of a musical work.	Do the melody and rhythm change during the work? Do the changes show a pattern?
Content: the subject matter of a musical work.	Is the music "about" a story or some other topic? Do the sounds show a pattern?

HOW CAN I EXPLORE MUSICAL ELEMENTS?

To explore the effects of rhythm, hum the song "When the Saints Go Marching In." At the beginning, the rhythm is regular, with every other beat being stressed:

"Oh WHEN the SAINTS go MARCH-ing IN. . . ."

The steady, relatively quick tempo gives the march a jaunty mood.

You can experiment with the effects of rhythm, melody, and harmony by singing a round with one or two other people. During a round, one voice sings the first line (such as the classic "Row, row, row your boat"), another voice begins the first line while the first voice sings the second line—and then a third voice may begin. Though the tune for each line is different, the rhythm remains the same; and the overall effect is harmonious.

The form of a musical work influences its other elements. For instance, a simple advertising jingle usually combines a short, bright melody with lively rhythm and pleasant harmony. At the other extreme, a symphony, a very complex work, usually includes four movements, built around different melodies and rhythms. Melodic themes repeated with variations from movement to movement help tie the whole work together.

The content of a musical work may be suggested by the title: Tchaikovsky's *1812 Overture* celebrates a stirring victory; Edvard Grieg's *Peer Gynt Suite* weaves the story of a Scandinavian legend, with various themes representing different characters. Other works may explore melodies, rhythms, and instrumental qualities for their own sake.

All elements of music—rhythm, melody, key, harmony, form, and content—join to create works of art that have strong emotional effects. When you listen carefully to music, you experience its emotional effect and recognize how all the elements combine to create it.

For more about listening to music, see the following books: *Encyclopedia of Pop, Rock, and Soul* (9–12), edited by Irwin Stambler, illustrated, © 1989, St. Martin's Press, New York.

The Joy of Classical Music, by Joan Bennett Kennedy, © 1992, Nan A. Talese/Doubleday, New York.

ACKNOWLEDGMENTS (continued)

Macmillan Publishing Company
Reprinted with permission of Charles Scribner's Sons, an imprint of Macmillan Publishing Company from *The Spirit of St. Louis* by Charles A. Lindbergh. Copyright © 1953 Charles Scribner's Sons; copyright renewed © 1981 Anne Morrow Lindberg.

Naomi Long Madgett
Excerpt from "Alabama Centennial" from *Pink Ladies in the Afternoon* by Naomi Long Madgett (Lotus 1972, 1990). Reprinted by permission of the author.

Elaine Markson Literary Agency, Inc.
Reprinted by permission of Grace Paley. From *Later the Same Day*, Farrar, Straus, & Giroux: 1985. Copyright © 1985, 1994 by Grace Paley. All rights reserved.

Merlyn's Pen
From the issue of Oct./Nov. 1993: letter by Andrew Franklin; Dara Horn; "Old Bridge" by Klinton Crispin; "Exhibition of Chinese Jade" by Edward Kai Chiu. From the issue of Feb./March 1993: "Coward" by Drake Bennett; Summer Woodford. From the issue of Dec./Jan. 1993: book review by Jessamy Millican. From the issue of Oct./Nov. 1992: "The Sea" by Michelle Johnson. From the issue of Apr./May 1991: "Through My Picture Window" by Ami Palmer; letter by Carrie Hernandez. From the issue of Dec./Jan. 1991: "Road Trip" by Alice Reagan. From the issue of Oct./Nov. 1990: "Huff and Puff and Blow Your Life Down" by Carrie Hernandez; book review by Chris Green. From the issue of Dec./Jan. 1990: "Ashes in the Grate" by Cynthia Lewis. From the issue of Oct./Nov. 1989: "Homer" by Mike Arbagi; Van Ngo. From the issue of May/June 1986: "The Last Mustangs" by Kelly Dane.

Merriam-Webster Inc.
By permission. From *Merriam-Webster Collegiate® Dictionary* © 1993 by Merriam-Webster Inc., publisher of Merriam-Webster ® dictionaries.

New Directions Publishing Corp.
Dylan Thomas: *A Child's Christmas in Wales*. Copyright © 1952 by New Directions Publishing Corp. William Carlos Williams: *The Collected Poems of William Carlos Williams, 1901–1939*, vol. 1. Copyright © 1938 by New Directions Publishing Corp. Reprinted by permission of New Directions Publishing Corp.

The New York Times
Excerpt from *The New York Times*, Feb. 8, 1994, "Taking the Commuter For More Than A Ride" by Evelyn Nieves. Excerpt from *The New York Times*, May 11, 1994, "Japan's Premier Say Reform Effort Is in Danger" by David E. Sanger. Copyright © 1994 *The New York Times*. Reprinted by permission.

The New Yorker Magazine, Inc.
Excerpt from "Before the End of Summer" by Grant Moss, Jr. Reprinted by permission. Copyright © 1960, 1988 The New Yorker Magazine, Inc.

Harold Ober Associates
Excerpt from "Civil Peace" from *Girls At War and Other Stories* by Chinua Achebe. Copyright © 1972, 1973 by Chinua Achebe. Reprinted by permission of Harold Ober Associates. (For Canadian distribution rights.)

Simon J. Ortiz
Excerpt from "Hunger in New York City" from *Going for the Rain: Poems* by Simon J. Ortiz. Published by Harper & Row, 1976. Copyright © 1976 by Simon J. Ortiz. Reprinted by permission of the author.

Osborn McGraw-Hill
From *Microsoft Word Made Easy for the Macintosh* by Paul Hoffman. Copyright © 1988 by McGraw-Hill, Inc. Reprinted by permission of the publisher.

Penguin Books USA Inc.
Excerpt from "The Worlds's Biggest Membrane" copyright © 1971, 1972, 1973, by The Massachusetts Medical Society, from *The Lives of a Cell* by Lewis Thomas. Excerpt from *The Medusa and the Snail* by Lewis Thomas. Copyright © 1974, 1975, 1976, 1977, 1978, 1979 by Lewis Thomas. Excerpt from *The Green Consumer*. Revised edition by John Elkington and Julia Hailes, and Viking Penguin. Copyright © 1993 by Viking Penguin. Used by permission of Viking

Penguin, a division of Penguin Books USA Inc.

Putnam Publishing Group, Inc.
Reprinted by permission of G. P. Putnam's Sons Excerpts from *The Joy Luck Club* by Amy Tan. Copyright © 1989 by Amy Tan.

Random House, Inc.
Excerpt from *End of the Game and Other Stories* by Julio Cortazar, translated by Paul Blackburn. Copyright © 1967 by Random House, Inc. Reprinted by permission of Pantheon Books, a division of Random House, Inc. Excerpt from *And Justice for All* by John Tateishi. Copyright © 1984 by John Tateishi. Excerpt from *The Road from Coorain* by Jill Ker Conway. Copyright © 1989 by Jill Conway. Reprinted by permission of Alfred A. Knopf, Inc., a division of Random House, Inc. Excerpt from "Katherine Comes to Yellow Sky" from *A Dove of the East and Other Stories* by Mark Helprin. Copyright © 1975 by Mark Helprin. Reprinted by permission of Alfred A. Knopf, Inc., a division of Random House, Inc. Excerpt from "A Ride Through Spain" from *Selected Writings* by Truman Capote. Copyright © 1963. Reprinted by permission of Random House, Inc.

Marian Reiner
Excerpt from *More Cricket Songs*, Japanese haiku translated by Harry Behn. Copyright © 1971 Harry Behn. Reprinted by permission of Marian Reiner.

Scholastic Inc.
Excerpt from *Humor: Making People Laugh*. Copyright © 1976 by Scholastic Inc. Reprinted by permission of Scholastic Inc.

Sara B. Stein
Excerpt from *My Weeds* by Sara B. Stein. Copyright © 1988 by Sara B. Stein. Reprinted by permission of Sara B. Stein, c/o Wallace Literary Agency.

The University of Nebraska Press
Excerpt from *Black Elk Speaks* by John G. Neihardt. Published by The University of Nebraska Press.

The University of New Mexico Press
Reprinted from *The Way to Rainy Mountain* by N. Scott Momaday. First published in *The Reporter*, January 26, 1967. Copyright © 1969 The University of New Mexico Press. Reprinted with their permission.

Wylie, Aitken & Stone, Inc.
Excerpt from "The Man to Send Rain Clouds" from *Storyteller* by Leslie Marmon Silko. Copyright © 1981 by Leslie Marmon Silko. Reprinted by permission of Wylie, Aitken & Stone, Inc,

Note: Every effort has been made to locate the copyright owner of material reprinted in this book. Omissions brought to our attention will be corrected in subsequent editions.

ART CREDITS

1 Section One Opener: *Julian Bell Writing*, 1928, Duncan Grant/Charleston Trust; 8 Van Gogh Self Portrait, Musée D'Orsay/Giraudon/Art Resource, N.Y.; *Self-Portrait*, Vincent Van Gogh, Vienna Kunsthistorisches Museum, Neue Galerie/Art Resource, N.Y.; *Self-Portrait*, Vincent Van Gogh, Rijksmuseum Kroller-Muller; *Self-Portrait*, Vincent Van Gogh, Otterloo/ Bridgeman/Art Resource, N.Y.; 34 *Portrait of Van Gogh Painting Sunflowers* (top), Gauguin, The Israel Museum, Jerusalem/Art Resource, N.Y. and (bottom) Van Gogh Museum, Amsterdam/Art Resource, N.Y.; 57 Section Two Opener: *Emblems*, 1913, Roger de la Fresnaye, © The Phillips Collection, Washington, D.C.; 85 *Water Lilies at Giverny*, Claude Monet, Giraudon/Art Resource, N.Y.; 90 © 1993 by John Shanks/Phi Delta Kappa; 93 *Selling Fruit, Highway, Barbados*, Jill Walker/Best of Barbados Ltd., Welches, St. Thomas, Barbados, West Indies; 102 Section Three Opener: *Girl Writing*, 1941, Milton Avery, The Phillips Collection, Washington, D.C.; 113 *The Shipwreck*, Tate Gallery, London/Art Resource, N.Y.; 123 © Henley & Savage/The Stock Market; 192 Copyright © Harley L. Schwadron; 198 P. Jennis from the TOR Book edition of *The Red Badge of Courage*; 216 *Landscape*, Sasahide, Paris, Musée Guimet,/© Giraudon/Art Resource, N.Y.; 217

The Starry Night, 1859, Vincent Van Gogh, oil on canvas, 29 x 36¼", The Museum of Modern Art, N.Y. Acquired through the Lillie P. Bliss Bequest. Photograph © 1994 The Museum of Modern Art, N.Y.; 258 Section Four Opener: *The Window*, Pierre Bonnard, 1925, Tate Gallery, London. Presented by Lord Ivor Spenser Churchill through the Contemporary Society; 416 Section Five Opener: *Libraries Are Appreciated*, 1943, Jacob Lawrence, Philadelphia Museum of Art; 392 Copyright © 1991 by Art Bouthillier; 442 Copyright © 1989 by Randy Glasbergen; 454 *The Studio*, Jacob Lawrence, © Seattle Art Museum/Paul Macapier.

PHOTOGRAPH CREDITS

5 NASA, JFK Space Center, Fla.; 10 © Tom Stewart 1991/ The Stock Market; 13 © Anne Marie Weber/The Stock Market; 20 Jeff Isaac Greenberg/ Photo Researchers, Inc.; 22 Frederica Georgia/ Photo Researchers, Inc.; 31 © American Museum of Natural History; 41 © Gabe Palmer/The Stock Market; 44 Jeff Isaac Greenberg/Photo Researchers, Inc.; 58 Jeff Isaac Greenberg/Photo Researchers, Inc.; 69 © Michael J. Okoniewski/Gamma-Liaison; 71 Danila Boschung/Leo deWys, Inc.; 72 © Alex Stewart/The Image Bank; 75 © Hollege/The Stock Market; 97 Paramount/ Photofest; 106 © Eric Meola/ The Image Bank; 115 © Jean Anderson/ The Stock Market; 119 © J. Wilson/Gamma-Liaison; 126 Art Resource, N.Y.; 128 Archive Photos; 129 © Paul Metzger/Photo Researchers, Inc.; 132 © David Woods/ The Stock Market; 135 Brown Brothers, Sterling, Pa.; 147 © John Eastcott/ Yva Momatiuk/Animals Animals; 157 © Peter Berk/The Stock Market; 169 © NASA/ Starlight; 177 © Michael Heller/ New York Times Pictures; 183 Focus on Sports; 190 © Joan Menschenfreund/The Stock Market; 198 Archive Photos; 207 © C.C. Lockwood/Bruce Coleman Inc.; 213 © Giraudon/Art Resource, N.Y.; 223, 227 © Roger Ressmeyer/Starlight; 239 The Bettmann Archive; 244 © Ulf Andersen/ Gamma-Liaison; 250, 254 The Bettmann Archive; 276 William R. Sallaz/© Duomo; 283 © Jeff Gnass Photography/The Stock Market; 290 © Mark D. Phillips 1992/Photo Researchers, Inc.; 293 © M. Tamborino/ The Stock Market; 299 © Mugshots/ The Stock Market; 300 © Aquarium for Wildlife Conservation; 305–307 United States Postal Service; 381 © Stephen Dalton/ Photo Researchers, Inc.; 383 © Erich Lessing, Kunsthistorisches Museum, Vienna/Art Resource, N.Y.; 384 © Ray Coleman/ Photo Researchers, Inc. ; 389 © Harry Rodgers/ Photo Researchers, Inc.; 392 © 1991 by Art Bouthillier; 401 © Will McIntyre/Photo Researchers, Inc.; 445 The Bettmann Archive; 450 © Bill Wassman/ The Stock Market; 455 © Richard Hutchings/ Photo Researchers, Inc.; © Mandolin Bros./ Photo Researchers, Inc.; © Mary Allen, N.Y.

ILLUSTRATION CREDITS

Cover illustration by Theo Rudnak/Renard Represents
Joe Boddy: 6, 45, 84, 95, 115, 120, 132, 137, 138, 153, 171, 172, 178, 179, 184, 185, 200, 201, 205, 212, 216, 229, 249, 270, 279, 284, 316, 333, 356, 381, 368, 387, 391, 404, 422, 423, 426, 431, 434, 452
Eldon Doty/HK Portfolio: 63, 76, 78, 81, 136, 149, 163, 186, 261, 266, 273, 296, 303, 329, 351, 361, 373, 398, 411, 433, 444
Tara Framer: 417
Annie Matsick: 15, 25, 26, 46, 88, 100, 108, 164, 233, 289, 319, 332, 338, 358, 360, 362, 365, 371, 375, 377, 379
Steve Sullivan: 2, 11, 52, 56, 82, 103, 107, 123, 130, 150, 154, 158, 159, 165, 173, 199, 220, 221, 254, 330, 349, 418, 421, 439, 440, 441, 448

INDEX

rhetorical, 42
sentences begun with, 84

R

raise, rise, 319
Readers' Guide to Periodical Literature, 219, 424–425
Reading-comprehension questions, 444–445
Reading skills, 434–437
real, really, 319
Redundancy, 49
Reference books, 423
Reflective essay, 41, 96, 107–112
Reflexive pronouns, 361, 367, 378
regardless, irregardless, 320
Relative adverbs, 285, 299, 378
Relative clauses, 80–81, 299
Relative pronouns, 299, 351, 362–363, 368, 378, 388
Remote cause, 164
Repetition, 67
  in poems, 145
  in speeches, 240
Research report, 40–41, 217–228, 374, 376, 418
Resolution, 137
respectfully, respectively, 320
Restrictive appositives, 290, 307, 378
Restrictive clauses, 299–300, 306, 378
Restrictive phrases, 378
Résumé, 231–233
Reverse chronology, 167
Revising, 2, 46–51
Rhetorical question, 42
Rhyme, in poems, 143, 145
Rhythm
  in music, 455, 456
  in poems, 145
  in speeches, 240
Run-on sentences, 70–71, 259, 260, 306, 379

S

Scanning, 434
Secondary source, 219
Second person, 349, 379, 405
Semicolon, 379
Sensory details, 35, 36

Sentence completion questions, 443, 446
Sentence outline, 223
Sentences, 53, 68–69, 70–75, 76–81,82–83,94, 96, 292, 348, 380–390
  beginnings of, 49, 83–84
  choppy, 72, 76–81, 297
  combining, 76–81, 83, 276, 291, 326–328, 370
  complex, 82, 83, 321, 388
  compound, 82, 83, 271, 305–306, 321, 388
  compound-complex, 82, 321, 388
  concise, 68–69
  declarative, 320, 348, 386, 388
  empty, 73–74, 333
  exclamatory, 333, 334, 387
  faulty subordination in, 301–302, 334
  fragments, 70, 259, 261–262, 334, 380
  imperative, 337, 348, 387
  interrogative, 338, 368–369, 371, 386
  inverted, 339, 385–386
  numbers in, 345
  in paragraphs, 58–61
  parallelism in, 74, 334, 346
  prepositions ending, 357
  run-on, 70–71, 259, 260, 306, 379
  simple, 82, 83, 388, 390
  streamlining, 353
  stringy, 71, 326–328, 395
  variety in, 77, 82–84, 96, 241, 302, 389–390
  wordy, 72–73, 415
  see also Clauses; Predicate; Subject
Series, 78, 259, 271, 305, 390
Setting, 136, 137, 138
Short-answer questions, 443
Simile, 50, 100, 144
Simple predicate, 382–383, 390
Simple sentences, 82, 83, 388, 390
Simple subject, 380–381, 390
Single possessive, 352
Singular, 390
Singular nouns, 270, 342, 345, 350, 390
Skimming, 434
Slang, 90, 289
so, 325